Lecture Notes in Computer Science 15838

Founding Editors

Gerhard Goos
Juris Hartmanis

Editorial Board Members

Elisa Bertino, *Purdue University, West Lafayette, IN, USA*
Wen Gao, *Peking University, Beijing, China*
Bernhard Steffen⊙, *TU Dortmund University, Dortmund, Germany*
Moti Yung⊙, *Columbia University, New York, NY, USA*

The series Lecture Notes in Computer Science (LNCS), including its subseries Lecture Notes in Artificial Intelligence (LNAI) and Lecture Notes in Bioinformatics (LNBI), has established itself as a medium for the publication of new developments in computer science and information technology research, teaching, and education.

LNCS enjoys close cooperation with the computer science R & D community, the series counts many renowned academics among its volume editors and paper authors, and collaborates with prestigious societies. Its mission is to serve this international community by providing an invaluable service, mainly focused on the publication of conference and workshop proceedings and postproceedings. LNCS commenced publication in 1973.

Yu Liu · Longbiao Chen · Shaohua Wang ·
Min Deng · Bolong Zheng · Qiang Mei
Editors

Spatial Data and Intelligence

6th International Conference, SpatialDI 2025
Xiamen, China, April 17, 2025
Proceedings

Editors
Yu Liu
Peking University
Beijing, China

Longbiao Chen
Xiamen University
Xiamen, China

Shaohua Wang
Chinese Academy of Sciences
Beijing, China

Min Deng
Central South University
Changsha, China

Bolong Zheng
Huazhong University of Science
and Technology
Wuhan, China

Qiang Mei
Jimei University
Xiamen, China

ISSN 0302-9743   ISSN 1611-3349 (electronic)
Lecture Notes in Computer Science
ISBN 978-981-95-3101-1   ISBN 978-981-95-3102-8 (eBook)
https://doi.org/10.1007/978-981-95-3102-8

© The Editor(s) (if applicable) and The Author(s), under exclusive license
to Springer Nature Singapore Pte Ltd. 2026

This work is subject to copyright. All rights are solely and exclusively licensed by the Publisher, whether the whole or part of the material is concerned, specifically the rights of translation, reprinting, reuse of illustrations, recitation, broadcasting, reproduction on microfilms or in any other physical way, and transmission or information storage and retrieval, electronic adaptation, computer software, or by similar or dissimilar methodology now known or hereafter developed.

The use of general descriptive names, registered names, trademarks, service marks, etc. in this publication does not imply, even in the absence of a specific statement, that such names are exempt from the relevant protective laws and regulations and therefore free for general use.

The publisher, the authors and the editors are safe to assume that the advice and information in this book are believed to be true and accurate at the date of publication. Neither the publisher nor the authors or the editors give a warranty, expressed or implied, with respect to the material contained herein or for any errors or omissions that may have been made. The publisher remains neutral with regard to jurisdictional claims in published maps and institutional affiliations.

This Springer imprint is published by the registered company Springer Nature Singapore Pte Ltd.
The registered company address is: 152 Beach Road, #21-01/04 Gateway East, Singapore 189721, Singapore

If disposing of this product, please recycle the paper.

Preface

This volume contains the papers from the 6th China Spatial Data Intelligence (SpatialDI 2025), which was held at Xiamen University International Academic Exchange Center, Xiamen, during April 17–19, 2025.

SpatialDI 2025 was sponsored by the ACM SIGSPATIAL China Branch, organized by Xiamen University, and co-organized by the Academy of Digital China (ADC), Xiamen Institute of Data Intelligence (XIDI), and Jimei University.

SpatialDI serves as a premier forum for researchers and practitioners to explore the convergence of computer science, geographical information science, artificial intelligence, and emerging technologies. The conference highlights cutting-edge advancements and interdisciplinary collaborations in spatial data intelligence. The main topics of SpatialDI 2025 included generative AI and spatial data intelligence, spatiotemporal knowledge graphs and large geographic models, digital twins and smart cities, government spatiotemporal big data and data governance, emergency disaster reduction and sustainable development, spatial humanities and social geography computing, spatiotemporal data management and analysis, and intelligent processing of remote sensing images. Additionally, the conference featured the ACM China SIGSPATIAL Rising Star and Doctoral Dissertation Award Forum, fostering the growth of young researchers in the field.

This year, the conference received 100 submissions, each rigorously reviewed by at least three Program Committee members in a single-blind process. Based on the reviewers' evaluations, 17 papers were accepted for presentation, with an acceptance rate of 17%.

Beyond the technical program, SpatialDI 2025 hosted several invited talks by leading experts. Wenzhong Shi from Hong Kong Polytechnic University, China, delivered a talk titled "Urban Informatics and Spatial Analysis". Baoguo Yu from China Electronics Technology Group Corporation 54th Research Institute, China, addressed "Integrated Spatiotemporal Network and Intelligent Navigation for Underground Space". Yongjiu Feng from Tongji University, China, discussed "Key Technologies and Applications of Spatiotemporal Intelligent Services for Urban Spatial Monitoring and Planning Governance". Yu Zheng from JD.com, China, shared great insights on "Urban Computing: Unleash the Value of Urban Data with Spatiotemporal Intelligence".

We extend our sincere gratitude to the keynote and invited speakers, program committee members, and reviewers for their invaluable contributions to the conference. We also thank Springer for their continued trust and support in publishing the proceedings of SpatialDI 2025.

We hope this volume serves as a valuable resource for researchers and practitioners, inspiring further innovation in spatial data intelligence and its transformative applications.

April 2025

Yu Liu
Longbiao Chen
Shaohua Wang
Min Deng
Bolong Zheng
Qiang Mei

Organization

General Co-chairs

Cheng Wang	Xiamen University, China
Qingfeng Guan	China University of Geosciences (Wuhan), China
Yunjun Gao	Zhejiang University, China

Program Co-chairs

Longbiao Chen	Xiamen University, China
Shaohua Wang	Aerospace Information Research Institute, Chinese Academy of Sciences, China
Min Deng	Central South University, China

Publicity Co-chair

Bolong Zheng	Huazhong University of Science and Technology, China

Strategic Workshop Organizing Co-chair

Ziqiang Yu	Yantai University, China

Local Organizing Co-chairs

Sheng Wu	Fuzhou University, China
Guorong Cai	Jimei University, China
Qiang Mei	Jimei University, China
Zhaoge Liu	Xiamen University, China

Steering Committee

Xiaofeng Meng	Renmin University of China, China
Yunjun Gao	Zhejiang University, China
Yu Liu	Peking University, China
Guangzhong Sun	University of Science and Technology of China, China
Huayi Wu	Wuhan University, China
Xin Xie	Microsoft Research Asia, China
Feng Lu	Institute of Geographic Sciences and Natural Resource Research, Chinese Academy of Sciences, China
Zhiming Ding	Institute of Software, Chinese Academy of Sciences, China
Yong Li	Tsinghua University, China
Yang Yue	Shenzhen University, China
Xiao Pan	Shijiazhuang Tiedao University, China
Zhipeng Gui	Wuhan University, China

Contents

BuildingView: Constructing Urban Building Exteriors Databases
with Street View Imagery and Multimodal Large Language Model 1
  Zongrong Li, Yunlei Su, Hongrong Wang, and Wufan Zhao

Urban Fire Risk Prediction and Spatiotemporal Analysis Based
on Machine Learning 20
  Weijie Song and Zhaoge Liu

Spatio-Temporal Diffusion Attention Networks for Vessel Flow Prediction 35
  Yuanyuan Pang, Yong Li, Qiang Mei, and Peng Wang

Study on Pollutants and Greenhouse Gases Emission Inventory Making
and Emission Prediction of Tianjin Port 54
  Tong Xue, Yong Li, Qiang Mei, and Peng Wang

Automatic Landslide Identification Based on High-Resolution Remote
Sensing Images Using Lightweight Deep Learning Network 70
  Xiangzhong Guo, Guolong Wu, and Yimin Lu

LCformer: Enhancing Multivariate Time Series Forecasting
with Transformer Based on Lagged Correlations 86
  Lihua Wang, Zipei Fan, and Xuan Song

SignalingTraj: A Signaling Data Based Trajectory Generation
with Diffusion Model 99
  Linzi Zou, Li Li, Junting Lu, Junjun Si, and Yiduo Mei

Research on Estimation Time of Arrival in Marine Traffic Based on Large
Language Model 118
  Junyou Su, Yi Yuan, Yu Liang, Bin Tan, Xuan Song, and Zipei Fan

HTDiff: Self-Guiding Diffusion Models for Hand Trajectory Prediction 139
  Yu Liu, Zipei Fan, Tianlv Huang, Wei Han, and Meiqi Zhou

A Method for Ship Trajectory Repair Based on Feature Correlation
and SHAP Model Interpretability 150
  *Lin Ye, Xiaohui Chen, Haiyan Liu, Ran Zhang, Bing Zhang,
  and Mingqi Zheng*

A Maritime Route Prediction Method for Large Oil Tankers Based
on IMO-MMSI Matching and Encoder-LSTM Model 167
 *Xiaohui Chen, Ran Zhang, Deze Wang, Bing Zhang, Yunpeng Zhao,
Lin Ye and Mingqi Zheng*

Learning Sequential Features of Check-Ins for User Relationship Inference 191
 Zhihui Ma, Hongmei Chen, Lihua Zhou, and Qing Xiao

Spatial Optimization of Fire Stations in Beijing Based on Multi-factor Fire
Risk Analysis and Covering Problem Model 202
 *Chang Liu, Shaohua Wang, Cheng Su, Xiao Li, Yang Zhong,
Junyuan Zhou, Dachuan Xu, Haojian Liang, and Jiayi Zheng*

A Location Label Optimization Method for Crowdsourcing Trajectory Data ... 219
 Kehong Xiao, Xiang Li, Fang Ren, and Jiaqi Li

Leveraging Data Augmentation Through Contrastive Self-supervised
Learning for Next Point-of-Interest Recommendation 245
 Limin Guo, Weijia Liu, Zhi Cai, and Xing Su

Deductive Inference of How Urbanization Shaped by Governmental
Policy in Beijing from 2005 to 2022 267
 Zhi Cai, Hanming Fan, Sheng Li, Hanwen Liao, and Haiyan Gao

LERI Evaluation and Driving Mechanism Analysis via GWRF Model 295
 *Chenfeng Xu, Zhihao Kang, Min Li, Yike Hu, Zhengyang Zou,
Xing Geng, Haolan Huang, Zibo Zhu, Fenglei Chen, Ziruo Feng,
and Yan Cheng*

Author Index 313

BuildingView: Constructing Urban Building Exteriors Databases with Street View Imagery and Multimodal Large Language Model

Zongrong Li[1,2], Yunlei Su[1], Hongrong Wang[1], and Wufan Zhao[1]

[1] Thrust of Urban Governance and Design, The Hong Kong University of Science and Technology (Guangzhou), Guangzhou, China
zongrong@usc.edu, ysu186@connect.hkust-gz.edu.cn,
wufanzhao@hkust-gz.edu.cn
[2] Spatial Sciences Institute, University of Southern California, Los Angeles, USA

Abstract. Urban Building Exteriors are increasingly important in urban analytics, driven by advancements in Street View Imagery and its integration with urban research. Multimodal Large Language Models (LLMs) offer powerful tools for urban annotation, enabling deeper insights into urban environments. However, challenges remain in creating accurate and detailed urban building exterior databases, identifying critical indicators for energy efficiency, environmental sustainability, and human-centric design, and systematically organizing these indicators. To address these challenges, we propose BuildingView, a novel approach that integrates high-resolution visual data from Google Street View with spatial information from OpenStreetMap via the Overpass API. This research improves the accuracy of urban building exterior data, identifies key sustainability and design indicators, and develops a framework for their extraction and categorization. Our methodology includes a systematic literature review, building and Street View sampling, and annotation using the ChatGPT-4O API. The resulting database, validated with data from New York City, Amsterdam, and Singapore, provides a comprehensive tool for urban studies, supporting informed decision-making in urban planning, architectural design, and environmental policy. The code for BuildingView is available at https://github.com/Jasper0122/BuildingView.

Keywords: Building exteriors · Street-View imagery · Multimodal large language model · GeoAI · Urban analytics

1 Introduction

Urban environments are increasingly becoming the focus of interdisciplinary research, where the integration of spatial and visual data is essential for understanding various aspects of urban life. Within this context, the study of building exteriors has gained significant attention due to its direct impact on critical areas such as energy efficiency [1], environmental sustainability [2], and human-centric urban design [3]. Specifically, analyzing building exteriors involves extracting detailed spatial and visual features, which are crucial for evaluating urban heat islands, energy consumption, and overall aesthetic coherence. Moreover, building exteriors serve not only as the physical interface between a structure and its environment but also play a crucial role in determining the overall energy performance and aesthetic appeal of urban spaces.

In this regard, Street View imagery has emerged as an effective tool for extracting detailed features of building exteriors, providing a unique perspective that traditional remote sensing methods often overlook. [4]. Unlike remote sensing imagery, which provides a top-down view of urban landscapes, street view imagery captures buildings at eye level, revealing intricate details of their spatial attributes, materials, and architectural styles [5]. This granular level of detail is vital for assessing the impact of building exteriors on factors such as urban heat islands, energy consumption, and the overall aesthetic coherence of neighborhoods. Therefore, integrating street view imagery with advanced feature extraction techniques is essential for a comprehensive analysis of building exteriors. While street view imagery offers these advantages, its potential remains underutilized in urban research, particularly when it comes to integrating this visual data with other spatial datasets to provide a comprehensive understanding of building exteriors and their broader urban implications. This highlights the growing need to harness street view imagery more effectively to address the multifaceted challenges of modern urban environments.

Through a systematic search of the urban building exterior research, it is evident that there is a significant gap in the availability of comprehensive databases that integrate street view imagery with detailed building exterior information. Existing studies tend to focus on either the spatial characteristics of buildings—such as their geographic positioning and interactions with surrounding infrastructure—or the aesthetic and material aspects, including innovations in architectural design and material usage [6] [7]. However, these perspectives are rarely combined to offer a full understanding of urban building exteriors. The lack of integrated databases that unify spatial data with visual and material information limits the ability to conduct in-depth analyses necessary for informed decision-making in urban planning, architectural design, and environmental policy. Additionally, while recent advancements have leveraged street view imagery for various urban analyses, they primarily focus on environmental factors or general urban features rather than systematically extracting and organizing building exterior information [8]. The integration of large language models with street view imagery for detailed urban analysis remains in its nascent stages, highlighting the need for a more integrated approach to understanding urban building exteriors.

To address these knowledge deficits, we propose BuildingView, an innovative approach that integrates Street View imagery with multimodal large language models to create a comprehensive urban building exteriors database. By leveraging high-resolution visual data from Google Street View, combined with spatial and structural data obtained through the Overpass API and OpenStreetMap, this research sets a new standard for the integration of visual and spatial data in urban informatics, significantly advancing the field. Our key contributions include:

1. **Systematic collection and organization of urban building exteriors indicators**, providing a comprehensive understanding of critical factors such as energy efficiency, environmental sustainability, and human-centric design.
2. **Development of BuildingView**, a reusable tool that utilizes Street View imagery and multimodal large language models to construct detailed urban building exterior databases for any urban area globally.
3. **Construction of extensive urban building exterior databases** for New York, Amsterdam, and Singapore, enabling more informed decision-making in urban planning, architectural design, and environmental policy.

To outline the structure of this paper, the remainder is organized as follows. Section 2 provides a review of relevant literature on building exteriors, discussing both traditional and emerging research in this domain. Section 3 introduces our methodological framework, including the systematic literature review, the sampling approach using Overpass and Google Street View APIs, as well as the annotation process with large language models. Section 4 presents experimental details and results, followed by a comprehensive analysis of findings. Section 5 discusses the implications and limitations of our study. Finally, Sect. 6 concludes the paper and offers perspectives for future research.

2 Related Work

The current section surveys prior research on building exteriors, discussing the indicators commonly examined in the context of urban informatics, architecture, and sustainability. We divide the related work into two major subsections. Subsection 2.1 reviews various building exterior indicators—ranging from structural attributes to energy and environmental aspects—while Subsect. 2.1 focuses on how Street View Imagery (SVI) and large language models (LLMs) have been leveraged in urban building analysis. This structured overview helps in identifying knowledge gaps that our proposed approach aims to address.

2.1 Indicators of Building Exteriors Indicators

In the realm of urban informatics and geoscience, the development of spatiotemporal databases pertaining to buildings has garnered significant attention. Researchers within the disciplines of urban planning and geography typically concentrate on the spatial characteristics of buildings, such as their geographic positioning and the dynamics of their interaction with adjacent infrastructure. For instance, the architectural and urban planning processes must meticulously consider the spatial interplay between buildings and their adjacent parking facilities to optimize energy efficiency [1].In contrast, architects and designers are more inclined to examine the intrinsic elements of buildings, including materials and aesthetic design. Recently, the architectural style and the materials used for the exterior of buildings are continually subject to innovation and enhancement [6,7].

The academic discourse has increasingly pivoted towards the examination of the connections between buildings and other indicators, with a particular emphasis on their impact on energy consumption and environmental sustainability. Especially, researchers are actively exploring ways to harness more energy from natural sources through building design, thereby reducing the energy costs associated with buildings. Additionally, they are working to mitigate the thermal impacts caused by the urban heat island effect, which is exacerbated by the heat generated within urban environments [9]. Concurrently, there is a burgeoning interest in the human-centric aspects of building design, particularly how it fosters engagement and interaction with the public from a participatory perspective [3].

While numerous open-source databases exist that cater to specific domains of building information, they are often limited to a single aspect of building data. The foundational building attribute knowledge within these databases is typically derived from field surveys or footprint data extracted from remote sensing imagery [10]. To date, no open-source database has been developed that integrates street view imagery to provide a comprehensive, visually-driven repository encompassing the spatial. Thus, we want to build a spatial database with fundamental, and external surface properties of buildings, with a focus on their relevance to energy, environmental, and human-centric dimensions.

2.2 SVI and LLMs in Urban Building Analysis

The advent of street view imagery (SVI) has revolutionized the way urban environments are analyzed, offering a rich and dynamic geospatial data source that rivals traditional remote sensing methods such as satellite imagery [5]. The comprehensive visual data captured by SVI allows for detailed analysis and understanding of urban environments at the street level, providing critical insights into various urban characteristics and phenomena.

Previous research has demonstrated the utility of SVI in urban studies by integrating it with other urban data sources such as street networks, building information, demographic and socioeconomic data, and survey responses. For instance, SVI has been utilized to audit neighborhood environments [8], and analyze the effects of green view indices on pedestrian activity [11]. Additionally, studies have explored the use of SVI and machine learning to measure the built environment's impact on crime [12], as well as investigating the relationship between neighborhood walkability factors and walking behaviors using big data approaches [13]. Furthermore, SVI has been applied at a global scale, as seen in the creation of extensive datasets that cover millions of street-level images across hundreds of cities, facilitating large-scale urban science and analytics [14].

However, to date, there has been no significant work that focuses on using SVI in conjunction with LLMs to construct a comprehensive database of urban building exteriors. The proposed BuildingView project aims to fill this gap by harnessing the combined power of SVI and multimodal LLMs to create an extensive and detailed urban building exteriors database, which can serve as a valuable resource for a wide range of urban studies, including architectural analysis, urban planning, and environmental assessment.

3 Method

In this study, we introduce BuildingView, a novel framework for constructing urban building exterior databases using Street View imagery and multimodal large language models. The research framework is divided into three primary steps, as illustrated in Fig. 1, Subsect. 3.1: a systematic literature review of building exterior indicators; Subsection 3.2: sampling of buildings and street view imagery using the Overpass and Google Street View APIs to gather data points; and Subsect. 3.3: annotation of street view images using the ChatGPT-4O API to create the Urban Building Exteriors Database. Further details on each of these steps are provided below.

3.1 Systematic Literature Review of Building Exteriors Indicators

Global building morphology indicators database has concluded many indicators for urban data science [15]. However, a database of buildings directly covering energy, green, and human-centred buildings has not yet been created. Our goal is to establish a building database that encompasses the majority of indicators of interest to researchers. This database will include comprehensive spatial information on buildings and knowledge extracted from street view images through advanced vision analytics and vision-based reasoning techniques.

For that, we have done a systematic literature review on building exteriors Fig. 2. The initial step is to identify emerging topics concerning building exteriors over the past five years. To achieve this, we conduct a keyword search on "building envelope," "exterior of building," and "building exterior" within the Web of Science database. Specifically, this search was performed on November 15, 2024, and restricted to publications from 2019 to 2024, yielding 6,285 relevant scholarly works. There is a growing discussion about the intelligent design of external surfaces of buildings. The integration of innovative materials and intelligent technologies has the potential to significantly enhance the comfort of indoor environments [16].

In addition to fundamental building information and its spatial attributes, we have categorized the concept of "smart building exterior design" into three primary areas that are most frequently discussed by scholars: "human," "energy," and "green." Incorporating these keywords into our search criteria, we have identified a total of 4,683 relevant works, with the distribution being 544 for "human," 4,115 for "energy," and 523 for "green."

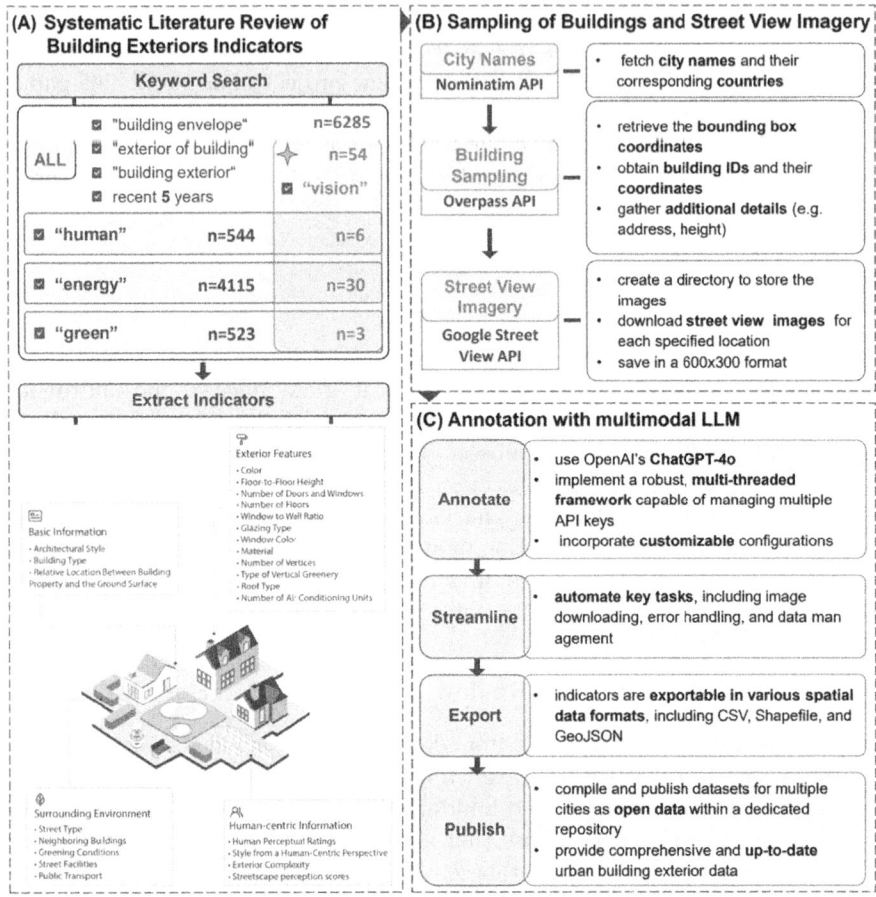

Fig. 1. BuildingView Workflow: (A) Indicator Review; (B) Sampling; (C) Annotation with ChatGPT-4.0.

Given our focus on indicators that can be discerned through visual analysis, we have narrowed down the total literature on building exteriors to 54 relevant pieces. Within this subset, only 39 pieces specifically address the hot topic of human-centric, energy fuel and engineering environmental fields. We reviewed these works and we found that among these, the topic of glazing has garnered significant attention. Specific indicators such as glazing type, colour, and Window-Wall Ratio (WWR) are recognized as crucial factors influencing energy absorption [17,18]. Outdoor air conditioners, as significant contributors to heat, and their placement methods are also central topics in discussions about energy conservation [19]. The rooftop, as the uppermost exterior of the building, plays a pivotal role in capturing solar energy. Its design and materials can significantly influence the building's energy efficiency by absorbing and utilizing solar radiation [20]. From a human-centric perspective, building styles exhibit

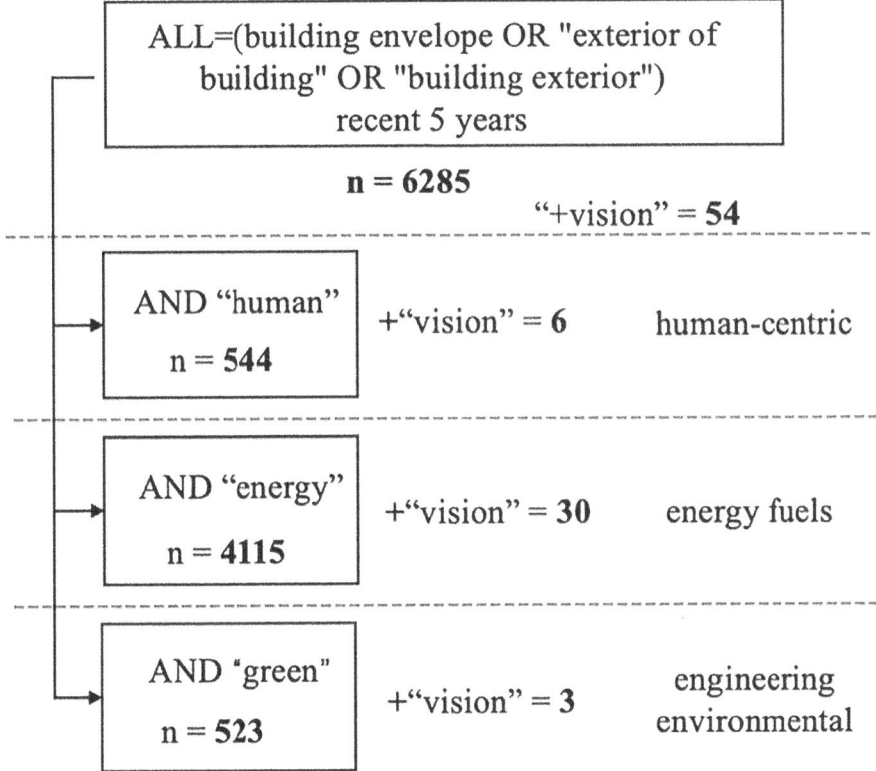

Fig. 2. Literature Review of Building Exteriors.

considerable variation, influenced by factors such as culture, climate, and history [21]. They are commonly recognized as falling into categories such as Historical, Somewhat Historical, No Significant Style, Somewhat Modern, and Modern [3]. Vertical greenery not only contributes to aesthetics but also has a positive impact on the thermal insulation of building facades [22]. Meanwhile, the surrounding infrastructure, such as transport stations and parking lots, can significantly influence the design of building exteriors and is, in turn, affected by them [1, 23]. Consequently, we will also consider these elements.

Subsequently, we have identified and summarized the key indicators that researchers find intriguing, which are presented in Table. 1. The indicators, which can be derived through vision-based reasoning from street view maps, are predominantly self-explanatory. However, some may not be readily distinguishable by AI technology, and thus, we provide additional explanations for a few that require further clarification. We have considered a range of indicators for

Table 1. Building Exteriors Indicators

Indicator	Value Example	Explanation
Architectural style	Haussman, Neoclassical, Renaissance, Modernism, Others,	
Building type	single-family houses, multiple-family houses, non-residential buildings	based on the number of units
Relative location	on the surface, in the air, underground, across the surface	relative location between building property and the ground surface
Colour	red, grey, light brown, unknown.	the colour of the building exteriors
Floor-to-Floor height	3 m, approximately 2 m, unknown.	inferences based on prior knowledge
Number of Doors and Windows	3 doors and approximately 2 windows, unknown.	
Number of Floors	2, approximately 2, unknown.	inferences based on prior knowledge
WWR	Approximately 0.25, 30%, unknown.	the ratio of the total area of windows to the total wall area
Glazing type	single, double, or triple, unknown	types refer to the number of glass layers in windows
Window colour	grey, light brown, unknown.	the colour of the exterior glazing of windows
Material	stone, glass product, metallic materials, or indistinguishable due to exterior paint	the material of building exteriors
Classification of the building materials	alternative materials, natural materials, or secondary raw materials	the classification based on building exterior materials
Number of vertices	-	-
Vertical greenery type	panel type, mini planter, cage system box, unknown	the type of vertical greenery system on the building exteriors
Roof type	lightweight, green, photovoltaic, vents, rubber	the classification of roof types from an energy-saving perspective
Number of air-con units	3, approximately 3, unknown	number of outdoor air conditioning units
Air-con placement type	horizontal, vertical	placement type of outdoor air-con units
Street type	residential street, local street, etc.	-
Neighbouring buildings	3 similar buildings, none, etc.	-
Greening conditions	3 trees, 3 grasslands, unknown, etc.	-
Street facilities	3 roads, 3 parking lots, unknown, etc.	-
Public transport	3 subway stations, 3 bus stops, none, unknown, etc.	-
Human perceptual ratings	complex, original, ordered, pleasing, boring	-
Building style	Historical, somewhat historical, no significant style, somewhat modern, modern	Style of the building from a human-centric perspective
Exterior complexity	complex, moderate, simple	inferences based on prior knowledge
Streetscape perception scores	Safer, wealthier, livelier, more beautiful, more depressing, more boring	-

our research on building exteriors, encompassing basic building information such as architectural style, building type, and relative location, as well as characteristics like colour. We have also included energy-saving indicators, environmental friendliness indicators—such as Window-Wall Ratio (WWR) and building exterior materials, vertical vegetation type, and human-centric indicators visible on the exteriors, including streetscape perception scores and exterior complexity, etc. Additionally, we have taken into account indicators of the surrounding environment that may influence the design of building exteriors. In parallel, we have integrated useful information for 3D building analysis, including details about neighbouring buildings and greening conditions. Subsequently, we have developed systematic and comprehensive prompts to assist ChatGPT in extracting these indicators from Street View images, aiming to obtain an accurate, detailed, and structured description of the attributes of our building exteriors to fulfill our global spatial database about building exteriors.

3.2 Sampling of Buildings and Street View Imagery

We begin by using the Nominatim API to fetch city names and their corresponding countries based on a query provided through the command line. Nominatim, an open-source geocoding service, outputs a list of cities and countries that match the query, allowing for accurate identification of the desired city and country [24]. This makes it easier to directly locate the corresponding bounding box by simply inputting the city and country names, streamlining the data collection process.

For the building sampling, we employ the Overpass API to retrieve and store building data for the specified city and country. The Overpass API [25], which queries the OpenStreetMap (OSM) database, returns building footprints, latitude/longitude coordinates, and occasional attributes (e.g., address, height). While this information is valuable for establishing each building's spatial context, OSM data generally lacks detailed façade descriptors—such as window-to-wall ratio or materials—that are essential for our analysis. Consequently, we integrate street-view imagery to capture more fine-grained exterior attributes. The Overpass-sourced building records are saved in JSONL format by building types, providing a structured foundation for subsequent merging with street-view data.

Finally, to match the buildings with their corresponding street view exteriors, we use the Google Street View API to download images for the locations specified in the JSONL file. This process involves creating a directory to store the images based on the name of the JSONL file, reading the latitude and longitude coordinates from the file, and downloading images using the Google Street View API for each specified location. To ensure that each downloaded street-view image captures the correct building exterior (rather than facing the opposite side of the street), we adopt the following strategy to determine the camera orientation (heading) when querying the Google Street View API. First, we compute the bearing from the street-view panorama's GPS coordinate to the building's centroid. Specifically, we retrieve the panorama's latitude and longitude returned by the Street View API (the closest panorama to our target building), and then calculate the azimuth angle toward the building's coordinates. This angle is subsequently used as the heading parameter in our Street View API request, ensuring that the image is oriented to face the building.

Additionally, if no panorama is found within 30 meters of the building's coordinate, we expand the search radius in incremental steps (e.g., up to 50 meters), ensuring a higher likelihood of acquiring at least one valid image in dense urban areas. Through this bearing-based approach, we minimize errors where the camera might otherwise capture the opposite side of the street or irrelevant surroundings. The final images, saved at 600×300 resolution, are thus more likely to depict the intended building facade.

3.3 Annotation with Multimodal Large Language Model

We annotate the street view imagery using OpenAI's ChatGPT-4o, a state-of-the-art language model designed to generate human-like text based on tailored prompts [26]. To ensure stability and efficiency in API requests, we implement a robust, multi-threaded framework capable of managing multiple API keys to optimize the distribution of API calls. The prompts for annotation are meticulously developed based on urban building exterior indicators identified during our preliminary research. To maintain flexibility and adaptability in the annotation process, we incorporate customizable configurations, allowing modifications to suit specific research objectives.

We further streamline the annotation process by automating key tasks, including image downloading, error handling, and data management. This automation framework facilitates the execution of tasks according to predefined parameters, manages failed download attempts, consolidates data into a unified dataset while eliminating duplicate records, and tracks processed data to prevent redundancy.

The indicators resulting from our annotation process are designed to be exportable in various spatial data formats, including CSV, Shapefile, and GeoJSON. Our accompanying documentation provides several examples for querying and exporting data into both tabular and geospatial formats, ensuring compatibility with a wide range of analytical tools.

To promote accessibility and facilitate the distribution of ready-to-use datasets, we compile and publish datasets for multiple cities as open data within a dedicated repository. This repository includes datasets for cities and countries with detailed mapping available in OpenStreetMap (OSM), and it continues to expand as we add new locations. The ongoing development of this repository reflects our commitment to providing comprehensive and up-to-date urban building exterior data.

4 Experiment

This section describes the experimental setup, including data selection, sampling strategy, and validation of the proposed approach. Subsection 4.1 details the data collection from Amsterdam, New York City, and Singapore, along with the associated building and Street View datasets. Subsection 4.2 outlines the result analysis and evaluates the performance of our indicators using both manual inspection and quantitative metrics. By examining these diverse case studies, we highlight the strengths and limitations of our method.

4.1 Study Area and Dataset

We construct an Urban Building Exteriors Database using Street View Imagery, theoretically applicable to any urban area with street views. For this project, we select three representative cities: New York City (NYC), Amsterdam, and Singapore. The distribution of data points for the three cities is shown in Fig. 3.

Fig. 3. The Distribution of Sampling Points

Each city is chosen based on its unique architectural characteristics and urban landscape. New York City is renowned for its iconic skyscrapers and diverse architectural styles, ranging from historic brownstones to modern glass towers [27]. Amsterdam offers a distinct contrast with its picturesque canal houses, narrow buildings, and intricate facades, reflecting a historic and compact urban design [28]. Singapore, known for its modernist high-rise buildings and innovative architectural solutions, represents a dynamic and evolving urban environment that blends tradition with cutting-edge design [29].

To collect building information, we employ the Overpass API, a powerful tool for querying OpenStreetMap [30] data, which enables us to compile comprehensive datasets for each city. From these, we sample buildings and collect their building IDs, latitude and longitude coordinates, and address information. For the SVI, we utilize Google Street View Imagery [31] to capture panoramic images of individual building exteriors. To standardize the collection process, we center the building ID coordinates within a 30-meter buffer and select the closest street view image to each building. This method ensures consistency and precision in capturing building exteriors. The dataset comprises 8,130 building images for NYC, 6,422 building images for Singapore, and 7,758 building images for Amsterdam. Additionally, sample street view images for each city have been included to provide visual context for the building exterior data collected, as shown in Fig. 4.

Fig. 4. Representative Street View Images from Selected Cities.

4.2 Result and Analysis

We collected building exterior datasets from Amsterdam, New York City, and Singapore, comprising a total of 22,310 records. For most extracted indicators, the effective generation rate exceeds 99.90%. However, the generation rate for streetscape perception scores is relatively lower at 86.05%. This reduced rate is attributed to the inherent randomness in ChatGPT's generation process and the challenges associated with complex regular expression matching.

In terms of efficiency, the entire GPT4O-based annotation process across all records incurred a total cost of approximately $220, while covering 26 indicators per building. This breaks down to roughly $0.01 per building annotation. Each API call required only a few seconds on average. By deploying parallel processing, we managed to complete the entire annotation task within several hours. These results not only highlight the cost-effectiveness of our approach but also demonstrate its potential for scaling to large datasets in urban building data analysis.

To evaluate the model's predictive performance, we select four key variables: Floor-to-Floor Height Numeric Only, Window-to-Wall Ratio (WWR), Vertices, and Tree Coverage. Using manual inspection as the benchmark, we randomly sample 200 instances from the three cities and calculate three key statistical indicators: Mean Absolute Error (MAE), Root Mean Square Error (RMSE), and R^2. The results show that while predictive accuracy varies among different variables, the overall performance remains strong, as shown in Table 2. Notably, the R^2 values for Floor-to-Floor Height Numeric Only and WWR are 0.83036 and 0.74679, respectively. Although the Vertices variable presents certain challenges, its R^2 value of 0.69767 still indicates a reasonable level of predictive capability.

In the accompanying figures, we select the following indicators from three perspectives—environment, energy, and human—to visualize the results: 'A' represents the parking lot scale, 'B' represents the tree coverage scale, and 'C' represents the Window-to-Wall Ratio (WWR) scale, while the numbers 1, 2, and 3 correspond to Amsterdam, Singapore, and New York City, respectively. In Fig. 5, the color of the dots transitions from red to green, indicating the scale of the

Table 2. Performance Metrics for Different Variables

Variable	MAE	RMSE	R^2
Floor-to-Floor Height	0.01724	0.09285	0.83036
WWR	0.01355	0.04130	0.74679
Vertices	0.82209	2.24292	0.69767
Tree	0.13462	0.50000	0.66215
Total	0.24687	0.71927	0.73424

metrics from small to large. Deeper red signifies a smaller scale, while deeper green indicates a larger scale.

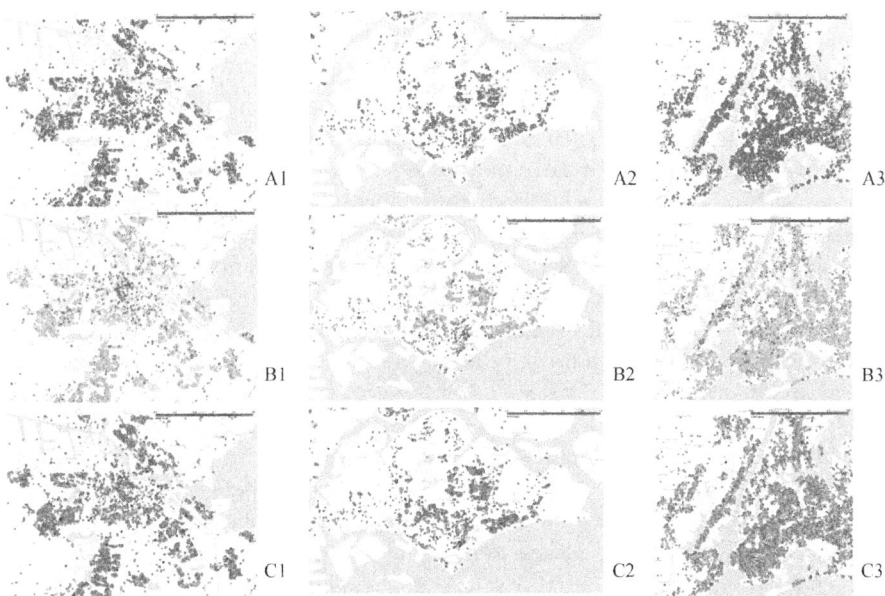

Fig. 5. Visualization of Result: The Number of Parking Lots (A), Trees (b) and Window-to-Wall Ratio (c)

For parking lot scale (A1, A2, A3), deeper red areas in city centers typically indicate smaller or fewer parking lots due to higher population densities and constrained land use, while peripheral or suburban districts appear in lighter or deeper shades of green, suggesting larger or more abundant parking facilities. Tree coverage (B1, B2, B3) shows predominantly green hues, with darker greens indicating denser or more extensive tree presence. Amsterdam maintains balanced tree distribution across its canal networks and suburban edges, Singapore showcases dense greenery in residential neighborhoods (aligned with its garden city initiative), and New York City presents significant variation among boroughs, with some zones rich in street trees and others more built-up. For Window-to-Wall Ratio (C1, C2, C3), intense green signifies high ratios of windows to wall surfaces, commonly found in modern or renovated buildings favoring natural light and large windowpanes, while historic districts display red or lighter green hues due to smaller or fewer windows reflective of older architectural styles.

We also create word clouds that capture the diversity of architectural styles across the studied cities. The word clouds reveal that modern and somewhat modern architectural styles are common in some regions, whereas somewhat historical styles prevail in others (see Fig. 6).

The word cloud reveals notable differences in architectural styles across the three cities. In Figures A and C, the terms "somewhat modern" and "modern somewhat" are most prominent, indicating a widespread presence of contemporary architectural designs. This suggests ongoing urban development and renovation activities, which contribute to a modernized cityscape. These areas likely feature more recent constructions with streamlined facades, larger windows, and minimalist aesthetics. In contrast, Figure B shows a strong prevalence of "somewhat historical," pointing to a significant influence of heritage architecture and preservation efforts. This pattern suggests that historical conservation policies or cultural preferences for traditional styles are more influential in this region. Consequently, the urban landscape here is characterized by older buildings with ornate facades, smaller windows, and classic architectural elements.

Additionally, the term "significant style" appears across all three maps, though its relative prominence varies. In Figures A and C, it suggests distinctive design elements that enhance visual appeal and architectural identity. In Figure B, however, its presence is more subdued, possibly indicating a more uniform historical architectural style. This variation reflects the interplay between modern development and historical preservation across the cities. The word clouds not only highlight stylistic differences but also reveal underlying cultural, historical, and socioeconomic factors that shape urban architectural identity. The diversity in architectural styles underscores how urban planning policies, cultural heritage values, and contemporary design trends contribute to the distinct character of each city.

5 Discussion

BuildingView provides an automated, scalable, and open-source framework for extracting building-facade attributes and contextual features from street-view imagery. In what follows, we discuss its value for various fields of built environment research in Subsect. 5.1, outline the role of sustainability and crowd intelligence in dataset maintenance and enhancement in Subsect. 5.2, and consider future directions and implementation strategies to further expand its scope and applicability in Subsect. 5.3.

Fig. 6. The Visualization of Result: Human Style Wordclouds.

5.1 Potential Benefits to Existing Built Environment Research

Human-Centered Urban Research. Current studies on walkability, aesthetics, and perceived safety are often limited by labor-intensive data collection, reducing research scope and comparability. BuildingView streamlines this by automatically extracting attributes like façade articulation, greenery, window transparency, and pedestrian-scale infrastructure from street-view imagery. These details provide insights into how architectural and environmental elements influence human experiences, such as neighborhood safety and public space quality, supporting evidence-based urban design to enhance walkability and visual appeal.

Scalability and Standardization in Built Environment Data. Built-environment research often lacks standardized, large-scale datasets that capture architectural complexity across different contexts. BuildingView addresses this by systematically extracting and labeling features from street-view images using fine-tuned large language models, ensuring consistent data across regions. Its open-source and modular design allows users to add new indicators or customize the framework, facilitating comparative studies and promoting standardized urban data analytics.

Urban Morphology. Traditional urban morphology studies rely on simplified datasets or field surveys with limited building details. BuildingView enhances this by using street-view imagery to capture detailed façade geometry, window-to-wall ratios, and architectural elements, offering high-resolution morphological indicators. These observations reveal architectural patterns, urban density impacts on livability, and adaptations to cultural or climatic contexts, enabling precise cross-city morphological comparisons and better classification of architectural styles.

5.2 Sustainability and Crowd Intelligence

BuildingView is fully automated and reproducible, ensuring continuous updates and responsiveness to urban changes. Scripts for data acquisition, annotation, and enrichment are openly available, enabling scheduled re-runs when new street-view imagery becomes available. As urban environments evolve—new buildings emerge, façades are updated, or land-use patterns change—these automated updates keep the data relevant. Future improvements can integrate advanced building attribute prediction models for greater accuracy and richer metadata.

In addition to automated updates, BuildingView leverages crowd intelligence, turning data users into contributors. In areas with limited street-view coverage, local communities or researchers can enhance the dataset using open mapping platforms like Mapillary or KartaView. An interactive web-based validation tool could also allow volunteers to verify or refine architectural labels, ensuring higher data quality through community participation. This collaborative, open-source approach supports global open-data principles, making BuildingView a valuable resource for urban researchers, planners, and policymakers.

5.3 Future Directions and Implementation Considerations

BuildingView is designed to accommodate a variety of urban contexts and building types using street-view data. Ongoing and future enhancements can amplify its robustness, usability, and overall impact. First, broadening geographic reach remains a key priority for capturing buildings in regions where street-view coverage is limited or inconsistent, a process that may benefit from partnerships with local institutions or community-driven imagery initiatives. Second, refining classification algorithms and annotation prompts can help distinguish subtle features and address any class imbalances, especially for rare building elements. Third, volunteer-driven validation tools could allow local users to verify automated labels in challenging scenarios, strengthening data reliability and inclusiveness. Lastly, reducing reliance on proprietary APIs can facilitate more equitable access and sustainability by leveraging open-source or collaborative data platforms where feasible. Through these incremental improvements, BuildingView can serve as a valuable resource for built environment research, policy-making, and community engagement, supporting a clearer understanding of how façades and streetscapes shape the social, environmental, and energy dimensions of cities.

6 Conclusion

In this study, we have compiled a list of hot topics related to building exteriors for the last five years. Twenty-six metrics are summarised and categorized into disciplines. Our study presents a novel spatial database for building exteriors, demonstrating the feasibility of integrating AI and street view imagery to enhance the completeness of the database. The validation of our approach highlights its potential for efficiency and accuracy, setting a precedent for similar endeavors. Such a workflow can be replicated for global regions, resulting in a worldwide database of building exteriors.

Upon enhancing the building classification approach through the integration of multi-source datasets, we anticipate the development of a comprehensive and accurate global building exteriors database. This envisioned database will serve as a solid foundation, providing invaluable insights and data to researchers and industry experts alike.

Acknowledgments. This work is supported by the National Natural Science Foundation of China (Grant No. 42401567), the Tertiary Education Scientific Research Project of the Guangzhou Municipal Education Bureau (Grant No. 2024312159), and the Guangzhou Municipal Science and Technology Bureau Program (Grant No. 2025A03J3640).

Disclosure of Interests. The authors have no competing interests to declare that are relevant to the content of this article.

References

1. Xie, D., Gou, Z.: Dissipating surplus solar photovoltaics capacity from net-zero energy buildings to electric vehicle charging stations in nearby parking lots: a study in new York city. Energy and Buildings **303** (2024)
2. Orsini, F., Marrone, P.: Approaches for a low-carbon production of building materials: a review. J. Cleaner Prod. **241** 2019
3. Liang, X., Chang, J. H., Gao, S., Zhao, T., Biljecki, F.: Evaluating human perception of building exteriors using street view imagery. Build. Environ. **263** (2024)
4. Liang, X., Chang, J. H., Gao, S., Zhao, T., Biljecki, F.: Evaluating human perception of building exteriors using street view imagery. Build. Environ. 111875 (2024)
5. Biljecki, F., Ito, K.: Street view imagery in urban analytics and GIS: a review. Landsc. Urban Plan. **215**, 104217 (2021)
6. Zhao, P., Miao, Q., Song, J., Qi, Y., Liu, R., Ge, D.: Architectural style classification based on feature extraction module. IEEE Access **6**, 52598–52606 (2018)

7. Xiao Hong Ding and Hai Hong Hu: Analysis of the building's exterior color and material. Appl. Mech. Mater. **409–410**, 388–391 (2013)
8. Rundle, A.G., Bader, M.D., Richards, C.A., Neckerman, K.M., Teitler, J.O.: Using google street view to audit neighborhood environments. Am. J. Preven. Med. **40**(1), 94–100 (2011)
9. Gupta, V., Deb, C.: Envelope design for low-energy buildings in the tropics: a review. Renew. Sustain. Energy Rev. **186** (2023)
10. Chen, S., Ogawa, Y., Zhao, C., Sekimoto, Y.: Large-scale building footprint extraction from open-sourced satellite imagery via instance segmentation approach. In: IGARSS 2022-2022 IEEE International Geoscience and Remote Sensing Symposium, pp. 6284–6287. IEEE (2022)
11. Ki, D., Lee, S.: Analyzing the effects of green view index of neighborhood streets on walking time using google street view and deep learning. Landsc. Urban Plan. **205**, 103920 (2021)
12. Kim, J.H., Lee, S., Hipp, J.R., Ki, D.: Measuring the built environment with google street view and machine learning: consequences for crime on street segments. J. Quantitative Criminol. 1–29 (2021)
13. Koo, B.W., Guhathakurta, S., Botchwey, N.: How are neighborhood and street-level walkability factors associated with walking behaviors? a big data approach using street view images. Environ. Behav. **54**(1), 211–241 (2022)
14. Hou, Y., et al.: Global streetscapes-a comprehensive dataset of 10 million street-level images across 688 cities for urban science and analytics. ISPRS J. Photogramm. Remote. Sens. **215**, 216–238 (2024)
15. Biljecki, F., Chow, Y.S.: Global building morphology indicators. Comput. Environ. Urban Syst. **95** (2022)
16. Wang, G., Fang, J., Yan, C., Huang, D., Hu, K., Zhou, K.: Advancements in smart building envelopes: a comprehensive review. Energy Build., 114190 (2024)
17. Alsehail, A., Almhafdy, A.: The effect of window-to-wall ratio (WWR) and window orientation (wo) on the thermal performance: a preliminary overview. Environ. Behav. Proc. J. **5**(15), 165–173 (2020)
18. Ayşe, F.A.: Determination of optimum building envelope parameters of a room concerning window-to-wall ratio, orientation, insulation thickness and window type. Buildings **12**(3) (2022)
19. Han, M., Chen, H.: Effect of external air-conditioner units' heat release modes and positions on energy consumption in large public buildings. Build. Environ. **111**, 47–60 (2017)
20. Sadineni, S.B., Madala, S., Boehm, R.F.: Passive building energy savings: a review of building envelope components. Renew. Sustain. Energy Rev. **15**(8), 3617–3631 (2011)
21. Cheuk, F.N.: Perception and evaluation of buildings: the effects of style and frequency of exposure. Collabra: Psychol. **6**(1), 44 (2020)
22. Carlo, A.C., et al.: Vertical greenery as natural tool for improving energy efficiency of buildings. Horticulturae **8**(6), 526 (2022)
23. Champagne, M.P., Dubé, J., Barla, P.: Build it and they will come: how does a new public transit station influence building construction? J. Transp. Geography **100** (2022)
24. Clemens, K.: Geocoding with openstreetmap data. GEOProcessing **2015**, 10 (2015)
25. Roland, O., et al.: Overpass api. Anwenderkonferenz für Freie und Open Source Software für Geoinformationssysteme (2011)

26. OpenAI. Chatgpt, Large language model (2023)
27. Richard, L.: The city in literature: an intellectual and cultural history. Univ of California Press (2023)
28. Havinga, L., Colenbrander, B., Schellen, H.: Heritage attributes of post-war housing in amsterdam. Front. Architectural Res. **9**(1), 1–19 (2020)
29. Yan, H., Ji, G., Yan, K.: Data-driven prediction and optimization of residential building performance in singapore considering the impact of climate change. Build. Environ. **226**, 109735 (2022)
30. Jonathan, B.: OpenStreetMap. Packt Publishing Ltd (2010)
31. Anguelov, D., et al.: Google street view: capturing the world at street level. Computer **43**(6), 32–38 (2010)

Urban Fire Risk Prediction and Spatiotemporal Analysis Based on Machine Learning

Weijie Song[✉] and Zhaoge Liu[✉]

Xiamen University, Xiamen, Fujian, China
36920241153247@stu.xmu.edu.cn, zhaogeliu@xmu.edu.cn

Abstract. Urban fires occur frequently, posing significant threats to public safety in modern cities. Although previous studies have attempted to predict fire risks using regression analysis, traditional regression models are limited in handling complex nonlinear relationships among variables and accurately assessing the weight of each indicator. Additionally, at the level of prefecture-level cities and above in China, a comprehensive fire risk prediction indicator system has not yet been established. This study aims to enhance the accuracy and practicality of urban fire risk prediction. Based on multi-source data from prefecture-level and above cities in China, this research integrates fire risk, social economy, natural meteorology and spatial location to construct a fire risk prediction indicator system from three dimensions: hazard, vulnerability, and exposure. Five machine learning algorithms were employed for modeling and comparison to quantify fire risks and explore their spatiotemporal distribution. The findings reveal that XGBoost performs the best in predicting fire frequency and direct losses, demonstrating strong generalization and reliability. Further spatiotemporal analysis indicates that fire risks fluctuate upward over time, particularly in years with lower humidity, higher sunlight and high wind speed exposure. Spatially, coastal economically developed cities exhibit higher fire-related economic losses, while fire frequency is more concentrated in the central and eastern regions. Conversely, fire risks are relatively lower in the western and northeastern regions.

Keywords: Machine learning · Fire risk prediction · Fire risk prediction index system · Spatio-temporal analysis

1 Introduction

Urban fires pose a significant threat to the safety and development of modern cities, constituting a critical public safety issue. With the continuous advancement of urbanization and the rapid development of the Chinese economy, the population size of prefecture-level cities has steadily increased, leading to a higher frequency of fire incidents. Statistical data indicate that, in recent years, urban fire risks in China have shown a general upward trend. Simultaneously, localized fire risks caused by climate change, urban expansion, and imbalanced regional development have become particularly prominent, exhibiting strong spatiotemporal heterogeneity [4,16]. Consequently, achieving cross-year fire risk prediction for prefecture-level and above cities and revealing the spatiotemporal distribution patterns of fire risks hold significant value in providing precise decision-making support for both local and central governments [7].

Existing studies on fire risk prediction primarily utilize regression-based methods. While traditional regression models excel at explaining risk factors, they struggle to address the complex and diverse fire data observed in Chinese prefecture-level and above cities [15]. These limitations include capturing nonlinear relationships among variables and determining the precise weights of individual factors. Recently, with advancements in artificial intelligence, the application of machine learning to fire risk prediction has effectively addressed these challenges [10,17].

Although some studies have adopted machine learning algorithms to enhance predictive performance, research on fire risk prediction for prefecture-level and above cities in China still lacks a comprehensive indicator system and a systematic comparison of algorithmic performance [20,21,26]. Further exploration is required for datasets characterized by small sample sizes, high dimensionality, and heterogeneity to develop more efficient and robust predictive models.

Among machine learning approaches for fire risk prediction, Support Vector Regression (SVR), Random Forest (RF), Extreme Gradient Boosting (XGBoost), K-Nearest Neighbors (KNN) and Bayesian Ridge Regression (BRR) all show good performance with their own advantages [1–3,6,25]. Accordingly, this research selects SVR, RF, KNN, XGBoost, and BRR as the primary machine learning algorithms for fire risk prediction.

In summary, this study focuses on prefecture-level cities across mainland China, utilizing urban fire risk, socio-economic, meteorological, and spatial location to construct a comprehensive fire risk prediction indicator system from the dimensions of hazard, vulnerability, and exposure. Five machine learning models are systematically evaluated to identify the optimal algorithm for predicting annual fire risks across these cities. The research also explores the spatiotemporal distribution patterns of fire risks, offering data-driven recommendations for the allocation of firefighting resources. The findings aim to support central and local governments in optimizing resource deployment, improving fire risk management, and formulating disaster prevention and mitigation strategies.

2 Data Sources and Processing

2.1 Research Area and Data Sources

This study focuses on analyzing prefecture-level and above cities in mainland China (excluding Hong Kong, Macau, and Taiwan). The dataset encompasses socio-economic characteristics, meteorological conditions, and spatial location from 2012 to 2019, urban fire risk from 2013 to 2020. Each record combines fire characteristics of a given year with fire risk data for the following year, including fire frequency and direct economic losses. This structure creates a cross-year dataset. According to the *China Urban Statistical Yearbook*, as of the end of 2020, mainland China had 297 prefecture-level and above cities, including 4 municipalities, 15 sub-provincial cities, and 278 prefecture-level cities. The sampled cities cover all provinces and autonomous regions in mainland China, ensuring that the findings comprehensively reflect the current state and regional disparities of urban fire risks across the country.

Socio-economic statistics in this study are primarily derived from the *China Urban Statistical Yearbook*. To predict and analyze urban fire risks, four indicators were selected: casualties, fire frequency, and direct economic losses, with the latter two serving as target variables in the predictive models. These data are sourced from the *China Fire Services Yearbook*. Meteorological data were primarily obtained from the National Environmental Information Center (NCEI) under the National Oceanic and Atmospheric Administration (NOAA), with average annual humidity and cumulative annual sunshine derived from the China Surface Climate Data Daily Dataset (V3.0). To incorporate spatial weightings into the fire risk evaluation model, enabling identification of regional fire patterns and enhancing prediction accuracy, city-level geographic coordinates were included. These data were obtained from Baidu Maps. The comprehensiveness and accuracy of the data sources were thereby ensured.

2.2 Data Processing

First, if all indicators for a city in a given year are missing, the data is deleted. In the case that a few data points of the indicator data of a certain year of individual cities are missing, this study adopts the average interpolation method to average the data according to the sub-city group and the year group [13,24].

Before conducting data analysis and model training or prediction, min-max normalization was applied to standardize the original data into dimensionless variables [23]. This step eliminates the influence of differing units across indicators, facilitating comparisons and analyses. Min-max normalization is particularly suited for indicators with varying scales and magnitudes. The normalization formula is as follows:

$$z^* = \frac{z - z_{\min}}{z_{\max} - z_{\min}} \quad (1)$$

where z^* represents the normalized value, z is the actual value, $z_{\max}$ is the maximum observed value, and $z_{\min}$ is the minimum observed value. After normalization, all indicators were converted into unitless values ranging between 0 and 1. This ensures that the influence of different indicators is balanced during statistical analysis, thereby improving the accuracy and reliability of the results.

3 Methodology

This study adopts a systematic approach to predict urban fire risks accurately while addressing their complex nature. The methodology includes the

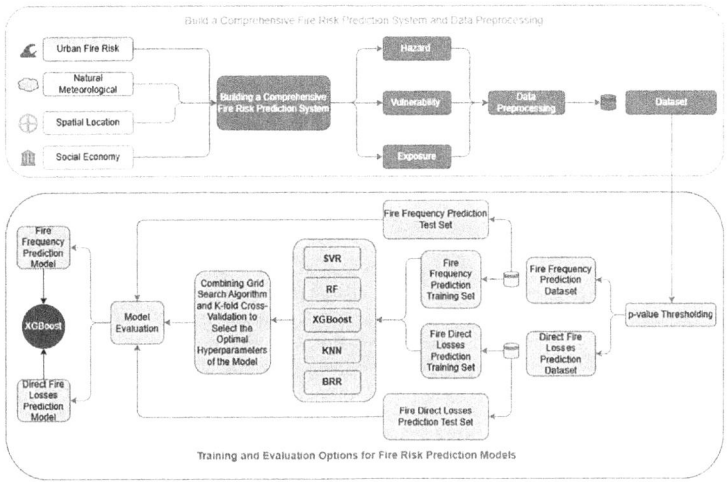

Fig. 1. Urban Fire Risk Prediction Process Architecture.

following steps. First, a comprehensive fire risk prediction indicator system was constructed to select the predictive and target variables for machine learning models. Then, in order to analyze the correlation between fire frequency and direct loss and fire characteristics, in this paper, based on the pre-processed data, we used Pearson correlation coefficient and p-value significance threshold limit to screen the indicators, and selected the corresponding variables significantly correlated with fire frequency and direct loss as predictors [18].Following this, the dataset was divided into training and testing sets, with five machine learning algorithms trained on the training set and evaluated on the testing set. The best-performing algorithm was selected for predicting fire frequency and direct losses. Finally, combined with the test results, the temporal and spatial analysis of fire risk is conducted. The workflow is illustrated in Fig. 1.

3.1 Fire Risk Assessment Index System

Fire risk is a multidimensional concept influenced by social economy, natural meteorology and spatial location factors [11,27,28]. This study categorizes indicators into three dimensions: hazard, vulnerability, and exposure. These dimensions capture various aspects of fire risk, providing a scientific basis for prevention, preparedness, and response. The detailed indicator system is shown in Table 1.

Hazard refers to the intensity and likelihood of fire-causing factors. Meteorological conditions directly affect fire occurrence and spread, acting as critical factors. Combining the fire conceptual framework proposed by Charles R. Jennings [11] and the evaluation indices system suggested by Weiyi Ju et al. [12],

Table 1. Comprehensive Fire Risk Prediction Index System

Primary Index	Secondary Index	Indicator Description (Unit)	Variable Index
Hazard	LPG Supply Volume	Liquefied Petroleum Gas Supply Volume (tons)	X_1
	Gas Supply Volume	Artificial and Natural Gas Supply Volume (10^4 m^3)	X_2
	Cumulative Sunshine Duration	Annual Total Sunshine Duration (hours)	X_3
	Average Humidity	Annual Mean Daily Humidity (%)	X_4
	Annual Precipitation	Total Annual Precipitation (mm)	X_5
	Average Temperature	Annual Average Temperature (°C)	X_6
	Average Wind Speed	Annual Mean Wind Speed (km/h)	X_7
	Highest Temperature	Annual Mean Daily Maximum Temperature (°C)	X_8
	Lowest Temperature	Annual Mean Daily Minimum Temperature (°C)	X_9
	Industrial Development Level	Number of Industrial Enterprises	X_{10}
	Fatalities	Number of Fire-Related Deaths	X_{11}
	Injuries	Number of Fire-Related Injuries	X_{12}
	Fire Frequency	Number of Next Year's Fire Occurrences	Y_1
	Fire Loss	Next Year's Fire Direct Losses (ten thousand yuan)	Y_2
Vulnerability	Education Level	Proportion of Primary and Secondary School Students	X_{13}
	Per Capita GDP	Per Capita GDP (yuan)	X_{14}
	Vulnerable Group Area	Number of Primary Schools, Secondary Schools, Hospitals	X_{15}
	Per Capita Housing Area	Per Capita Residential Area (km^2)	X_{16}
	Per Capita Road Area	Per Capita Urban Road Area (m^2)	X_{17}
	Per Capita Green Area	Per Capita Green Area (hectares)	X_{18}
	Urban Water Supply Capacity	Per Capita Water Resource Volume (10^4 tons)	X_{19}
	Urban Unemployment Rate	Proportion of Registered Unemployed Population	X_{20}
	Infrastructure Dependence	Proportion Employed in Transportation/Storage/Postal	X_{21}
	Social Management Level	Proportion Employed in Public Administration	X_{22}
	Per Capita Income	Average Salary of Employees (yuan)	X_{23}
	Private and Individual Ratio	Proportion of Urban Private and Individual Employees	X_{24}
	Unit Employment Ratio	Proportion of Urban Unit Employees (10^4 persons)	X_{25}
Exposure	Urban Population Scale	Average Annual Population (10^4 persons)	X_{26}
	Urbanization Level	Administrative Area (km^2)	X_{27}
	Urban Area	Land Area (km^2)	X_{28}
	Consumption Capability	Per Capita Consumption (10^4 yuan)	X_{29}
	Latitude	Baidu Latitude	X_{30}
	Longitude	Baidu Longitude	X_{31}

this study selects seven meteorological conditions as hazard indicators. Additionally, Jun Hu et al. [9] identified significant correlations between industrial development levels and urban fire risks. Liquefied petroleum gas (LPG) and coal gas contribute to fire risks during storage, transportation, and use. Therefore, the total supply of LPG and coal gas is included as hazard indicators. Casualties, fire frequency, and direct economic losses reflect the severity of annual fires in a city and are included as hazard indicators.

Vulnerability reflects the degree to which the exposed population, properties, and environment are susceptible to fire damage. This paper, in light of the indicators encompassed in the five dimensions of the resilient city evaluation system and the socio-economic determinants determined by Jun Hu et al. through correlation analysis, and by integrating the characteristics of various cities in China and the collection circumstances of basic data, selected 13 socio-economic factors as vulnerability indicators [19].

Exposure refers to the quantity or value of elements at risk within the fire-affected area. This study uses population size, urbanization level, city area, and consumption capacity as exposure indicators. Since city coordinates, as spatial location information, are directly related to the distribution of urban buildings, population density, resource distribution, etc. , this study selected city coordinates as an exposure index [8].

3.2 Fire Risk Prediction Algorithms

This section details the implementation of five machine learning algorithms: Support Vector Regression (SVR), Random Forest (RF), K-Nearest Neighbors (KNN), Extreme Gradient Boosting (XGBoost), and Bayesian Ridge Regression (BRR).

SVR model aims to find a prediction function:

$$f(x) = w^T \phi(x) + b \tag{2}$$

where w and b are parameters to be optimized. The objective function is:

$$\min_{w,b,\xi,\xi^*} \frac{1}{2}\|w\|^2 + C \sum_{i=1}^{n}(\xi_i + \xi_i^*) \tag{3}$$

Here, $\|w\|^2$ controls model complexity, ξ_i and ξ_i^* are slack variables representing deviations, and C balances complexity and fitting accuracy.

RF builds multiple decision trees using the following steps:

1. Randomly sample subsets from the training set and randomly select a portion of the features from each subset.
2. Construct decision trees, optimizing split points and features by minimizing Mean Squared Error (MSE):

$$\text{MSE}(t) = \frac{1}{|t|} \sum_{x_i \in t}(y_i - \bar{y})^2 \tag{4}$$

   where t represents a tree node, x_i is denotes the fire indicators for the ith sample, y_i is the fire direct loss or frequency for sample i, and $\bar{y}$ denotes the direct fire loss or frequency mean in the node.
3. Aggregate predictions from T trees by averaging, the formula is as follows:

$$\hat{y} = \frac{1}{T} \sum_{t=1}^{T} f_t(x) \tag{5}$$

   where $\hat{y}$ denotes the prediction result and $f_t(x)$ denotes the predicted value of sample x for the tth tree.

XGBoost optimizes a loss function iteratively:

1. Initialize the model with a constant value and compute the initial error.
2. In each iteration t, the objective function for XGBoost is:

$$\text{Obj}(t) = \sum_{i=1}^{n} L(y_i, \hat{y}_i^{(t)}) + \sum_{k=1}^{l} \Omega(f_k) \tag{6}$$

where $L(y_i, \hat{y}_i^{(t)})$ is the loss function and $\Omega(f_k)$ is the regularization term. The loss function is approximated using a second-order Taylor expansion:

$$L(y_i, \hat{y}_i^{(t)}) \approx L(y_i, \hat{y}_i^{(t-1)}) + g_i f_t(x_i) + \frac{1}{2} h_i f_t^2(x_i) \tag{7}$$

Here, $g_i = \frac{\partial L(y_i, \hat{y}_i^{(t-1)})}{\partial \hat{y}_i^{(t-1)}}$ is the first derivative (gradient), and $h_i = \frac{\partial^2 L(y_i, \hat{y}_i^{(t-1)})}{\partial (\hat{y}_i^{(t-1)})^2}$ is the second derivative (Hessian). Finally, fit a new regression tree $f_t(x)$ to approximate the negative gradient of the current error (residuals):

$$r_i^{(t-1)} = -g_i \tag{8}$$

3. Update the model according to the contribution of each tree (controlled by the learning rate η):

$$\hat{y}_i^{(t)} = \hat{y}_i^{(t-1)} + \eta f_t(x_i) \tag{9}$$

where η is the learning rate, typically in the range $(0, 1]$.

4. Stop when the error converges, that is, the error change in successive iterations is less than a set threshold.

KNN predicts by:

1. For each test sample, calculate its Manhattan distance from all the training samples with the following equation:

$$d(x, x_i) = \sum_{j=1}^{m} |x_j - x_{i,j}| \tag{10}$$

Here, $d(x, x_i)$ denotes the Manhattan distance between the test sample x and the i-th training sample x_i, x_j represents the j-th feature of the test sample x, $x_{i,j}$ represents the j-th feature of the training sample x_i, m is the total number of features.

2. Selecting k nearest neighbors.
3. The average of the k nearest neighbor fire target values is calculated as the prediction result $\hat{y}$ with the following equation:

$$\hat{y} = \frac{1}{k} \sum_{i \in \text{NN}(x)} y_i \tag{11}$$

where $\text{NN}(x)$ denotes the index set of the k closest training samples.

BRR. The following are the main algorithm steps:

1. Assume a regression model:
$$y = Xw + \epsilon \quad (12)$$
where $X \in \mathbb{R}^{n \times m}$ is the feature matrix, $w \in \mathbb{R}^m$ is the regression weight vector, and $\epsilon \sim \mathcal{N}(0, \sigma^2)$ represents Gaussian noise.

2. Impose a Gaussian prior:
$$p(w \mid \lambda) = \mathcal{N}(0, \lambda^{-1} I) \quad (13)$$
where λ is the regularization parameter that controls the width of the weight distribution, and I is the identity matrix.

3. Compute the likelihood function:
$$p(y \mid X, w, \alpha) = \mathcal{N}(Xw, \alpha^{-1} I) \quad (14)$$
where α is a hyperparameter representing the precision of the data.

4. Compute the posterior distribution:
$$p(w \mid X, y, \alpha, \lambda) \propto p(y \mid X, w, \alpha) p(w \mid \lambda) \quad (15)$$

5. Use empirical Bayes method to maximize the marginal likelihood $p(y \mid X, \alpha, \lambda)$, updating α and λ.

6. For a new input fire feature vector x, predict the corresponding target value $\hat{y}$:
$$p(\hat{y} \mid x, y, X, \alpha, \lambda) = \int p(\hat{y} \mid x, w) p(w \mid y, X, \alpha, \lambda) \, dw \quad (16)$$

3.3 Model Evaluation Metrics

To comprehensively evaluate the model's performance, this paper uses the coefficient of determination (R^2) and the Pearson correlation coefficient (r) as evaluation metrics [13,22]. R^2 can be quantitative model for fire loss directly, fire frequency data such as the explanation power fluctuations, reflect the overall model fitting effect, R^2 value in the range of [0, 1], numerical value is close to 1, the said model can explain the change of the target variable. The Pearson correlation coefficient can measure the consistency of the trend between the predicted value and the actual value, reflecting the model's ability to capture the data law. The value range of r is $[-1, 1]$, where a positive value indicates positive correlation, a negative value indicates negative correlation, and the closer the absolute value is to 1, the stronger the linear correlation is. The model needs to both accurately predict the magnitude of the fluctuations in fire data, R^2, and ensure that the predicted trend is consistent with reality, r.

4 Experiments and Results

4.1 Experimental Setup

This study employed the Pearson correlation coefficient to calculate the correlation coefficients between each fire risk prediction indicator and the target variables (fire frequency and direct fire loss), to initially understand the degree of linear correlation between them. Then, a significance test was conducted on each correlation coefficient, and the corresponding p-value was calculated. By setting the significance level threshold at 0.05, the indicators with a p-value less than 0.05 were screened out. The p-value was calculated to ensure that the correlation between the selected indicators and the target variables was not accidental but statistically reliable. In the prediction of fire frequency, the indicators X_2, X_3, X_4, X_6, X_8, X_9, X_{13}ïïjŇ X_{14}ïïjŇ X_{16}, X_{17}, X_{19}, X_{20}, X_{22} and X_{28} were removed. In the prediction of direct fire loss, the indicators X_{13}, X_{14}, X_{17}, X_{19}, X_{20}, X_{22} and X_{28} were removed.

In the experiment, we divided the fire data set into the training set and the test set according to the 8:2 ratio. To achieve optimal model performance, a combination of Bayesian search and k-fold cross-validation is employed to fine-tune hyperparameters, using the average R^2 value obtained during cross-validation as the selection criterion for the best parameter combination [5,14]. In this study, k is set to 10, as it balances bias and variance effectively. To ensure reproducibility, a random seed of 42 is used. Once the optimal hyperparameters are identified, the models are trained on the training set and evaluated on the test set.

4.2 Model Validation and Testing

Table 2. Model Validation and Testing Results

Model	Fire Direct Losses Prediction			Fire Frequency Prediction		
	CV R^2	Test R^2	Test r	CV R^2	Test R^2	Test r
SVR	0.4432	0.4812	0.7313	0.5323	0.4060	0.7125
BRR	0.5036	0.5543	0.7465	0.5199	0.5323	0.7310
KNN	0.5467	0.5891	0.7682	0.6473	0.6597	0.8225
RF	0.5664	**0.6240**	0.7913	0.6624	0.6749	0.8325
XGBoost	**0.5629**	0.6216	**0.7924**	**0.6988**	**0.7298**	**0.8583**

Five kinds of prediction models were obtained through 10-fold cross-validation. The trained prediction models were tested by using 2/8 fire data of prefecture-level and above cities in China as test sets. The cross-validation and test results are shown in Table 2.

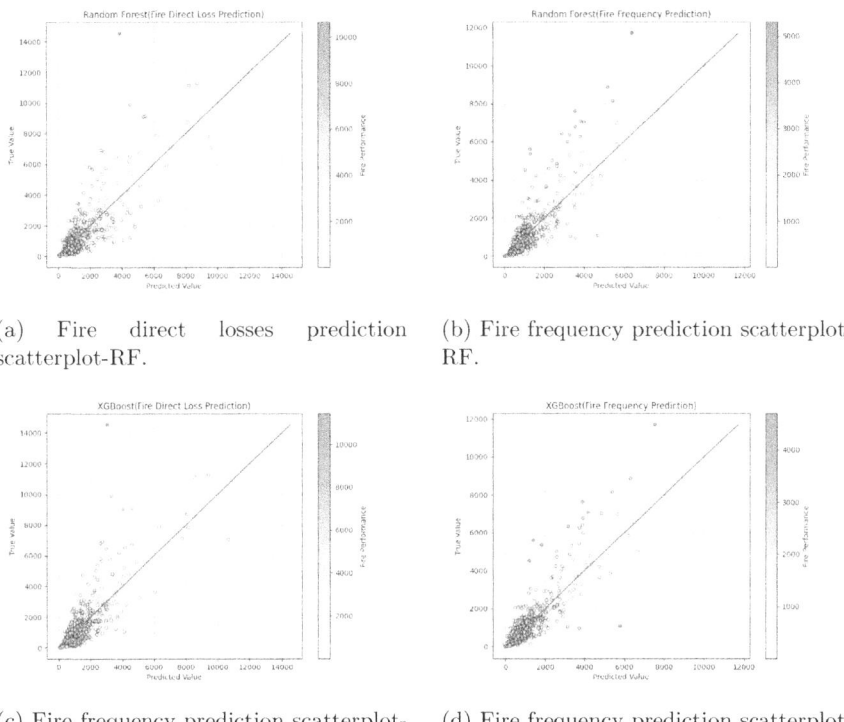

(a) Fire direct losses prediction scatterplot-RF.

(b) Fire frequency prediction scatterplot-RF.

(c) Fire frequency prediction scatterplot-XGBoost.

(d) Fire frequency prediction scatterplot-XGBoost.

Fig. 2. Fire risk prediction scatterplot.

As shown in Table 2, in fire direct losses prediction, the R^2 value of XGBoost and RF in the cross-validation and testing phase is similar to the r value. As shown in Fig. 2-c, the points between the predicted value and the true value of XGBoost are more closely distributed along the diagonal, and there are almost no obvious outliers or outliers. The excellent prediction performance is further confirmed, indicating that its ability to explain the fire direct losses and prediction accuracy are better than other models.

In the fire frequency prediction, XGBoost performs best, with R^2 values of 0.6988 and 0.7298 in cross validation and test phase, and r values of 0.8583 in test phase. The Fig. 2-d shows that the points between the predicted and true values of XGBoost are equally closely distributed along the diagonal, with almost no obvious outliers or outliers, indicating its high accuracy and stability in fire frequency prediction.

Although RF shows the same prediction performance as XGBoost in fire direct losses prediction, both R^2 and r values in fire frequency prediction are significantly lower than XGBoost. As shown in Fig. 2-a and Fig. 2-b, it can be seen that the points between the predicted value and the real value of RF are

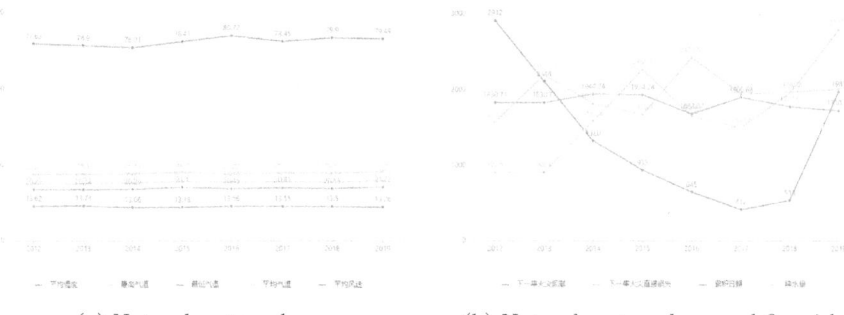

(a) Natural meteorology.   (b) Natural meteorology and fire risk.

Fig. 3. Natural meteorology and fire risk time series Analysis.

also relatively closely distributed near the diagonal, and the model does not have obvious over-fitting phenomenon, but the actual effect is still worse than XGBoost. Considering the performance of the model in the cross-validation and testing phase, as well as the visualization results of the scatter plot, XGBoost shows more accurate prediction performance in the prediction of fire direct losses and fire frequency. Therefore, based on the above analysis, XGBoost is selected as the prediction model of annual direct fire loss and fire frequency in Chinese cities.

5 Analysis of Spatial and Temporal Distribution of Fire Risk

This study selected meteorological data from Zhongshan City between 2012 and 2019 to analyze trends in fire risk over time. Based on the line chart in Fig. 3, it can be observed that the direct fire losses in the following year show a general upward trend with fluctuations, while starting from 2017, the frequency of fires in the following year has also shown a steady increase. Humidity is significantly negatively correlated with direct fire losses and fire frequency, while cumulative sunlight shows a positive correlation with both. On the other hand, rainfall and temperature have a relatively low correlation with fire risk, indicating that variations in these factors have a limited impact on fires. Meanwhile, average wind speed is positively correlated with both direct fire losses and fire frequency, suggesting that higher wind speeds may contribute to the spread of fire. These patterns indicate that central and local governments should prioritize fire prevention measures during years with low humidity, high sunlight and high wind speed, to enhance fire response capabilities.

Based on the 2020 urban fire data in mainland China, the fire risk distribution was plotted in Fig. 4, which illustrates the actual and predicted spatial distribution of fire risks (including fire frequency and direct losses). From the spatial distribution patterns shown in Fig. 4, the following observations can be made:

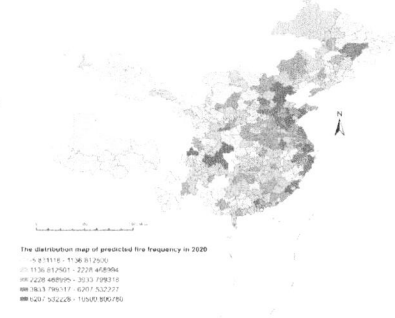

(a) The distribution map of actual fire frequency in 2020.

(b) The distribution map of predicted fire frequency in 2020.

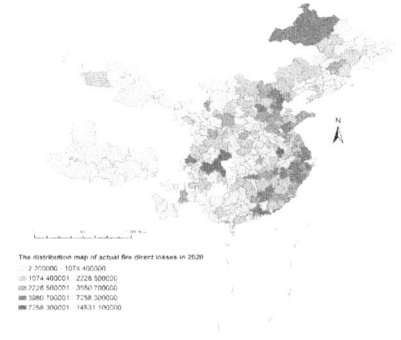
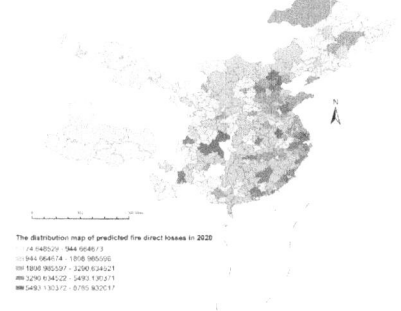

(c) The distribution map of actual fire direct losses in 2020.

(d) The distribution map of predicted fire direct losses in 2020.

Fig. 4. Fire risk distribution.

Coastal economically developed cities such as Shanghai, Guangzhou, Wenzhou, and Ningbo exhibit significantly higher fire direct losses, which can be attributed to higher economic density, concentrated buildings, and the distribution of high-value assets. In contrast, cities in the central and eastern regions, such as Beijing, Tianjin, and Hangzhou, exhibit higher fire frequencies, especially in urban clusters like the Bohai Economic Rim and the Yangtze River Delta. This concentration may be related to large population size and industrial activity in these areas.

On the other hand, cities in the western region experience relatively lower fire direct losses and frequencies. For instance, cities in provinces like Yunnan and Gansu exhibit both low fire frequency and losses, reflecting weaker economic activity in these regions. Similarly, northeastern cities, such as Shenyang, Changchun and Jilin, show limited fire-related impacts, possibly reflecting regional economic contraction.

In summary, the spatial distribution of fire risks reveals a concentration of high values along the coast, higher frequency in central and eastern regions, and relatively lower levels in the western and northeastern regions. These findings highlight the influence of economic development, population size, and urbanization on fire risks, further underscoring the importance of implementing targeted fire prevention measures and emergency response strategies in high-risk areas.

6 Conclusion

This study uses multi-source data from prefecture-level and above cities to predict and analyze urban fire risks through multiple machine learning algorithms. The findings reveal significant differences in model performance for predicting fire frequency and direct losses, with XGBoost and Random Forest demonstrating the best overall performance. These models exhibited significantly lower prediction errors compared to others, suggesting that tree-based algorithms, due to their ability to capture nonlinear feature relationships and robustness, are better suited for modeling complex fire data. Finally, this study selects the XGBoost algorithm with optimal comprehensive performance to realize fire risk prediction.

Further spatiotemporal distribution analysis highlights that the geographic distribution of fire risks is closely linked to climatic conditions and socioeconomic characteristics. Regions with high fire frequency are often concentrated in areas with dry climates and large population size, while economically developed regions suffer more severe property losses due to asset concentration. These results underscore the evident regional characteristics of fire risks, emphasizing the need for localized management strategies. This study contributes by integrating multi-source data and employing advanced machine learning methods, providing a scientific and quantitative analytical framework for urban fire risk prediction and assessment. The findings can assist fire management agencies in optimizing resource allocation, formulating targeted prevention strategies, and offering a basis for future research on algorithm selection and feature analysis.

Despite its achievements in fire risk prediction, this study has certain limitations. First, the data primarily span the years 2012âĂŞ2020, a relatively short time frame that may not fully capture the long-term trends of fire risks. Second, although multi-source data were integrated, there is still room for improvement in data fusion and feature engineering, as some potential fire risk factors may not have been fully identified or utilized. Additionally, the generalizability of the models may vary across regions and fire scenarios, requiring further validation and optimization.

Future research can be expanded in the following directions: (1) Extend the temporal and spatial coverage of the dataset to include more years and regions, enhancing the stability and generalizability of the models. (2) Further explore and integrate data from additional dimensions, such as urban infrastructure, cultural practices, and emergency response capabilities, to enrich the fire risk assessment indicator system. (3) Investigate more advanced machine learning algorithms and deep learning models, such as ensemble learning and neural networks, to improve the accuracy and efficiency of fire risk predictions. (4) Strengthen research on model interpretability by analyzing the driving factors and mechanisms behind prediction results, providing more intuitive and comprehensible insights for fire risk management and decision-making. Through continuous optimization and innovation, fire risk prediction research will offer stronger support for urban safety and development.

References

1. Breiman, L.: Random forests. Mach. Learn. **45**, 5–32 (2001). https://doi.org/10.1023/A:1010933404324
2. Chen, T., Guestrin, C.: Xgboost: a scalable tree boosting system. In: Proceedings of the 22nd ACM SIGKDD International Conference on Knowledge Discovery and Data Mining (2016). https://api.semanticscholar.org/CorpusID:4650265
3. Cover, T., Hart, P.: Nearest neighbor pattern classification. IEEE Trans. Inf. Theory **13**(1), 21–27 (1967). https://doi.org/10.1109/TIT.1967.1053964
4. D'Angelo, N., Albano, A., Gilardi, A., Adelfio, G.: Spatio-temporal point process modelling of fires in sicily exploring human and environmental factors (2024). https://arxiv.org/abs/2402.10859
5. Dewancker, I., McCourt, M., Clark, S.: Bayesian optimization for machine learning : a practical guidebook (2016). https://arxiv.org/abs/1612.04858
6. Drucker, H., Burges, C.J.C., Kaufman, L., Smola, A., Vapnik, V.N.: Support vector regression machines. In: Neural Information Processing Systems (1996). https://api.semanticscholar.org/CorpusID:743542
7. Guo-liang, C.: Study on comprehensive assessment index system of urban fire risk in Beijing city. China Safety Sci. J. (2007). https://api.semanticscholar.org/CorpusID:111468258
8. Hao, A.: Thoughts on the current situation, problems and development of urban area fire risk assessment. In: Proceedings of the 2014 Annual Conference of Science and Technology of China Fire Protection Association, pp. 595–597. Tianjin Fire Research Institute of the Ministry of Public Security, Beijing (2014)
9. Hu, J., Shu, X., Xie, S., Tang, S., Wu, J., Deng, B.: Socioeconomic determinants of urban fire risk: a city-wide analysis of 283 Chinese cities from 2013 to 2016. Fire Saf. J. **110**, 102890 (2019). https://doi.org/10.1016/j.firesaf.2019.102890, https://www.sciencedirect.com/science/article/pii/S037971121830537X
10. Huang, S., Ji, J., Wang, Y., Li, W., Zheng, Y.: Development and validation of a soft voting-based model for urban fire risk prediction. Int. J. Disaster Risk Red. **101**, 104224 (2024). https://doi.org/10.1016/j.ijdrr.2023.104224, https://www.sciencedirect.com/science/article/pii/S2212420923007045
11. Jennings, C.R.: Social and economic characteristics as determinants of residential fire risk in urban neighborhoods: A review of the literature. Fire Saf. J. **62**, 13–19 (2013). https://doi.org/10.1016/j.firesaf.2013.07.002, https://www.sciencedirect.com/science/article/pii/S0379711213001136
12. Ju, W., Xing, Z., Wu, J.: Comprehensive risk assessment of natural disasters based on machine learning in Changzhou city, China. Environment, Development and Sustainability (2024). https://api.semanticscholar.org/CorpusID:273246477
13. Kirch, W.: Pearson's Correlation Coefficient, pp. 1090–1091. Springer Netherlands, Dordrecht (2008). https://doi.org/10.1007/978-1-4020-5614-7_2569

14. Kohavi, R.: A study of cross-validation and bootstrap for accuracy estimation and model selection. In: International Joint Conference on Artificial Intelligence (1995). https://api.semanticscholar.org/CorpusID:2702042
15. Liu, Z.G., Li, X.Y., Jomaas, G.: Effects of governmental data governance on urban fire risk: a city wide analysis in china. Int. J. Disaster Risk Red. **78**, 103138 (2022). https://doi.org/10.1016/j.ijdrr.2022.103138, https://www.sciencedirect.com/science/article/pii/S2212420922003570
16. xin Luo, Y., Li, Q., rui Jiang, L., hao Zhou, Y.: Analysis of Chinese fire statistics during the period 1997–2017. Fire Safety J. **125**, 103400 (2021). https://doi.org/10.1016/j.firesaf.2021.103400, https://www.sciencedirect.com/science/article/pii/S0379711221001417
17. Madaio, M.A., et al.: Firebird: predicting fire risk and prioritizing fire inspections in atlanta. In: Proceedings of the 22nd ACM SIGKDD International Conference on Knowledge Discovery and Data Mining (2016). https://api.semanticscholar.org/CorpusID:11161557
18. Mansournia, M.A., Nazemipour, M., Etminan, M.: P-value, compatibility, and s-value. Global Epidemiol. **4**, 100085 (2022). https://doi.org/10.1016/j.gloepi.2022.100085, https://www.sciencedirect.com/science/article/pii/S2590113322000153
19. Miao, H., Wang, N., Wang, Y., Lin, P.: An urban resilience measurement system based on decomposing post-disaster recovery process. J. Nat. Disasters **30**, 10–27 (2021)
20. Michail, D., et al.: Seasonal fire prediction using spatio-temporal deep neural networks (2024). https://arxiv.org/abs/2404.06437
21. Mishra, M., et al.: Spatial analysis and machine learning prediction of forest fire susceptibility: a comprehensive approach for effective management and mitigation. Sci. Total Environ. **926**, 171713 (2024). https://doi.org/10.1016/j.scitotenv.2024.171713, https://www.sciencedirect.com/science/article/pii/S0048969724018552
22. Nagelkerke, N.J.D.: A note on a general definition of the coefficient of determination. Biometrika **78**, 691–692 (1991). https://api.semanticscholar.org/CorpusID:123723097
23. Nogueira, A.L.: The effect of data standardization in cluster analysis. Brazilian J. Radiation Sci. **9** (2021). https://api.semanticscholar.org/CorpusID:210138589
24. Rymes, M.D., Myers, D.R.: Mean preserving algorithm for smoothly interpolating averaged data. Solar Energy **71**, 225–231 (2001). https://api.semanticscholar.org/CorpusID:121266909
25. Tipping, M.E.: Sparse bayesian learning and the relevance vector machine. J. Mach. Learn. Res. **1**, 211–244 (2001). https://doi.org/10.1162/15324430152748236
26. Yuan, Y., Wylie, A.G.: Comparing machine learning and time series approaches in predictive modeling of urban fire incidents: a case study of austin, texas. ISPRS Int. J. Geo-Inf. **13**(5) (2024). https://doi.org/10.3390/ijgi13050149
27. Zhang, Y.: Analysis on comprehensive risk assessment for urban fire: the case of Haikou city. Procedia Eng. **52**, 618–623 (2013). https://api.semanticscholar.org/CorpusID:111010710
28. Zhao, B., Zhuang, L., Wang, K.: Spatial characteristics and existing problems of china's prefecture-level cities since reform and opening-up. Tropical Geography **43**(5), 795–807 (2023). https://doi.org/10.13284/j.cnki.rddl.003676

Spatio-Temporal Diffusion Attention Networks for Vessel Flow Prediction

Yuanyuan Pang[1](✉), Yong Li[1], Qiang Mei[2,3], and Peng Wang[2,4]

[1] Beijing University of Technology, Beijing 100124, China
pangyuanyuan@emails.bjut.edu.cn
[2] Shanghai Maritime University, Shanghai 201306, China
[3] Jimei University, Xiamen 361021, China
[4] Institute of Computing Technology, Chinese Academy, Beijing 100086, China

Abstract. To improve the efficiency of traffic information prediction, prevent traffic congestion, and reduce navigation conflicts, a mid-to-long-term ship traffic prediction method based on a spatiotemporal diffusion attention network is proposed. First, a method for constructing a maritime network is proposed, addressing the different structural characteristics of waterways and road networks. Next, a spatiotemporal diffusion attention network is built to enhance prediction accuracy. Then, using AIS data from the Huangpu River region as an example, a comparative analysis is conducted with a baseline model under the LibCity traffic prediction framework. Finally, the prediction results are visualized and analyzed. Experimental results show that the proposed model improves the evaluation metrics (MAE, $MAPE$, $RMSE$, R^2) compared to SOTA, with an improvement range of 1.6%–14.9%. The method surpasses the comparison models, thus validating its feasibility and effectiveness.

Keywords: Vessel flow prediction · Maritime road · Automatic identification system · Spatio-Temporal Diffusion Attention Network

1 Introduction

Maritime transportation is vital to global trade due to its cost-effectiveness and capacity to handle large volumes of goods. As maritime traffic grows, port congestion has become a major issue, leading to longer cargo turnover times and reduced navigation efficiency [21]. A 2021 survey by Xinde Marine News [9] found severe congestion at major global ports, with vessels waiting for clearance. As traffic increases, congestion risks rise, and if port authorities fail to quickly address these issues, accidents may occur. Optimizing vessel scheduling and port management is crucial for reducing congestion and improving efficiency [8]. Early traffic forecasting is key to mitigating congestion and enhancing system performance. Thus, forecasting vessel traffic flow has become a priority for maritime regulators to improve operations and efficiency.

Maritime traffic data differs significantly from urban traffic flow data, with larger statistical periods, broader spatial coverage, and greater fluctuations, making prediction more challenging. Unlike urban road networks, waterways lack strict structural constraints, and their complex spatial relationships further complicate predictions. Additionally, the spatiotemporal characteristics are influenced by spatial and temporal heterogeneity, where adjacent regions can impact each other. Vessel traffic data, based on AIS, combines static timeline information with dynamic vessel data such as MMSI(Maritime Mobile Service Identity), timestamps, coordinates, heading, and speed. Effectively processing this multidimensional spatiotemporal data is crucial for improving traffic prediction performance.

The challenges above have garnered significant attention and research from scholars. Maritime traffic prediction, being a form of medium- to long-term forecasting, has traditionally been approached through two main categories of methods: dynamic modeling and data-driven approaches. Dynamic modeling utilizes mathematical tools and physical principles to address traffic issues through computational simulations [12]. However, such simulations require complex system programming, consume substantial computational resources, and often suffer from unrealistic assumptions and simplifications, which can reduce the accuracy of predictions. In contrast, data-driven methods forecast traffic flow through classical statistical models and machine learning algorithms. Autoregressive Integrated Moving Average (ARIMA) and its variants are classic representatives of statistical approaches [14]. For instance, Sadeghi et al. [10] used ARIMA to predict container ship traffic flow, while Fan et al. employed gray theory in combination with Markov chains to refine ship traffic flow predictions. These methods have achieved relatively good results. However, due to the static assumptions inherent in time series analysis, they fail to account for spatiotemporal correlations, limiting their performance in handling highly nonlinear traffic flows. Machine learning methods, on the other hand, have demonstrated superior performance in traffic prediction tasks. For example, Wang et al. [13] combined Backpropagation Neural Networks (BP) with residual analysis to predict vessel flow, and Zhang et al. [20] enhanced BP using Particle Swarm Optimization (PSO) for vessel traffic analysis and prediction. These approaches overcome the limitations of statistical methods and are more effective in addressing nonlinear issues.

In the field of deep learning, networks such as Recurrent Neural Networks (RNN) [19] and Long Short-Term Memory (LSTM) networks [3] have been widely applied in traffic prediction. For example, Xie [17] and Zhao [4] used LSTM for predicting inland vessel traffic flow. However, these methods face challenges in jointly extracting spatiotemporal features from the input data. To fully leverage spatial features, researchers have adopted Convolutional Neural Networks (CNN) to capture spatial relationships within traffic networks, while utilizing RNN to model temporal dependencies. For instance, Wu et al. [15] proposed a feature-level fusion architecture, CLTFP, which combines LSTM and 1D CNN for short-term traffic prediction. This approach marked the first attempt to model both spatial and temporal regularities in a unified manner. Graph Neural Networks (GNNs) have gained significant attention, especially models based on spatial convolution, such as Graph Convolutional Networks (GCN) and Graph Attention Networks (GAT) [5,11].

In recent years, Spatiotemporal Graph Neural Networks (STGNNs) have become a mainstream method for modeling complex spatiotemporal dependencies in traffic data [6,16]. STGNNs typically combine GCNs [6,16] with sequence models [1,18] to jointly capture spatial and temporal features.

This study shifts the traffic prediction task from urban to maritime environments, exploring whether existing models can be adapted for maritime traffic. To address the unique challenges, we construct a maritime vessel traffic dataset, introduce trajectory pixelization [7], and propose a method for building maritime road networks. Additionally, we introduce a new spatiotemporal graph neural network, the Spatiotemporal Diffusion Attention Network (ST-DAN), for vessel traffic prediction. A case study on the Huangpu River region illustrates the approach, with a schematic shown in Fig. 1.

Fig. 1. Map of the Bending Area of the Huangpu River.

The contributions of this paper are as follows:

1. **Vessel Traffic Dataset Construction**: We use AIS data to build a daily vessel traffic dataset for the Huangpu River's bending area, assessing the reliability of various traffic flow prediction models in maritime scenarios.
2. **Maritime Road Network Construction**: The sea surface is divided into a regular grid, with vessel trajectories mapped onto the grid cells as geographic units. This approach simplifies traffic prediction by using grid cells to collect historical in and out-flow data for future predictions.
3. **Spatiotemporal Graph Convolution Models**: We propose a novel spatiotemporal graph neural network, ST-DAN, which integrates diffusion and self-attention mechanisms.

4. **Objective and Fair Model Comparison**: We perform a standardized comparison of traffic prediction models using the unified LibCity codebase, consistent evaluation criteria, testing environments, and datasets to ensure a fair assessment of model performance.

2 Technical Framework

The model implemented in this paper consists of three parts: maritime road network construction, spatiotemporal graph construction, and Spatiotemporal Diffusion Attention Network. These components will be detailed in the following sections.

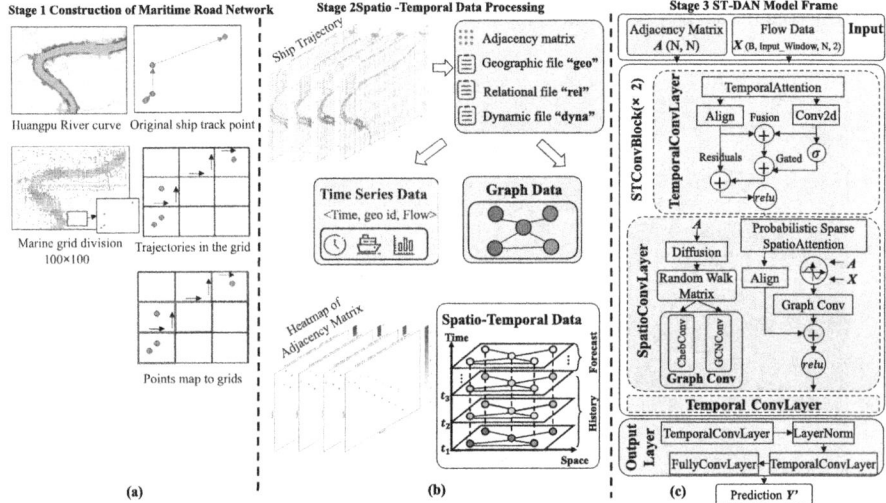

Fig. 2. Framework of ST-DAN.

2.1 Construction of Maritime Road Network

Unlike land vehicles, which are confined to road networks, ships have greater freedom of movement, resulting in more sparse trajectories and less similarity between paths. To address this, we introduce the concept of a maritime road network. This involves dividing the sea surface into equal-sized grids and mapping ship nodes to these grid cells. Ships within a certain range are assigned to the same network node, transforming ship trajectories into network node-based representations that reflect their sailing routes. This approach is similar to a land-based road network. By constructing this maritime network, we can capture traffic signals and relevant information. The construction process will be detailed in the following section.

AIS Data Preprocessing. Each raw AIS record contains multiple fields. To reduce redundancy, we retain only the longitude, latitude, timestamp, dynamic sailing information, and the unique MMSI number. Records within a specific time frame are grouped by MMSI and sorted by timestamp. Abnormal values are identified and removed by assessing the speed between consecutive points in each trajectory. A schematic of the preprocessing process is shown in Fig. 3.

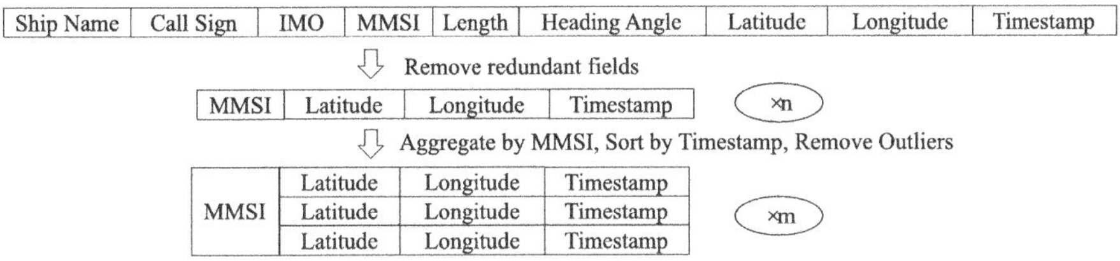

Ship Name	Call Sign	IMO	MMSI	Length	Heading Angle	Latitude	Longitude	Timestamp

⇩ Remove redundant fields

MMSI	Latitude	Longitude	Timestamp

xn

⇩ Aggregate by MMSI, Sort by Timestamp, Remove Outliers

MMSI	Latitude	Longitude	Timestamp
	Latitude	Longitude	Timestamp
	Latitude	Longitude	Timestamp

xm

Fig. 3. A schematic of the AIS data preprocessing process.

Sea Surface Grid Division and Trajectory Mapping. The Huangpu River bends are divided into 100 × 100 grid network. Ship trajectory data, with MMSI as the primary key, is mapped to these grids. Ships within the same region are assigned to the same grid cell (Fig. 2(a)), transforming ship trajectories into grid node representations. The vector data is exported in Mercator coordinates using PostGIS and Postgres, then converted to WGS84 format for graph construction.

Trajectory Data Processing. The grid node trajectory data is processed chronologically, forming a sequence with grid entity IDs as the primary key. The geographical boundaries of each grid are calculated, and their center points' latitude and longitude serve as the coordinates for each grid entity. This results in a set of ship trajectories, with each timestamp linked to a specific trajectory. A schematic of ship trajectories within the grid is shown in Fig. 4.

2.2 Construction of Spatio-Temporal Graph

After constructing the maritime road network, a set of ship trajectories within the grid is obtained (Fig. 2(b)), with each timestamp corresponding to a ship trajectory map. A weighted adjacency matrix of a directed graph is then created from these trajectories. Geographical, relational, and dynamic atomic files are extracted from the matrix, with the dynamic files containing key time-series data. Finally, a spatiotemporal graph is constructed. The next section will detail the process of constructing this spatiotemporal graph.

Construction of the Adjacency Matrix. A weighted adjacency matrix for a 100 ×100 grid is constructed from ship trajectories, where the weight represents the number of connections between nodes. For example, Fig. 5 shows a topology diagram and heatmap for 15 grid nodes, illustrating the connectivity and

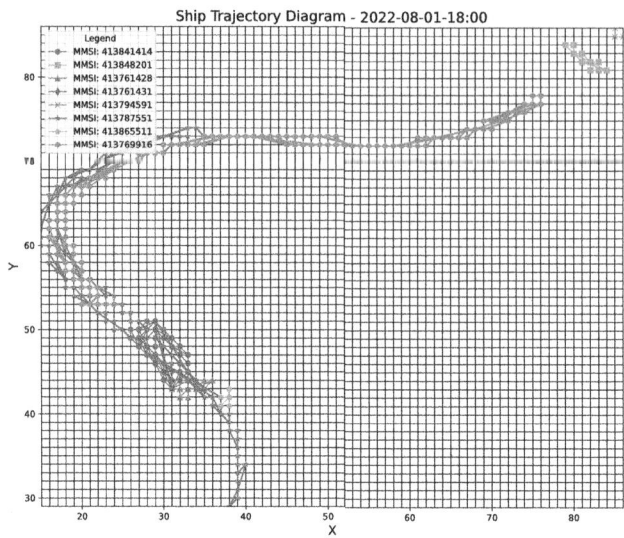

Fig. 4. Schematic of Ship Trajectories within the Grid.

weight information between them. The adjacency matrix captures the geographical relationships between nodes and serves as a key component in the prediction of traffic flow.

Extraction of Atomic Files. Using the weighted directed adjacency matrix, we extract valid information to generate atomic files. The format of these files is shown in Table 1. The Geographical File (geo) includes node ID, type, and spatial coordinates. The Relational File (rel) captures the many-to-many relationships between nodes. Together, the geographical and relational files form the graph structure, detailing node and edge connectivity. The Dynamic File (dyna) stores time-series data for each node, including incoming (in_flow) and outgoing (out_flow) traffic.

Table 1. The Data Structure of Atomic Files

File Name	Content	Example
Dataset.geo	Geographic entity attribute	geo_id, type, coordinates
Dataset.rel	Relationship of entity	rel_id, type, origin_id, destination_id, link_weight
Dataset.dyna	Traffic status	dyna_id, type, time, entity_id, in_flow, out_flow

We extract the network entities from the non-zero rows of the adjacency matrix as geographical entities for the "geo" atomic file. The corresponding source and destination entities, along with their weights, are recorded in the "rel" atomic file. The "dyna" file includes time-based information, with inbound and outbound

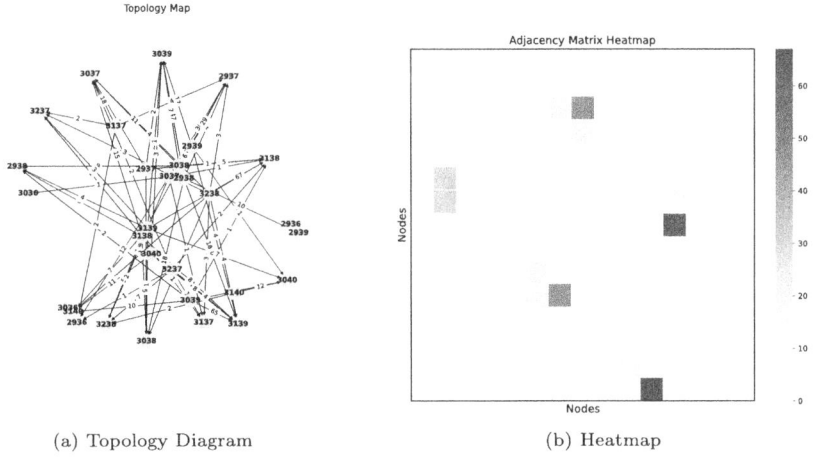

(a) Topology Diagram (b) Heatmap

Fig. 5. The Topology Diagram and Heatmap Corresponding to the Adjacency Matrix.

flow values calculated for each geographical entity node. This file is crucial for flow prediction. Relevant details of the Huangpu River bend data are shown in Table 2.

Table 2. The Data Scale of Atomic Files in the Huangpu River Bend Dataset

Item	Content
Date Range	20200801–20201031
Geographic Range	(31°16'N, 121°28'E), (31°11'N, 121°33'E)
Number of Network Nodes	10,000
Number of Entity Nodes	1,861
Number of Entity Relationships	101,983
Number of State Records	171,212
Time Interval	86400 s
Number of Time Stamps	92

2.3 Spatio-Temporal Diffusion Attention Networks

This section details the proposed Spatiotemporal Diffusion Attention Network (ST-DAN) architecture. As shown in Fig. 2(c), ST-DAN consists of three modules: input, spatiotemporal convolution, and output. The input module processes atomic files and standardizes the dataset, including the maritime road network's directed, weighted adjacency matrix and time-series traffic flow data. The spatiotemporal convolution module applies convolutional operations to capture spatiotemporal features. The output module then generates traffic flow predictions for future time steps based on the extracted features.

Input Module. The input module loads the atomic files from the spatiotemporal data processing stage and normalizes the data. It then uses the Pytorch Dataloader class to convert the data into batches for the spatiotemporal convolution module.

(1) Loading Atomic Files. The dyna atomic files are loaded to extract traffic data (e.g., inflow, outflow) and corresponding time series. Time series samples are generated using a sliding window approach, with defined input and output windows.

(2) Normalization. The data undergoes normalization using methods such as Z-score, Min-Max, or Log normalization. This process scales the data to a consistent range, eliminating dimensional discrepancies and improving model performance and stability.

Spatio-Tenporal Unit Module. The spatiotemporal convolution module consists of two ST-Conv blocks, each containing two temporal convolution layers and one spatial convolution layer.

Temporal Convolution Captures Temporal Features. The temporal convolution layer captures temporal features by applying convolution operations along the time axis to model dynamic traffic flow behavior. As shown in Fig. 2(c), it consists of a temporal attention layer, a 2D causal convolution with kernel size K_t, and a gated linear unit (GLU) [2] for nonlinear transformation.

First, the input features pass through the temporal attention layer, which highlights key time steps by learning correlations between different time points, while suppressing irrelevant or noisy information. This improves the model's ability to represent temporal patterns. Next, the output is processed by an Align operation and 2D causal convolution. The Align operation adjusts the input tensor's dimensions and channels, allowing the model to handle data with varying time steps or scales, ensuring feature consistency across different time intervals.

The 2D causal convolution, guided by the causal structure, ensures that each time step only depends on past data, preventing information leakage. This operation captures local temporal dependencies, strengthening the model's representation of dynamic changes. The aligned results are then combined with the partial outputs from the 2D convolution, enhancing temporal feature representation.

To control feature fusion, the combined output passes through a sigmoid function, which constrains the values between 0 and 1, acting as a gating mechanism. This mechanism learns the dependencies between time steps and dynamically adjusts the influence of the fused features. The gated output is then added to the aligned input, producing the final output.

To prevent issues like gradient vanishing or explosion, residual connections are used between the gated output and the aligned input, ensuring smooth gradient flow and preserving original features. Finally, a ReLU activation introduces nonlinearity, further enhancing the model's ability to capture temporal dynamics and fine-grained features in traffic flow.

Spatial Convolution Captures Spatial Features. **(1) Graph Convolution**

In our model, graph convolution is directly applied to graph-structured data to capture spatial patterns. To reduce complexity, we use two approximation strategies: the Chebyshev polynomial and first-order graph Laplacian approximations.

We apply the Chebyshev polynomial approximation to localize the filter and reduce the number of parameters. The filter $\Theta(\Lambda)$ is represented as a polynomial of the graph Laplacian Λ, i.e., $\Theta(\Lambda) = \sum_{k=0}^{K-1} \theta_k \Lambda^k$, where $\theta \in \mathbb{R}^K$ is a sparse vector of polynomial coefficients. K is the size of the graph convolution kernel, defining the maximum radius of convolution from the central node. The Chebyshev polynomial $T_k(x)$ approximates the kernel as a truncated expansion of order $k-1$, i.e., $\Theta(\Lambda) \approx \sum_{k=0}^{K-1} \theta_k T_k(\tilde{\Lambda})$, where $\tilde{\Lambda} = \frac{2\Lambda}{\lambda_{max}} - I_n$, and λ_{max} is the largest eigenvalue of L. Consequently, graph convolution is simplified as:

$$\Theta *_G x = \Theta(L)x \approx \sum_{k=0}^{K-1} \theta_k T_k(\tilde{L})x, \quad (1)$$

Here, $T_k(\tilde{L}) \in \mathbb{R}^{n \times n}$ is the k-th Chebyshev polynomial evaluated at the scaled Laplacian $\tilde{L}$. This approximation reduces the graph convolution cost to $\mathcal{O}(K|\mathcal{E}|)$ by recursively computing k local convolutions.

The first-order approximation simplifies the graph Laplacian, stacking multiple local graph convolution layers to define a hierarchical linear representation [5]. This allows for deeper architectures that recover spatial information without being restricted by polynomial parameterization. Assuming $\lambda_{max} \approx 2$ due to normalization, Eq. 1 simplifies to:

$$\Theta_G^* x \approx \theta_0 x + \theta_1 \left(\frac{2}{\lambda_{max}} L - I_n \right) x \approx \theta_0 x - \theta_1 \left(D^{-\frac{1}{2}} W D^{-\frac{1}{2}} \right) x, \quad (2)$$

where θ_0 and θ_1 are shared kernel parameters. To stabilize the model, we set $\theta_0 = -\theta_1 = \theta$. The weight matrix W and degree matrix D are re-normalized as $\tilde{W} = W + I_n$ and $\tilde{D}_{ii} = \sum_j \tilde{W}_{ij}$, respectively. Thus, the graph convolution becomes:

$$\Theta *_G x = \theta \left(I_n + D^{-\frac{1}{2}} W D^{-\frac{1}{2}} \right) x = \theta \left(\tilde{D}^{-\frac{1}{2}} \tilde{W} \tilde{D}^{-\frac{1}{2}} \right) x \quad (3)$$

This formulation efficiently captures the spatial dependencies in graph-structured data.

(2) Diffusion

By incorporating the diffusion mechanism from DCRNN [6], we establish connections between multi-hop neighboring nodes to capture the graph structure. The diffusion process is modeled as a weighted combination of infinite random walks of the graph signal. After several steps, it converges to a stationary distribution $P \in \mathbb{R}^{N \times N}$ (Eq. 4), where the i-th row, $P_{(i,:)} \in \mathbb{R}^N$, represents the diffusion probability from node v_i:

$$\mathcal{P} = \sum_{k=0}^{\infty} \alpha(1-\alpha)^k (D_O^{-1} W)^k \tag{4}$$

The graph signal $X \in \mathbb{R}^{N \times P}$ and filter f_θ produce a diffusion convolution $X_{(:,p)} \star_\mathcal{G} f_\theta$:

$$X_{:,p} \star_\mathcal{G} f_\theta = \sum_{k=0}^{K-1} \left(\theta_{k,1} (D_O^{-1} W)^k + \theta_{k,2} (D_I^{-1} W^\mathsf{T})^k \right) X_{:,p} \tag{5}$$

for $p \in \{1, \cdots, P\}$

The diffusion convolution layer $H_{(:,q)}$ maps the P-dimensional input features to the Q-dimensional output:

$$H_{:,q} = a \left(\sum_{p=1}^{P} X_{:,p} \star_\mathcal{G} f_{\Theta_{q,p,:,:}} \right) \text{ for } q \in \{1, \cdots, Q\}, \tag{6}$$

Here, $\alpha \in [0,1]$ is the restart probability, $D_O^{-1} W$ is the state transition matrix, and D_O is the out-degree diagonal matrix. In the diffusion convolution, $\theta \in \mathbb{R}^{K \times 2}$ represents the filter parameters, while $D_O^{-1} W$ and $D_I^{-1} W^\mathsf{T}$ are the transition matrices for the diffusion and reverse diffusion processes. The parameter tensor $\Theta \in \mathbb{R}^{Q \times P \times K \times 2}$ parameterizes the convolution filter between the p-th input and q-th output. $X \in \mathbb{R}^{N \times P}$ is the input, and $H \in \mathbb{R}^{N \times Q}$ is the output. $f_{\Theta_{(q,p,:,:)}}$ is the filter, and a is the activation function.

(3) The Probabilistic Sparse Attention Mechanism
The spatial convolution layer uses a probabilistic sparse self-attention mechanism, as proposed by [22], to address the long-tail distribution of traditional self-attention scores. In this distribution, only a few vectors contribute significantly, while most contribute minimally. The probabilistic sparse attention mechanism uses Kullback-Leibler (KL) divergence to identify and discard low-contribution vectors, reducing computational load while preserving key spatial features for large-scale traffic networks.

The attention probability distribution of the query vector is first calculated. If a value vector significantly impacts the attention weight, its distribution p deviates from the uniform distribution q; otherwise, it aligns with q. The attention score for the i-th query vector is computed probabilistically as:

$$A(q_i, K, V) = \sum_j p(k_j | q_i) \nu_j = E_{p(k_j | q_i)}[\nu_j] \tag{7}$$

The probability distribution of the query vector and the uniform distribution is calculated as shown in Eq. 8 and Eq. 9, respectively:

$$p(k_j|q_i) = \frac{k(q_i, k_j)}{\sum_l k(q_i, k_l)}, \tag{8}$$

$$q(k_j|q_i) = \frac{1}{L_K}, \tag{9}$$

Here, $k(q_i, k_j)$ is the asymmetric exponential kernel function $\exp\left(\frac{q_i k_j^T}{\sqrt{d}}\right)$, and L_K is the length of the query vector. The sparsity is then measured using the following KL divergence formula:

$$M(q_i, K) = \ln \sum_{j=1}^{L_k} e^{\frac{q_i k_j^T}{\sqrt{d}}} - \frac{1}{L_k} \sum_{j=1}^{L_k} \frac{q_i k_j^T}{\sqrt{d}}, \tag{10}$$

Here, j represents the j-th key vector of the key matrix. The first term calculates the logarithm sum over all keys, and the second term computes the arithmetic mean. Suppose the sparsity score of the i-th query vector is higher. In that case, its attention probability becomes more diversified, with a higher likelihood of including the key dot products that dominate the long-tail self-attention distribution. Therefore, the query vectors with the highest $M(q_i, K)$ values are selected as the main vectors for the attention computation.

Output Module. As shown in Fig. 2(c), the output module consists of several layers, starting with the first temporal convolution layer. This layer extracts temporal features from the input spatio-temporal data, which are crucial for subsequent predictions. Afterward, a layer normalization operation stabilizes the training process by preventing issues like gradient vanishing or explosion. The second temporal convolution layer further refines the temporal features, enhancing the model's ability to capture spatio-temporal patterns. Finally, a fully convolutional layer processes the output from the temporal convolutions, integrating multi-level feature information to improve prediction accuracy.

3 Experiment Results and Analysis

In this section, we present experiments showing that ST-DAN outperforms other models in maritime traffic prediction. Using the Huangpu River dataset from Chapter 3, we perform quantitative analysis by comparing evaluation metrics with baseline models and provide qualitative analysis through predicted vs. actual value plots.

3.1 Evaluation Metrics

We use five evaluation metrics for traffic flow prediction: *MAE*, *MAPE*, *RMSE*, and R^2. *MAE*, defined in Eq. 11, measures the mean absolute error between actual and predicted values, commonly used in regression tasks. *MAPE* (Eq. 12) calculates the mean absolute percentage error. *RMSE* (Eq. 13) represents the root mean square error, which is more sensitive to large errors and reflects model stability. R^2 (Eq. 14) measures how well the independent variable explains the variance in the dependent variable, with a higher R^2 indicating a better fit of the model.

$$MAE = \frac{1}{n}\sum_{i=1}^{n}|\widehat{y}_i - y_i| \tag{11}$$

$$MAPE = \frac{1}{n}\sum_{i=1}^{n}\left|\frac{\widehat{y}_i - y_i}{y_i}\right| * 100\% \tag{12}$$

$$RMSE = \sqrt{\frac{1}{n}\sum_{i=1}^{n}(\widehat{y}_i - y_i)^2} \tag{13}$$

$$R^2 = 1 - \frac{\sum_{i=1}^{n}(y_i - \widehat{y}_i)^2}{\sum_{i=1}^{n}(y_i - \bar{y})^2} \tag{14}$$

Here, the true values are $y = \{y_1, y_2, \ldots, y_n\}$, and the predicted values are $\hat{y} = \{\hat{y}_1, \hat{y}_2, \ldots, \hat{y}_n\}$, where n is the number of samples. The mean is $\bar{y} = \frac{1}{n}\sum_{i=1}^{n} y_i$, and the variance is $\text{Var}(y_i) = \frac{1}{n}\sum_{i=1}^{n}(y_i - \bar{y})^2$.

3.2 Baselines

To demonstrate the superiority of the proposed model, we compare it with several baseline models, categorized into three types: temporal models, spatiotemporal separation models, and spatiotemporal block stacking models. Temporal models, including RNN, Seq2Seq, and Transformer, are effective in fields like NLP and traffic forecasting. Spatiotemporal separation models, such as DCRNN, GWNET, and MTGNN, focus on handling spatial and temporal features separately. Spatiotemporal block stacking models, including STGCN, ASTGCN, and STSGCN, combine spatiotemporal features using stacked blocks.

- DCRNN: Uses diffusion-based graph convolution to capture temporal dependencies and an encoder-decoder framework for spatial dependencies.
- GWNET: Combines diffusion convolution with 1D dilated causal convolution to capture spatiotemporal dependencies.
- MTGNN: A framework for multivariate time series, using graph convolution and mixed-hop propagation with dilated composite convolutions for spatiotemporal dependencies.
- STGCN: Integrates graph convolution with gated temporal convolution to capture spatiotemporal correlations.
- STSGCN: Designed for spatiotemporal network data, it extracts complex spatiotemporal correlations via synchronous modeling.
- ASTGCN: Combines spatiotemporal attention mechanisms with convolutions to capture dynamic spatiotemporal features.

3.3 Experimental Settings

The dataset was split into training, testing, and validation sets at a 7:2:1 ratio. The time sampling interval was 1 day, with an input window of 12 days and an output window of 6 days, meaning data from the past 12 days predicted traffic for the next 6 days. All models were trained for up to 100 epochs, with baseline models using optimal parameters from the original papers. In the Huangpu River dataset experiments, the output dimension was set to 2 (inflow and outflow). The ST-DAN model used an initial learning rate of 0.001, the RMSProp optimizer, and StepLR for learning rate scheduling. All experiments were run on an NVIDIA TESLA V100.

3.4 Result and Analysis

The experimental results on the Huangpu River test set are shown in Table 3, which presents evaluation metrics for all baseline models and our proposed ST-DAN, along with predictions at steps 1, 3, and 6. These results show that ST-DAN outperforms most baseline models.

Table 3. Experimental Results on the Huangpu River Test Set

Time	Metrics	ST-DAN	RNN	Seq2Seq	Transformer	DCRNN	GWNET	MTGNN	STGCN	ASTGCN	STSGCN
No. 1 step	MAE	**5.584**	12.542	12.166	7.917	8.378	7.096	8.885	6.360	6.077	1.542×10^{-13}
	MAPE	0.576	0.804	0.858	0.909	0.788	**0.552**	0.790	0.622	0.805	1.748×10^{-12}
	RMSE	**11.343**	20.059	20.258	15.802	15.960	12.140	12.710	11.962	12.509	3.985×10^{-13}
	R^2	0.896	0.617	0.609	0.764	0.797	0.892	0.846	**0.907**	0.885	-1.512×10^{-24}
No. 3 step	MAE	**5.584**	11.943	12.747	8.116	8.378	7.096	22.713	6.360	6.077	3.683×10^{-13}
	MAPE	**0.576**	0.871	1.106	1.055	0.788	0.552	1.912	0.622	0.805	4.853×10^{-12}
	RMSE	**11.343**	18.649	20.896	16.007	15.960	12.140	30.789	11.962	12.509	9.607×10^{-13}
	R^2	**0.907**	0.589	0.484	0.730	0.797	0.892	−0.121	0.896	0.885	-1.092×10^{-25}
No. 6 step	MAE	**5.584**	12.528	12.207	7.890	8.378	7.096	23.401	6.360	6.077	2.452×10^{-13}
	MAPE	**0.552**	0.853	0.884	0.905	0.788	0.576	2.034	0.622	0.805	2.859×10^{-12}
	RMSE	**11.343**	19.946	20.360	15.759	15.960	12.140	29.193	11.962	12.509	6.053×10^{-13}
	R^2	**0.907**	0.614	0.598	0.762	0.797	0.892	0.184	0.896	0.885	-3.551×10^{-24}

Next, we will discuss the performance of each model and demonstrate the superiority of ST-DAN. The three-time steps mentioned earlier are defined as short-term, mid-term, and long-term predictions, with performance evaluation metrics considered separately. Regarding short-term prediction, ST-DAN did not outperform STGCN but surpassed most of the baseline models. For mid-term prediction, our model achieved reductions of 1.6%, 7.5%, and 5.8% in MAE, MAPE, and RMSE, respectively, while R^2 increased by 4.3%. In the case of long-term prediction, MAE, MAPE, and RMSE decreased by 3.9%, 7.5%, and 14.9%, respectively, while R^2 improved by 4.5%. ST-DAN performs better in long-term predictions.

We also compared the traffic prediction performance of our model with other SOTA methods and presented the results visually. As shown in Fig. 6, the plot includes the prediction curves of multiple models, including ST-DAN and the Baseline models. Each model's prediction curve is compared with the true values to assess its prediction accuracy. It can be observed that the prediction curve of the ST-DAN model closely follows the actual values.

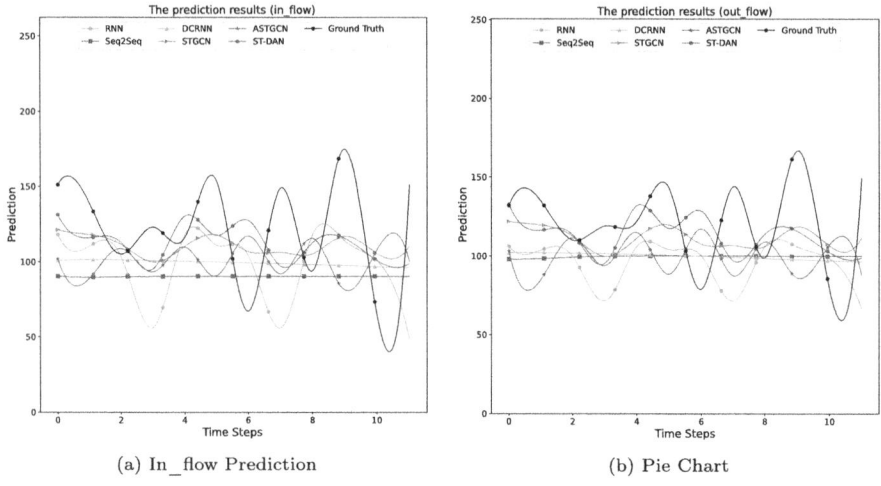

Fig. 6. Model Prediction Performance Comparison Curve.

Additionally, using inflow traffic as an example, we visualized the prediction errors of ST-DAN compared to three categories of Baseline models (as shown in Fig. 7), with the shaded areas representing the errors. The first two plots compare ST-DAN errors with RNN, Seq2Seq, Transformer, DCRNN, GWNET, and MTGNN. ST-DAN has the smallest error area, indicating higher prediction accuracy. The third graph compares the errors of ST-DAN with those of STGCN and ASTGCN, and it is clear that the ST-DAN model error is also superior to the others.

3.5 Hyperparameter Experiments

We conducted experiments on ST-DAN with different batch sizes to observe changes in predictive performance. Table 4 presents the evaluation metrics from these experiments. By comparing the metrics across different batch sizes, we found that the model performed best with a batch size of 8 for most time steps. In particular, at time steps 2, 3, and 4, the model achieved superior MAE, MAPE, and RMSE results while also exhibiting higher R^2 values. This indicates that the model had better predictive accuracy and goodness of fit under this configuration. In contrast, a batch size of 16 led to a significant performance

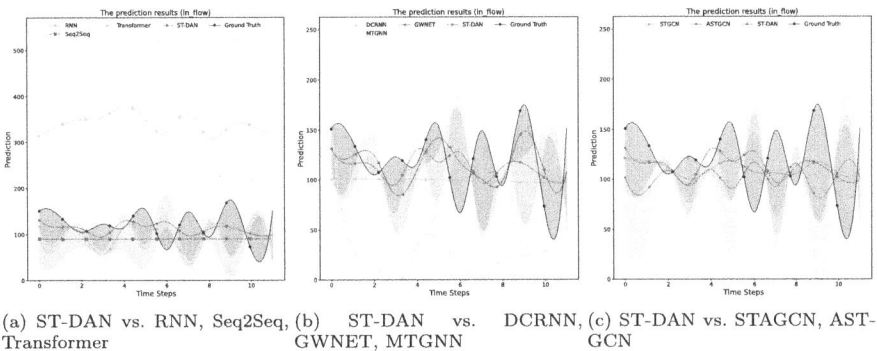

Fig. 7. Comparison of Prediction Errors Between ST-DAN and Three Types of Baseline Models.

decline at certain time steps, potentially due to gradient estimation bias caused by the larger batch size. Although a batch size of 4 offered a slight advantage in training time, its predictive performance was neither as stable nor as effective as that of a batch size of 8.

In addition, we have collected and visualized the changes in training loss, validation loss, learning rate, and training time across training batches under different batch_size settings. These analyses provide a deeper understanding of how batch size affects model performance, enabling us to select the optimal experimental parameters accordingly.

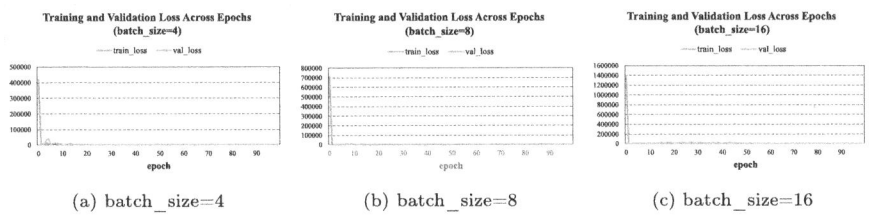

Fig. 8. Training and Validation Loss Across Epochs for Batch_sizes 4, 8, and 16.

As shown in Fig. 8, the training and validation losses exhibit distinct trends under different batch size settings. When the batch size is set to 4, both training and validation losses decrease rapidly in the early stages but eventually stabilize at relatively higher values. This may be attributed to the smaller batch size leading to less stable gradient estimates during training, thereby affecting the model's convergence performance. In contrast, with a batch size of 8, the training and validation losses decrease more rapidly compared to a batch size of 4, and the final loss values are significantly lower. For a batch size of 16, both training and validation losses also decrease rapidly in the early stages, with smaller fluctuations thereafter, and the final loss values are comparable to those achieved with

Table 4. Model Prediction Evaluation Metrics under Different Batch Sizes

Batch_size	Time_step	MAE	MAPE	RMSE	R2
4	1	8.572	1.096	16.154	0.755
	2	8.527	1.097	16.083	0.757
	3	8.559	1.103	16.129	0.754
	4	8.542	1.103	16.061	0.756
	5	8.550	1.102	16.074	0.756
	6	8.539	1.098	16.065	0.756
8	1	5.360	0.476	10.962	0.886
	2	4.134	0.416	9.093	0.920
	3	4.405	0.474	9.483	0.894
	4	4.678	0.392	9.567	0.925
	5	5.657	0.505	11.188	0.879
	6	5.201	0.475	10.585	0.891
16	1	7.917	0.909	15.802	0.764
	2	39.254	3.937	75.003	-4.370
	3	8.116	1.055	16.007	0.730
	4	8.382	0.889	16.826	0.753
	5	70.627	7.945	105.416	-9.649
	6	7.890	0.905	15.759	0.762

a batch size of 8. This suggests that a larger batch size can contribute to more stable training; however, it may not necessarily result in additional performance improvements in certain cases.

Figure 9(a) shows that the learning rate decreases progressively with the number of epochs, promoting stable training and convergence. The learning rate trends are similar across different batch sizes due to the shared initial learning rate of 0.001, RMSProp optimizer, and StepLR schedule.

Figure 9(b) indicates that training times remain stable across batch sizes, with batch size 4 being slightly faster, likely due to smaller batches enabling quicker iterations, depending on hardware and model complexity.

Considering training/validation loss trends, learning rate adjustments, and Table 4 metrics, batch size 8 achieves the best balance, with faster loss reduction, lower final loss, effective learning rate adjustment, and relatively short training time. This makes it a favorable choice for balancing performance and efficiency.

3.6 Ablation Study

In addition to the comparative experiments, we also conducted ablation studies on ST-DAN, designing the following three variants to validate the effectiveness of the spatiotemporal diffusion attention network:

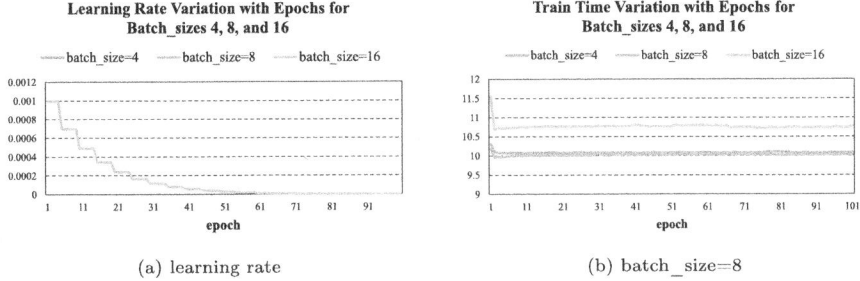

(a) learning rate (b) batch_size=8

Fig. 9. The Variation of Learning Rate and Training Time with Epochs under Different Batch Size Settings.

- **ST-AN**: Removes the diffusion mechanism from the original model, neglecting the random walk of graph signals in spatial feature extraction.
- **ST-DSAN**: Removes the temporal attention mechanism from the original model.
- **ST-DTAN**: Removes the spatial probabilistic sparse attention mechanism from the original model.

We gathered the experimental results of the three variants and the original model. As shown in Fig. 10, ST-DAN with the diffusion and spatiotemporal attention mechanisms outperforms all ablation versions by a significant margin. The results for MAE, RMSE, and MAPE show that ST-DAN's performance is more than twice as good as that of the three variant models, indicating a considerable improvement in model accuracy. The R^2 correlation metric shows that ST-DAN is nearly three times higher than the variants, suggesting enhanced model interpretability. These findings confirm that the diffusion mechanism, temporal attention mechanism, and spatial probabilistic sparse attention mechanism are indispensable components of ST-DAN. In conclusion, these ablation experiments validate the effectiveness, interpretability, and predictive accuracy of the ST-DAN design.

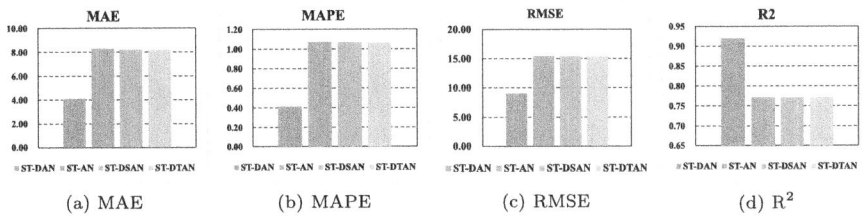

(a) MAE (b) MAPE (c) RMSE (d) R^2

Fig. 10. Comparison of Metrics for Three Ablation Variants and the Original Model.

4 Conclusions and Future

This study proposes ST-DAN, a novel spatiotemporal diffusion attention network for maritime vessel traffic prediction. We simplify vessel trajectory and traffic forecasting by mapping ships to grid nodes within a maritime road network. AIS data processing and spatiotemporal graph construction are built on the open-source LibCity framework. Integrating spatiotemporal graph neural networks, diffusion mechanisms, temporal attention, and spatial probabilistic sparse attention enhances the model's ability to capture vessel traffic patterns.

During the experimental phase, prediction experiments on grid nodes were conducted for short-term, medium-term, and long-term forecasting using the Huangpu River dataset. Comparisons with nine baseline models and ablation studies both demonstrated the superiority of ST-DAN. It was concluded that ST-DAN performs best in long-term forecasting.

ST-DAN can be applied in decision support systems to forecast future traffic conditions, helping to identify potential congestion and enhance maritime safety and efficiency.

Future work will focus on analyzing traffic prediction across different maritime regions, improving short-term prediction capabilities, and expanding the dataset for a broader sample.

References

1. Cho, K., van Merriënboer, B., Bahdanau, D., Bengio, Y.: On the properties of neural machine translation: encoder–decoder approaches. In: Proceedings of SSST-8, Eighth Workshop on Syntax, Semantics and Structure in Statistical Translation, pp. 103–111. Association for Computational Linguistics (2014)
2. Dauphin, Y.N., Fan, A., Auli, M., Grangier, D.: Language modeling with gated convolutional networks. In: International Conference on Machine Learning, pp. 933–941. PMLR (2017)
3. Hochreiter, S.: Long Short-Term Memory. Neural Computation MIT-Press (1997)
4. Ji, Z., Wang, L., Zhang, X., Wang, F.: Ship traffic flow forecast of Qingdao port based on LSTM. In: Sixth International Conference on Electromechanical Control Technology and Transportation (ICECTT 2021), vol. 12081, pp. 587–595. SPIE (2022)
5. Kipf, T.N., Welling, M.: Semi-supervised classification with graph convolutional networks. In: International Conference on Learning Representations (2017). https://openreview.net/forum?id=SJU4ayYgl
6. Li, Y., Yu, R., Shahabi, C., Liu, Y.: Diffusion convolutional recurrent neural network: Data-driven traffic forecasting. In: International Conference on Learning Representations (2018)
7. Lin, Y., et al.: Origin-destination travel time oracle for map-based services. Proc. ACM Manag. Data **1**(3), 1–27 (2023)
8. Lind, M., Ward, R., Watson, R.T., Haraldson, S., Zerem, A., Paulsen, S.: Decision support for port visits. In: Maritime informatics, pp. 167–186. Springer (2020)
9. Network, S.M.: Sindh maritime network (2021). https://www.xindemarinenews.com/en/index.html. Accessed 15 Dec 2024

10. Sadeghi Gargari, N., Akbari, H., Panahi, R.: Forecasting short-term container vessel traffic volume using hybrid arima-nn model. Int. J. Coast. Offshore Environ. Eng. (IJCOE) **4**(3), 47–52 (2019)
11. Velickovic, P., Cucurull, G., Casanova, A., Romero, A., Lio, P., Bengio, Y., et al.: Graph attention networks. stat **1050**(20), 10–48550 (2017)
12. Vlahogianni, E.I.: Computational intelligence and optimization for transportation big data: challenges and opportunities. Engineering and Applied Sciences Optimization: Dedicated to the Memory of Professor MG Karlaftis pp. 107–128 (2015)
13. Wang, C., Zhang, X., Chen, X., Li, R., Li, G.: Vessel traffic flow forecasting based on BP neural network and residual analysis. In: 2017 4th International Conference on Information, Cybernetics and Computational Social Systems (ICCSS), pp. 350–354. IEEE (2017)
14. Williams, B.M., Hoel, L.A.: Modeling and forecasting vehicular traffic flow as a seasonal Arima process: theoretical basis and empirical results. J. Transp. Eng. **129**(6), 664–672 (2003)
15. Wu, Y., Tan, H.: Short-term traffic flow forecasting with spatial-temporal correlation in a hybrid deep learning framework. arXiv preprint arXiv:1612.01022 (2016)
16. Wu, Z., Pan, S., Long, G., Jiang, J., Zhang, C.: Graph Wavenet for deep spatial-temporal graph modeling. In: Proceedings of the 28th International Joint Conference on Artificial Intelligence, pp. 1907–1913 (2019)
17. Xie, Z., Liu, Q.: LSTM networks for vessel traffic flow prediction in inland waterway. In: 2018 IEEE International Conference on Big Data and Smart Computing (BigComp), pp. 418–425. IEEE (2018)
18. Yu, F., Koltun, V.: Multi-scale context aggregation by dilated convolutions. In: ICLR (2016)
19. Zaremba, W.: Recurrent neural network regularization. arXiv preprint arXiv:1409.2329 (2014)
20. Zhang, J., Shi, X., Xie, J., Ma, H., King, I., Yeung, D.Y.: GAAN: gated attention networks for learning on large and spatiotemporal graphs. In: 34th Conference on Uncertainty in Artificial Intelligence 2018, UAI 2018 (2018)
21. Zhang, X., Fu, X., Xiao, Z., Xu, H., Qin, Z.: Vessel trajectory prediction in maritime transportation: current approaches and beyond. IEEE Trans. Intell. Transp. Syst. **23**(11), 19980–19998 (2022)
22. Zhou, H., et al.: Informer: beyond efficient transformer for long sequence time-series forecasting. In: Proceedings of the AAAI Conference on Artificial Intelligence, vol. 35, pp. 11106–11115 (2021)

Study on Pollutants and Greenhouse Gases Emission Inventory Making and Emission Prediction of Tianjin Port

Tong Xue[1(✉)], Yong Li[1], Qiang Mei[2,3], and Peng Wang[2,4]

[1] College of Computer Science, Beijing University of Technology, 100124 Beijing, China
xuetong@emails.bjut.edu.cn
[2] Merchant Marine Academy, Shanghai Maritime University, 200210 Shanghai, China
[3] Navigation College, Jimei University, 361021 Jimei, China
[4] Institute of Computing Technology, Chinese Academy of Sciences, 100190 Beijing, China

Abstract. Objectives: Pollutants emitted from ships pose significant environmental challenges, particularly to air quality in port-adjacent regions, while greenhouse gas (GHG) emissions exacerbate global warming. Existing emission inventories for Tianjin Port often overlook the Domestic Emission Control Areas (DECA) policy. Additionally, forecasting models relying on multiple data sources face practical constraints. **Methods:** This study compiled a high spatial-temporal resolution emission inventory of pollutants and GHGs from ships in Tianjin Port in 2018, using AIS data and DECA policies. Four types of time series models—based on Transformer, MLP, TCN, and RNN—were employed to predict emissions. **Results:** The results showed that SO_X and CO_2 are the primary pollutants and GHGs, with oil tankers, dry bulk carriers, and container ships being the main emission sources. Emissions from the main engine accounted for over 80% in channels, while auxiliary engine and boiler emissions were lower. However, in berths and anchorages, main engine emissions were almost negligible. Anchoring and docking contributed significantly, with emissions from these areas accounting for 94.94% of total emissions. Time series prediction results indicated that SCINet outperformed other models in low-value emission prediction. **Conclusions:** This study aligned with the DECA policy to develop an emissions inventory for Tianjin Port in 2018, examining the emission patterns of pollutants and GHGs from multiple perspectives. It also achieved emissions forecasting under a single data source condition.

Keywords: pollutant · greenhouse gas · emission inventory · AIS · emission prediction

1 Introduction

Shipping is a significant anthropogenic source of air pollutants and greenhouse gases (GHGs) [1,7]. Recent studies indicate that in 2017, CO_2 emissions from global shipping accounted for approximately 3% of anthropogenic CO_2 emissions [11], while the proportion of reactive gas emissions was even higher, with NO_X emissions contributing 20% and SO_2 emissions 12% of anthropogenic totals [10,16]. Air pollution has substantial impacts on human health and the environment, particularly in areas near ports [13], while GHGs contribute to global warming. As the largest comprehensive port in northern China, Tianjin Port ranked eighth worldwide in container throughput in 2023, facing severe environmental challenges.

In recent years, numerous researchers have sought to quantify pollutants and GHGs emitted from ships in ports to provide a scientific basis for emission reduction strategies. Against this backdrop, the Ministry of Transport of the People's Republic of China issued the Marine Emission Control Area Plan for Pearl River Delta, Yangtzy River Delta, Bohai Rim Area. The plan mandated that, starting January 1, 2018, ships berthed at all ports within the emission control areas (including Tianjin Port) must use fuel with a sulfur content $\leq 0.5\%$ m/m [3]. However, some existing studies developing the 2018 emissions inventory for ships at Tianjin Port did not fully account for the practical impacts of the DECA (Domestic Emission Control Areas) policy [17]. To address this gap, we integrated the strengths of existing emission models while incorporating the improvements introduced by the DECA policy to provide a more comprehensive 2018 emissions inventory. This inventory includes pollutants (PM_{10}, $PM_{2.5}$, DPM, NO_X, SO_X, CO, and HC) and GHGs (CO_2, CH_4, and N_2O) from shipping activities.

There are currently many methods for predicting air pollutant and GHG emissions [5,6,13,18]. Taking $PM_{2.5}$ concentration forecasting as an example, hybrid deep learning models have demonstrated superior performance among existing pollutant prediction approaches. These models typically combine CNN, LSTM, or GRU architectures, with some incorporating attention mechanisms [19]. However, these models not only rely on historical pollutant data but also integrate meteorological variables such as temperature, pressure, wind speed, and wind direction, spatial features among monitoring stations, traffic data, and even specific characteristics of street canyons and background pollutant domains [4,8]. While the use of multiple data sources enhances prediction accuracy, it also limits the practical applicability of hybrid deep learning models in real world scenarios. This limitation arises from increased computational requirements and the need for high resolution data, which may not be readily available at the city, regional, or port levels [12]. Based on the emissions inventory we developed, we aim to perform predictions using only the pollutant and GHG data from the inventory. To achieve this, we plan to leverage existing excellent time series models for forecasting.

To compare the effectiveness of various time series forecasting methods for pollutant and GHG emissions, we selected seven models, maintaining identical parameter settings as much as possible to ensure fairness. We chose several advanced and representative Transformer based models, including iTransformer, Informer, and Transformer, to evaluate performance. In addition, we selected DLinear as a representative MLP based model, and SCINet and TS2Vec as TCN based comparative models. Finally, for the RNN based models, we included LSTM for comparison.

In this study, we synthesized previous research [9,15] and existing ship emissions inventory models, incorporating ship emission control strategies, to develop a detailed high-resolution emissions inventory for ship pollutants and GHGs at Tianjin Port in 2018. Based on this emissions inventory, we conducted a comprehensive analysis of the emission patterns of ship pollutants and GHGs from the perspectives of time, ship type, engine type, and operational conditions. Finally, we created datasets and used seven models to predict the pollutant and GHG emissions from ships in the region.

2 Materials and Methods

2.1 Overview of the Study Area and Data Sources

Tianjin Port, located in the Binhai New Area of Tianjin, China, serves as the maritime gateway to the Beijing-Tianjin-Hebei region and is the largest comprehensive port in northern China [2,17]. In 2023, the container throughput at Tianjin Port reached 22.19 million TEUs, ranking eighth in the world. The geographic area covered in this study is primarily defined by the Tianjin Port Vessel Traffic Service (VTS) area, as designated by the China Maritime Safety Administration. The area spans from 117.35°E to 118.34°E and from 38.64°N to 39.24°N.

The research data includes AIS data from 7 channels, 8 anchorages and 205 berths at Tianjin Port in 2018, along with Lloyd's data and emission parameters for pollutants and GHGs. According to statistics, the raw 2018 AIS data for Tianjin Port consists of 70,572 data points for channels, 47,145 data points for berths and 20,361 data points for anchorages.

2.2 Model of Ship Emission Inventory

In previous studies [9,15], we provided a detailed introduction to the key technical methodologies employed in the development of the 2018 Tianjin Port ship emissions inventory. These methodologies included data cleaning, trajectory aggregation, data integration, calculation formulas, emission factors, and default parameter settings. The calculation formulas primarily accounted for air pollutant and GHG emissions from ship main engines, auxiliary engines, and boilers. Building on this foundation, the present study further refined ship type classifications and incorporates adjustments to emission parameters in alignment with the DECA policy, aiming to reduce uncertainties in emission calculations. The following sections will focus on the specific advancements made in the development of the 2018 ship emissions inventory.

1, The ship types in the original AIS ledger data are reclassified in this study. The original data, represented in Chinese, exhibit inconsistencies in naming, such as records with different names but similar meanings. These inconsistencies potentially affect the accuracy of pollutant and GHG emissions calculations, as critical parameters, including the ratio of the power of auxiliary engine to the maximum continuous rated power of the main engine (AMR) and the load factor of the auxiliary engine (LF_a), are closely related to ship type. To address this issue, ship type classifications were standardized by referencing ship registry records and considering practical requirements, consolidating them into nine categories: bulk carriers, container ships, cruise ships, general cargo ships, tugs, ro-ro ships, tankers, fishing vessels, and other types. Notably, tankers included oil tankers, chemical tankers, LPG carriers and LNG carriers. This standardized classification approach not only enhanced the consistency of ship type definitions but also provided more accurate baseline data for emissions calculations.

2. Match the missing static information. The AIS raw data lacks certain static information, including rotation speed of main engine (RPM), the maximum continuous rated power of the main engine (MCR), the maximum continuous rated power of the auxiliary engine (A_MCR), ship construction year, and maximum design speed ($Speed\_Max$). Among these, RPM is used to determine the ship's operational state, whether at low speed or even speed. The ship's operational state and construction year together determine the emission factor for pollutants and GHGs. In this study, a multi-step matching process was employed to fill in the missing information. First, the global main engine dataset was utilized, with the MMSI number serving as the matching criterion to associate it with the IMO number. Then, using the IMO number as the key, information on RPM, MCR, A_MCR, and the ship's construction year was extracted from the global main engine dataset. The design speed was matched via the ship's registry using the MMSI number as the key. To ensure data consistency and traceability, this study clearly identified the global main engine dataset and ship registry, integrated by Lloyd's Register Data, as the primary data sources for the above five categories of information. This matching process significantly enhanced the completeness of the AIS data, providing crucial static parameters for the subsequent calculation of ship emissions.

3, Calculate the missing static information. To supplement the static information missing in AIS records that could not be matched, this study estimated the remaining missing data through calculation. Taking the channel data as an example, records sourced from Lloyd's Register Data were first filtered. The average values for RPM, MCR, ship construction year, and design speed were calculated for each ship type, along with the overall average values regardless of ship type. Then, based on typical stay times for ships at different locations (e.g., berth stay times of no more than 4 days, anchorage stay times not exceeding 20 days, and channel transit times of less than 2 h), channel transit records with a duration of less than 2 h were selected and stored in a new table for subsequent analysis. Following this, the ship's attribute information was completed, and outliers were removed. The completion of static information followed these principles: for instance, in the case of design speed, if the information was already present and greater than 0, it was retained; if missing, the average design speed for the relevant ship type was selected from Lloyd's Register Data to complete the data. If no match was found, the overall average design speed for all ships was used instead. The completion of RPM, MCR, and ship construction year followed similar procedures. In contrast, for A_MCR, if missing, it was calculated as the product of AMR and MCR. Regarding the removal of outliers, the method involved filtering out AIS records where the average speed exceeded the design speed, which were then deleted. Through these methods, the static information was completed, and outliers were removed, providing a reliable data foundation for subsequent pollutant emission calculations.

4, Adjust the fuel correction factor and calculate pollutant and GHG emissions. For ships entering the Ship Emission Control Area, this study adjusted the fuel used according to relevant policy requirements, specifically switching to low-sulfur fuel (LSF). More precisely, ships entering the Bohai Sea Area (BSA) berths in 2018 used low-sulfur marine diesel oil (MGO-0.5%), while most ships in other conditions continued to use heavy fuel oil (HFO) [14]. In this study, we assumed that ships entering the channel in 2018 used HFO (1.5% sulfur) fuel, while those entering berths and anchorages used MGO (0.5% sulfur) fuel. The fuel correction factor (FCF) was adjusted based on the type of fuel to ensure more accurate results. Following this, emissions of various pollutants and GHGs from the main engine, auxiliary engine, and boiler were calculated using relevant formulas, thereby generating an emission inventory. This method enhanced the accuracy of emissions estimation by incorporating the fuel type used in different operating scenarios.

Steps 1 and 4 in the above description represented the main innovations of our approach. Figure 1 illustrated the AIS data preprocessing workflow, consisting of several key modules: trajectory integration, data preprocessing, policy-compliant modification, emission calculation, and post-processing. First, trajectory integration was performed to extract key trajectory points that describe the ship's original path, and the data points were then sorted in chronological order. Next, the raw AIS data collected from multiple sources, along with Lloyd's Register data, were combined to form the ship activity database. Following this, pollutant and GHG emissions were calculated based on the ship's static technical parameters, dynamic load variations, additional parameters and factors. In particular, policy-compliant modifications were applied to ships entering the DECA, switching them to low-sulfur fuel (LSF) [14]. Finally, the emission inventory dataset was established from multiple perspectives for visualization and analysis.

2.3 Model of Ship Emission Inventory

The problem of predicting pollutant and GHG emissions from ships is defined as follows: In the port environment, given a long time series X, which represents the records of pollutant emissions and GHG emissions related to ship activities, and a fixed-length look-back window T. The objective is to predict emissions for the next τ time steps at timestamp t. Specifically, based on the past T

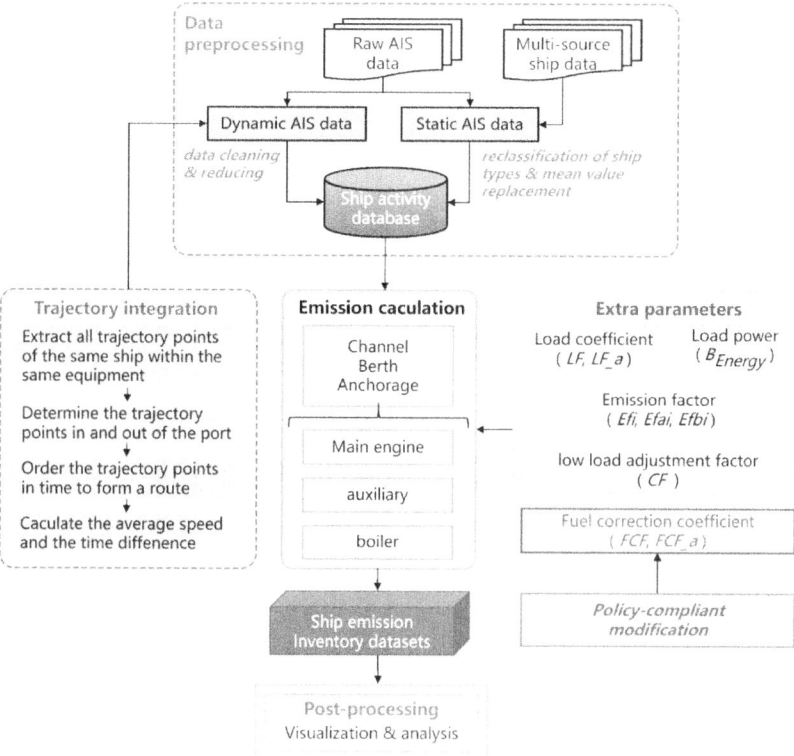

Fig. 1. Data preprocessing flow chart. FCF and FCF_a represent fuel correction factors of main engine and auxiliary engine respectively.

time steps of the sequence $\boldsymbol{X}_{t-T+1:t} = \{x_{t-T+1}, \ldots, x_t\}$, the task is to forecast the future emissions $\hat{\boldsymbol{X}}_{t+1:t+\tau} = \{\hat{x}_{t+1}, \hat{x}_{t+2}, \ldots, \hat{x}_{t+\tau}\}$. Here, τ denotes the prediction horizon, $x_t \in \mathbb{R}^d$ represents the value at time step t, and d is the number of variables corresponding to the emission data of different kinds of pollutants and GHGs.

Problem Generation: In addition to the critical importance of accurately obtaining ship pollutant and GHG emission datasets, evaluating the accuracy and reliability of forecasting models is equally vital. Among commonly used model evaluation metrics, Mean Squared Error (MSE) and Mean Absolute Error (MAE) are widely employed for overall error analysis in time series forecasting. However, due to the complexity of data characteristics, relying solely on these metrics may fail to fully capture the performance of forecasting models. Therefore, it is necessary to explore the rationality and effectiveness of MSE and MAE in specific application scenarios. Furthermore, incorporating visualization methods to compare actual data with predicted results can serve as a valuable supplement for quantifying evaluation outcomes. Based on the above background, this study proposes and aims to address the following two questions:

Question 1: How can different deep learning methods be employed to accurately predict future pollutant and GHG emissions based on historical emission data from ships?

To achieve accurate predictions of ship pollutant and GHG emissions and systematically compare different forecasting methods, this study selects seven mainstream forecasting methods. In the experimental design, the time step of historical data input is set to 96, meaning that data from the past 96 time points are used to forecast emissions for the next τ time points. The forecasting process is as follows:

$$\hat{X}_{t+1:t+\tau} = f_x(X_{t-T+1:t}) = f_x(x_{t-T+1}, \ldots, x_t),$$
$$T = \{1, 2, \cdots, 96\}, \quad \tau = \{48, 96, 192, 336, 720\},$$
$$x \in \{\text{iTransformer, Informer, Transformer, Dlinear, SCINet, TS2Vec, LSTM}\} \tag{1}$$

where $f_x()$ represents a prediction function based on seven different prediction methods.

Question 2: How to measure the predictive performance of different methods?

To comprehensively assess the forecasting performance of ship pollutant and GHG emissions, an integrated evaluation method combining global error analysis and visual explanation is proposed. This method conducts a thorough analysis of the prediction accuracy through both quantitative and qualitative approaches. The overall error of the seven forecasting methods is quantified using MSE and MAE, while visualization techniques are employed to interpret the rationality and effectiveness of these metrics. Ultimately, the model with the smallest error across three evaluation criteria is selected as the optimal model. The optimal model is:

$$Optimal f \leftarrow \min\{\text{MSE} \cap \text{MAE}\} \cap \text{optimal}\{\text{Visualisation Results}\} \tag{2}$$

3 Results

3.1 Total Emissions

Based on the results of the emission inventory, the emissions of GHGs and pollutants were first statistically analyzed. For GHG emissions, the total ship emissions of CO_2, N_2O, and CH_4 in 2018 were estimated to be 1.35×10^6 tons, 93.6 tons, and 8.53 tons, respectively. CO_2 was the major component of GHGs. For pollutant emissions, the total ship emissions of SO_X, NO_X, PM_{10}, $PM_{2.5}$, CO, DPM, and HC in 2018 were estimated to be 1.74×10^4 tons, 9.6×10^3 tons, 1.08×10^3 tons, 902 tons, 922 tons, 444 tons, and 372 tons, respectively. As shown in Fig. 2, among the various pollutants emitted in 2018, SO_X was the dominant pollutant, followed by NO_X.

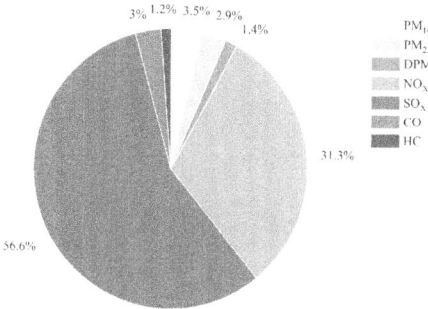

Fig. 2. Pollutant emission ratios at Tianjin Port in 2018.

3.2 Contribution of Different Types of Vessels and Different Months

For CO_2 and SO_X emissions from various types of ships, the trends in emissions were generally consistent. As shown in Fig. 3, emissions from tankers were the highest, followed by bulk carriers and container ships. For NO_X emissions, bulk carriers had the highest emissions, while tankers and container ships had comparable emissions.

For total monthly emissions of CO_2, SO_X and NO_X, July, August, September and October were the highest overall, with total monthly emissions of CO_2 and NO_X peaking in July, and total monthly emissions of SO_X peaking in September. The lowest overall emissions were recorded in February and March, possibly due to the Chinese New Year in China and the trade disputes between China and the United States, which collectively reduced the supply and demand for various cargoes, and these events not only affected trading volumes, but also reduced ship carbon emissions.

3.3 Contribution of Different Engine Types and Different Operating Conditions

Emissions from main engines, auxiliary engines and boilers were quantified under different operating conditions for ships in the channel, berths and anchorages in the area designated for the Tianjin Port study. The percentage of pollutant and GHG emissions for different engine types and different operating conditions are shown in Fig. 4 and Fig. 5.

As can be seen in Fig. 4, in 2018, the main engine accounted for more than 80% of the emissions in the channel, and the rest was the auxiliary engine emissions. In berths and anchorages, the main engine accounted for almost 0% of the emissions. the auxiliary engine emission share of DPM, NO_X, HC and CH_4 was significantly higher than that of boilers, while the boiler emission share of SO_X, CO_2, N_2O, PM_{10} and $PM_{2.5}$ was significantly higher than that of auxiliary engines. As can be seen from Fig. 5, the emission shares of different pollutants and GHGs under different operating conditions were similar with small changes.

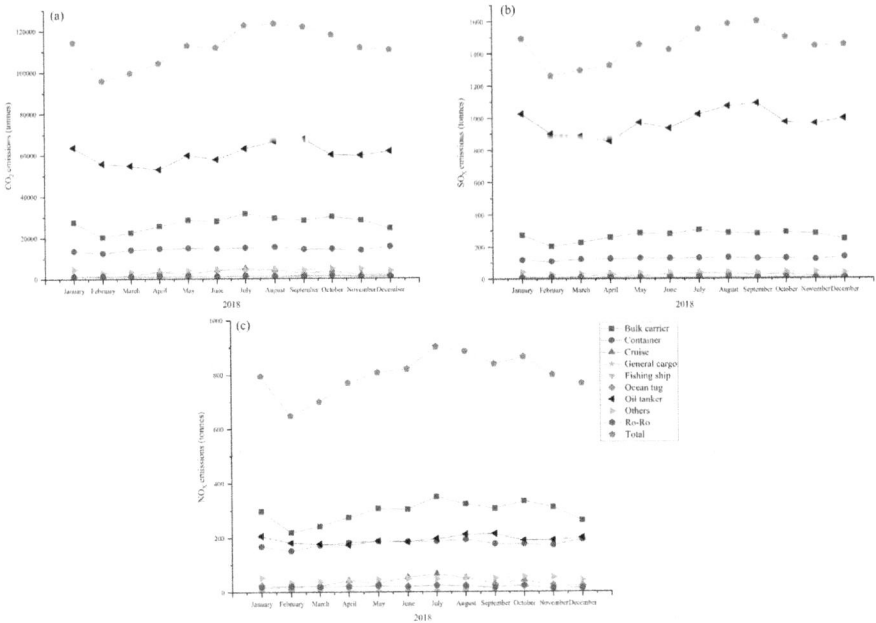

Fig. 3. (a), (b) and (c) represents the monthly CO_2, SO_X and NO_X emissions of different types of ships in Tianjin Port in 2018, respectively.

In practice, the boiler is usually switched off during normal sailing. When the ship is cruising or sailing slowly, the boiler is under no load. Since ships spend most of their time cruising or sailing slowly in the channel, the percentage of predicted boiler pollutant and GHG emissions in the channel is close to 0%. However, when a ship is maneuvering, mooring, or berthed, it is usually at anchorage or berth, when the main engine stops working and auxiliary engine and boiler emissions begin to increase. During maneuvering, the ship's speed is lower and the voyage time is shorter, resulting in the least amount of pollutant and GHG emissions. On the contrary, emissions during the mooring and berthed call phases increase significantly and become the main source of total pollutant and GHG emissions from ships. Based on this characterization, the rate of pollutant and GHG emissions in the vicinity of harbor berths and anchorages is significantly greater than the rate of emissions from channels. Specifically, emissions from berths and anchorages accounted for 94.94% of total emissions in 2018. This change reflects the fact that the cumulative effect of total emissions becomes more significant with the increase in ship berthing time.

3.4 Prediction Model

To examine the advantages and limitations of various methods for the prediction of pollutant and GHG emissions in Tianjin harbor in 2018, we selected seven advanced and representative models.

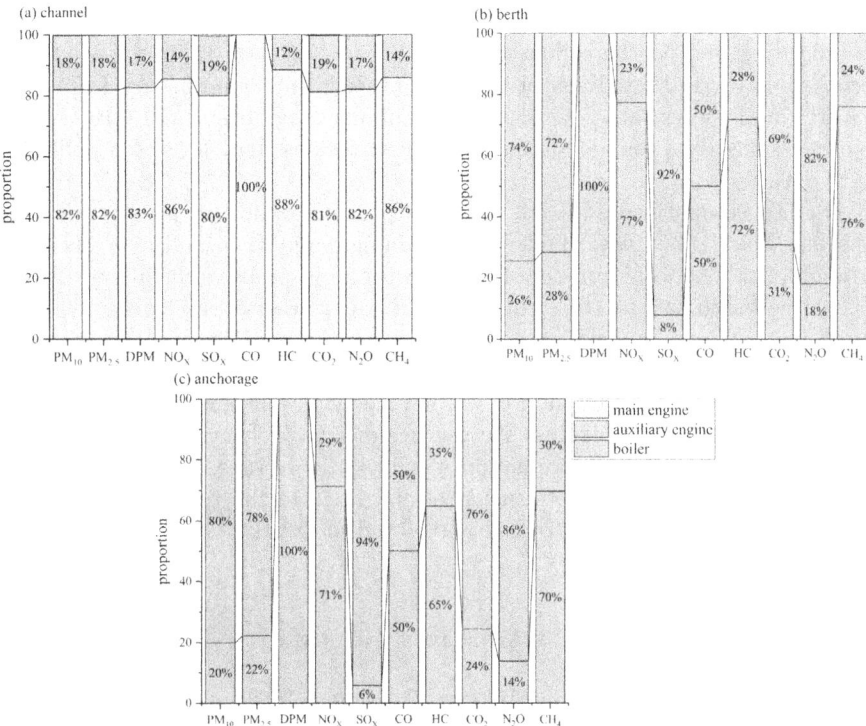

Fig. 4. (a), (b) and (c) represent the proportion of pollutants and GHG emissions from different engine types in the Tianjin Port channel, berth and anchorage in 2018, respectively.

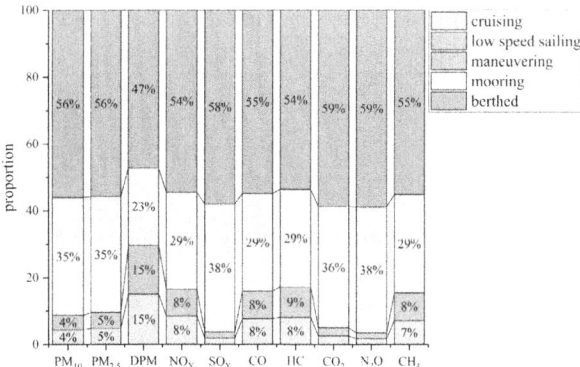

Fig. 5. The proportion of pollutants and GHG emissions in Tianjin Port under different operating conditions in 2018.

For the production of the experimental dataset, we integrated the 2018 Tianjin port channel, berth, and anchorage data and reclassified them into 15-minute granularity based on the sailing time to obtain a total of 31348 data, which is recorded as merge2018. Each of them contains 1 time column and 11 variable features, and the variables consist of 10 columns of pollutant and GHG respective emissions data and 1 column of total emissions data for these pollutants and GHGs.

For fair comparisons, we set the same parameters for all models whenever possible. The dataset was divided into training, validation, and test sets in the ratio of 6:2:2. The total number of epochs with appropriate early stops is 10, and we set the batch size to 16 as suggested. **Hyperparameter tuning:** Our proposed method is optimized using the Adam Optimizer. **Parameter settings:** The inputs for each dataset are zero-mean normalized. Under the LSTF setting, we gradually extend the prediction window size. The specific parameter settings are shown in Table 1. **Metrics:** We use two evaluation metrics, including MSE and MAE applied on each prediction window (the average of multivariate predictions), and will continue to visualize and analyze the results subsequently. **Platform:** all models were trained and tested on NVIDIA GeForce RTX 4080 GPUs.

Table 1. Model parameter Settings.

Model	iTransformer	Informer	Transformer	Dlinear	SCINet	TS2Vec	LSTM
lookback length	96						
label length	48						
horizon	{48, 96, 192, 336, 720}						
num of heads	8			/			
batch size	16						
learning rate	0.0005						
train epochs	10					600	10
dropout	0.1						/
factor	/	3		/			
stacks		/			1	/	
levels		/			2	/	
num of encoder layers	2			/			
num of decoder layers	/	1		/			

The experimental results are shown in Table 2. Smaller MSE/MAE represents more accurate prediction results. The Transformer model shows superior performance in terms of MSE values, and SCINet achieves a crushing overtake in terms of MAE values. However, iTransformer and Dlinear have the best combined MAE and MSE results.

Table 2. Prediction results of each model on the dataset merge2018.

Models	iTransformer		Informer		Transformer		Dlinear		SCINet		TS2Vec		LSTM	
Metric	MSE	MAE	MSE	MAE	MSE	MAE	MSE	MAE	MSE	MAE	MSE	MAE	MSE	MAE
Horizon 48	1.086	0.511	1.086	0.543	**1.079**	0.547	1.084	0.521	1.156	**0.454**	1.090	0.568	1.114	0.545
96	1.094	0.514	1.088	0.553	**1.078**	0.535	1.093	0.523	1.156	**0.456**	1.093	0.562	1.115	0.542
192	1.107	0.518	1.100	0.549	**1.089**	0.532	1.101	0.524	1.166	**0.456**	1.101	0.559	1.115	0.538
336	1.111	0.518	**1.105**	0.551	1.117	0.540	1.106	0.523	1.175	**0.456**	1.107	0.556	1.115	0.536
720	1.133	0.517	1.134	0.555	**1.116**	0.542	1.126	0.522	1.203	**0.455**	1.128	0.553	1.135	0.536
Avg	1.106	0.516	1.103	0.550	**1.096**	0.539	1.102	0.523	1.171	**0.455**	1.104	0.560	1.119	0.539

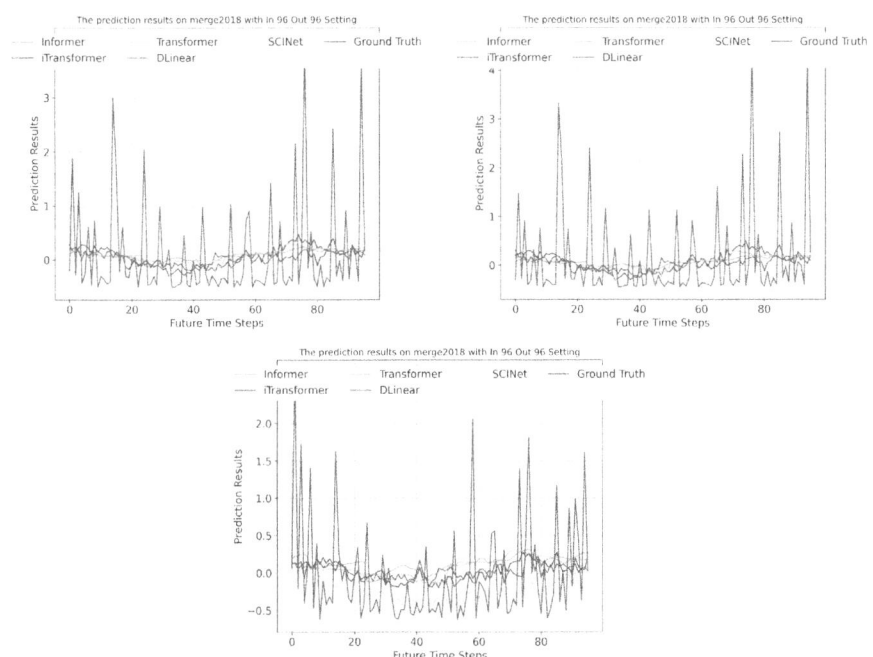

Fig. 6. Standardized CO_2, SO_X and NO_X emission projections, respectively.

Based on the combined results of 2018, we selected the models iTransformer, Informer, Transformer, and Dlinear SCINet with a prediction length of 96 for the visualization of the prediction results, in order to more intuitively show the prediction effect of the models. As shown in Fig. 6, SCINet has the best prediction ability for low values. Dlinear and iTransformer predict similar trends, taking into account the effects of low and high values, but they do not perform well due to the fact that low values account for the vast majority of the data. Transformer favors predicting the overall trend of the data and mining the data for implied cyclical patterns. The Informer model captures localized mutations in some of the data, and its potential for capturing data features can be observed.

We further divided the dataset into smaller granularity to show more accurate results. We make separate datasets for channel, berth and anchorage, with time columns as the real time when the ship enters the harbor, and conduct the experiment again. There are 43,763, 45,376, and 20,342 data for channel, berth, and anchorage in 2018, and the datasets are denoted as channel2018, berth2018, and anchorage2018, respectively. Similarly, each of their each data entry contains 1 time column and 11 variable features. All experimental settings are kept consistent with Table 1. The results of the experiments are shown in Table 3, and unsurprisingly, SCINet shows the most superior prediction results in terms of MAE values. Informer outperforms the Transformer model on the channel2018 dataset, and Dlinear outperforms the Transformer model on the berth2018 dataset.

Table 3. Forecast results of channel, berth and anchorage respectively.

Models		iTransformer		Informer		Transformer		Dlinear		SCINet	
Metric		MSE	MAE	MSE	MAE	MSE	MAE	MSE	MAE	MSE	MAE
Horizon	48	1.013	0.651	1.001	0.657	**0.999**	0.636	1.002	0.660	1.089	**0.591**
	96	1.012	0.647	**1.000**	0.654	1.003	0.653	1.002	0.659	1.082	**0.592**
	192	1.009	0.647	1.001	0.637	**0.997**	0.649	1.001	0.658	1.085	**0.592**
	336	1.003	0.645	**0.992**	0.642	**0.992**	0.632	0.996	0.658	1.076	**0.590**
	720	0.993	0.642	**0.983**	0.634	0.989	0.651	0.987	0.656	1.069	**0.588**
	Avg	1.006	0.646	**0.995**	0.645	0.996	0.644	0.998	0.658	1.080	**0.591**
Models		iTransformer		Informer		Transformer		Dlinear		SCINet	
Metric		MSE	MAE	MSE	MAE	MSE	MAE	MSE	MAE	MSE	MAE
Horizon	48	0.903	0.540	0.895	0.569	**0.892**	0.568	**0.892**	0.550	0.989	**0.470**
	96	0.904	0.548	0.900	0.583	0.896	0.568	**0.895**	0.551	0.999	**0.472**
	192	0.909	0.547	0.903	0.580	0.902	0.571	**0.901**	0.552	1.004	**0.474**
	336	0.915	0.543	0.909	0.572	0.907	0.564	**0.906**	0.553	1.014	**0.474**
	720	0.913	0.548	0.909	0.579	0.907	0.586	**0.905**	0.552	1.007	**0.474**
	Avg	0.909	0.545	0.903	0.577	0.901	0.571	**0.900**	0.552	1.003	**0.473**
Models		iTransformer		Informer		Transformer		Dlinear		SCINet	
Metric		MSE	MAE	MSE	MAE	MSE	MAE	MSE	MAE	MSE	MAE
Horizon	48	0.708	0.390	0.697	0.403	**0.693**	0.391	0.699	0.443	0.741	**0.308**
	96	0.715	0.394	**0.702**	0.413	0.706	0.403	0.707	0.450	0.754	**0.309**
	192	0.722	0.394	0.711	0.420	**0.709**	0.410	0.714	0.448	0.762	**0.311**
	336	0.735	0.394	**0.723**	0.416	**0.723**	0.401	0.727	0.450	0.771	**0.311**
	720	0.711	0.389	0.698	0.415	**0.696**	0.396	0.704	0.450	0.744	**0.306**
	Avg	0.718	0.392	0.706	0.413	**0.705**	0.400	0.710	0.448	0.754	**0.309**

The prediction length of 96 is selected to visualize the normalized CO_2 emissions. As shown in Fig. 7, it can be clearly seen that SCINet has the best prediction effect, which pays more attention to the low-value data with larger amount of data, and is more effective in low-value prediction. Due to the recursive downsampling-convolution-interaction architecture, SCINet effectively captures the changes in the low-value smooth data of the time series without relying too much on the historical averages like most other networks. However, the drawbacks are the slow training speed of the model, the training time is about 3 to 6 times of the DLinear model, and the high MSE value in the prediction results, which is not enough to capture the mutation values. However, from the comprehensive results in the figure, SCINet still predicts the best results at present. The other models tend to synthesize the effects of high and low values, and have average prediction results for both high and low values. On the berth and anchorage dataset, the predicted values of Informer and Transformer are too flat, and although the values are lower in terms of MSE, the prediction effect is not good as observed in the figure.

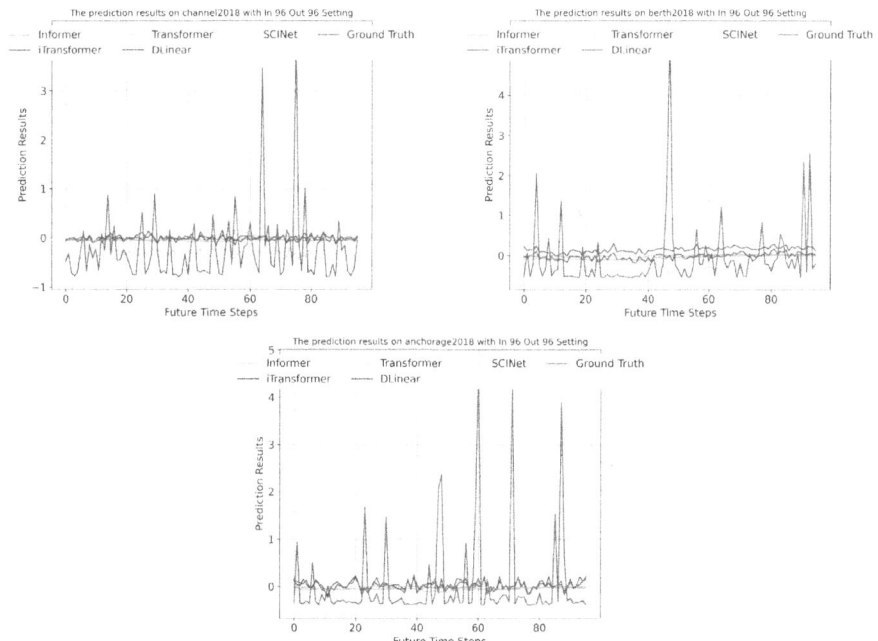

Fig. 7. Standardized CO_2 emission prediction results representing channel, berth and anchorage respectively.

4 Conclusions

In this study, we improved the production method of ship emission inventories to obtain an inventory of pollutant and GHG emissions from ships with high flows in Tianjin port in 2018. Specifically, ship types were first re-normalized, while missing static information was added. Subsequently, the fuel correction factor was adjusted according to different fuel types in combination with the DECA policy. Finally, formulas were used to calculate the emissions of different types of pollutants and GHGs from main engines, auxiliary engines and boilers, from which emission inventories were constructed.

Next, we discussed the emission patterns of pollutants and GHGs from ships. Overall, CO_2 was the main component of GHGs and SO_X was the main pollutant. In terms of ship types, for CO_2 and SO_X emissions from various ships, tankers had the highest emissions, followed by dry bulk carriers and container ships. For NO_X emissions, dry bulk carriers had the highest emissions, with tankers and container ships not far behind. From a temporal perspective, in 2018, for total monthly emissions of CO_2, SO_X and NO_X, July, August, September, and October had the highest overall emissions, and February and March had the lowest overall emissions. In terms of engine type, in channels, main engine emissions accounted for more than 80% of the total emissions. In berths and anchorages, the proportion of main engine emissions is almost 0%. The proportion of auxiliary engine emissions of DPM, NO_X, HC and CH_4 was significantly higher than that of boilers, while the proportion of boiler emissions of SO_X, CO_2, N_2O, PM_{10} and $PM_{2.5}$ was significantly higher than that of auxiliary engines. From the point of view of operating conditions, anchoring and berthing brought most of the pollutant and GHG emissions from ships, with berths and anchorages accounting for 94.94% of the total emissions.

Finally, we used models based on Transformer, MLP, TCN and RNN to predict pollutant and GHG emissions from ships in the region. For the dataset merge2018, Transformer and SCINet showed superior performance to other models. For more fine-grained datasets, SCINet had the best prediction, which focused more on low value data with larger amount of data, and was better at predicting low values. In addition, Dlinear outperformed the Transformer model on the berth2018 dataset, and Informer outperformed the Transformer model on the channel2018 dataset.

There are some limitations in our study. In the future, more and more effective prediction models can be explored, and the model can be improved for the dataset to balance prediction accuracy and efficiency. There is much room for improvement in this area.

References

1. Capaldo, K., Corbett, J.J., Kasibhatla, P., Fischbeck, P., Pandis, S.N.: Effects of ship emissions on Sulphur cycling and radiative climate forcing over the ocean. Nature **400**(6746), 743–746 (1999)
2. Chen, D., et al.: Estimating ship emissions based on AIS data for port of Tianjin, china. Atmos. Environ. **145**, 10–18 (2016)
3. Chen, J., Wan, Z., Zhang, H., Liu, X., Zhu, Y., Zheng, A.: Governance of shipping emission of so x in china's coastal waters: the Seca policy, challenges, and directions. Coast. Manag. **46**(3), 191–209 (2018)

4. Chiang, P.W., Horng, S.J.: Hybrid time-series framework for daily-based pm 2.5 forecasting. IEEE Access **9**, 104162–104176 (2021)
5. Gao, H., et al.: A review of building carbon emission accounting and prediction models. Buildings **13**(7), 1617 (2023)
6. Jin, Y., Sharifi, A., Li, Z., Chen, S., Zeng, S., Zhao, S.: Carbon emission prediction models: a review. Science of the Total Environment, p. 172319 (2024)
7. Lawrence, M.G., Crutzen, P.J.: Influence of no x emissions from ships on tropospheric photochemistry and climate. Nature **402**(6758), 167–170 (1999)
8. Li, D., Liu, J., Zhao, Y.: Forecasting of pm2. 5 concentration in beijing using hybrid deep learning framework based on attention mechanism. Appl. Sci. **12**(21), 11155 (2022)
9. Li, Y., et al.: Research on the carbon emissions traceability inventory and multi-horizon prediction of ship carbon emissions: a case study of Tianjin port. Front. Mar. Sci. **10**, 1174411 (2023)
10. McDuffie, E.E., et al.: A global anthropogenic emission inventory of atmospheric pollutants from sector-and fuel-specific sources (1970–2017): an application of the community emissions data system (CEDS). Earth Syst. Sci. Data **12**(4), 3413–3442 (2020)
11. Meng, L., Liu, K., He, J., Han, C., Liu, P.: Carbon emission reduction behavior strategies in the shipping industry under government regulation: A tripartite evolutionary game analysis. J. Clean. Prod. **378**, 134556 (2022)
12. Jurado Martins de Oliveira, G., Lavieri, P.S., Cunha, A.L.: Integrating a non-gridded space representation into a graph neural networks model for citywide short-term crash risk prediction. Urban Inform. **2**(1), 7 (2023)
13. Shakya, D., Deshpande, V., Goyal, M.K., Agarwal, M.: Pm2. 5 air pollution prediction through deep learning using meteorological, vehicular, and emission data: A case study of new Delhi, India. J. Cleaner Prod. **427**, 139278 (2023)
14. Wang, X., et al.: Ship emissions around china under gradually promoted control policies from 2016 to 2019. Atmos. Chem. Phys. **21**(18), 13835–13853 (2021)
15. Xie, W., et al.: Maritime greenhouse gas emission estimation and forecasting through AIS data analytics: a case study of Tianjin port in the context of sustainable development. Front. Mar. Sci. **10**, 1308981 (2023)
16. Yang, L., et al.: Real world emission characteristics of Chinese fleet and the current situation of underestimated ship emissions. J. Clean. Prod. **418**, 138107 (2023)
17. Yang, L., et al.: An AIS-based emission inventory and the impact on air quality in Tianjin port based on localized emission factors. Sci. Total Environ. **783**, 146869 (2021)
18. Zhang, Q., Han, Y., Li, V.O., Lam, J.C.: Deep-air: A hybrid CNN-LSTM framework for fine-grained air pollution estimation and forecast in metropolitan cities. IEEE Access **10**, 55818–55841 (2022)
19. Zhou, S., Wang, W., Zhu, L., Qiao, Q., Kang, Y.: Deep-learning architecture for pm2. 5 concentration prediction: a review. Environmental Science and Ecotechnology p. 100400 (2024)

Automatic Landslide Identification Based on High-Resolution Remote Sensing Images Using Lightweight Deep Learning Network

Xiangzhong Guo[1,2], Guolong Wu[1], and Yimin Lu[1(✉)]

[1] Key Laboratory of Spatial Data Mining & Information Sharing of Ministry of Education, Academy of Digital China (Fujian), Fuzhou University, Fuzhou 350116, China
luym@fzu.edu.cn
[2] State Key Laboratory of Regional and Urban Ecology, Institute of Urban Environment, Chinese Academy of Sciences, Xiamen 361021, China

Abstract. Automatic identification of landslide disasters from remote sensing images based on deep learning models is an effective method, but most of the existing models use multi-temporal images or geological data to improve the accuracy, which suffers from problems of high model complexity and data acquisition difficulty. We proposed a Mv2_SA_DeepLabv3+ model, which is a lightweight deep learning network for detecting landslide disaster occurrence areas from remote sensing images captured in a single temporal image. Mv2_SA_DeepLabv3+ model is based on the Deeplabv3+ network structure. Firstly, it used the lightweight MobileNetV2 network as the backbone network for feature extraction to reduce the complexity of the model. Secondly, it improves the Atrous Spatial Pyramid Pooling (ASPP) module to obtain more features to improve the model accuracy. Finally, the loss function is optimized by combining CrossEntropy Loss and Dice Loss to solve the problem of positive and negative category imbalance of the samples. Furthermore, two publicly available landslide disaster remote sensing image datasets were utilized to validate the proposed model. The experiment results indicated that the Mv2_SA_DeepLabv3+ model shows a good performance, with the Kappa coefficient and the F1 score of 0.83 and 86.84%, which outperforms the original UNet (improved of 0.11 and 8.34%). These results demonstrate the model can obviously overcome the interference of irrelevant information, so as to accurately recognize the landslide area. Besides, the model has a low computational complexity, which facilitates the rapid deployment of the model and provides data support for further disaster emergency rescue.

Keywords: Automatic landslide identification · Remote sensing images · Deep learning · Lightweight

1 Introduction

Landslides disaster is a common and destructive natural disaster, causing great threats and losses to human society [1, 2]. According to the governmental information disclosure of the Ministry of Natural Resources of China, it is known that 5,659 geologic disasters occurred nationwide in 2022, of which 3,919 were landslides, accounting for 69.3% of the total number of geologic disasters. Quick and accurate identification and monitoring of landslide disaster areas is important for disaster prevention and management [3, 4]. With the development of remote sensing technology and the application of deep learning algorithms, automatic landslide disaster identification using remote sensing images has become an effective and frontier research direction [5, 6].

High-resolution remote sensing images, with their broad spatial coverage and multi-temporal observation capability, provide a valuable data source for landslide disaster research [7–9]. Remote sensing images can provide rich surface information, including spectra, vegetation cover, land use types, etc., which are crucial for landslide disaster identification and analysis [10]. The traditional method for landslide disaster identification and analysis based on remote sensing images is manual visual interpretation by geologists, which has problems such as subjectivity and limitations, so the automatic identification of landslide disaster areas using computer algorithms has become a hotpot for research [11, 12].

Deep learning, as a powerful artificial intelligence technology with the ability to process large-scale data and automatically learn features, provides a new research idea for automatic landslide disaster identification [13, 14]. The deep learning model can automatically extract and analyze the semantic features in the image. These semantic features are learned from many remote sensing images and label datasets produced by geologists through visual interpretation. So as to realize the accurate segmentation and identification of landslide disaster areas [15, 16]. In recent years, automatic landslide disaster identification methods based on deep learning have made significant progress, providing powerful support for landslide disaster monitoring and early warning [17].

However, traditional deep learning models face some challenges in automatic landslide disaster identification. Due to the large volume of remote sensing image data, traditional deep learning models often require a large number of parameters and computational resources, resulting in increased model complexity and computing time, and it is difficult to meet the timeliness requirements of disaster response [18]. Therefore, researchers began to focus on the design and application of lightweight deep learning networks, aiming to reduce the computational complexity of models and the difficulty of data acquisition, while maintaining the accuracy and robustness of automatic identification of landslide disasters [19, 20]. In this study, a lightweight deep learning model was proposed with the aim of exploring the automatic landslide disaster identification method based on a lightweight deep learning network to solve the problems of traditional models in landslide disaster identification.

The main contributions of this study are the following.

1) A lightweight deep learning network: Mv2_SA_DeepLabv3+ is proposed for detecting landslide disaster occurrence areas from high-resolution remote sensing images. Compared with the traditional semantic segmentation model for landslide identification, the Mv2_SA_DeepLabv3+ model has higher accuracy and lower model complexity, effectively balancing the accuracy and speed of landslide disaster extraction contradiction.

2) Based on the DeepLabv3+ network structure, using the lightweight MobileNetV2 network as the backbone network can greatly reduce the model complexity without

decreasing the model accuracy, which verifies the advantages of the lightweight deep learning network in automatic landslide disaster identification.
3) Improve the ASPP module and optimize the loss function to enhance the model's ability to identify landslide disasters, the Shuffle Attention module enhances the model's attention to landslide features and improves the effect of multi-scale semantic feature extraction, and the Dice Loss function corrects the sample imbalance problem to improve the model's classification accuracy. In addition, adding the Shuffle Attention module and combining the improvement of the Dice Loss function does not increase the model complexity.

2 Method

In this study, we take landslide disaster high-resolution remote sensing images as the data source, and based on Deeplabv3+ deep learning network architecture, we adopt the lightweight MobileNetV2 network as the backbone network for feature extraction and further improve the ASPP module and optimize the loss function, to establish a deep learning semantic segmentation model for the end-to-end automatic landslide disaster identification. The model in this study has the following three main stages: 1) Dataset preparation: fusing the two datasets, normalizing the dataset image and labeled data so that the range of values is within the interval of [0,1], and further cropping the data to the standard size of 256 × 256 while dividing it into the training, validation, and testing sets; 2) Model construction: establishing a neural network structure to construct a deep learning model for the landslide disaster image feature; 3) Model training and validation: the model is accelerated by GPU to learn the landslide disaster image features, and the comparison and ablation experiments are conducted to verify that model has a better performance in landslide identification (Fig. 1).

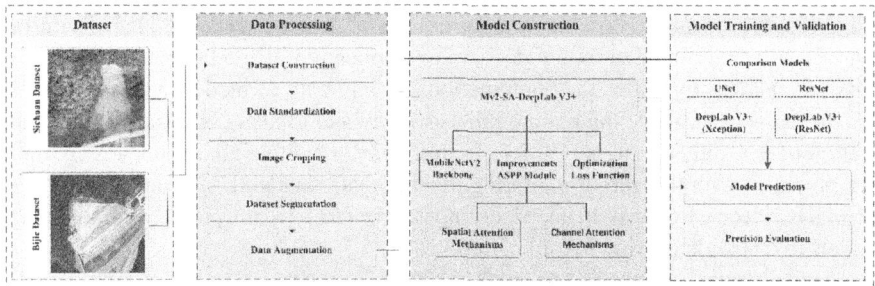

Fig. 1. Framework diagram of semantic segmentation.

2.1 Structure of the Model

DeepLabv3+ is based on DeepLabv3, which introduces a decode module, further fuses the bottom features and high features, improves the accuracy of segmentation boundary, and has been widely used in automatic landslide disaster identification [38]. The core idea of the DeepLabv3+ model is to introduce the Atrous Convolution operation to enlarge the field of view of the sensory field and keep the computational amount small. While traditional convolutional operations use a fixed receptive field size, Atrous Convolution extends the range of the receptive field by introducing Atrous Convolution in the convolutional kernel. This operation captures a larger range of contextual information while keeping the number of network parameters and computational cost relatively low, which helps improve the accuracy of semantic segmentation. Another key feature of the DeepLabv3+ model is the use of encoder-decoder structures to capture feature representations at different scales through feature pyramid pooling and spatial pyramid pooling. The feature pyramid pooling module can extract multi-scale context information, which comes from feature maps of different levels. This multi-scale feature fusion helps to improve the accuracy of semantic segmentation and the preservation of edge details. The spatial pyramid pooling module can capture detailed information about the target.

In this study, based on the DeepLabv3+ network structure, a lightweight deep learning network (Mv2_SA_DeepLabv3+) was proposed to realize end-to-end detection of landslide disaster areas from remote sensing images captured in a single temporal image. The network structure of the Mv2_SA_DeepLabv3+ model is shown in Fig. 2, which have the following three main improvements: 1) Lightweight backbone network: the deep convolutional neural network (DCNN) part of the encoder process of DeepLabv3+ network structure adopts the lightweight MobileNetV2 network as the backbone network, which reduces the number of parameters, reduces the computational complexity of the model, and improves the model's ability to be deployed in emergencies; 2) Improvements ASPP module: adding the Shuffle Attention module to enhance the model's attention to landslide features and improve the effect of multi-scale semantic feature extraction; 3) Optimize the loss function: the loss function part of the loss function adopts a combination of CrossEntropy Loss and Dice Loss to solve the problem of imbalance of positive and negative samples categories in the landslide segmentation task.

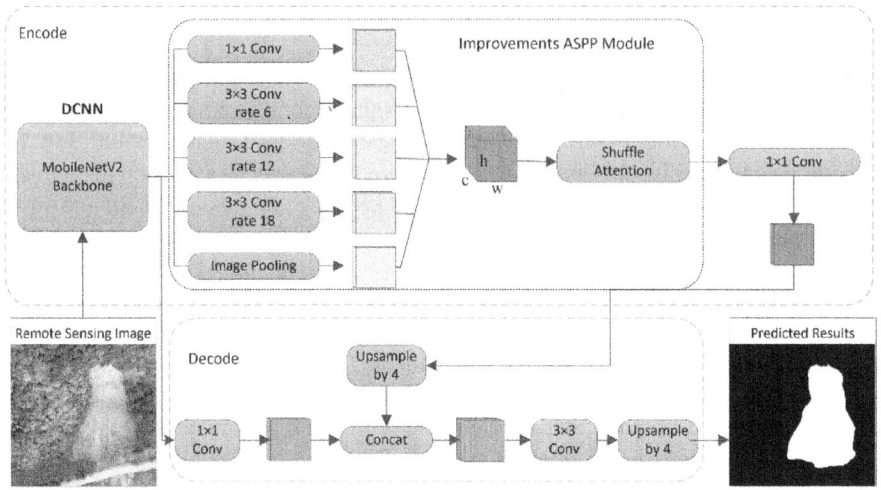

Fig. 2. Mv2_SA_DeepLabv3+ network structure.

2.2 Lightweight Backbone Network

This study is based on the DeepLabv3+ network architecture and uses the MobileNetV2 model as the backbone network for feature extraction [39]. The MobileNetV2 network model is a lightweight and efficient deep convolutional neural network. It is designed to solve the problems of the traditional deep learning models in terms of the number of parameters and the computational complexity so that the feature extraction can be realized on the resource-limited mobile devices. The main innovation of this model is the introduction of a lightweight depthwise convolution operation, which means that the depthwise separable convolutions are decomposed into two steps, namely depthwise convolution and pointwise convolution. Where depthwise convolution is used to learn spatial features and pointwise convolution is used to learn the feature representation between channels. Thus, realizing efficient computation on resource-limited devices. Another key feature of the MobileNetV2 model is the introduction of the inverted residual structure, which improves the expressiveness of the feature representation by adding a linear bottleneck layer and an activation function in the feature extraction process. This structure can effectively reduce the problems of information loss and gradient vanishing, and it is more effective in capturing details and semantic features in high-resolution remote sensing images. In addition, the MobileNetV2 model employs a combination of feature pyramid pooling and depthwise separable convolution to obtain feature representations at different scales. The feature pyramid pooling module can extract features with different semantic levels from feature maps at multiple scales, while depthwise separable convolution is used to integrate and fuse these features effectively. This multi-scale feature fusion helps to improve the identification accuracy of high-resolution remote sensing images (Fig. 3).

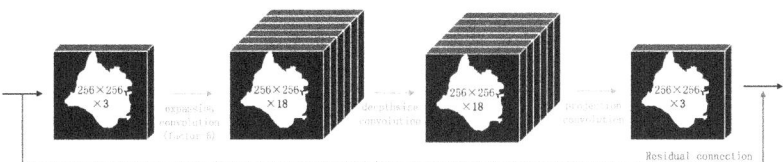

Fig. 3. MobileNetV2 network structure.

2.3 Improvements ASPP Module

In high-resolution remote sensing image processing, accurately understanding and analyzing the semantic information of images is crucial for tasks such as automatic identification of landslide disasters. To address these issues, researchers have proposed a deep learning network model called ASPP, which can effectively capture semantic information at different scales and improve the performance of high-resolution remote sensing image processing. The key feature of the ASPP model is the use of atrous convolution and spatial pyramid pooling structures. Atrous convolution is an operation that expands the receptive field by introducing an adjustable atrous rate during the convolution process. In addition, the ASPP model introduces a spatial pyramid pooling structure, which can perform multi-scale pooling operations on input feature maps to obtain contextual information at different scales. By cascading or combining pooling features of multiple scales, the ASPP model can more comprehensively capture the semantic information of images and improve the accuracy of high-resolution remote sensing image semantic segmentation. In the ASPP model, by parallel stacking multiple empty convolutions with different atrous rates and spatial pyramid pooling structures, the model can obtain richer multi-scale semantic information. This information is aggregated and fused in the feature map to generate the final semantic segmentation result. By using the ASPP model, the scale problem in remote sensing image processing can be effectively solved, and the accuracy of image understanding and analysis can be improved.

This study adds a Shuffle Attention module to the feature map after aggregation and fusion in the ASPP module to improve the efficiency and accuracy of deep convolutional neural networks in high-resolution remote sensing image processing. The Shuffle Attention module combines two operations: attention mechanism and channel rearrangement [40]. The attention mechanism includes two attention mechanisms: channel and spatial. The spatial attention mechanism maps the spatial feature information from the original feature map to other spaces and preserves key feature information. The channel attention mechanism can select and strengthen feature channels with important information by learning the weights of each channel, thereby improving the automatic identification performance of the high-resolution remote sensing images. The channel rearrangement operation divides the input feature map into multiple groups and rearranges the feature channels of each group. This operation can reduce model complexity and improve the efficiency of the high-resolution remote sensing image processing without significant performance loss (Fig. 4).

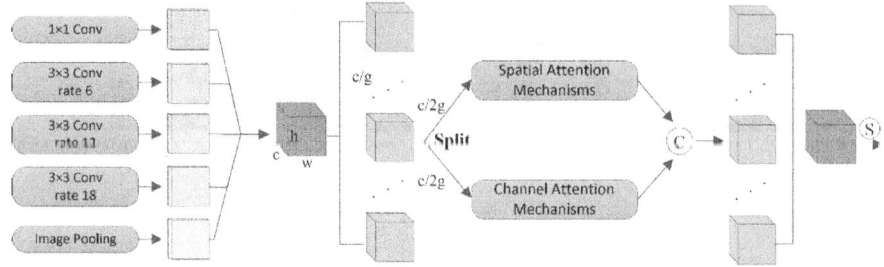

Fig. 4. Improved ASPP module structure.

2.4 Optimizing the Loss Function

The loss function is used to measure the robustness of the model and plays a crucial role in determining the quality of network learning, which is calculated by calculating the difference between the predicted and true values [21]. In the task of landslide disaster segmentation of the high-resolution remote sensing images, there is a situation where the number of pixels in the landslide area is less than the number of pixels in the background. The researchers propose a regional cost function called the Dice Loss function, in which all the outputs of the network affect the gradient of the samples, which can effectively solve the sample imbalance problem [22]. To obtain a high-quality landslide disaster segmentation map with clear boundaries, this study combines CrossEntropy Loss and Dice Loss to optimize the loss function. The loss function in this study is calculated as follows:

$$L = L_{BEC} + L_{DICE} \quad (1)$$

where L_{BEC} is CrossEntropy Loss function, and L_{DICE} is Dice Loss function.

3 Experiment

All the experiments in this study are carried out on a server equipped with NVIDIA GeForce RTX 2080Ti 11 GB GPU for deep learning model training, and the experimental models are implemented based on the PyTorch deep learning framework. The neural network training process uses a Stochastic Gradient Descent (SGD) optimizer; the initial learning rate is 0.001; the batch size is 8; and the iteration period is 100 times.

3.1 Experiment Data

The dataset used in this study is a fusion of two publicly available landslide disaster remote sensing image datasets, the Bijie landslide dataset and high-precision aerial imagery and interpretation of landslide and debris flow disaster in Sichuan and surrounding areas between 2008 and 2020 [23]. The two datasets have a wide spatial range, different types of landslide disaster-causing factors, and different scale levels, which make the disaster areas of different sizes. To cover the complete landslide area with one image data, the datasets provide non-uniform sizes of optical images and labeled data.

In this study, the optical images and labeled data of both datasets are converted to the image format of TIFF, and the images of both datasets are uniformly cropped to the standard size of 256 × 256 for training, validation, and testing of deep learning models. After cropping and correction, a total of 2379 pairs of (image-labeled) data were used in this study, which was divided into training set, validation set, and test set in the ratio of 6:2:2 according to the conventional ratio. Further data enhancement is performed for the divided training set, and the data enhancement methods are horizontal flipping, vertical flipping, and diagonal mirroring, to prevent the overfitting phenomenon during the training process. The size of the enhanced training set is enlarged to 7612 pairs of (image-labeled) data, which makes the training set have richer features, reduces the dependence on specific attributes of the original data, and can effectively improve the model generalization ability.

3.2 Experiment Results

To assess the good landslide disaster recognition capability of the Mv2_SA_DeepLabv3+ model proposed in this study, four traditional deep learning network models were selected for comparison experiments. These include the classical full convolutional neural network UNet model [24], the deep learning convolutional neural network ResNet model [25], and the DeepLabv3+ model for multi-scale feature extractions. Among them, the UNet model is a dual convolutional backbone network, the ResNet model is a ResNet101 backbone network, and the DeepLabv3+ model comes with the original Xception backbone network and ResNet101 backbone network, respectively.

Table 1. Extraction results of four evaluation indexes of different models.

Models (Backbone)	OA (%)	Kappa	F1 (%)	MIoU (%)
UNet (Dual-Conv)	90.32	0.72	78.49	76.42
ResNet (ResNet101)	93.29	0.80	84.46	82.45
DeepLabv3+ (Xception)	92.14	0.78	82.63	80.37
DeepLabv3+ (ResNet101)	93.69	0.82	86.47	84.13
Mv2_SA_DeepLabv3+ (MobileNetV2)	94.12	0.83	86.84	84.72

In this study, the segmentation results of the proposed Mv2_SA_DeepLabv3+ model and the traditional deep learning network model are quantitatively analyzed, and the experimental results are shown in Table 1. The results show that the Mv2_SA_DeepLabv3+ model achieves a more obvious improvement and achieves the highest values in the four metrics of OA, Kappa, F1, and MIoU, which are

94.12%, 0.83, 86.84%, and 84.72%, respectively. Compared to the original UNet, the Mv2_SA_DeepLabv3+ model improved by 3.80%, 0.11, 8.34% and 8.30% on the four-evaluation metrics. The DeepLabv3+ model with ResNet101 as the backbone network achieved the next best results, compared to which the Mv2_SA_DeepLabv3+ model also achieved an overall improvement of 0.42%, 0.01, 0.37%, and 0.58% in the four metrics. In summary, compared with the commonly used landslide disaster identification algorithms, the Mv2_SA_DeepLabv3+ model has good performance in the identification of landslide disasters, which can effectively avoid misclassification and omission, and the boundaries of landslide occurrence areas are clearer.

To verify the extraction ability of each model for landslide disaster areas, the Mv2_SA_DeepLabv3+ model proposed in this study was qualitatively analyzed with four comparison models using test set data. Five typical scenario regions were selected, where scenarios (a) and (b) are large landslide areas, scenario (c) is a bar-shaped landslide area, scenario (d) is a landslide area adjacent to a building, and scenario (e) is a typical non-landslide area that is prone to misclassification. The extraction results of each model for the five typical scene areas are shown in Fig. 5, where the first row is the real color image data, the second row is the labeled data of landslide areas visually interpreted by the experts, and the remaining rows represent the prediction results of different models for the areas where landslide disasters occur, respectively. According to the occurrence of misclassification, the red ellipse solid line and dotted line are used to mark the misclassification and omission areas, respectively; the misclassification represents the expert visual interpretation judgment for the non-landslide disaster occurrence area model incorrectly predicted as the landslide disaster occurrence area, and the omission represents the expert visual interpretation judgment for the landslide disaster occurrence area model incorrectly predicted as the non-landslide disaster occurrence area. The extraction results of the five typical scenarios show that the phenomena of misclassification and misclassification are more serious in the prediction results of the UNet model. The prediction results predicted by the ResNet model also have a certain degree of misclassification and misclassification. The misclassification phenomenon in the prediction results of the DeepLabv3+ model is relatively good, but there is also a slight misclassification, even though ResNet101 as the backbone network also has a misclassification exists. The Mv2_SA_DeepLabv3+ model proposed in this study predicts fewer results overall, but there is also a slight miss-scoring in complex scenarios, as shown in Scenario (c), there will be a small amount of landslide areas that have been omitted to be extracted.

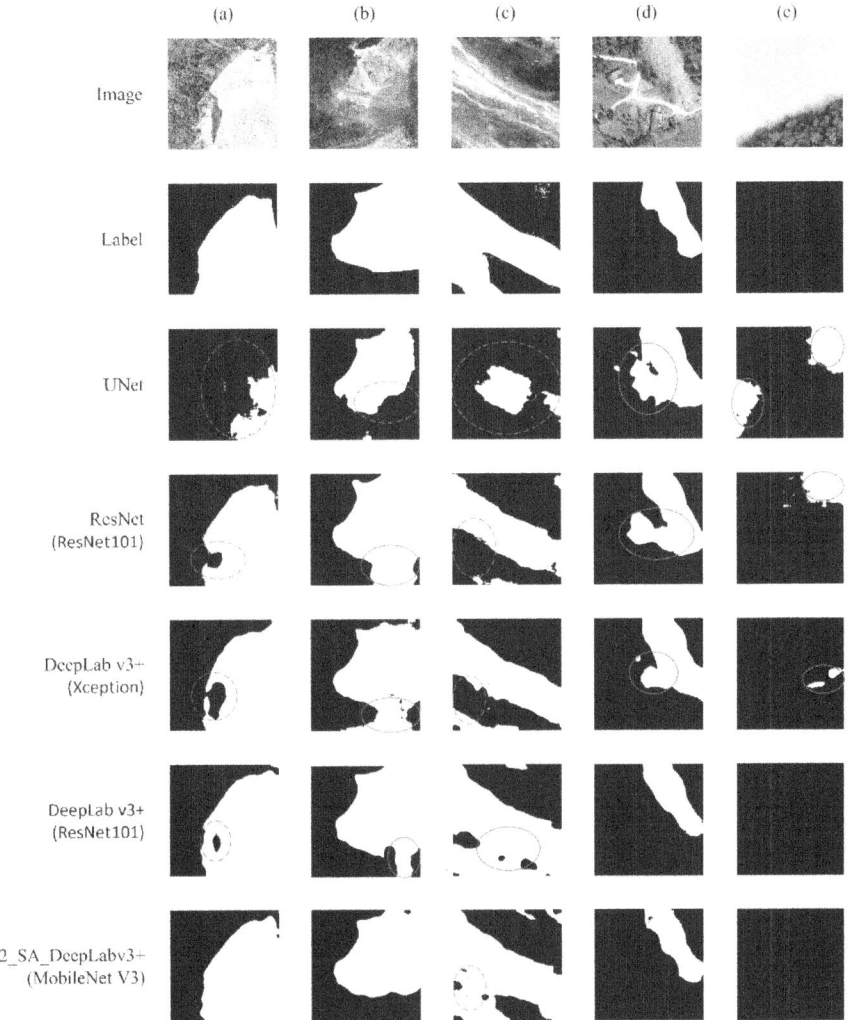

Fig. 5. Results of landslide disaster occurrence area of Mv2_SA_Deeolabv3+ model and other models. The white part in the image is the landslide disaster occurrence area extracted by the model.

3.3 Ablation Study

In this study, ablation experiments are conducted to verify the usefulness of each improvement module of the Mv2_SA_DeepLabv3+ model for extracting landslide disasters areas. A total of four sets of ablation experiments are set up, which are 1) Model 1: the original DeepLabv3+ model, using the Xception backbone network, with a pixel-by-pixel cross-entropy loss function; 2) Model 2: the original DeepLabv3+ model structure, with MobileNetV2 as the backbone network, and with a pixel-by-pixel cross-entropy loss function; 3) Model 3: the original DeepLabv3+ model structure, with MobileNetV2 as the backbone network, with a pixel-by-pixel cross-entropy loss function; 4) Model 4:

the Mv2_SA_DeepLabv3+ model, which adopts the original DeepLabv3+ model structure, using MobileNetV2 as the backbone network, adding the Shuffle Attention module to improve the ASPP module, and the loss function is the cross-entropy loss function combined with the Dice Loss function. Based on the same experimental setup, all four models are trained for 50 epochs, and ablation experiments are performed using the test set made from the same dataset, and the specific experimental results are shown in Table2.

Table 2. The experimental results of four evaluation indexes of each module in the model.

Models (Backbone)	OA (%)	Kappa	F1(%)	MIoU (%)
Model 1	92.14	0.78	82.63	80.37
Model 2	92.30	0.78	82.80	80.60
Model 3	93.70	0.82	86.16	83.93
Model 4	94.12	0.83	86.84	84.72

4 Discussion

4.1 Comparative Analysis of Model Complexity

In this study, the model complexity is evaluated for all the models of the comparison experiments, and the evaluation method used is the two evaluation indexes of computation amount and number of parameters, and the statistical results are shown in Table3. The results show that the complexity of the Mv2_SA_DeepLabv3+ model proposed in this study is the lowest among all the comparative experimental models, with a computational amount of 6.6 G Mac and a few parameters of 5.81 M. This is mainly due to the excellent network structure of DeepLabv3+ and the lightweight MobileNetV2 backbone network. From the statistical table, it can be observed that: 1) The computational amount of the UNet model is comparable to that of the ResNet model, but the parameter is 16.73 M lower; 2) Also using the ResNet101 as the backbone network, the Deeplabv3+ model decreases the computational amount by 31.68 G Mac and increases the parameter by 11.57 M compared to the ResNet model; 3) The Xception backbone network used in the original DeepLabv3+ model vs. ResNet101 backbone network has a slight decrease in both computation and parameter counts; 4) Also based on the DeepLabv3+ model structure, the model complexity using the lightweight MobileNetV2 backbone network vs. the original model Xception backbone network has been substantially optimization, the computational volume and the number of parameters decreased by 14.2 G Mac and 41.96 M, respectively; 5) the improved ASPP module and the added loss function of the Mv2_SA_DeepLabv3+ model did not increase the complexity of the model.

Table 3. Comparison of computational and parametric statistics of experimental models.

Models	Backbone	FLOPs (G Mac)	Params (M)
UNet	Dual-Conv	54.76	31.04
ResNet	ResNet101	53.89	47.77
Deeplabv3+	Xception	20.80	54.71
Deeplabv3+	ResNet101	22.21	59.34
Deeplabv3+	MobileNetV2	**6.6**	**5.81**
Mv2_SA_DeepLabv3+	MobileNetV2	**6.6**	**5.81**

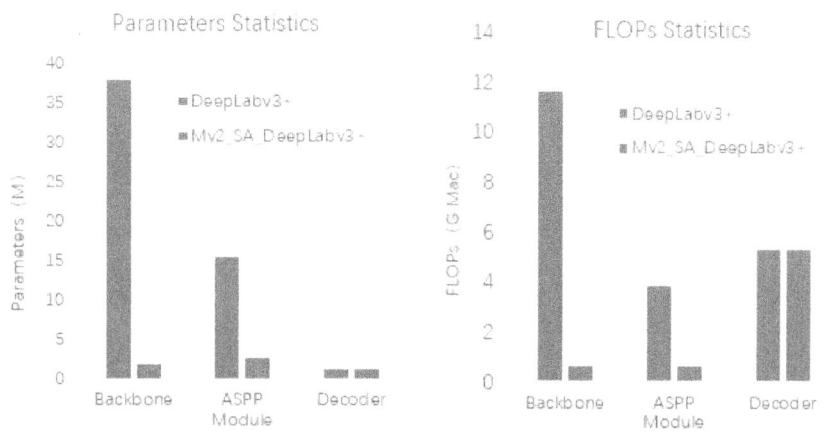

Fig. 6. Comparison of parametric quantities and computational statistics of the model's constituent structures.

4.2 Percentage Analysis of Model Complexity

To further explore the complexity of the proposed Mv2_SA_DeepLabv3+ model, the overall complexity of the model is divided into three main components, namely the MobileNetV2 backbone network, the improved ASPP module, and the decoder part. The computational and parameter counting results of the MobileNetV2 backbone network, the improved ASPP module, and the decoder parts of the Mv2_SA_DeepLabv3+ model are shown in Fig. 6. The computational volume and the number of parameters consumed by the MobileNetV2 backbone network is 0.61G Mac, accounting for 9.29%, and the number of parameters required is only 1.81M, accounting for 31.10%. The computation consumed by the improved ASPP module is 0.658G Mac (10.02%), and the number of parameters required is only 2.71M (46.56%). The decoder part consumed for 5.297G Mac is 80.69% and the number of required parameters is 1.31M or 22.34%. This study also shows the statistics of the specifics of the complexity of the original DeepLabv3+ model with Xception as the backbone network in Fig. 6.

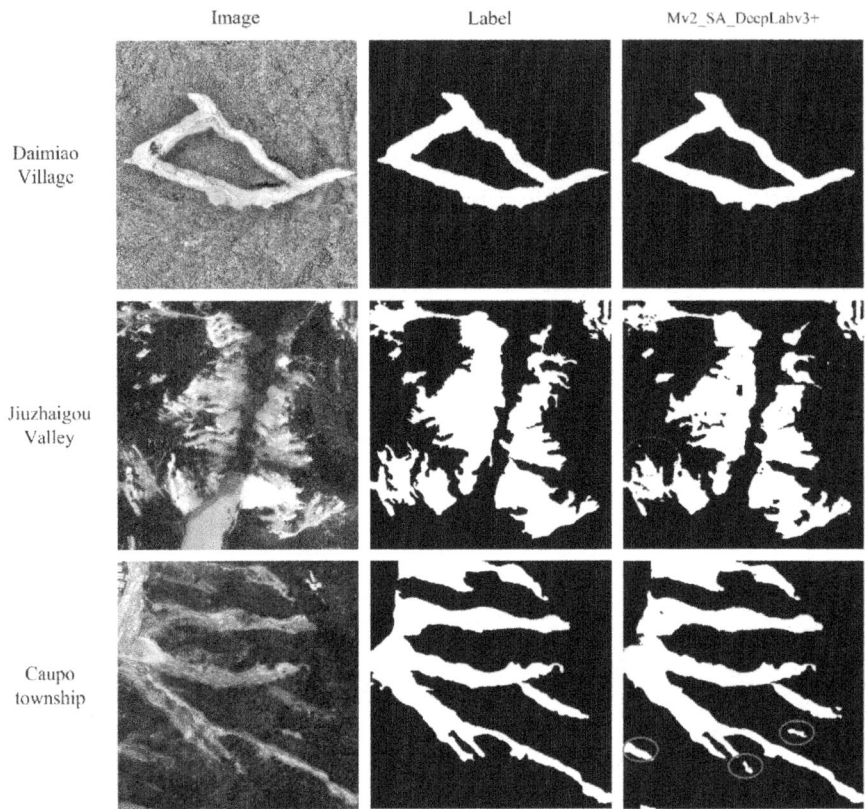

Fig. 7. Predicted results of model applications.

4.3 Model Applications

To further verify the extraction capability of the proposed model for landslide disaster areas, the results of landslide regional scale prediction were qualitatively analyzed. Three typical landslide disaster scenarios were selected from a dataset of high-precision aerial imagery and interpretation of landslide and debris flow disaster in Sichuan and surrounding areas between 2008 and 2020, and the extraction results of the Mv2_SA_DeepLabv3+ model for the three typical landslide disasters are shown in Fig. 7. The extraction results show that the lightweight deep learning network proposed in this study can automatically recognize the complete landslide disaster area, obviously overcome the interference of irrelevant information, and thus accurately identify the landslide area and its boundary. Through the analysis of the map of landslide disaster area prediction results of the model application found that the results of the extraction effect of the landslide in Daimiao Village, Laoshangchang, basically match with the labeled data, indicating that the extraction effect of the Mv2_SA_DeepLabv3+ model on seismic landslides is better than that of rainfall landslides. Therefore, the model needs to be further improved for the rainfall landslide type of landslide disasters to alleviate the effect of ground water on remote sensing reflectivity after rainfall.

5 Conclusion

In this study, a lightweight deep learning network named Mv2_SA_DeepLabv3+ is proposed to address the problem that landslide detection models based on remotely sensed images rely on multi-temporal or geologic data, and the models are complex and difficult to deploy. The model is based on the Deeplabv3+ network structure and uses the lightweight MobileNetV2 network as the backbone network to extract features and improves the ASPP module by adding the Shuffle Attention module, and further combining the Binary Cross Entropy Loss and Dice Loss to optimize the loss function. Comparison experiments and ablation experiments are further conducted based on two publicly available landslide disaster remote sensing image datasets with traditional deep learning models to analyze the performance difference between the Mv2_SA_DeepLabv3+ model and the traditional deep learning model in landslide disaster recognition and to validate the advantages and potentials of the lightweight deep learning network in automatic landslide disaster recognition. The Mv2_SA_DeepLabv3+ model and the traditional deep learning model are used to analyze the performance difference between the Mv2_SA_DeepLabv3+ model and the traditional deep learning model in landslide disaster recognition. DeepLabv3+ model reduces the computational complexity of the model while maintaining high extraction accuracy, better balances the contradiction between the extraction accuracy and speed of landslide disaster in high-resolution remote sensing imagery and meets the timeliness requirements of disaster emergency command for the model. In view of the slight misclassification and omission phenomenon that occurs when the model is applied, the next step of research needs to improve the generalization ability of the model to adapt to different resolutions of remote sensing image data and to improve the extraction accuracy of rainfall landslides.

Acknowledgments. This work was supported by the Strategic Priority Research Program of Chinese Academy of Sciences, grant number XDA23100504, and the National Key Research and Development Program of China, grant number 2017YFB0503500.

Disclosure of Interests. The authors have no competing interests to declare that are relevant to the content of this article.

References

1. Cheng, L., Li, J., Duan, P., Wang, M.: A small attentional YOLO model for landslide detection from satellite remote sensing images. Landslides **18**, 2751–2765 (2021). https://doi.org/10.1007/s10346-021-01694-6
2. Liu, T., Chen, T., Niu, R., Plaza, A.: Landslide detection mapping employing CNN, ResNet, and DenseNet in the three gorges reservoir. China. IEEE J. Sel. Top. Appl. Earth Obs. Remote Sens. **14**, 11417–11428 (2021). https://doi.org/10.1109/JSTARS.2021.3117975

3. Wang, H., Zhang, L., Yin, K., Luo, H., Li, J.: Landslide identification using machine learning. Geosci. Front. **12**, 351–364 (2021). https://doi.org/10.1016/j.gsf.2020.02.012
4. Li, Z., Shi, W., Lu, P., Yan, L., Wang, Q., Miao, Z.: Landslide mapping from aerial photographs using change detection-based Markov random field. Remote Sens. Environ. **187**, 76–90 (2016). https://doi.org/10.1016/j.rse.2016.10.008
5. Li, H., He, Y., Xu, Q., Deng, J., Li, W., Wei, Y.: Detection and segmentation of loess landslides via satellite images: a two-phase framework. Landslides **19**, 673–686 (2022). https://doi.org/10.1007/s10346-021-01789-0
6. Li, Z., Shi, W., Myint, S.W., Lu, P., Wang, Q.: Semi-automated landslide inventory mapping from bitemporal aerial photographs using change detection and level set method. Remote Sens. Environ. **175**, 215–230 (2016). https://doi.org/10.1016/j.rse.2016.01.003
7. Liu, X., et al.: Feature-fusion segmentation network for landslide detection using high-resolution remote sensing images and digital elevation model data. IEEE Trans. Geosci. Remote Sensing. **61**, 1–14 (2023). https://doi.org/10.1109/TGRS.2022.3233637
8. Keyport, R.N., Oommen, T., Martha, T.R., Sajinkumar, K.S., Gierke, J.S.: A comparative analysis of pixel- and object-based detection of landslides from very high-resolution images. Int. J. Appl. Earth Obs. Geoinf. **64**, 1–11 (2018). https://doi.org/10.1016/j.jag.2017.08.015
9. Liu, J., Lu, Y., Guo, X., Ke, W.: A deep learning method for offshore raft aquaculture extraction based on medium-resolution remote sensing images. IEEE J. Sel. Top. Appl. Earth Obs. Remote Sens. **16**, 6296–6309 (2023). https://doi.org/10.1109/JSTARS.2023.3291499
10. Xia, W., Chen, J., Liu, J., Ma, C., Liu, W.: Landslide extraction from high-resolution remote sensing imagery using fully convolutional spectral-topographic fusion network. Remote Sens. **13**, 5116 (2021). https://doi.org/10.3390/rs13245116
11. Ji, J., Zhou, Y., Cheng, Q., Jiang, S., Liu, S.: Landslide susceptibility mapping based on deep learning algorithms using information value analysis optimization. Land **12**, 1125 (2023). https://doi.org/10.3390/land12061125
12. Abraham, M.T., Satyam, N., Lokesh, R., Pradhan, B., Alamri, A.: Factors affecting landslide susceptibility mapping: assessing the influence of different machine learning approaches. Sampling Strat. Data Splitting. Land. **10**, 989 (2021). https://doi.org/10.3390/land10090989
13. Chen, X., Yao, X., Zhou, Z., Liu, Y., Yao, C., Ren, K.: DRs-UNet: a deep semantic segmentation network for the recognition of active landslides from InSAR imagery in the three rivers region of the Qinghai-Tibet plateau. Remote Sens. **14**, 1848 (2022). https://doi.org/10.3390/rs14081848
14. Nagendra, S., et al.: Constructing a large-scale landslide database across heterogeneous environments using task-specific model updates. IEEE J. Sel. Top. Appl. Earth Obs. Remote Sens. **15**, 4349–4370 (2022). https://doi.org/10.1109/JSTARS.2022.3177025
15. Lu, Y., Shao, W., Sun, J.: Extraction of offshore aquaculture areas from medium-resolution remote sensing images based on deep learning. Remote Sens. **13**, 3854 (2021). https://doi.org/10.3390/rs13193854
16. Xu, B., et al.: Landslide identification method based on the FKGRNet model for remote sensing images. Remote Sens. **15**, 3407 (2023). https://doi.org/10.3390/rs15133407
17. Meena, S.R., et al.: Rapid mapping of landslides in the Western Ghats (India) triggered by 2018 extreme monsoon rainfall using a deep learning approach. Landslides **18**, 1937–1950 (2021). https://doi.org/10.1007/s10346-020-01602-4
18. Ghorbanzadeh, O., Gholamnia, K., Ghamisi, P.: The application of ResU-net and OBIA for landslide detection from multi-temporal Sentinel-2 images. Big Earth Data. **7**, 961–985 (2023). https://doi.org/10.1080/20964471.2022.2031544
19. Liu, Q., Wu, T., Deng, Y., Liu, Z.: SE-YOLOv7 landslide detection algorithm based on attention mechanism and improved loss function. Land. **12**, 1522 (2023). https://doi.org/10.3390/land12081522

20. Niu, C., Gao, O., Lu, W., Liu, W., Lai, T.: Reg-SA–UNet++: a lightweight landslide detection network based on single-temporal images captured postlandslide. IEEE J. Sel. Top. Appl. Earth Obs. Remote Sens. **15**, 9746–9759 (2022). https://doi.org/10.1109/JSTARS.2022.3219897
21. Chen, L., Qu, H., Zhao, J., Chen, B., Principe, J.C.: Efficient and robust deep learning with correntropy-induced loss function. Neural Comput. Appl. **27**, 1019–1031 (2016). https://doi.org/10.1007/s00521-015-1916-x
22. Yang, Q.-L.Z.Y.-B.: SA-Net: shuffle attention for deep convolutional neural networks, http://arxiv.org/abs/2102.00240 (2021)
23. Ji, S., Yu, D., Shen, C., Li, W., Xu, Q.: Landslide detection from an open satellite imagery and digital elevation model dataset using attention boosted convolutional neural networks. Landslides **17**, 1337–1352 (2020). https://doi.org/10.1007/s10346-020-01353-2
24. Ronneberger, O., Fischer, P., Brox, T.: U-Net: convolutional networks for biomedical image segmentation (2015). http://arxiv.org/abs/1505.04597
25. He, K., Zhang, X., Ren, S., Sun, J.: Deep residual learning for image recognition. In: 2016 2020 IEEE/CVF Conference on Computer Vision and Pattern Recognition (CVPR), pp. 770–778 (2016)

LCformer: Enhancing Multivariate Time Series Forecasting with Transformer Based on Lagged Correlations

Lihua Wang, Zipei Fan, and Xuan Song[✉]

School of Artificial Intelligence, Jilin University, Changchun, China
lihua23@mails.jlu.edu.cn, {fanzipei,songxuan}@jlu.edu.cn

Abstract. Existing methods often ignore the correlations between variables or fail to consider their dynamic and delayed nature, which may affect the prediction accuracy. The main goal of this study is to address the challenges in time series prediction by effectively capturing the inter-dependencies between multiple variables. We propose the LCformer model, a new framework based on the Transformer architecture that integrates the lagged correlation information of multiple variables and its own historical information. The model identifies relevant exogenous variables using an exogenous variable filter (EVF), and employs a novel additive attention embedding (AAE) layer as well as cross-attention mechanism to simulate the lagged dependencies between these exogenous variables and the target variable. Experimental evaluation shows that the LCformer model is competitive with state-of-the-art methods, confirming its ability to accurately capture complex relationships in time series data, and learning multivariate lagged correlations, which can significantly improve prediction accuracy.

Keywords: Multivariate Time Series Forecasting · Deep Learning · Lagged Correlations

1 Introduction

Multivariate time series (MTS) forecasting is widely applied in various fields such as finance [2], transportation [16], meteorology [21], and energy [26]. The task involves multiple time series, each representing a key indicator of a complex real-world system that exhibits intricate dynamic relationships [17]. For example, weather includes various features such as temperature, humidity, and carbon dioxide concentration. In recent years, some studies have benefited from the ability of Transformer [3,5,21,23,26] to capture long-term dependencies and temporal relationships, achieving remarkable results. However, these models either embed all features into a feature vector at the same timestamp, implicitly considering the relationships among variables, or adopt a channel-independent strategy that completely disregards the influence of other variables. While both approaches can effectively capture temporal dependencies, they fail to account for the inter-dependencies among variables, which may limit their predictive capability. The iTransformer [14] model treats each time series variable as a separate token and uses an attention mechanism to address multivariate correlation, but it overlooks use of its own historical information. While recent studies [20,24] have explicitly addressed capturing temporal dependencies and multivariate correlations, their common approach is to learn these correlations within the same time window. These models overlook the dynamic and lagged characteristics of the dependencies between variables, as shown in Fig. 1.

Several studies have confirmed that using lagged dependencies between variables can enhance prediction accuracy. For instance, significant lagged correlations exist between precipitation and aerosol concentration [1], as well as between temperature and wind direction [4], which are beneficial for forecasting. Trading strategies can be developed based on lagged dependencies to profit from temporal delays between patterns [9,18]. Motivated by the above observations, we propose LCformer, a transformer-based model that explicitly leverages the temporal lagged dependencies between variables for prediction. Specifically, we partition the input sequence into non-overlapping subsequences and map them into feature space to obtain vector representations. Inspired by PETformer [11], we utilize placeholder enhancement techniques (PET) to initialize the target sequence and input it alongside the vector representations of historical information into the model. The model learns historical patterns through self-attention mechanisms and focuses on the lagged effects of variable information using cross-attention mechanisms to update the predicted values of the target sequence. However, the complexity of the attention mechanisms across multiple subsequences of several variables presents new challenges. This necessitates that the model coordinately considers the differences in correlations among multiple subsequences at different time steps while balancing model complexity and performance. To address these challenges, we designed an additive attention embedding (AAE) in conjunction with an exogenous variable filter (EVF) to achieve differential attention to multivariate information, effectively utilizing the temporal lagged dependencies between variables with low computational complexity.

In summary, the contributions of this paper are as follows:

- We propose the LCformer framework based on the Transformer architecture, which can simultaneously model the dual effects of lagged correlations across both time and variable dimensions.
- We introduce a novel additive attention embedding (AAE) that allows the prediction targets to differentially focus on information from exogenous variable sequences across time window while reducing computational complexity of the attention scores from $O(C^2)$ to $O(\frac{LT}{p^2})$, where C is the dimension of variable, L is the length of historical time series window, T is the length of prediction window, and p is the length of patch.
- Extensive experimental results on twelve real-world benchmarks demonstrate that LCformer outperforms previous state-of-the-art methods in both long-term and short-term time series forecasting.

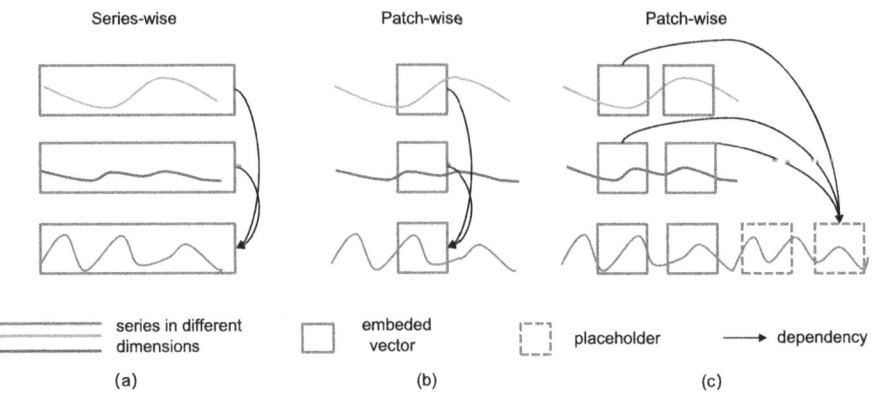

Fig. 1. Comparison of LCformer's embedded representation for modeling inter-variable dependencies with other methods. (a) The iTransformer [14] embeds each sequence into a vector, where the attention mechanism focuses on inter-sequence relationships. (b) Crossformer [24] embeds each segment of a sequence into a vector, where the attention mechanism focuses on segment-level relationships within the same time window. (c) Our LCformer also embeds each segment of a sequence into a vector, but the attention mechanism focuses on segment-level relationships across time windows.

2 Related Works

Transformer-Based Time Series Forecasting Models. In recent years, Transformers have garnered significant attention for their ability to capture long-term temporal dependencies and complex multivariate correlations. Many studies have focused on integrating Transformers with time series tasks, achieving remarkable progress. Notable works such as LogTrans, Pyraformer, Informer and FEDformer [8,13,26,27] have successfully reduced the computational complexity of the original Transformer by redesigning the attention mechanism (e.g., sparse attention and frequency domain attention), leading to efficient and accurate predictions. During this phase, multivariate information corresponding to each timestamp is mapped into a vector space for dot-product attention computation, where each embedding vector integrates information from multiple variables, primarily focusing on modeling temporal dependencies. To enable models to attend to semantic information, approaches like PatchTST [15] and Crossformer [24] segment each time series into multiple subsequences to capture the temporal dependencies between these subsequences. However, the channel-independent strategy adopted by PatchTST [15] completely overlooks the utilization of inter-variable dependencies. While Crossformer [24] addresses inter-variable dependencies, it models these relationships only within the same time slice, failing to account for the lagged nature of inter-variable relationships. Furthermore, methods such as iTransformer [14] and TimeXer [20] model inter-variable dependencies based on the attention mechanism of sequence-level embedding vectors. The iTransformer [14] model focuses solely on inter-variable dependencies, disregarding the influence of historical information. TimeXer [20] employs learnable global tokens to bridge endogenous and exogenous information, but its reliance on sequence-level embedding vectors neglects the dynamics and lagged nature of inter-variable correlations. Therefore, this paper continues to explore the application of Transformers in modeling inter-variable dependencies.

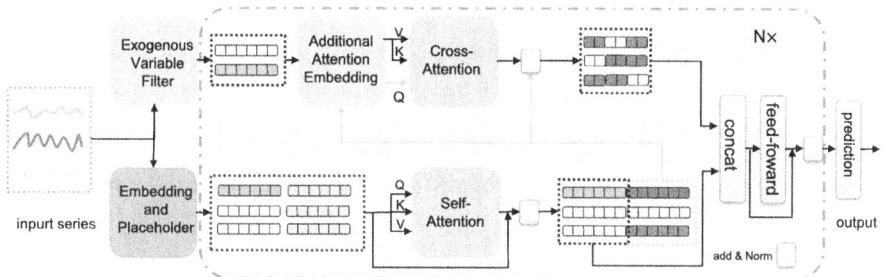

Fig. 2. The LCformer model architecture

3 Preliminaries

Definition 1 . An assumption is that there is a time-lag dependency relationship between variables i and j, i.e., variable j at a future time point $t + \delta$ can be affected by variable i at time t (e.g., $t + \delta, \delta \in [L]$, where L is the maximum time lag).

Definition 2 (Cross-correlation coefficient). The cross-correlation coefficient quantifies the strength of time lag relationships. Specifically, the larger the absolute value of the coefficient, the stronger the lagged correlation at the corresponding time step. Cross-correlation coefficient between the two variates at time t is defined as [25]:

$$R_{i,t}^{(j)}(\delta) = \frac{\text{Cov}(x_{t-L+1-\delta:t-\delta}^{(i)}, x_{t-L+1:t}^{(j)})}{\sigma^{(i)}\sigma^{(j)}} \quad (1)$$

$$= \frac{1}{L} \sum_{t'=t-L+1}^{t} \frac{x_{t'-\delta}^{(i)} - \mu^{(i)}}{\sigma^{(i)}} \cdot \frac{x_{t'}^{(j)} - \mu^{(j)}}{\sigma^{(j)}} \quad (2)$$

where $\mu^{(\cdot)} \in \mathbb{R}$ and $\sigma^{(\cdot)} \in \mathbb{R}$ represent the mean and standard variation of the univariate time series within the lookback window, respectively.

4 Methodology

In a multivariate time series prediction task, the goal is to forecast T furture values $Y = \{y_t^1, y_t^2, \cdots, y_t^c\}_{t=1}^T$, based on a given a collection of multivariate time series samples with lookback window L, $X = \{x_t^1, x_t^2, \cdots, x_t^c\}_{t=1}^L$, where each x_t^c time step t is a vector of variable. Our LCformer is illustrated in Fig. 2. This model utilizes a Transformer as its core architecture, where the input is composed of learnable vectors for the target sequence concatenated with the embedded representations of the historical sequence. Using self-attention, the model learns historical patterns and performs an initial update on the vector representation of the target sequence. Subsequently, the exogenous variables filtered by the EVF are processed through the AAE, employing cross-attention for a secondary update of the target sequence's vector representation, ultimately generating predictions through the prediction layer.

4.1 Embedding and Self-attention

We separates X into C independent feature sequences $X' = \{X^1, X^2, \cdots X^c\}$. The independent sequences X^i is divided into N sub-sequences $x_p^{(i)} \in \mathbb{R}^{P \times N}$, where N is determined by the sub-sequence window length P, i.e., $N = \lceil \frac{L}{P} \rceil$. The patches mapped to the Transfomer latent space of dimension D via a trainable linear projection $W_p \in \mathbb{R}^{P \times D}$ and the first N dimentions of the additive position encoding $W_{pos} \in \mathbb{R}^{(N+M) \times D}$, i.e., $X_d^{(i)} = (x_p^{(i)})^T W_p + W_{pos}[:N]$, $X_d^{(i)} \in \mathbb{R}^{N \times D}$. For continuity and consistency between the history window and the prediction window, the embedding is defined as $\hat{X}_d^{(i)} = \hat{X}_d^{(i)} + W_{pos}[-M:]$, $\hat{X}_d^{(i)} \in \mathbb{R}^{M \times D}$. This process generates m tokens for each independent sequence, amounting to a total of $(N+M)$ tokens $X_d^{(i)} = concat(X_d^{(i)}, \hat{X}_d^{(i)})$, $X_d^{(i)} \in \mathbb{R}^{(N+M) \times D}$, where $X_d^{(i)}$ denote input into the LCformer.

Self-attention will respectively transform $X_d^{(i)}$ into query matrices $Q_h^{(i)}$, key matrices $K_h^{(i)}$, and value matrices $V_h^{(i)}$. Afterwards, the initial update to the vector representation of the target sequence is obtained by combining residual connections and LayerNorm layers:

$$\left(O_h^{(i)}\right)^T = Attention(Q_h^{(i)}, K_h^{(i)}, V_h^{(i)}) = Softmax(\frac{Q_h^{(i)}(K_h^{(i)})^T}{\sqrt{d_k}})V_h^{(i)} \quad (3)$$

$$\left(O_h^{(i)}\right)^T = \left(O_h^{(i)}\right)^T + LayerNorm(\left(O_h^{(i)}\right)^T) \quad (4)$$

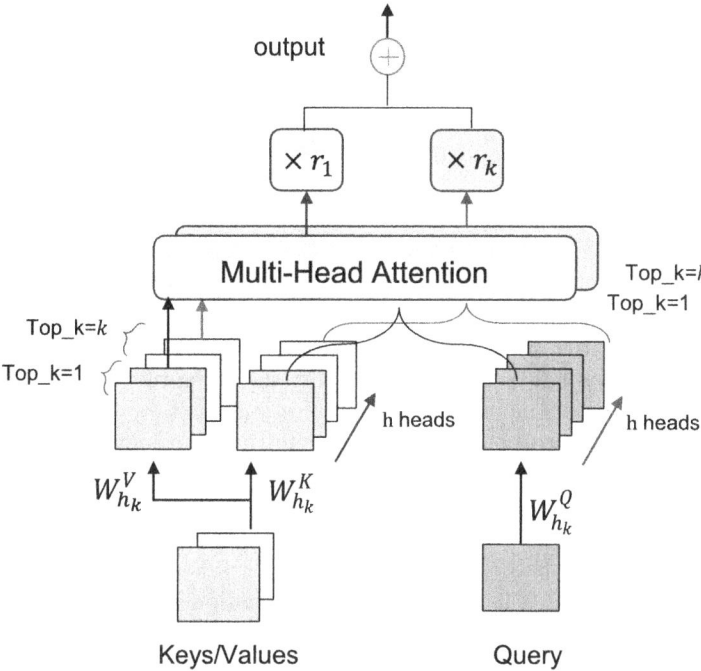

Fig. 3. The additional attention embedding layer

4.2 Exogenous Variable Filter and Additive Attention Embedding Layer

As shown in Fig. 1(b), existing methods divide the time series X' into segment and map them into a vector space to obtain the representations $H \in \mathbb{R}^{N \times C \times D}$, for the n-th segment, the attention mechanism focuses on the dependencies between the C vectors $\{h_n^{(1)}, h_n^{(2)}, \ldots, h_n^{(C)}\}$. Therefore, traditional Transformer-based models primarily focus on multivariate dependencies within the same time window when capturing multivariate relationships, which limits the model's predictive capability. However, directly implementing patch-based multivariate dependencies across time windows poses unacceptable complexity for high-dimensional datasets. Fortunately, not all variables influence the target variable. Based on this consideration, we use the EVF module to filter exogenous variables that impact the target variable with mutual correlation coefficients. This module is parameter-free and can be pre-computed in one go.

Specifically, the EVF calculates the correlation coefficient between each pair of variate i and variate j to filter the exogenous variables. For reducing the complexity, we apply the method proposed by LIFT [25], which use Fourier transform to estimate the coefficients for all possible leading steps in $\{0, \ldots, L-1\}$ at once. We choose Top_k variates that show the most signigicant lagging dependencies with target variate j. Then, we can get exogenous variates by the following equation: $X_{ex} = EVF(X')$, $X_{ex} \in \mathbb{R}^{C \times k \times L}$.

The exogenous variables $X_{ex}^{(i)}$ corresponding to each target variable is divided into patches and embedding $X_{ex}^{(i)} \in \mathbb{R}^{k \times N \times D}$. AAE layer will transform $\hat{X}_d^{(j)} \in \mathbb{R}^{D \times M}$ into query matrices $Q_{h_k}^{(j)} = (\hat{X}_d^{(j)})^T W_{h_k}^Q$, transform $X_{ex}^{(i)} \in \mathbb{R}^{D \times (k \times N)}$ into key matrices $K_{h_k}^{(i)} = (X_{ex}^{(i)})^T W_{h_k}^K$ and value matrices $V_{h_k}^{(i)} = (X_{ex}^{(i)})^T W_{h_k}^V$, where $W_{h_k}^V, W_{h_k}^K \in \mathbb{R}^{D \times d}$ and $W_{h_k}^Q \in \mathbb{R}^{D \times (k \times d)}$. Specifically, in AAE layer, we concatenate multiple exogenous variables along the head dimension. This processing allows the attention mechanism to focus on the relationships between patches, enabling the target variable to attend to information from multiple exogenous variables across time windows, thus modeling the lagged and dynamic dependencies between the exogenous variables and the target variable. Furthermore, it is important to note that we have multiple exogenous variables, which may have differing correlations with the target variable, meaning they exert varying degrees of influence on the future values of the target sequence. Therefore, as shown in Fig. 3, the obtained scaled product is multiplied by the weight $\gamma = \{\gamma_1, \gamma_i, \ldots, \gamma_k\}$, where γ_i is a learnable vector, k is the number of exogenous variables. This approach facilitates the quantification and adjustment of these influences during training, enabling the model to effectively coordinate the differences in correlations among multiple subsequences across different time steps. By weighting the influences of multiple exogenous variables, the final attention output $O_h^{(j)} \in \mathbb{R}^{D \times M}$ is obtained:

$$\left(O_h^{(j)}\right)^T = \sum_{i=1}^{k} \gamma_i (Softmax(\frac{Q_{h_k}^{(j)}(K_{h_k}^{(i)})^T}{\sqrt{d}}) V_{h_k}^{(i)}) \tag{5}$$

$$\left(O_h^{(j)}\right)^T = \left(O_h^{(j)}\right)^T + LayerNorm(\left(O_h^{(j)}\right)^T) \tag{6}$$

As a result, LCformer achieves a secondary update of the vector representation of the target sequence. In summary, by considering its historical information and differentiating the effects of lagged correlations from exogenous variables, the model's predictions will be more aligned with real-world situations and needs, leading to further improvements in performance.

Instance Normalization. The RevIN [7] framework introduces a novel technique that addresses the issue of data distribution drift by recovering non-stationary information. Specifically, each time series $X^{(i)}$ is zero-normalized, and the model output is then denormalized to obtain the final prediction results.

Loss Function. We choose to use the Mean Absolute Error (MAE) loss to measure the difference between the predicted values and the true values. The loss function is defined as follows:

$$L = \frac{1}{CT} \sum_{i=1}^{C} \sum_{j=1}^{T} |\hat{y}_j^{(i)} - y_j^{(i)}| \tag{7}$$

where $y_j^{(i)}$ is the true value for the *i-th* dimension at time j, $\hat{y}_j^{(i)}$ is the predicted value for the *i-th* dimension at time j, C is the number of variable dimensions and T is the prediction length.

5 Experiments

Datesets. We conduct experiments on real-world datasets following [20], including five short-term electricity price forecating datasets (EPF) and seven well-established public long-term multivariate forecasting benchmarks to evaluate the performance of LCformer in multivatiate forecasting. We adopt the same train/val/test splits ratio are same as [20].

Baselines. We select representative state-of-the-art deep forecasting models as baselines, including the following categories: Transformer-based models: iTransformer [14], PatchTST [15], TimeXer [20], and Crossformer [24]; CNN-based models: SCINet [12] and TimesNet [22]; linear-based models: TiDE [6], RLinear [10], and DLinear [23].

Setup. Using the same settings as in [20], for EPF, the input sequence length and prediction length are set to 168 and 24, respectively, with a patch length of 24. For the long-term forecasting dataset, we uniformly use a patch length of 16, and all models adopt the same lookback length of 96 and prediction lengths of $\{96, 192, 336, 720\}$.

5.1 Experimental Results

The results of EPF are presented in Table 1. The EPF dataset is derived from real-world scenarios, where there is a high correlation between the forecast targets and other variables. Model results indicate that in this task scenario, models focusing solely on historical information [15,23] perform relatively worse than those considering the relationships between variables. However, although TimeXer [20] improves upon iTransformer [14] by combining attention to historical information with multivariate dependencies through global tokens, its coarse-grained attention performs poorly on certain datasets. Similar to our work, Crossformer [24] employs a two-stage attention mechanism to capture multivariate dependencies based on patches, but it overlooks the lagged relationships between variables. In contrast, LCformer effectively addresses the lagged dependencies between variables through patch-based attention, achieving outstanding performance on most datasets and exhibiting a lower overall mean squared error compared to other baselines. As shown in Table 2, we also compared the average results of four different prediction lengths on the multivariate time series long-term forecasting benchmark. It can be observed that LCformer achieves state-of-the-art performance on most datasets, demonstrating its versatility and effectiveness. Experiments show that LCformer significantly improves the accuracy of multivariate long-term forecasting by effectively utilizing the lagged dependencies between variables. Detailed results are listed in Appendix A.

Table 1. Experimental results of the short-term forecasting task on EPF dataset. All baseline results are derived from [20]. Avg means the average results from all five datasets. Bold/underline indicates the best/second.

Models	LCformer	TimeXer	iTrans	RLinear	PatchTST	Cross	TiDE	TimesNet	DLinear	SCINet
Metric	MSE MAE	MSE MAE	MSE MAE	MSE MAE	MSE MAE	MSE MAE	MSE MAE	MSE MAE	MSE MAE	MSE MAE
NP	0.263 0.220	**0.236 0.268**	0.265 0.300	0.335 0.340	0.267 0.284	0.240 0.285	0.335 0.340	0.250 0.289	0.309 0.321	0.373 0.368
PJM	**0.080 0.176**	0.093 0.192	0.097 0.197	0.124 0.229	0.106 0.209	0.101 0.199	0.124 0.228	0.097 0.195	0.108 0.215	0.143 0.259
BE	**0.372 0.246**	0.379 0.243	0.394 0.270	0.520 0.337	0.400 0.262	0.420 0.290	0.523 0.336	0.419 0.288	0.463 0.313	0.731 0.412
FR	**0.355 0.195**	0.385 0.208	0.439 0.233	0.507 0.290	0.411 0.220	0.434 0.208	0.510 0.290	0.431 0.234	0.429 0.260	0.855 0.384
DE	0.470 0.425	**0.440 0.415**	0.479 0.443	0.574 0.498	0.461 0.432	0.574 0.430	0.568 0.496	0.502 0.446	0.520 0.463	0.565 0.497
AVG	**0.304 0.261**	0.307 0.265	0.335 0.289	0.412 0.339	0.330 0.282	0.354 0.284	0.412 0.338	0.340 0.290	0.366 0.314	0.533 0.384

Table 2. Long-term forecasting result. All baseline results are derived from [20]. Bold/underline indicates the best/second.

Models	LCformer	TimeXer	iTrans	RLinear	PatchTST	Cross	TiDE	TimesNet	DLinear	SCINet
Metric	MSE MAE	MSE MAE	MSE MAE	MSE MAE	MSE MAE	MSE MAE	MSE MAE	MSE MAE	MSE MAE	MSE MAE
ECL	0.193 0.279	**0.171 0.270**	0.178 0.270	0.219 0.298	0.205 0.290	0.244 0.334	0.251 0.244	0.192 0.295	0.212 0.300	0.268 0.365
Weather	0.251 0.270	**0.241 0.271**	0.258 0.278	0.272 0.291	0.259 0.281	0.259 0.315	0.271 0.320	0.259 0.287	0.265 0.317	0.292 0.363
ETTh1	**0.435 0.426**	0.437 0.437	0.454 0.447	0.446 0.434	0.469 0.454	0.529 0.522	0.541 0.507	0.458 0.450	0.456 0.452	0.747 0.647
ETTh2	0.358 0.387	0.367 0.396	0.383 0.407	0.374 0.398	0.387 0.407	0.942 0.684	0.611 0.550	0.414 0.427	0.559 0.515	0.954 0.723
ETTm1	**0.379 0.381**	0.382 0.397	0.407 0.410	0.414 0.407	0.387 0.400	0.512 0.496	0.419 0.419	0.400 0.406	0.403 0.407	0.485 0.481
ETTm2	**0.270 0.313**	0.274 0.322	0.288 0.332	0.286 0.327	0.281 0.326	0.757 0.610	0.358 0.404	0.291 0.333	0.350 0.401	0.571 0.537
Traffic	0.431 **0.257**	0.466 0.287	**0.428** 0.282	0.626 0.378	0.481 0.304	0.550 0.304	0.760 0.473	0.620 0.336	0.625 0.383	0.804 0.509

5.2 Ablation Study

The main components of our work include the EVF, AAE, and PET. To validate the effectiveness of these modules, we designed the following ablation experiments: "wo_AAE", indicating that the cross-attention embedding vectors are sequence-based representations rather than patch-based representations; "wo_EVF", indicating the removal of the EVF module, treating all variables as exogenous variables; and "wo_PET", indicating the removal of the PET. The results in Table 3 indicate that LCformer outperforms other designs on both the ETTh1, ETTh2 and Traffic datasets.

5.3 Hyperparameter Study

We evaluated the impact of the hyperparameter Top_k (representing the number of exogenous variables) on the model using the ETTh2 dataset. As shown in Fig. 4, $Top\_k = 2/3$ yields the best performance across all prediction lengths. Choosing a Top_k that is too small or too large results in decreased model performance. Overall, selecting Top_k as an approximation of $\log C$ tends to produce better results, and the model's overall performance remains stable when Top_k is close to $\log C$.

5.4 Model Analysis

Computational Efficiency Analysis. The Table 4 compares the theoretical complexity of computing attention scores at each layer of various transformer-based architectures. Assuming a historical time series window of length L and a prediction window of length T, with dimension C of the variable and length p of the patch, the model's computational complexity is $O((\frac{L+T}{p})^2)$ as introduction of the future window. Nevertheless, by dividing the time series into multiple patches, the model's complexity remains significantly lower than the original Transformer's complexity of $O(L^2)$. Additionally, benefiting from the design of the AAE layer, the computational complexity of the attention scores that capture lagged dependencies between patches of variables decreases from $O(C^2)$ to $O(\frac{LT}{p^2})$. In the case where L and T are of limited length, as the dimensionality of the variables increases, especially when dealing with datasets that contain a large number of variables, our model demonstrates a some advantage compared with the complexity C of TimeXer.

Table 3. Component ablation of LCformer

Models	LCformer		wo_AAE		wo_PET		wo_EVF	
Metric	MSE	MAE	MSE	MAE	MSE	MAE	MSE	MAE
ETTh1	**0.435**	**0.426**	0.441	0.432	0.439	0.429	0.439	0.428
ETTh2	**0.358**	**0.387**	0.369	0.393	0.370	0.396	0.368	0.394
Traffic	**0.431**	**0.257**	0.436	0.259	0.931	0.531	-	-

"-" indicates an out-of-memory situation.

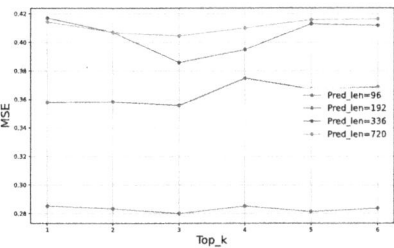

Fig. 4. Mean square error of all prediction lengths corresponding to different Top_k.

Table 4. Comparison of model theoretical complexity

Method	Encoder layer	Decoder layer
Trans. [19]	$O(L^2)$	$O(T(L+T))$
In. [26]	$O(L \log L)$	$O(T(T + \log L))$
Auto. [21]	$O(L \log L)$	$O((\frac{L}{2} + T)log(\frac{L}{2} + T))$
Pyra. [13]	$O(L)$	$O(L(L+T))$
FED. [27]	$O(L)$	$O(\frac{L}{2} + T))$
Cross. [24]	$O(\frac{C}{p^2}L^2)$	$O(\frac{4}{p^2}T(L+T))$
PET. [11]	$O((\frac{L}{p})^2)$	
Patch. [15]	$O((\frac{L}{p})^2)$	
PDF [5]	$O((\frac{max(p_i)}{p})^2)$	
TimeXer [20]	$O((\frac{L}{p})^2)$	
ours	$O((\frac{L+T}{p})^2)$	

6 Conclusions

The proposed method employs the Exogenous Variable Filter (EVF) to identify exogenous variables, while the Additive Attention Embedding Layer (AAE) enables the model to capture lagged dependencies between variables. Additionally, the use of Placeholder Enhancement Technique (PET) allows the model to directly simulate the interactions between historical and future information, achieving dual attention to both the temporal dimension and the lagged effects between variables.

A Experimental Results

The Table 5 presents all the experimental results for the long-term forecasting task. Clearly, our LCformer achieves the best results in 51 out of 70 different configurations of prediction lengths and metrics.

Table 5. Experimental results of the long-term multivariate forecasting task. All baseline results are derived from [20].

	Models	LCFormer		TimeXer		iTrans.		RLinear		PatchTST		Cross.		TiDE		TimesNet		DLinear		SCINet	
	Metric	MSE	MAE	MSE	MAE	MSE	MAE	MSE	MAE	MSE	MAE	MSE	MAE	MSE	MAE	MSE	MAE	MSE	MAE	MSE	MAE
ECL	96	0.155	0.247	**0.140**	**0.242**	0.148	**0.240**	0.201	0.281	0.195	0.285	0.219	0.314	0.237	0.329	0.168	0.272	0.197	0.282	0.247	0.345
	192	0.176	0.265	**0.157**	0.256	0.162	0.253	0.201	0.283	0.199	0.289	0.231	0.322	0.236	0.330	0.184	0.289	0.196	0.285	0.257	0.355
	336	0.205	0.291	**0.176**	**0.275**	0.178	0.269	0.215	0.298	0.215	0.305	0.246	0.337	0.249	0.344	0.198	0.300	0.209	0.301	0.269	0.369
	720	0.235	0.315	**0.211**	**0.306**	0.225	0.317	0.257	0.331	0.256	0.337	0.280	0.363	0.284	0.373	0.220	0.320	0.245	0.333	0.299	0.390
	Avg	0.193	0.279	**0.171**	**0.270**	0.178	0.270	0.219	0.298	0.216	0.304	0.244	0.334	0.251	0.344	0.192	0.295	0.212	0.300	0.268	0.365
Weather	96	**0.156**	**0.195**	0.157	0.205	0.174	0.214	0.192	0.232	0.177	0.218	0.158	0.230	0.202	0.261	0.172	0.220	0.196	0.255	0.221	0.306
	192	0.214	0.248	**0.204**	**0.247**	0.221	0.254	0.240	0.271	0.225	0.259	0.206	0.277	0.242	0.298	0.219	0.261	0.237	0.296	0.261	0.340
	336	**0.260**	**0.283**	0.261	0.290	0.278	0.296	0.292	0.307	0.278	0.297	0.272	0.335	0.287	0.335	0.280	0.306	0.283	0.335	0.309	0.378
	720	0.373	0.356	**0.340**	**0.341**	0.358	0.349	0.364	0.353	0.354	0.348	0.398	0.418	0.351	0.386	0.365	0.359	0.345	0.381	0.377	0.427
	Avg	0.251	**0.270**	**0.241**	0.271	0.258	0.279	0.272	0.291	0.259	0.281	0.259	0.315	0.271	0.320	0.259	0.287	0.265	0.317	0.292	0.363
ETTh1	96	**0.378**	**0.388**	0.382	0.403	0.386	0.405	0.386	0.395	0.414	0.419	0.423	0.448	0.479	0.464	0.384	0.402	0.386	0.400	0.654	0.599
	192	**0.429**	**0.418**	0.429	0.435	0.441	0.436	0.437	0.424	0.460	0.445	0.471	0.474	0.525	0.492	0.436	0.429	0.437	0.432	0.719	0.631
	336	**0.463**	**0.436**	0.468	0.448	0.487	0.458	0.479	0.446	0.501	0.466	0.570	0.546	0.565	0.515	0.491	0.469	0.481	0.459	0.778	0.659
	720	**0.469**	**0.460**	0.469	0.461	0.503	0.491	0.481	0.470	0.500	0.488	0.653	0.621	0.594	0.558	0.521	0.500	0.519	0.516	0.836	0.699
	Avg	**0.435**	**0.426**	0.437	0.437	0.454	0.447	0.446	0.434	0.469	0.454	0.529	0.522	0.541	0.507	0.458	0.450	0.456	0.452	0.747	0.647
ETTh2	96	**0.278**	**0.328**	0.286	0.338	0.297	0.349	0.288	0.338	0.302	0.348	0.745	0.584	0.400	0.440	0.340	0.374	0.333	0.387	0.707	0.621
	192	**0.355**	**0.379**	0.363	0.389	0.380	0.400	0.374	0.390	0.388	0.400	0.877	0.656	0.528	0.509	0.402	0.414	0.477	0.476	0.860	0.689
	336	**0.396**	**0.412**	0.414	0.423	0.428	0.432	0.415	0.426	0.426	0.433	1.043	0.731	0.643	0.571	0.452	0.452	0.594	0.541	1.000	0.744
	720	**0.404**	**0.427**	0.408	0.432	0.427	0.445	0.420	0.440	0.431	0.446	1.104	0.763	0.874	0.679	0.462	0.468	0.831	0.657	1.249	0.838
	Avg	**0.358**	**0.387**	0.367	0.396	0.383	0.407	0.374	0.398	0.387	0.407	0.942	0.684	0.611	0.550	0.414	0.427	0.559	0.515	0.954	0.723
ETTm1	96	**0.309**	**0.341**	0.318	0.356	0.334	0.368	0.355	0.376	0.329	0.367	0.404	0.426	0.364	0.387	0.338	0.375	0.345	0.372	0.418	0.438
	192	**0.361**	**0.367**	0.362	0.383	0.387	0.370	0.391	0.392	0.367	0.385	0.450	0.451	0.398	0.404	0.374	0.387	0.380	0.389	0.426	0.441
	336	**0.390**	**0.341**	0.395	0.407	0.426	0.420	0.424	0.415	0.399	0.410	0.532	0.515	0.428	0.425	0.410	0.411	0.413	0.413	0.445	0.459
	720	**0.456**	**0.428**	0.452	0.441	0.491	0.459	0.487	0.450	0.454	0.439	0.666	0.589	0.487	0.461	0.478	0.450	0.474	0.453	0.595	0.550
	Avg	**0.379**	**0.381**	0.382	0.397	0.407	0.410	0.414	0.407	0.387	0.400	0.513	0.496	0.419	0.419	0.400	0.406	0.403	0.407	0.485	0.481
ETTm2	96	**0.167**	**0.246**	0.171	0.256	0.180	0.264	0.182	0.265	0.175	0.259	0.287	0.366	0.207	0.305	0.187	0.267	0.193	0.292	0.286	0.377
	192	**0.233**	**0.290**	0.237	0.299	0.250	0.309	0.246	0.304	0.241	0.302	0.414	0.492	0.290	0.364	0.249	0.309	0.284	0.362	0.399	0.445
	336	**0.290**	**0.328**	0.296	0.338	0.311	0.348	0.307	0.342	0.305	0.343	0.597	0.542	0.377	0.422	0.321	0.351	0.369	0.427	0.637	0.591
	720	**0.389**	**0.389**	0.392	0.394	0.412	0.407	0.407	0.398	0.402	0.400	1.730	1.042	0.558	0.524	0.408	0.403	0.554	0.522	0.960	0.735
	Avg	**0.270**	**0.313**	0.274	0.322	0.288	0.332	0.286	0.327	0.281	0.326	0.757	0.610	0.358	0.404	0.291	0.333	0.350	0.401	0.571	0.537
Traffic	96	0.393	**0.238**	0.428	0.271	0.395	0.268	0.649	0.389	0.462	0.295	0.522	0.290	0.805	0.493	0.593	0.321	0.650	0.396	0.788	0.499
	192	**0.404**	**0.246**	0.448	0.282	0.417	0.276	0.601	0.366	0.466	0.296	0.530	0.293	0.756	0.474	0.617	0.336	0.598	0.370	0.789	0.505
	336	0.446	**0.263**	0.473	0.289	**0.433**	0.283	0.609	0.369	0.482	0.304	0.558	0.305	0.762	0.477	0.629	0.336	0.605	0.373	0.797	0.508
	720	0.479	**0.281**	0.516	0.307	**0.467**	0.302	0.647	0.387	0.514	0.322	0.589	0.328	0.719	0.449	0.640	0.350	0.645	0.394	0.841	0.523
	Avg	0.431	**0.257**	0.466	0.287	**0.428**	0.282	0.626	0.378	0.481	0.304	0.550	0.304	0.760	0.473	0.620	0.336	0.625	0.383	0.804	0.509
1ˢᵗ Count		51		15		7		0		0		0		0		0		0		0	

References

1. Alpert, P., Shafir, H., Elhacham, E.: An unknown maximum lag-correlation between rainfall and aerosols at 140–160 minutes. Geophys. Res. Lett. **48**(2), e2020GL089334 (2021)
2. Chen, C.W.S., Gerlach, R., Lin, E.M.H., Lee, W.C.W.: Bayesian forecasting for financial risk management, pre and post the global financial crisis. J. Forecast. **31**(8), 661–687 (2012)
3. Chen, P., et al.: Pathformer: multi-scale transformers with adaptive pathways for time series forecasting. arXiv preprint arXiv:2402.05956 (2024)
4. Chhin, R., Shwe, M.M., Yoden, S.: Time-lagged correlations associated with inter-annual variations of pre-monsoon and post-monsoon precipitation in myanmar and the indochina peninsula. Int. J. Climatol. **40**(8), 3792–3812 (2020)
5. Dai, T., et al.: Periodicity decoupling framework for long-term series forecasting. In: The Twelfth International Conference on Learning Representations (2024)
6. Das, A., Kong, W., Leach, A., Mathur, S., Sen, R., Yu, R.: Long-term forecasting with tide: time-series dense encoder. arXiv preprint arXiv:2304.08424 (2023)
7. Kim, T., Kim, J., Tae, Y., Park, C., Choi, J.H., Choo, J.: Reversible instance normalization for accurate time-series forecasting against distribution shift. In: International Conference on Learning Representations (2021)
8. Li, S., et al.: Enhancing the locality and breaking the memory bottleneck of transformer on time series forecasting. In: Advances in Neural Information Processing Systems, vol. 32 (2019)
9. Li, S., Sun, Y., Lin, Y., Gao, X., Shang, S., Yan, R.: Causalstock: deep end-to-end causal discovery for news-driven stock movement prediction. arXiv preprint arXiv:2411.06391 (2024)
10. Li, Z., Qi, S., Li, Y., Xu, Z.: Revisiting long-term time series forecasting: an investigation on linear mapping. arXiv preprint arXiv:2305.10721 (2023)
11. Lin, S., Lin, W., Wu, W., Wang, S., Wang, Y.: Petformer: long-term time series forecasting via placeholder-enhanced transformer. IEEE Trans. Emerg. Top. Comput. Intell. (2024)
12. Liu, M., et al.: Scinet: time series modeling and forecasting with sample convolution and interaction. In: Advances in Neural Information Processing Systems, vol. 35, pp. 5816–5828 (2022)
13. Liu, S., et al.: Pyraformer: low-complexity pyramidal attention for long-range time series modeling and forecasting. In: The Tenth International Conference on Learning Representations (2022)
14. Liu, Y., et al.: itransformer: inverted transformers are effective for time series forecasting. arXiv preprint arXiv:2310.06625 (2023)
15. Nie, Y., Nguyen, N.M., Sinthong, P., Kalagnanam, J.: A time series is worth 64 words: long-term forecasting with transformers. arXiv preprint arXiv:2211.14730 (2022)
16. Shao, Z., et al.: Decoupled dynamic spatial-temporal graph neural network for traffic forecasting. arXiv preprint arXiv:2206.09112 (2022)
17. Shao, Z., et al. Exploring progress in multivariate time series forecasting: comprehensive benchmarking and heterogeneity analysis. IEEE Trans. Knowl. Data Eng. (2024)
18. Shi, D., Calliess, J.P., Cucuringu, M.: Multireference alignment for lead-lag detection in multivariate time series and equity trading. In: Proceedings of the Fourth ACM International Conference on AI in Finance, pp. 507–515 (2023)

19. Vaswani, A.: Attention is all you need. In: Advances in Neural Information Processing Systems (2017)
20. Wang, Y., et al. Timexer: empowering transformers for time series forecasting with exogenous variables. arXiv preprint arXiv:2402.19072 (2024)
21. Haixu, W., Jiehui, X., Wang, J., Long, M.: Autoformer: decomposition transformers with auto-correlation for long-term series forecasting. In: Advances in Neural Information Processing Systems, vol. 34, pp. 22419–22430 (2021)
22. Wu, H., Hu, T., Liu, Y., Zhou, H., Wang, J., Long, M.: Timesnet: temporal 2D-variation modeling for general time series analysis. arXiv preprint arXiv:2210.02186 (2022)
23. Zeng, A., Chen, M., Zhang, L., Qiang, X.: Are transformers effective for time series forecasting? In: Proceedings of the AAAI Conference on Artificial Intelligence, vol. 37, pp. 11121–11128 (2023)
24. Zhang Y., Yan, J.: Crossformer: transformer utilizing cross-dimension dependency for multivariate time series forecasting. In: The Eleventh International Conference on Learning Representations (2023)
25. Zhao, L., Shen, Y.: Rethinking channel dependence for multivariate time series forecasting: learning from leading indicators. arXiv preprint arXiv:2401.17548 (2024)
26. Zhou, H., et al.: Informer: beyond efficient transformer for long sequence time-series forecasting. In: Proceedings of the AAAI Conference On Artificial Intelligence, vol. 35, pp. 11106–11115 (2021)
27. Zhou, T., Ma, Z., Wen, Q., Wang, X., Sun, L., Jin, R.: Fedformer: frequency enhanced decomposed transformer for long-term series forecasting. In: International Conference on Machine Learning, pp. 27268–27286. PMLR (2022)

SignalingTraj: A Signaling Data Based Trajectory Generation with Diffusion Model

Linzi Zou[1], Li Li[1(✉)], Junting Lu[1], Junjun Si[2], and Yiduo Mei[3]

[1] College of Computer Science, Beijing Information Science and Technology University, Beijing, China
{2024021013,lili_bistu,lujunting}@bistu.edu.cn
[2] School of Computer and Cyber Sciences, Communication University of China, Beijing, China
sijunjun@cuc.edu.cn
[3] Inspur Yunzhou Industrial Internet Co., Ltd., Jinan City, Shandong Province, China
meiyiduo@inspur.com

Abstract. The ubiquity of mobile phone signaling data (SD) plays a pivotal role in mobility analysis; however, privacy policies and public concerns over personal location exposure severely limit the availability of public SD trajectory datasets. To address privacy concerns in human mobility analysis, synthetic trajectory generation has emerged as a promising solution. Existing trajectory generation methods primarily target GPS data, which exhibits high spatiotemporal continuity, leaving a critical gap in SD-specific trajectory synthesis. To bridge this gap, we propose SignalingTraj, a diffusion-based framework tailored for high-fidelity SD trajectory generation. Leveraging the generative capacity of diffusion models, SignalingTraj addresses the unique challenges of SD data, including low spatial resolution and irregular sampling. Specifically, we integrate spatial attributes and handover correlations of base stations (BSs) into a pre-training strategy using Variational Graph Autoencoders (VGAE), converting BSs into continuous representation vectors. Experiments on real-world SD datasets demonstrate that SignalingTraj synthesizes high-fidelity, privacy-preserving trajectories that closely mirror original data distributions. SignalingTraj outperforms existing methods in data fidelity and utility, positioning it as a robust solution for generating scalable, synthetic SD trajectories to support diverse mobility analysis applications.

Keywords: Spatial-temporal data mining · mobile phone signaling data · diffusion model · trajectory generation

1 Introduction

With the development of mobile communication technologies and the prosperity of mobile devices, massive GPS trajectories are generated along with the mobility of humans. GPS trajectories have been widely applied in various fields, including urban computing [36], smart transportation [18,32,37], and urban planning [23,29,30]. However, GPS data collection is constrained by the requirement for users who actively enable location tracking or grant explicit permissions, limiting its applications and coverage of the broader population. Furthermore, this limitation is particularly significant when attempting to estimate the movement patterns of the whole city. In contrast, mobile phone signaling data (SD) collected by Mobile Network Operators (MNOs) in the form of Call Detail Records (CDRs) provide a more comprehensive alternative. SD trajectories are automatically generated when mobile phones interact with cell towers—including during calls, text messages, or cell handovers. Consequently, SD trajectories are characterized by low cost and extensive spatiotemporal coverage. As a result, SD trajectories have become a primary data source for smart city applications, including urban planning, traffic management, public health monitoring, and travel mode identification. [7,13,17] Despite the significant potential of SD trajectory data, publicly available datasets are often limited due to privacy policies and public concerns over the disclosure of personal location information contained within trajectories. To address these privacy concerns while leveraging the benefits of mobility data, synthetic trajectory data generation has emerged as a promising solution. Synthetic data can mimic real-world mobility patterns without compromising individual privacy, thereby serving as a valuable resource for researchers and policy-makers.

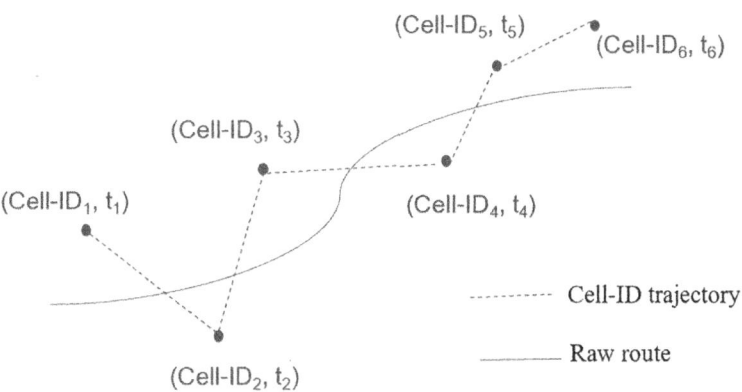

Fig. 1. An example of SD trajectory.

However, current methods for generating synthetic trajectories [12,20,38,39] are primarily designed for GPS trajectory, which is typically characterized by high spatiotemporal continuity. Unlike GPS trajectory, SD trajectory is characterized by lower spatial resolution and irregular sampling intervals, making the generation of realistic trajectories significantly more challenging. Note that GPS trajectories are recorded as explicit numerical coordinates, enabling GPS trajectory generation methods to synthesize continuous trajectories. As shown in Fig. 1, the collected SD trajectory data lack explicit location information, such as geographic coordinates, but instead only include the Cell-ID (the unique identifier of a base station) and timestamps for each recording point. While some MNOs may provide the locations of base stations, the precise geographic coordinates of all BSs are often unavailable due to technical, legal, or privacy-related constraints [16]. Therefore, existing GPS trajectory generation methods cannot be directly applied to generate SD trajectories.

In order to overcome the above limitations, we propose a novel task called SignalingTraj, specifically designed for SD trajectory generation. Firstly, we utilize a graph neural network to learn the representation of each BS, which can capture both the attributes and the spatial correlations between BSs. Then, the representation of each BS serves as the input to the diffusion model, as the diffusion model's capability to generate high-quality, realistic data has been proven in GPS trajectory generation. Finally, SignalingTraj fuses the conditional BS handover constraints into the diffusion model to achieve controlled, high-fidelity SD trajectory generation.

- We define a new task, SignalingTraj, specifically aimed at generating high-quality synthetic SD trajectories. This task addresses the gap in existing research focused primarily on GPS-based trajectory generation, providing a tailored solution for the unique characteristics of SD data.
- SignalingTraj incorporates a pre-training strategy using Variational Graph Autoencoders (VGAE) to embed BSs into continuous representations, enhancing the model's ability to generate SD trajectories.
- We propose a novel spatial validity loss function to ensure that the generated trajectories adhere to realistic spatial distributions, improving the overall fidelity of the generated data.
- We conducted extensive experiments using three SD trajectory datasets to evaluate the model performance. The results demonstrate that our model significantly outperforms existing methods in terms of data fidelity and utility, making it a promising solution for generating large-scale synthetic SD trajectories for diverse mobility analysis tasks.

2 Related Work

2.1 GPS Trajectory Generation

Existing work on GPS trajectory generation methods can broadly be divided into two categories: non-generative and generative approaches. Non-generative methods, such as Markov-based models and simulation techniques [1,11,24], rely heavily on historical data and predefined rules, disregarding the inherent randomness and complexity of human movement. As a result, the generated trajectories fail to capture real-world human movement patterns accurately. For example, TimeGeo [11] leverages data-driven methods to estimate parameters from real-world data and generates trajectories via Markov-based models, assuming simplistically that users' mobility states depend solely on their presence at home. Despite achieving promising performance in some cases, these methods cannot model the complexity of real-world mobility due to their simplified assumptions. In contrast, generative approaches take advantage of advances in deep neural networks, such as Generative Adversarial Networks (GANs) [8,12,28,34], Variational Autoencoders (VAEs) [5,27], and diffusion models [6,31,35,38], to model complex GPS trajectories more effectively.

MoveSim [8] synthesizes trajectories based on a GAN framework, of which the discriminator requires inputs with discrete temporal distributions and fixed lengths. To address this limitation, some studies resort to preprocessing human trajectories by discretizing timestamps and segmenting trajectories into fixed-length sub-trajectories, resulting in a limited ability to model fine-grained behaviors or long-term correlations in human mobility. TS-TrajGen [12] is also based on a GAN architecture. It matches trajectory points to the road network and generates continuous trajectories via a path search algorithm. Beyond generating continuous GPS trajectories, some studies divide the city map into grids and employ GANs to produce matrix-based trajectory data [21,34]. However, this approach faces a trade-off between generation accuracy and grid size, resulting in coarse-grained behavioral patterns. Meanwhile, some researchers leverage GANs' image-generation capabilities by transforming trajectories into images for synthesis [3,28], though the image-trajectory conversion imposes significant computational overhead. TrajVAE [5] adopts a VAE framework, employing LSTM networks to capture temporal dependencies and model trajectory data as Gaussian distributions. TrajSynVAE [27] integrates classical temporal point processes with variational temporal point processes to synthesize human mobility trajectories.

Recently, diffusion models [9,25,26], noted for their ability to model randomness and uncertainty, have gained prominence in diverse domains, including image generation, text generation, and time-series modeling. As a result, numerous diffusion-based trajectory generation models have emerged, establishing a promising frontier in generative modeling. DiffTraj [38] employs a diffusion-based framework for trajectory generation, iteratively adding and removing noise to synthesize trajectories. CoDiffMob [35] integrates individual movement patterns and population-level dynamics into the diffusion process. To ensure geographical fidelity, recent studies focus on generating road-level trajectories [4,31,39], utilizing diffusion models to synthesize trajectories while incorporating road network topology constraints.

However, because raw GPS trajectories are recorded as explicit numerical coordinates, most diffusion-based trajectory generation models can directly adopt the original structure and training methods of conventional diffusion models. In contrast, SD trajectories are not recorded in numerical coordinate format; instead, locations are represented by Base Station (BS) IDs. Therefore, existing diffusion-based trajectory generation models cannot be directly applied. Unlike existing diffusion-model-based approaches, we propose a novel framework that generates SD trajectories represented by BS IDs, thereby enhancing extensibility and adaptability to broader geospatial datasets.

2.2 Human Mobility Application with SD Trajectory

The proliferation of mobile networks and the increasing use of mobile devices have led to a surge in research on human mobility using signaling data. Signaling data provides valuable insights into the movement patterns of individuals. Signaling data are characterized by their high penetration rates and wide spatio-temporal coverage, making them suitable for large-scale human mobility studies.

CellPred [22] investigates cellular data usage prediction by dividing users into several groups based on mobility patterns identified using an additional dataset. SUME [33] enhances user profiling by incorporating semantic information of the areas through which users pass, as this information is deeply influenced by user demographics. To address the issue of low spatial accuracy in SD trajectories, numerous map-matching algorithms [10,13] have been developed to estimate the actual positions of travelers from SD trajectories, thereby improving spatial-temporal accuracy. [2] created a synthetic CDR dataset based on real-life GPS trajectories, which involves training two Transformers sequentially—one used for map matching to obtain the road-level path from GPS traces, and the other tasked with reconstructing road segment sequences from the cell-level trajectory. In [13], the conventional data cleaning method is modified to eliminate outliers in raw SD trajectory to improve data quality. In addition, the HMM-based map-matching algorithm is designed to estimate the actual position of travelers from MPSD for spatial-temporal accuracy improvement. Similarly, our framework also leverages the high penetration rates of SD.

3 Preliminaries and Problem Statement

In this section, we first define the notations used in this paper. Then, based on these notations, we formally define the SD trajectory generation problem.

Definition 1: Trajectory. According to [36], a trajectory $\mathcal{X}$ refers to an ordered sequence of geographical points that are chronologically sampled during a time period, denoted:

$$\mathcal{X} = \{p_1, p_2, \cdots, p_{|\mathcal{X}|}\} \quad (1)$$

where p_i is the i-th trajectory point, for GPS trajectory p_i is presented as $p_i = \langle lon_i, lat_i, t_i \rangle$, where lon_i and lat_i are the longitude and latitude of p_i, t_i is the timestamp when the trajectory point is recorded, $|\mathcal{X}|$ denotes the length of $\mathcal{X}$.

Signaling Data Format. In general, the data format of the SD records contains user ID (anonymous ID), $Cell\text{-}ID$, time, as well as the signaling type. Among them, the $Cell\text{-}ID$ or Cell Global Identity (CGI), is an identification of the cell tower associated with the cellular record, with a polygon-shaped coverage area provided by the MNOs, and the user ID is an identification of the corresponding user of the cellular record. And both IDs are unique. The signaling type records the type of services for the signaling record, which has little to do with our investigation.

Definition 2: SD Trajectory. A SD trajectory can be presented as a base station identity sequence with the visiting time information at each recorded point, namely,

$$\mathcal{X}_{SD} = \{rp_1, rp_2, \cdots, rp_{|\mathcal{X}_{SD}|}\} \tag{2}$$

where $rp_i = \langle Cell\text{-}ID_i, t_i \rangle$ is the i-th is the location of a cellular tower $Cell\text{-}ID_i$ at the time t_i the cell phone interacts with the cellular tower. In a city, the number and location of cell towers are fixed. Therefore the possible locations of each observation in the SD trajectory are fixed and known. $|\mathcal{X}_{SD}|$ is the total number of trajectory points.

Problem Statement: SD Trajectory Generation. Given real-world SD trajectory datasets, the goal of this problem is to train $\theta-$parameterized generative model G, which can generate a SD trajectory dataset that follows the distribution of original trajectory data.

4 Methodology

In this section, we will introduce the SignalingTraj framework, which is a novel method for generating SD trajectories using diffusion models. As illustrated in Fig. 2, SignalingTraj consists of three main modules: SD trajectory pretraining module, Diffusion module, and SD trajectory generator module. The SD trajectory pretraining module converts SD trajectory into continuous vector representations, which serve as the input process for subsequent diffusion. The Diffusion Module models the data distribution of SD trajectories through an iterative process of noise addition and denoising. After training, the model is capable of generating vectorized SD trajectories into continuous space by sampling Gaussian noise. Finally, the SD Trajectory Generator Module maps the generated continuous representations back to the original format.

4.1 SD Trajectory Pretraining

During the collection process, SD data often contain numerous errors and are typically unsuitable for direct use in human mobility-related applications. Therefore, rather than using raw data directly, preprocessing is necessary. To further enhance the spatial consistency of the generated trajectories, we introduced the BS Graph to constrain the spatial constraints of the model in generating trajectories. Moreover, when exploring continuous diffusion models, transforming SD trajectories into continuous representations is essential to fully harness their potential. Thus, SD trajectory pretraining is divided into two steps: preprocessing and trajectory representation learning.

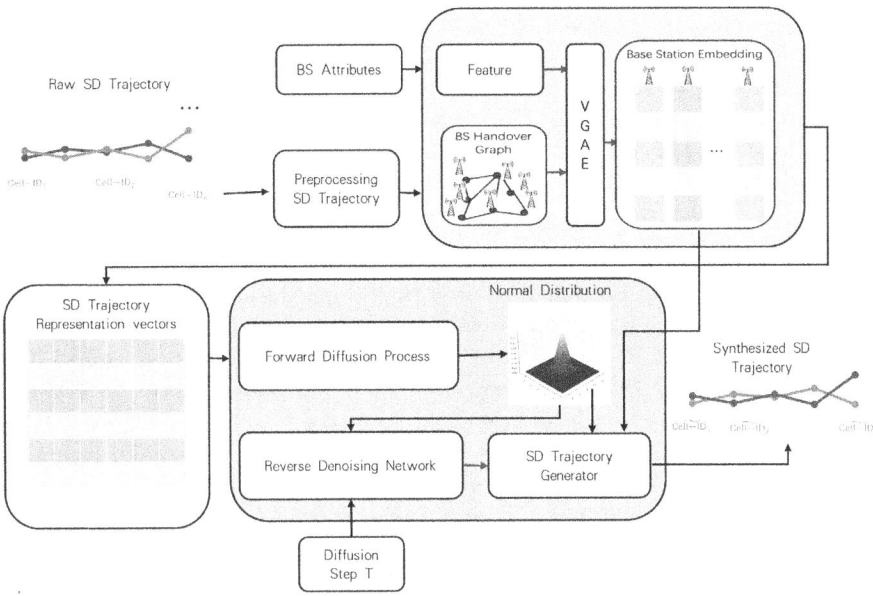

Fig. 2. The overview of the proposed SignalingTraj framework.

4.1.1 SD Trajectory Preprocessing

Raw SD trajectories collected in real-world settings often contain significant noise and errors, such as sudden, implausible jumps to distant cell towers followed by a return to a cell tower near the starting point. Preprocessing is essential to mitigate the negative impact of these errors on experiments and to prepare the input data for subsequent models and tasks. In this framework, we use the SD data cleaning method, which has been proven to be effective in [13], to eliminate outliers of the raw SD trajectory, thus improving the quality of the data.

First, we define a valid SD trajectory as one that includes a minimum of 30 base stations (BSs) and lasts at least 5 min.

Next, calculate the speed v_{i+1} between $Cell\text{-}ID_i$ and $Cell\text{-}ID_{i+1}$ in order, and compare v_{i+1} with maximum speed threshold v_{max}. If $v_{i+1} > v_{max}$, stop calculation and select $Cell\text{-}ID_i$ and $Cell\text{-}ID_{i+1}$ as potential outliers. Otherwise, $Cell\text{-}ID_i$ and $Cell\text{-}ID_{i+1}$ are regardedrmal points. Meanwhile, i is set to $i+1$ and the next iteration starts. Then claculate the frequency of $Cell\text{-}ID_i$ and $Cell\text{-}ID_{i+1}$. According to the assumption that the frequency of outliers is always less than normal points, if the frequency of $Cell\text{-}ID_i$ exceeds $Cell\text{-}ID_{i+1}$, label $Cell-ID_{i+1}$ as an outlier and eliminate. Then, if $Cell\text{-}ID_i = Cell\text{-}ID_{i+1}$, $Cell\text{-}ID_{i+1}$ is removed.

However, unlike existing SD trajectory preprocessing methods, we omitted the step of eliminating ping-pong data, a common phenomenon in SD data. The presence of ping-pong data in SD trajectories arises because cell phones are not always connected to the nearest cell tower due to load balancing considerations.

As a result, they may connect to any available cell tower based on real-world network loads. We chose not to filter out ping-pong data because it reflects the actual handover patterns between BSs, and these handover correlations play a crucial role in constructing the BS Graph.

The final trajectories used in the subsequent procedures were selected based on these criteria.

4.1.2 SD Trajectory Representation Vectors

First, we leverage an unsupervised deep graph embedding technique to convert each BSs into BSs representation vector to capture both the network structure between BSs and the BSs spatial attributes such as Location Area Code(LAC), Longitude, Latitude, track occurrence count identification. Existing GPS trajectory generation approaches employ the topology of road networks to define these relationships based on physical connections. However, BSs differ from road networks in that there are no roads connecting each base station to the topology of a road network, which makes it impossible to establish the topological relationships of BSs. For this reason, we build the BS Graph to address the above limitations, which is a new segmented connectivity graph constructed based on real user trajectories. Unlike existing topology-based approaches, BSs Graph builds connections directly based on base station handover correlations in SD trajectories. This data-driven approach enables the learned BS representations to better reflect the actual mobility patterns, providing a more realistic and effective basis for BS representation vectors. Once the BS representation vectors obtained, the representation vectors can be also obtained. After obtaining the BS representation vectors from the unsupervised deep graph embedding technique, we convert BSs representation vectors into trajectory representation vectors.

BS Handover Graph: BSs handover graph is represented as a weighted graph $\mathcal{G} = \{\mathcal{V}, \mathcal{E}, \mathcal{F}\}$ with $\mathcal{V}$ represents BSs with spatial attributes $\mathcal{F}$, and $\mathcal{E}$ represents edge between BSs. A is the adjacent matrix extracted from *Cell-ID* trajectories which reveals the handover relationships. Once the handover occurs from BS v_i to BS v_j, there is an edge connected between them, $A_{ij} = 1$, else $A_{ij} = 0$. To this end, the original base station representation problem is converted to the node embedding problem of the handover graph $\mathcal{G}$.

BS Attributes: The *Cell-ID* contains features such as Areacode, longitude and latitude, and BSs statistics. The Areacode indicates the area code of the base station, the longitude and latitude are the location information of the BSs, and the BSs statistics are the number of times the BSs appears in all trajectories. In this study, the Areacode label denoted as e_l is represented with one-hot vector, longitude and latitude, and BSs statistics are represented as a normalized one-dimensional vector.

Then, we utilize the Variational Graph Auto-Encoders(VGAE) [14] algorithm to embed the graph nodes in a representation $E \in \mathbb{R}^{N \times D}$, where N is the number of BSs, D is the BSs embedding dimension.

Based on the BSs representation vectors, we can represent a SD trajectory $\mathcal{X}_{SD}$ with length $|\mathcal{X}_{SD}|$ as a tensor $X \in \mathbb{R}^D$.

With this approach, we can represent SD trajectories in continuous space. Next, we employ the continuous diffusion model to generate the vectorized SD trajectories.

4.2 Diffusion Model for Vectorized SD Trajectory Generation

In this section, we introduce our model framework, which applies the diffusion model for trajectory generation. The framework is structured around two key phases: Add Noise (forward diffusion process) and Denoise (reverse denoising process). Our model generates SD trajectories by simulating the process of gradually introducing noise to the trajectory and then reversing this noise to recover the original trajectory.

4.2.1 Adding Noise: Forward Diffusion Process

The forward diffusion process is used to progressively add Gaussian noise to the trajectory data over several steps. The goal of this phase is to transform an original trajectory X_0 into a noisy version X_T by gradually introducing noise at adding noise steps T.

We begin with the original trajectory X_0 and at each step t, noise is added according to the following distribution:

$$q(X_t|X_{t-1}) = \mathcal{N}(X_t; \sqrt{\alpha_t}X_{t-1}, (1-\alpha_t)I) \tag{3}$$

where α_t controls the amount of noise introduced at each step. As t increases, the trajectory becomes progressively noisier, with the final step X_T approximating a standard Gaussian noise distribution:

$$q(X_T|X_0) = \prod_{t=1}^{T} q(X_t|X_{t-1}) \tag{4}$$

This results in a noisy trajectory X_T that is increasingly unrecognizable from the original trajectory $\hat{X}_0$.

4.2.2 Denoising: Reverse Diffusion Process

The denoising process aims to reverse the added noise and recover the original trajectory. Starting from the noisy trajectory X_T, we iteratively remove the noise at each step to recover the original trajectory $\hat{X}_0$. This is accomplished using a reverse diffusion process, which learns to predict and remove the noise added during the forward diffusion process.

The reverse process is defined as follows:

$$p_\theta(\hat{X}_{t-1}|\hat{X}_t) = \mathcal{N}(\hat{X}_{t-1}; \mu_\theta(\hat{X}_t), \Sigma_\theta(\hat{X}_t)) \tag{5}$$

where the reverse denoise process $p_\theta(\hat{X}_{t-1}|\hat{X}_t)$ at each step follows a Gaussian distribution. $\mu_\theta(\hat{X}_t)$ and $\Sigma_\theta(\hat{X}_t)$ represent the predicted mean and variance of the denoised trajectory $\hat{X}_t$ each step, learned by the model.

The reverse process is applied iteratively from $t = T$ to $t = 1$, gradually removing the noise at each step.

$$p(\hat{X}_0|X_T) = p(X_T) \prod_{t=T}^{1} p(\hat{X}_{t-1}|\hat{X}_t), \tag{6}$$

Since X_T follows a standard Gaussian distribution, we can directly obtain the original vectorized SD trajectory $\hat{X}_0$ in continuous space from random Gaussian noise through a T-step reverse denoising process.

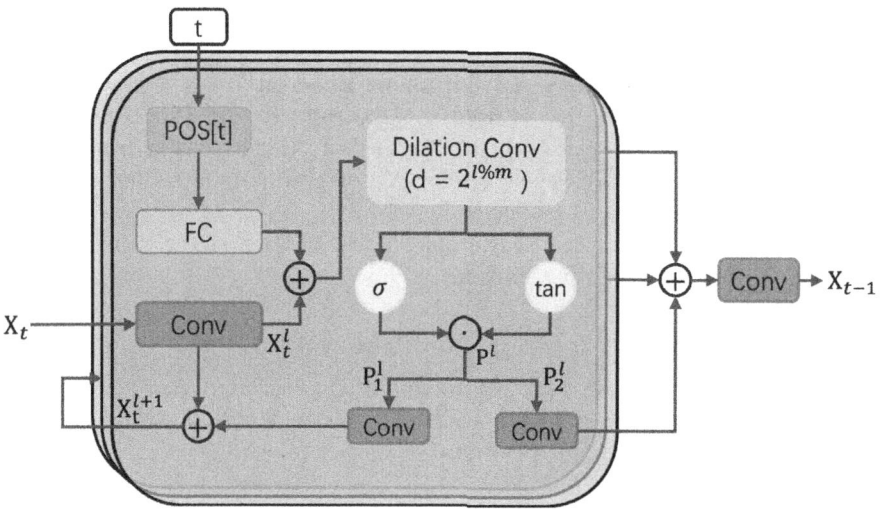

Fig. 3. Denoising network consisting of a stack of L residual dilated convolutional layer blocks(RDCLs)

4.2.3 Denoising Network

The general diffusion model usually uses U-Net as a denoising network, which is widely used in tasks such as image generation, image restoration, and speech generation [9,15,19]. In SignalingTraj, we use a residual dilation convolutional network as a component of the denoising network to capture the distribution of trajectory data. The specific architecture is shown in Fig. 3.

In the model, in order to map time step t to an F-dimensional vector, we implemented the position encoding proposed by Diffwave [15].

$$POS[t] = \left[\sin\left(10^{\frac{0+4}{F/2}}t\right), \sin\left(10^{\frac{1+4}{F/2}}t\right), \cdots, \sin\left(10^{\frac{(F/2-1)+4}{F/2}}t\right),\right.$$
$$\left.\cos\left(10^{\frac{0+4}{F/2}}t\right), \cos\left(10^{\frac{1+4}{F/2}}t\right), \cdots, \cos\left(10^{\frac{(F/2-1)+4}{F/2}}t\right)\right]. \tag{7}$$

This vector is then passed through two fully connected layers to further refine its representation. To capture the distribution of SD trajectories, we stack L Residual Dilation Convolution Layers (RDCLs). These layers are organized into $\frac{L}{m}$ blocks, with each block containing m layers. The input data will undergo Dilation Convolution and a gating mechanism to obtain $\mathbf{P}^l$:

$$\begin{aligned}\mathbf{H}^l &= \text{Conv}\left(\hat{\mathbf{X}}_n^{l-1} + \text{FC}(POS[t])\right) \in \mathbb{R}^{Q \times 2C},\\ \mathbf{P}^l &= \sigma\left(\mathbf{H}^l\right) \odot \tanh\left(\mathbf{H}^l\right) \in \mathbb{R}^{Q \times 2C},\end{aligned} \tag{8}$$

where $\text{FC}(\cdot): \mathbb{R}^F \to \mathbb{R}^C$ represents a fully connected layer, and C denotes the number of channels in the RDCL. The output $\mathbf{P}^l$ is split along the channel dimension into two components:

$$\mathbf{P_1}^l = \mathbf{P}^l[:, 0:C] \in \mathbb{R}^{Q \times C} \tag{9}$$

$$\mathbf{P_2}^l = \mathbf{P}^l[:, C:2C] \in \mathbb{R}^{Q \times C} \tag{10}$$

The first component, P_1^l, is combined with the input X_t^{l-1} through a residual connection to produce the output of the l-th layer:

$$\hat{X}_t^l = \hat{X}_t^{l-1} + \text{Conv}(\mathbf{P_1}^l) \tag{11}$$

Finally, the second component, P_2^l, from each layer is aggregated to estimate the noise:

$$\epsilon_\theta(\hat{X}_t, t) = \text{Conv}\left(\sum_{i=1}^{L} \text{Conv}(\mathbf{P_2}^l)\right) \in \mathbb{R}^{Q \times D} \tag{12}$$

Once the noise is estimated, the denoised trajectory $\hat{X}_{n-1}$ is computed using the reparameterization formula:

$$\hat{X}_{t-1} = \frac{1}{\sqrt{\bar{\alpha}_n}}\left(\hat{X}_t - \frac{\beta_n}{\sqrt{1-\bar{\alpha}_n}}\epsilon_\theta(\hat{X}_t, t)\right) + \sqrt{\frac{1-\bar{\alpha}_{n-1}}{1-\bar{\alpha}_n}}\beta_n \tag{13}$$

4.2.4 Model Training

Due to the spatial handover relationships between base stations, a constraint on the spatial handover relationships of base stations is incorporated to ensure that the generated trajectory data retains the original handover spatial relationships between adjacent base stations. The model loss consists of three parts: the predicted noise loss L_{noise}, the reconstruction loss L_{rec}, and the base station handover constraint loss L_{control}.

The predicted noise loss L_{noise} is the mean squared error between the predicted noise $\varepsilon_\theta(X_t, t)$ and the white noise ε_t, expressed as:

$$L_{\text{noise}} = \|\varepsilon_\theta(X_t, t) - \varepsilon_t\|^2 \tag{14}$$

The reconstruction loss L_{rec} is the mean squared error between the recovered $\hat{X}_0$ and the original X_0, expressed as:

$$L_{\text{rec}} = \|\hat{X}_0 - X_0\|^2 \tag{15}$$

For the generated SD trajectories, traverse adjacent base stations rp_i and rp_{i+1}. If two adjacent base stations rp_i and rp_{i+1} have no edges in the BS Graph, that is, there is no handover relationship the loss value is 1; otherwise, the loss value is 0. The cumulative sum of all loss values gives L_{control}. The final model loss function is:

$$L = L_{\text{noise}} + L_{\text{rec}} + L_{\text{control}} \tag{16}$$

4.3 SD Trajectory Generator

To discretize the sampled vectorized SD trajectory $\hat{X}_0 \in \mathbb{R}^{M \times D}$, we compute the cosine similarity between the pre-trained continuous base station representations E and $\hat{X}_0$.

$$S = \frac{\hat{X}_0 \cdot E^T}{\|\hat{X}_0\| \cdot \|E\|} \in \mathbb{R}^{M \times N} \tag{17}$$

Subsequently, in order to obtain the discrete base station representation $Cell - ID_i$, we apply the $argmax$ function to identify the most similar discrete base station representation, ensuring that the generated trajectory aligns with the communication infrastructure of the real world.

This method effectively bridges the gap between continuous diffusion models and the discreteness of base station locations, enhancing the spatial coherence and practicality of synthesized trajectories.

5 Experiments

We first describe the experimental settings and then compare the effectiveness of SignalingTraj with popular and state-of-the-art baselines. Next, we evaluate the efficiency and scalability of the model.

5.1 Datasets

We conduct our experiments on real-world signaling data trajectory datasets from our industrial partners, including China Mobile, China Unicom, and China Telecom, the duration is from Oct 1st to Oct 7th, 2024, covering the whole metropolitan area of Nanning, Guangxi province. Each dataset records the anonymous user ID, accessed cellular base station, and timestamp of each access.

To ensure data reliability and capture meaningful motion patterns, we removed base stations with fewer than 30 occurrences in the dataset and retained only trajectories with lengths between 25 and 120. For better comparing and understanding different datasets, we show their statistic information in Table 1.

Table 1. Dataset Summary.

Dataset	Base Station Number	Users Number	Trajectory Number	Avg. length
Mobile	6053	165996	241317	47
Unicom	7085	105311	173710	37
Telecom	9042	224351	322420	58

5.2 Baseline Methods

We compare our proposed model with the following baselines:

- **Markov.** Markov treats the road segments as states and constructs a transition matrix to capture the first-order transition probabilities between these road segments.
- **Movesim** [8]. A generative adversarial framework that uses insights from prior knowledge and physical regularities for human mobility generation.
- **TimeGeo** [11]. TimeGeo combines temporal non-chiral Markov chains, hierarchical exploration based with a preferred return spatial choice model, and a land use analysis framework to model urban mobility.

5.3 Evaluation Metrics

Our goal is to generate a realistic synthetic SD trajectory dataset that can support various trajectory mining tasks. To achieve this, it is critical to evaluate the similarity between the generated dataset and the real dataset from a macro-level perspective.

However, conventional distance-based metrics are unsuitable for measuring similarity in SD trajectory generation comparisons [12]. This is because raw signaling data records contain only the $Cell\text{-}ID$ of the base station, rather than the explicit longitude or latitude coordinates of mobile users, such as GPS points. Even when MNOs provide approximate base station coordinates, these locations are often unreliable due to inherent inaccuracies or deliberate obfuscation to protect user privacy. As a result, precise geographic distance calculations are impractical. To address this, we evaluate the quality of synthetic SD trajectories by calculating the JSD using the following metrics across four perspectives:

- **DailyLoc:** daily visited locations, which is calculated as the number of visited locations per day for each user.

- G-rank: the number of visits per BS, calculated as the visiting frequency of top-100 BSs.
- I-rank: an individual version of G-rank.
- Arealoc (JSD-Arealoc): quantifies the Arealoc distribution of our generated trajectory based on the areacode of each BS.

5.4 Experiment Settings

SignalingTraj is implemented using Python 3.8 and PyTorch (version 1.10.0+cu113). We employ the AdamW optimizer to train the SignalingTraj model and conduct experiments on a server equipped with a NVIDIA GeForce RTX 4090D GPU with 24 GB of memory. The batch size is set to 256. The learning rate is set to 5e-4 and is halved every 3 epochs. For the denoising network, we set the channel dimensional C = 512, and positional encoding dimensional F = 512. In order to use the VGAE model to obtain a pre-trained representation of the base station E, we used the de-duplicated base station transfer relation and the Lac field of the base station as the features of the base station for training, with a total of 200 epoch. Because the denoising network can only batch process fixed-length shapes, the trajectories with the same length are selected in each batch for training. At the sampling stage, the number of generated trajectories of each length is equal to the number of fish in the original dataset (Table 2).

Table 2. The model and baseline are compared for performance on signaling data from three operators. The best results are highlighted in **bold**.

Methods	Mobile				Unicom				Telecom			
	Dailyloc	G-rank	I-rank	Arealoc	Dailyloc	G-rank	I-rank	Arealoc	Dailyloc	G-rank	I-rank	Arealoc
Markov	0.2010	0.0287	0.01956	0.0442	**0.0875**	0.0567	**0.0025**	0.0603	0.2038	**0.0183**	**0.0056**	0.0463
Movesim	0.2145	0.2844	0.0394	0.3410	0.1101	0.2572	0.0238	0.3050	0.6031	0.6931	0.1891	0.2606
TimeGeo	0.3826	0.1065	0.1153	0.0927	0.4333	0.1022	0.1279	0.1283	0.4021	0.1093	0.1190	0.1133
SignalingTraj	**0.1284**	**0.0205**	**0.0086**	**0.0225**	0.1609	**0.0226**	0.0106	**0.0299**	**0.1242**	0.1873	0.0076	**0.0228**

5.5 Experimental Results

In our experiments, we chose SignalingTraj to compare with several other baselines and chose Dailyloc, G-rank, I-rank, and Arealoc as the resulting metrics.

The SignalingTraj model demonstrates superior performance across most metrics in the datasets of the three operators. Specifically, in terms of macro-similarity, SignalingTraj achieves notable improvements in the Arealoc metrics compared to the second best model. The improvements are 50.02%, 50.41%, and 50.76% respectively in the three operators' datasets. This indicates that SignalingTraj is highly effective in capturing the daily location patterns of users, which is a crucial aspect for understanding and predicting user mobility.

Some of the results reach the optimal or sub-optimal level, but there are still cases where the global and individual access location frequencies cannot be fully modeled on some data, such as 0.0205 for mobile's G-rank metrics, and 0.0086 for Unicom's I-rank metrics, but from most of the metrics, the model's effectiveness and superiority in signaling data processing and trajectory generation are demonstrated. From the data in the table, Movesim has outstanding performance in the I-rank indicator on the SD trajectories of China Mobile and China Unicom. TimeGeo has relatively good performance in the G-rank, I-rank and Arealoc indicators, but its effect on the actual base station arrival frequency of the simulated SD trajectory for one day is poor.

Then, Markov has a significant advantage in maintaining the spatial validity of the data. Because the original data exists in a number of time to return to the base station previously traveled. i.e., $\mathcal{X}_{SD} = \{\langle 2694, t_1\rangle, \langle 726, t_2\rangle, \langle 2539, t_3\rangle, \langle 2694, t_4\rangle, \langle 339, t_5\rangle, \langle 2694, t_6\rangle\}$. As in the above example of a signaling trajectory, at the moment t_4, the trajectory reverts back to the base station where t_1 is located. This cyclic pattern makes the Markov model produce a lot of ping-pong data, which leads to the existence of many loops in the trajectory it generates, such as for a certain two points back and forth round-trip, which makes the Markov in the Arealoc index of the performance of a significant, but for the simulation of the distribution of the data, there is often a significant difference with the actual situation.

Table 3. The model and baseline are compared for performance on signaling data from three operators. The best results are highlighted in **bold**.

Methods	Mobile				Unicom				Telecom			
	Dailyloc	G-rank	I-rank	Arealoc	Dailyloc	G-rank	I-rank	Arealoc	Dailyloc	G-rank	I-rank	Arealoc
SignalingTraj/Embed	0.4937	0.0468	0.0695	0.0194	0.5875	0.4844	0.0688	0.3545	0.5039	0.4422	0.0554	0.3837
SignalingTraj/Graph	0.1933	0.0687	0.0592	0.0341	0.2784	0.3931	0.1404	0.3689	0.3630	0.2931	0.1314	0.2623
SignalingTraj/Node2vec	0.1410	0.0266	0.0412	0.0705	0.1194	**0.0216**	**0.0085**	0.0675	0.1955	**0.0620**	0.1192	0.0360
SignalingTraj	0.1284	**0.0205**	**0.0086**	**0.0225**	0.1609	0.0226	0.0106	**0.0299**	0.1242	0.1873	**0.0076**	**0.0228**

5.6 Ablation Study

In order to verify the effectiveness of the different components of SignalingTraj, we did three ablation experiments, which include:

- SignalingTraj/Embed: removing the pre-training strategy of the BS and feeding it directly to the discrete base station IDs for training.
- SignalingTraj/Graph: removing the spatial constraints of BS Graph on SD trajectories generation
- SignalingTraj/Node2vec: pre-training the BS using the Node2Vec algorithm

As can be seen from Table 3, SignalingTraj/Node2vec performs relatively well in the G-rank indicator on Telecom data, which is 66.90% higher than SignalingTraj. It also performs well in G-rank and I-rank on Unicom data. However, in general, SignalingTraj performs better in more indicators and has better comprehensive performance. However, SignalingTraj/Embed and SignalingTraj/Graph perform poorly in different indicators, cannot effectively simulate the distribution of data, and the generated data is less practical. Overall, the SignalingTraj model performs better than other variants on multiple data sets, proving its effectiveness and competitiveness in processing complex signaling data.

6 Conclusion

In this paper, we propose SignalingTraj, a novel framework for generating high-quality synthetic SD trajectories. By leveraging a pre-trained Variational Graph Autoencoder (VGAE) and integrating the generative power of diffusion models, our framework effectively addresses challenges inherent to SD data, such as low spatial resolution and irregular sampling intervals. The proposed spatial validity loss function ensures that generated trajectories adhere to realistic spatial distributions, thereby enhancing the fidelity and utility of the synthetic data. Future work will incorporate temporal dynamics into the framework and extend its application to downstream tasks, such as demographic analysis or urban mobility forecasting.

Acknowledgments. This work is funded by the Young Backbone Teacher Support Plan of Beijing Information Science and Technology University.

References

1. Bindschaedler, V., Shokri, R.: Synthesizing plausible privacy-preserving location traces. In: 2016 IEEE Symposium on Security and Privacy (SP), pp. 546–563 (2016). https://doi.org/10.1109/SP.2016.39
2. Bollverk, O., Hadachi, A.: CDR-based trajectory reconstruction of mobile network data using transformers. In: 2023 8th International Conference on Models and Technologies for Intelligent Transportation Systems (MT-ITS), pp. 1–6 (2023). https://doi.org/10.1109/MT-ITS56129.2023.10241747
3. Cao, C., Li, M.: Generating mobility trajectories with retained data utility. In: Proceedings of the 27th ACM SIGKDD Conference on Knowledge Discovery & Data Mining. KDD 2021, pp. 2610–2620. Association for Computing Machinery, New York (2021). https://doi.org/10.1145/3447548.3467158
4. Cao, J., et al.: Holistic semantic representation for navigational trajectory generation. ArXiv **abs/2501.02737** (2025). https://api.semanticscholar.org/CorpusID:275336842
5. Chen, X., Xu, J., Zhou, R., Chen, W., Fang, J., Liu, C.: Trajvae: a variational autoencoder model for trajectory generation. Neurocomputing **428**, 332–339 (2021)
6. Chu, C., Zhang, H., Wang, P., Lu, F.: Simulating human mobility with a trajectory generation framework based on diffusion model. Int. J. Geogr. Inf. Sci. **38**, 1–32 (2024). https://doi.org/10.1080/13658816.2024.2312199

7. Doyle, C., Herga, Z., Dipple, S., Szymanski, B.K., Korniss, G., Mladenić, D.: Predicting complex user behavior from CDR based social networks. Inf. Sci. Int. J. **500** (2019)
8. Feng, J., Yang, Z., Xu, F., Yu, H., Wang, M., Li, Y.: Learning to simulate human mobility. In: Proceedings of the 26th ACM SIGKDD International Conference on Knowledge Discovery & Data Mining, pp. 3426–3433. ACM https://doi.org/10.1145/3394486.3412862
9. Ho, J., Jain, A., Abbeel, P.: Denoising diffusion probabilistic models. In: Proceedings of the 34th International Conference on Neural Information Processing Systems. NIPS '20, Curran Associates Inc., Red Hook, NY, USA (2020)
10. Huang, Y., Wang, D., Xu, W., Cai, Z., Fu, F.: Accurate map matching method for mobile phone signaling data under spatio-temporal uncertainty. IEEE Trans. Intell. Transp. Syst. **25**(2), 1418–1429 (2024). https://doi.org/10.1109/TITS.2023.3314631
11. Jiang, S., Yang, Y., Gupta, S., Veneziano, D., Athavale, S., González, M.C.: The timegeo modeling framework for urban mobility without travel surveys. Proc. Natl. Acad. Sci. **113**(37), E5370–E5378 (2016)
12. Jiang, W., Zhao, W.X., Wang, J., Jiang, J.: Continuous trajectory generation based on two-stage GAN. In: Proceedings of the AAAI Conference on Artificial Intelligence, vol. 37, pp. 4374–4382 (2023)
13. Jiang, Z., Huang, A., Qi, G., Guan, W.: A framework of travel mode identification fusing deep learning and map-matching algorithm. IEEE Trans. Intell. Transp. Syst. **24**(6), 6401–6415 (2023). https://doi.org/10.1109/TITS.2023.3250660
14. Kipf, T.N., Welling, M.: Variational graph auto-encoders. arXiv preprint arXiv:1611.07308 (2016)
15. Kong, Z., Ping, W., Huang, J., Zhao, K., Catanzaro, B.: Diffwave: a versatile diffusion model for audio synthesis. arXiv preprint arXiv:2009.09761 (2020)
16. Li, L., Si, J., Yang, J., Dai, S., Zhang, J., Bo, T.: Bs2vec: a spatial representation learning model for large scale base stations. In: 2022 IEEE 24th International Conference on High Performance Computing & Communications; 8th International Conference on Data Science & Systems; 20th International Conference on Smart City; 8th International Conference on Dependability in Sensor, Cloud & Big Data Systems & Application (HPCC/DSS/SmartCity/DependSys), pp. 1661–1667 (2022). https://doi.org/10.1109/HPCC-DSS-SmartCity-DependSys57074.2022.00252
17. Li, M., Gao, S., Lu, F., Zhang, H.: Reconstruction of human movement trajectories from large-scale low- frequency mobile phone data. Comput. Environ. Urban Syst. **77** (2019)
18. Liu, Z., Wang, J., Li, Z., He, Y.: Full Bayesian significance testing for neural networks in traffic forecasting. In: Larson, K. (ed.) Proceedings of the Thirty-Third International Joint Conference on Artificial Intelligence, IJCAI-24, pp. 2216–2224. International Joint Conferences on Artificial Intelligence Organization (2024). https://doi.org/10.24963/ijcai.2024/245
19. Lugmayr, A., Danelljan, M., Romero, A., Yu, F., Timofte, R., Van Gool, L.: Repaint: inpainting using denoising diffusion probabilistic models. In: Proceedings of the IEEE/CVF Conference on Computer Vision and Pattern Recognition, pp. 11461–11471 (2022)
20. Merhi, J., Buchholz, E., Kanhere, S.S.: Synthetic trajectory generation through convolutional neural networks . In: 2024 21st Annual International Conference on

Privacy, Security and Trust (PST), pp. 1–12. IEEE Computer Society, Los Alamitos, CA, USA (2024). https://doi.org/10.1109/PST62714.2024.10788061, https://doi.ieeecomputersociety.org/10.1109/PST62714.2024.10788061
21. Ouyang, K., Shokri, R., Rosenblum, D.S., Yang, W.: A non-parametric generative model for human trajectories. IJCAI 2018, pp. 3812–3817. AAAI Press (2018)
22. Qin, Z., et al.: CellPred: a behavior-aware scheme for cellular data usage prediction **4**(1) (2020). https://doi.org/10.1145/3380982
23. Ruan, S., Long, C., Bao, J., Li, C., Zheng, Y.: Learning to generate maps from trajectories. In: AAAI Conference on Artificial Intelligence, pp. 890–897 (2020)
24. Simini, F., Barlacchi, G., Luca, M., Pappalardo, L.: A deep gravity model for mobility flows generation. Nat. Commun. **12** (2021). https://doi.org/10.1038/s41467-021-26752-4
25. Song, J., Meng, C., Ermon, S.: Denoising diffusion implicit models. In: International Conference on Learning Representations (2021). https://openreview.net/forum?id=St1giarCHLP
26. Song, Y., Sohl-Dickstein, J.N., Kingma, D.P., Kumar, A., Ermon, S., Poole, B.: Score-based generative modeling through stochastic differential equations. ArXiv **abs/2011.13456** (2020). https://api.semanticscholar.org/CorpusID:227209335
27. Wang, H., et al.: Synthesizing human trajectories based on variational point processes **36**(4), 1785–1799 (2024). https://doi.org/10.1109/TKDE.2023.3312209
28. Wang, X., Liu, X., Lu, Z., Yang, H.: Large scale GPS trajectory generation using map based on two stage GAN, pp. 126–141. https://doi.org/10.6339/21-JDS1004
29. Wang, Y., Zheng, T., Liang, Y., Liu, S., Song, M.: Cola: cross-city mobility transformer for human trajectory simulation. In: Proceedings of the ACM Web Conference 2024. WWW 2024, pp. 3509–3520. Association for Computing Machinery, New York (2024). https://doi.org/10.1145/3589334.3645469
30. Wang, Y., et al.: Spatiotemporal-augmented graph neural networks for human mobility simulation. IEEE Trans. on Knowl. Data Eng. **36**(11), 7074–7086 (2024). https://doi.org/10.1109/TKDE.2024.3409071
31. Wei, T., et al.: Diff-RNTraj: a structure-aware diffusion model for road network-constrained trajectory generation. IEEE Trans. Knowl. Data Eng. **36**(12), 7940–7953 (2024). https://doi.org/10.1109/TKDE.2024.3460051
32. Wu, N., Wang, J., Zhao, W.X., Jin, Y.: Learning to effectively estimate the travel time for fastest route recommendation. In: Proceedings of the 28th ACM International Conference on Information and Knowledge Management. CIKM 2019, pp. 1923–1932. Association for Computing Machinery, New York (2019). https://doi.org/10.1145/3357384.3357907
33. Xu, F., Lin, Z., Xia, T., Guo, D., Li, Y.: Sume: semantic-enhanced urban mobility network embedding for user demographic inference. Proc. ACM Interact. Mob. Wearable Ubiquitous Technol. **4**(3) (2020)
34. Zhang, J., Huang, Q., Huang, Y., Ding, Q., Tsai, P.W.: Dp-trajgan: a privacy-aware trajectory generation model with differential privacy. Futur. Gener. Comput. Syst. **142**, 25–40 (2023)
35. Zhang, Y., Yuan, Y., Ding, J., Yuan, J., Li, Y.: Noise matters: Diffusion model-based urban mobility generation with collaborative noise priors. In: Proceedings of the ACM Web Conference 2025 (WWW 2025) (2025)
36. Zheng, Y.: Trajectory data mining: an overview. ACM Trans. Intell. Syst. Technol. (TIST) **6**(3), 1–41 (2015). https://doi.org/10.1145/2743025
37. Zheng, Y., Liu, L., Wang, L., Xie, X.: Learning transportation mode from raw GPS data for geographic applications on the web. In: WWW, pp. 247–256 (2008)

38. Zhu, Y., Ye, Y., Zhang, S., Zhao, X., Yu, J.: Difftraj: generating GPS trajectory with diffusion probabilistic model. In: Thirty-seventh Conference on Neural Information Processing Systems (2023). https://openreview.net/forum?id=ykMdzevPkJ
39. Zhu, Y., et al.: Controltraj: controllable trajectory generation with topology-constrained diffusion model. In: Proceedings of the 30th ACM SIGKDD Conference on Knowledge Discovery and Data Mining. KDD 2024, pp. 4676–4687. Association for Computing Machinery, New York (2024). https://doi.org/10.1145/3637528.3671866

Research on Estimation Time of Arrival in Marine Traffic Based on Large Language Model

Junyou Su[1], Yi Yuan[2], Yu Liang[1], Bin Tan[1], Xuan Song[1,2], and Zipei Fan[2,3(✉)]

[1] Department of Computer Science and Engineering, Southern University of Science and Technology, Shenzhen 518055, China
[2] School of Artificial Intelligence, Jilin University, Changchun 130012, Jilin, China
fanzipei@jlu.edu.cn
[3] LocationMind Inc., Tokyo 101-0048, Japan

Abstract. The prediction of the Estimated Time of Arrival (ETA) in maritime traffic plays a crucial role in enhancing voyage planning, logistics efficiency, and overall maritime safety. This study introduces a segmented labeling approach leveraging Large Language Models (LLMs) for ETA prediction, highlighting their advanced reasoning capabilities. Building on recent progress in time-series forecasting, we propose a novel framework that utilizes LLMs for ship trajectory prediction and ETA estimation. The framework employs a few-shot in-context learning approach, structured prompt generation, and iterative refinement mechanisms to enhance prediction accuracy and reliability. Comprehensive experiments on a large-scale maritime dataset demonstrate the framework's strong performance, particularly for short-distance routes, achieving notable improvements in prediction accuracy compared to traditional and deep learning-based methods. These results suggest that LLMs offer a promising direction for advancing time-series forecasting in the maritime sector.

Keywords: Large Language Models · Estimated Time of Arrival · Time-Series Forecasting · Maritime Traffic · Intelligent Transportation Systems

1 Introduction

Efficient maritime traffic management is a cornerstone of global trade, ensuring the safe and timely transportation of goods. Among the metrics vital to this domain, the Estimated Time of Arrival (ETA) of vessels stands out as a critical factor, facilitating effective voyage planning, resource allocation, and logistics management. Despite its importance, accurately predicting ETA remains a formidable challenge due to the dynamic and complex nature of maritime environments, which are influenced by factors such as weather conditions, traffic density, and operational variability.

Historically, ETA estimation relied on heuristic methods and sparse trajectory datasets, which often failed to account for the nuanced and multifaceted nature of real-world scenarios. The introduction of machine learning and deep learning models, including Long Short-Term Memory (LSTM) networks and Gradient Boosted Decision Trees (GBDT), marked a significant leap forward in time-series forecasting by effectively capturing spatiotemporal dependencies in maritime data. However, these methods still grapple with inherent limitations such as handling data sparsity and incorporating contextual information comprehensively.

Nowadays, Large Language Models (LLMs) have emerged as transformative tools, showcasing unparalleled capabilities in natural language processing and time-series forecasting tasks. Their ability to leverage vast pre-trained knowledge and adapt through few-shot or zero-shot paradigms makes them particularly suited for complex applications like ETA prediction. However, applying LLMs to this domain necessitates addressing challenges such as trajectory anomalies, data sparsity, and the need for models that are both interpretable and adaptive.

This paper introduces a pioneering framework for ship ETA prediction that leverages LLMs through a segmented labeling approach—a novel strategy specifically designed to enhance prediction accuracy. Central to this framework are techniques such as few-shot in-context learning, structured prompt engineering, and iterative conditional output refinement. By integrating historical trajectory data and vessel-specific attributes, the proposed method achieves not only accurate but also consistent ETA predictions. Notably, our approach demonstrates exceptional performance on short-distance routes, highlighting its practical value in maritime operations.

2 Related Work

2.1 Time-Series Forecasting

The research on time-series forecasting has made rapid progress, encompassing a variety of deep learning methods. Deep learning models, especially Convolutional Neural Networks (CNNs) and Long Short-Term Memory (LSTM) networks, are favored for their ability to capture complex patterns and nonlinear relationships in data. For example, the LSTNet model [13] combines CNNs for feature extraction and LSTMs for sequence modeling, utilizing an adaptive weight learning mechanism to balance the importance of long-term and short-term time-series information. Additionally, time-series forecasting models such as TCN-LSTM integrate Temporal Convolutional Networks (TCN [2]) and LSTMs to extract short-term features and capture long-term dependencies. The NeuralProphet framework [21] combines deep neural networks with the Prophet decomposition model, enhancing forecasting accuracy for time-series data with complex nonlinear trends and seasonality. These methods have achieved significant performance improvements in time-series forecasting across various domains, demonstrating the potential and application prospects of deep learning in this area.

2.2 ETA Forecasting

Estimated time of arrival (ETA) or travel time estimation (TTE) has been a critical topic in intelligent transportation systems, with various methods and advancements developed over decades. Early foundational work by Messer et al. (1973) explored real-time travel time prediction during freeway incidents, marking the inception of TTE research [14]. Traditional approaches, such as Wang et al. (2014), utilized sparse trajectory data for path travel time estimation, addressing challenges like data sparsity [24]. More recent studies, like Shen et al. (2022), integrated tensor decomposition and graph embedding (TTPNet) to enhance prediction accuracy by modeling latent relationships in spatiotemporal data [18].

With the proliferation of deep learning techniques, numerous end-to-end models have emerged. For example, DeepTTE (Wang et al., 2018) leveraged deep neural networks to directly estimate travel time from raw GPS sequences, significantly outperforming conventional methods [23]. Similarly, HetETA (Hong et al., 2020) applied heterogeneous information network embeddings to refine TTE [10], while MetaTTE (Wang et al., 2022) incorporated deep meta-learning to adapt predictions dynamically across cities [22]. Advanced spatial-temporal modeling frameworks, such as STGNN-TTE (Jin et al., 2022) [11] and 3DGAT (Fang et al., 2020) [7], employed graph neural networks (GNNs) to capture complex spatiotemporal dependencies, achieving state-of-the-art performance.

Privacy preservation and personalization have also become focal points of recent research. Federated learning frameworks like GOF-TTE (Zhang et al., 2022) [25] and cross-area privacy-preserving models (Zhu et al., 2022) [27] enable decentralized model training, safeguarding user privacy while maintaining robust prediction capabilities. In addition, models such as SSML (Fang et al., 2021) [8] and MetaER-TTE (Fan et al., 2022) [6] utilized meta-learning to address en-route TTE, effectively adapting to real-time traffic and personalized driving behaviors. These advancements collectively highlight the evolution of TTE from heuristic methods to sophisticated data-driven models, emphasizing the integration of privacy, personalization, and scalability.

2.3 LLM in Time-Serise Forecasting

Large Language Models (LLMs), such as the GPT series [1,3,15,16] and LLaMa [20], have demonstrated remarkable success across a variety of natural language processing (NLP) tasks. Their extensive parameter sets enable them to acquire vast general knowledge and reasoning capabilities during pre-training, which is essential for building intelligent systems with common sense reasoning. Increasingly, LLM architectures are being applied to time series processing and forecasting, where they show considerable promise.

For example, TEMPO [4] adapts GPT architectures to learn dynamic temporal representations, while TIME-LLM [12] leverages LLMs for time series forecasting by reprogramming input data and using Prompt-as-Prefix techniques. FPT [26] highlights that even when LLMs are frozen, they can still perform effectively in time series tasks, capitalizing on the versatility of self-attention mechanisms. Similarly, Lag-LLaMa [17] employs a decoder-only transformer to perform univariate probabilistic forecasting, and Gruver et al. [9] demonstrate that framing time series forecasting as a next-token prediction task allows LLMs to outperform traditional models through effective tokenization and adaptation.

Despite these advances, most existing studies primarily focus on leveraging the mapping capabilities of LLMs for numerical regression tasks. They have not yet fully integrated external textual inputs or utilized the reasoning abilities of LLMs in understanding complex language. To address this, TEST [19] proposes a time series embedding method tailored specifically for LLMs, generating embeddings that capture instance-wise, feature-wise, and text-prototype alignment for time series tokens.

Given the challenge of limited training data, recent research has increasingly turned to pre-trained LLMs to address cross-domain applications. LLM4TS [5] is a pioneering method that aligns pre-trained LLMs with temporal characteristics, introducing a two-level aggregation approach to effectively incorporate multi-scale temporal data into LLMs. This approach demonstrates the potential for large language models to adapt and excel in time series analysis tasks, opening new avenues for improving the accuracy and efficiency of time series forecasting.

3 Data Processing and Data Analysis

3.1 Raw Data Overview

The raw data (see Fig. 1) is AIS (Automatic Identification System) data sourced from SPIRE, with a total size of 45.8 GB in CSV file format lasting 3 months in 2021/02/01-2021/04/30. Specifically, each row contains the following attributes: {timestamp, mmsi, latitude, longitude, status, eta, destination, ship_and_cargo_type, draught, speed, course, heading, rot, imo, name, call_sign, flag, length, width}. The data is a concatenation of information from different maritime routes, which ensures that the data for a single route is chronologically ordered. However, there is no explicit relationship between different routes within the same file. The data visualization is shown in Fig. 2.

timestamp	mmsi	latitude	longitude	status	eta	destinatio	ship_and_	draught	speed	course	heading	rot	imo	name	call_sign	flag	length	width
2021/2/10 11:40	210065000	55.65378	21.15756	5	2020-12-(	TBA	70	6.3	0	331	103	0	9333369	QUEEN B	5BPK5	CY	0	0
2021/2/10 11:45	210065000	55.65378	21.15757	5	2020-12-(	TBA	70	6.3	0	7	103	0	9333369	QUEEN B	5BPK5	CY	0	0
2021/2/10 11:50	210065000	55.65383	21.1575	5	2020-12-(	TBA	70	6.3	0	27	103	0	9333369	QUEEN B	5BPK5	CY	0	0
2021/2/10 11:55	210065000	55.65379	21.15752	5	2020-12-(	TBA	70	6.3	0	272	103	0	9333369	QUEEN B	5BPK5	CY	0	0
2021/2/10 12:00	210065000	55.65377	21.15754	5	2020-12-(	TBA	70	6.3	0	235	103	0	9333369	QUEEN B	5BPK5	CY	0	0
2021/2/10 12:05	210065000	55.65378	21.15753	5	2020-12-(	TBA	70	6.3	0	322	103	0	9333369	QUEEN B	5BPK5	CY	0	0
2021/2/10 12:10	210065000	55.65378	21.15753	5	2020-12-(	TBA	70	6.3	0	27	103	0	9333369	QUEEN B	5BPK5	CY	0	0
2021/2/10 12:15	210065000	55.65379	21.15752	5	2020-12-(	TBA	70	6.3	0	58	103	0	9333369	QUEEN B	5BPK5	CY	0	0
2021/2/10 12:20	210065000	55.65378	21.15753	5	2020-12-(	TBA	70	6.3	0	281	103	0	9333369	QUEEN B	5BPK5	CY	0	0
2021/2/10 12:25	210065000	55.65379	21.15753	5	2020-12-(	TBA	70	6.3	0	297	103	0	9333369	QUEEN B	5BPK5	CY	0	0
2021/2/10 12:30	210065000	55.65379	21.15755	5	2020-12-(	TBA	70	6.3	0	165	103	0	9333369	QUEEN B	5BPK5	CY	0	0
2021/2/10 12:35	210065000	55.6538	21.15754	5	2020-12-(	TBA	70	6.3	0	316	103	0	9333369	QUEEN B	5BPK5	CY	0	0
2021/2/10 12:40	210065000	55.65383	21.1575	5	2020-12-(	TBA	70	6.3	0	219	103	0	9333369	QUEEN B	5BPK5	CY	0	0
2021/2/10 12:45	210065000	55.65374	21.15756	5	2020-12-(	TBA	70	6.3	0	18	103	0	9333369	QUEEN B	5BPK5	CY	0	0
2021/2/10 12:50	210065000	55.65378	21.15756	5	2020-12-(	TBA	70	6.3	0	300	103	0	9333369	QUEEN B	5BPK5	CY	0	0
2021/2/10 12:55	210065000	55.65379	21.15755	5	2020-12-(	TBA	70	6.3	0	166	103	0	9333369	QUEEN B	5BPK5	CY	0	0
2021/2/10 13:00	210065000	55.65377	21.15755	5	2020-12-(	TBA	70	6.3	0	13	103	0	9333369	QUEEN B	5BPK5	CY	0	0
2021/2/10 13:05	210065000	55.65377	21.15755	5	2020-12-(	TBA	70	6.3	0	211	103	0	9333369	QUEEN B	5BPK5	CY	0	0
2021/2/10 13:10	210065000	55.65378	21.15755	5	2020-12-(	TBA	70	6.3	0	270	103	0	9333369	QUEEN B	5BPK5	CY	0	0
2021/2/10 13:15	210065000	55.65379	21.15754	5	2020-12-(	TBA	70	6.3	0	47	103	0	9333369	QUEEN B	5BPK5	CY	0	0
2021/2/10 13:20	210065000	55.65383	21.1575	5	2020-12-(	TBA	70	6.3	0	151	103	0	9333369	QUEEN B	5BPK5	CY	0	0
2021/2/10 13:25	210065000	55.65373	21.15754	5	2020-12-(	TBA	70	6.3	0	83	103	0	9333369	QUEEN B	5BPK5	CY	0	0
2021/2/10 13:30	210065000	55.65378	21.15754	5	2020-12-(	TBA	70	6.3	0	347	103	0	9333369	QUEEN B	5BPK5	CY	0	0
2021/2/10 13:35	210065000	55.65378	21.15755	5	2020-12-(	TBA	70	6.3	0	145	103	0	9333369	QUEEN B	5BPK5	CY	0	0
2021/2/10 13:40	210065000	55.65378	21.15755	5	2020-12-(	TBA	70	6.3	0	178	103	0	9333369	QUEEN B	5BPK5	CY	0	0

Fig. 1. AIS Data Example

Fig. 2. AIS Data Visualization

3.2 Data Preprocessing

Due to the presence of missing values and the insufficiently clear and accurate segmentation of the maritime routes, anomalies data processing and data segmentation are necessary.

Anomalies Data Processing. The raw data contains numerous instances where heading and rot are recorded as NaN (Not a Number), and fewer instances where eta is NaN. To maintain the integrity of the time series after handling the missing values, the missing heading values are typically filled with the value from the previous record within the same route. Since the instances where eta is NaN are relatively few, these records can be directly deleted.

Data Segmentation. The status attribute in the raw data can initially reflect whether the vessel is in motion or docked at a port. However, this is not always accurate. For example, the vessel's speed may remain at 0 for a period of time before the status is changed to 5 (indicating that the vessel is docked). By considering both the status and speed attributes simultaneously, a very effective segmentation can be achieved. Specifically, data is initially segmented based on the transitions of status from 5 to 0 and back to 5. Subsequently, the speed values are used to identify appropriate critical points near the start and end of the segments, resulting in the final segmented data.

3.3 Data Analysis

In this section, we analyze the ETA data originally marked in the AIS data and manually uploaded by the captain and compare with the actual situation.

Relationship Between Vessel Type and Delay Time. We analyzed the relationship between the original estimated arrival time and the actual arrival time of different ship types, as shown in the Fig. 3. Cargo ships and passenger ships are two types that are more likely to arrive later than expected, accounting for about two-thirds of all delayed ships.

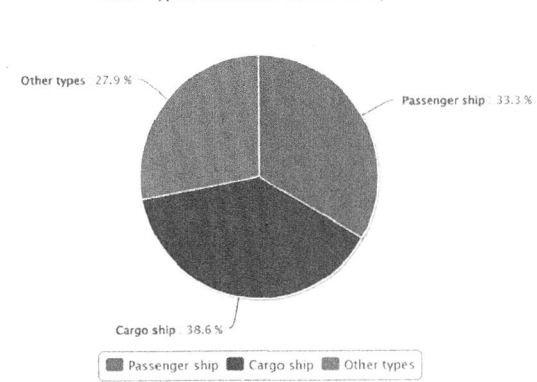

Fig. 3. ETA Delay Rate

ETA Changes During Route. We then analyzed the frequency of changes in the ETA data in the original AIS data as Fig. 4. Generally, ships sail according to fixed schedules. If the captain expects a delay during the voyage, the ETA will be manually changed and uploaded by the AIS device. From the data analysis, it can be seen that less than half of the ships did not change the ETA during the voyage, that is, the captain expected the ship to arrive according to the initial ETA, but there are still some ships that may change the arrival time due to weather/emergency reasons during the voyage.

3.4 Data Transformation

To facilitate interactions with the Large Language Model (LLM), one good way is to transform the data into the format illustrated as follows. This standardized data structure enables more efficient processing and seamless integration with the LLM, enhancing the overall accuracy and effectiveness of the system.

The most fundamental information for each route is the coordinates of its origin and destination. Therefore, this information should be extracted initially. Utilizing global port data obtained from MSI (Maritime Safety Information), details pertaining to the ports at both the starting and ending points are retrieved, including the port names, identifiers, and the distances between the actual coordinates and the port coordinates listed in the dataset.

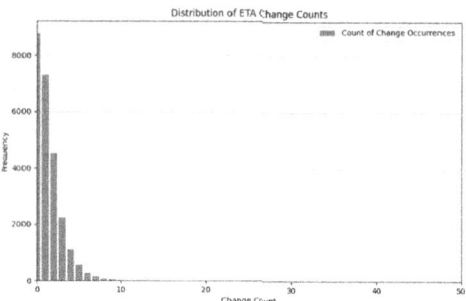

Fig. 4. ETA Change Count

Furthermore, to facilitate subsequent interactions with the Large Language Model (LLM) based on individual coordinate grid cells—each measuring 1×1 in the corresponding latitude and longitude units - a label attribute is also incorporated.

Subsequently, the data processing for each route addresses issues such as excessively large intervals between consecutive data points within the same route. Interpolation becomes essential in this context. The interpolation algorithm operates by calculating the average values of various attributes at the edges of each grid cell to add the corresponding points. Additionally, while retaining the origin and destination points, a point is preserved near each integer latitude and longitude, and all remaining points are filtered out.

In this way, the data are transformed into the target format:

```
jsonl: # Each object in jsonl is a route.
{
    "StartPort": (Name, ID, distance),
    "StartLongitude":"",
    "StartLatitude":"",
    "StartX":"",
    "StartY":"",
    "EndPort": (Name, ID, distance),
    "EndLongitude":"",
    "EndLatitude":"",
    "EndX":"",
    "EndY":"",
    "Len":"" # represents the number of items in the Path
    "Path": [
        {
            "longitude":"",
            "latitude":"",
            "timestamps":"",
            ... # other info
        },
```

...
  ]
}

4 Method

4.1 Problem Definition

Definition 1. (Location Area Label): The location area label l_i is the unique identifier of a specific grid cell on the map, where the map is partitioned into uniform grid cells based on latitude and longitude. Each grid cell covers an area of $n \times n$ degrees. The label l_i for a location is determined by dividing the latitude and longitude of the vessel's position by n as follows:

$$l_i = \lfloor \frac{\text{lat}_i}{n} \rfloor \sim \lfloor \frac{\text{lon}_i}{n} \rfloor, \tag{1}$$

where lat_i and lon_i are the latitude and longitude of the vessel. Example see Fig. 5

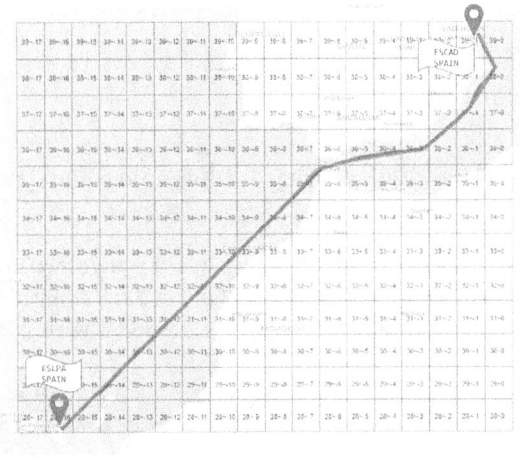

Fig. 5. Grid Label Example

Definition 2. (Trajectory): A ship trajectory represents the movement of a vessel, characterized by a sequence of spatiotemporal records that capture its location and motion attributes at specific timestamps. Formally, it is defined as:

$$T = ((l_i, s_i, h_i, t_i) \mid i = 1, \ldots, n), \tag{2}$$

where l_i denotes the location area label at time t_i, s_i represents the speed, h_i indicates the heading, and n is the length of the trajectory.

Definition 3. (Ship Trajectory Prediction): Given the past n records T_{t-n+1}^{t} of a trajectory T, the objective of ship trajectory prediction is to determine a mapping function $f(\cdot)$ with parameters θ, which predicts the entire route from the current position to the final destination:

$$f(T_{t-n+1}^{t}) = \{(l_j, s_j, h_j, t_j) \mid j = t+1, \ldots, t_{\text{end}}\}, \tag{3}$$

where

$$T_{t-n+1}^{t} = \{(l_i, s_i, h_i, t_i) \mid i = t-n+1, \ldots, t\}, \tag{4}$$

and t_{end} represents the timestamp of the final destination.

Definition 4. (Estimated Time of Arrival, ETA): The ETA refers to the predicted timestamp at which the vessel will reach its final destination. Formally, for a given trajectory T, the ETA is defined as:

$$\text{ETA} = t_{\text{end}}, \tag{5}$$

where t_{end} represents the timestamp corresponding to the predicted final location l_{end} of the ship. Accurately predicting the ETA is a critical aspect of ship trajectory prediction, as it supports effective voyage planning and logistics management.

4.2 Model Architecture

The architecture of the proposed model consists of 3 stages to predict the trajectory of a vessel. The overall workflow is broken down into the following steps (Fig. 6):

Few-Shot in-Context-Learning Setup. In this stage, we gather n historical trajectories that share the same starting and ending points. These historical trajectories are used as examples to provide the model with context for making predictions.

Alongside the trajectory data, we also collect basic vessel attributes, such as vessel MMSI(Maritime Mobile Service Identify), size. However, it's important to note that some of this additional information may have minimal direct impact on the prediction performance, though it could be helpful in refining the model's output under certain conditions.

Additionally, for the trajectory that needs to be predicted, we provide the first m data points. These initial points not only help the model infer the vessel's departure time but also provide context on the vessel's early trajectory, such as its initial direction, speed, and environmental factors influencing its movement. This information is essential for the model to correctly understand the structure of the trajectory and the output format.

Prompt Generation and Exact Response. Once the historical trajectory data is collected, we use a *Prompt Template* to formulate a structured prompt. This prompt is based on the input historical trajectory data and is formatted to

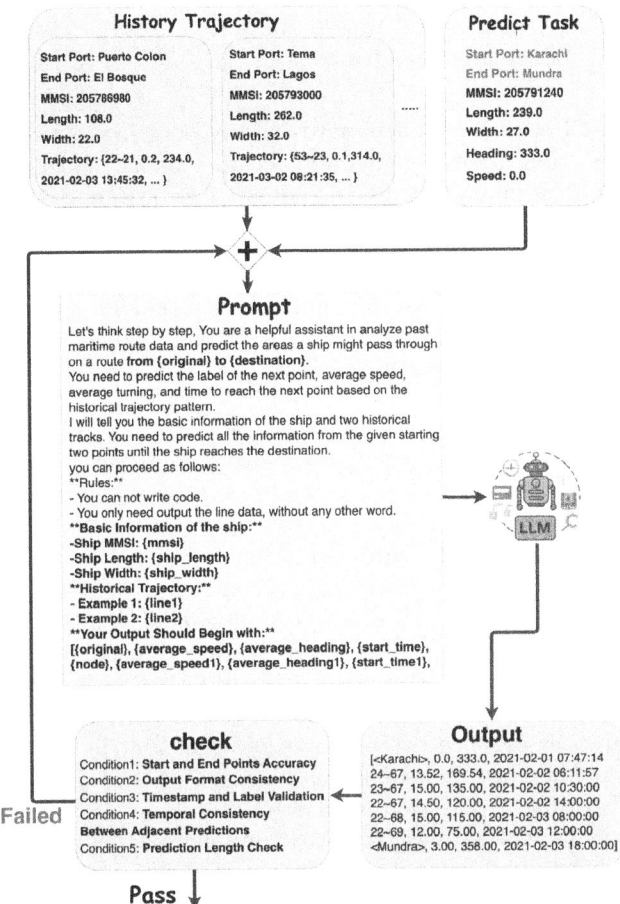

Fig. 6. Overview of Model Architecture

ensure the model receives the relevant information in a consistent manner. The prompt is then processed by the model to generate a corresponding response, which represents the predicted trajectory of the vessel. The LLM generates the predicted trajectory based on the temporal and spatial patterns observed in the historical data.

The generated response from the LLM is unstructured to provide the predicted trajectory in a consistent format, where each line corresponds to a trajectory data point. For example, each line might follow a format similar to:

$$39 \sim 0, 11.73, 48.0, 2021-02-09 18:06:46$$

To ensure the model output is properly processed, we employ regular expressions to extract each line of the predicted trajectory. These regular expressions are designed to capture the relevant components of each predicted point, including the index, coordinates, and timestamp. This enables accurate parsing and further analysis of the predicted trajectory.

Conditional Check and Refinement. In this stage, we perform several conditional checks to ensure the quality and accuracy of the model's output. These checks help to identify and correct any potential inconsistencies or errors in the predicted trajectory. The following checks are carried out:

1. **Start and End Points Accuracy**: The model's predicted start and end points are verified to ensure they match the actual start and end points of the vessel's journey. Additionally, we check if the predicted departure time aligns with the actual departure time of the vessel, as discrepancies here may indicate a misprediction.
2. **Output Format Consistency**: We verify that the overall structure of the LLM output matches the predefined format. This includes ensuring that each line follows the expected structure of a data point, as described earlier, and that the relevant information is properly represented.
3. **Timestamp and Label Validation**: Each predicted timestamp is checked to confirm it adheres to the correct time format (i.e. YYYY-MM-DD HH:MM:SS). Similarly, we validate that all labels, including index numbers and coordinate values, are formatted correctly and consistently throughout the output.
4. **Temporal Consistency Between Adjacent Predictions**: We analyze the time intervals between consecutive predicted positions. Large discrepancies in time intervals between two adjacent locations may indicate unrealistic or erroneous predictions. This check helps to ensure that the predicted trajectory follows a plausible progression in terms of time.
5. **Prediction Length Check**: We check for abnormal deviations in the length of the predicted trajectory, specifically for predictions that are either excessively long or short compared to the expected range. Such anomalies could suggest potential issues with the model's output, such as incorrect time frames or unrealistic movements.

These conditional checks are essential for refining the model's output and ensuring its reliability. If any of the checks fail, the model will be asked to re-predict the trajectory, then back to the first step. This iterative refinement process ensures that the model generates accurate and consistent trajectory predictions under various conditions.

5 Experiment

5.1 Experimental Setup

Environment. The experiments were conducted using the Qwen2.5-7B-Instruction model, which is a large language model optimized for instruction-based tasks. The model was run on four RTX 4090 GPUs, which provided the necessary computational power for efficient running of the large language model.

The following parameter settings were used for the model during experimentation:

- **Temperature** = 0: This setting ensures deterministic outputs, eliminating randomness in the model's predictions.
 - **Top-p** = 0.95: This parameter defines nucleus sampling, where the model considers the smallest set of possible next tokens whose cumulative probability mass is greater than or equal to 0.95.
 - **Max tokens** = 4096: The maximum number of tokens the model is allowed to generate in a single response. This ensures that long trajectories can be predicted in a single pass.
 - **Max model length** = 8192: This defines the total token length available for both input and output combined, ensuring that longer historical trajectory data can be provided to the model without truncation.

Baseline. To evaluate the practical application capabilities of LLMs and to assess their advantages and disadvantages compared to traditional machine learning methods (using Gradient Boosting Decision Trees, GBDT, as an example) and neural networks (using Long Short-Term Memory networks, LSTM, as an example), we designed two baseline models and conducted a series of experiments.

 - **GBDT** The selected or computed features for X and y are detailed in Tables 1 and 2, respectively. To prevent data leakage, the dataset is divided into training and testing sets in chronological order without shuffling. The model used for training is derived by wrapping the base Gradient Boosting Decision Trees (GBDT) model with a MultiOutputRegressor.
   The mean absolute error (MAE) of the timestamp predictions is presented in Table 3. Additionally, the feature importance derived from the Gradient Boosting Decision Tree (GBDT) model is illustrated in Fig. 7. Some sample route predictions are shown in Fig. 8, where the red line represents the predicted route and the blue line denotes the actual route.
 - **LSTM** This model is designed to predict the motion characteristics of vessels. It processes time series data, detailed in Tables 4, to learn the historical motion characteristics of vessels in order to forecast their future motion states. The model employs normalization and denormalization procedures to ensure data stability during the training process and to revert to the original scale post-prediction. The model's output is multi-objective, detailed in Tables 5, encompassing predictions of speed, heading, longitude, latitude, and timestamps.

Metrics. In this study, we evaluate the model's performance using two primary metrics: Mean Absolute Error (MAE) and Dynamic Time Warping (DTW), with a modified DTW metric that incorporates both spatial and temporal factors.

 - **MAE (Mean Absolute Error)**: This metric calculates the absolute time difference between the predicted and actual final trajectory points.

Table 1. X Features

Feature Name	Description
route_id	Identifier for the specific route
cur_lat	Current latitude of the ship
cur_lon	Current longitude of the ship
cur_speed	Current speed of the ship in knots or specified units
cur_heading	Current heading direction of the ship in degrees
cur_timestamp	Current timestamp indicating the time of the measurement
target_lat	Latitude of the target destination
target_lon	Longitude of the target destination
start_lat	Latitude of the starting point of the route
start_lon	Longitude of the starting point of the route
start_timestamp	Timestamp indicating the start time of the route
end_lat	Latitude of the ending point of the route
end_lon	Longitude of the ending point of the route
ship_length	Length of the ship in meters
ship_width	Width of the ship in meters
prev_lat	Latitude of the previous position of the ship
prev_lon	Longitude of the previous position of the ship
prev_speed	Speed of the ship at the previous position
prev_heading	Heading direction of the ship at the previous position in degrees
prev_timestamp	Timestamp of the previous position measurement

Specifically, it is used to compute the error in the predicted vessel arrival time. The formula for MAE is:

$$\text{MAE} = \frac{1}{n} \sum_{i=1}^{n} |t_{\text{pred},i} - t_{\text{true},i}|$$

where $t_{\text{pred},i}$ and $t_{\text{true},i}$ are the predicted and true timestamps of the i-th line's end point, respectively.

- **DTW (Dynamic Time Warping with Distance and Time):** This modified DTW metric measures the alignment of two sequences, considering both spatial (Euclidean distance between coordinates) and temporal (time difference between timestamps). The trajectory label is decomposed into pairs of coordinates and timestamps, represented as x ~ y. The DTW distance between two points (x_1, y_1, t_1) and (x_2, y_2, t_2) is computed as:

$$\text{DTW}(x_1, y_1, t_1, x_2, y_2, t_2) = \text{Euclidean}((x_1, y_1), (x_2, y_2)) + 0.5 \times |t_2 - t_1|$$

where Euclidean calculates the spatial distance between two points, and the term $0.5 \times |t_2 - t_1|$ adds a penalty for the temporal difference between the

Table 2. y Features

Feature Name	Description
next_lat	Predicted latitude coordinate for the next point
next_lon	Predicted longitude coordinate for the next point
next_speed	Predicted speed for the next time step
next_heading	Predicted heading direction for the next time step
next_timestamp	Predicted timestamp for the next data point

Table 3. GBDT Timestamp Result

Name	MAE(h)
Training_timestamp	201836 (56.1)
Testing_timestamp	207258 (57.6)

predicted and actual timestamps. This modified DTW takes both the spatial path and temporal alignment into account when evaluating the predicted trajectory.

6 Result

6.1 Initial Data Number

In this section, we analyze the relationship between the number of initial data points provided for trajectory prediction and the final prediction results. We compare scenarios where 1, 2, 3, or 50% of the trajectory's initial points are given.

As shown in Table 6, providing only one initial data point results in significant variability in the output format of the LLM, leading to a lower Correct Rate. On the other hand, providing 2 or 3 initial points yields similar performance. When 50% of the initial trajectory is provided, there is a significant improvement in MAE and DTW, as the predicted portion of the trajectory becomes shorter. However, we observe a corresponding decrease in the Correct Rate. An analysis of the anomalous outputs reveals that this decrease is due to discrepancies between the provided initial half of the trajectory and the historical trajectory, increasing the model's perplexity and leading to prediction failures.

6.2 Few-Shot Comparison

In this section, we examine how the number of provided historical trajectories influences the prediction performance of our method. Through extensive analysis, we determined that using two historical trajectories achieves an optimal balance between prediction accuracy and computational efficiency.

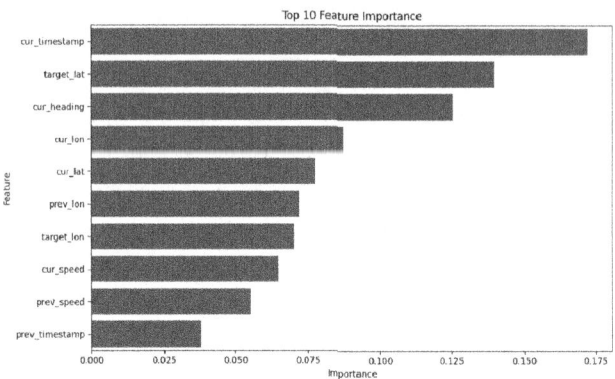

Fig. 7. Feature Importance

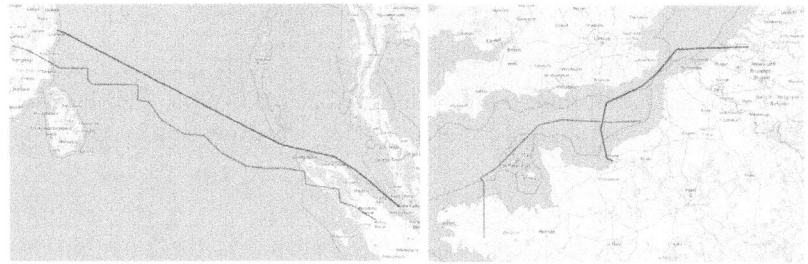

Fig. 8. Some examples of GBDT

The key observations are as follows. When only a single trajectory is provided, the model lacks sufficient data diversity. This scarcity forces the model to heavily mimic the single example, limiting its ability to generalize and adapt to varying scenarios during prediction. In this case, the model's outputs are overly dependent on the specific characteristics of the single trajectory, leading to reduced robustness and higher errors.

On the other hand, when two or more trajectories are provided, the model benefits from in-context learning. With two trajectories, the model can identify patterns and commonalities between the examples, enabling it to make more informed predictions. As the number of trajectories increases beyond two, slight improvements in metrics such as MAE and DTW are observed. However, the improvements diminish as the context length grows, and the computational cost of processing longer sequences increases significantly. This additional cost includes both the time required for inference and the memory overhead associated with handling larger inputs.

In summary, while providing more than two trajectories offers marginal gains in accuracy, the diminishing returns and increased computational burden make it less practical. Therefore, using two historical trajectories strikes the best compromise, as it provides sufficient data diversity for effective learning while main-

Table 4. X Features

Feature Name	Description
current_speed	Current speed of the vessel or vehicle
current_heading	Current heading direction in degrees
lat	Current latitude coordinate
lon	Current longitude coordinate
time_since_start	Elapsed time since the start of the route

Table 5. y Features

Feature Name	Description
next_lat	Predicted latitude coordinate for the next point
next_lon	Predicted longitude coordinate for the next point
next_speed	Predicted speed for the next time step
next_heading	Predicted heading direction for the next time step
next_timestamp	Predicted timestamp for the next data point

taining reasonable computational requirements. This choice ensures that the model can deliver accurate predictions efficiently in real-world applications.

6.3 Regenerate

During the regeneration process, both MAE and DTW initially show a slight increase before gradually stabilizing, while the rate at which the number of errors decreases also slows down over time (see Fig. 9). This phenomenon can be attributed to the fact that the instances where the LLM fails to provide a correct response on the first attempt are often associated with significant discrepancies between historical trajectories. These discrepancies may arise from the presence of anomalous trajectories in the data. As a result, the LLM faces difficulty in identifying common patterns across the trajectories, leading to the generation of erroneous outputs in the initial stages. Furthermore, this issue may be exacerbated by the model inadvertently learning from the anomalous trajectories, which could further distort the regeneration process. As the model iterates, it gradually stabilizes as it refines its understanding and reduces the impact of the anomalies, but the rate of error reduction becomes slower as the system reaches its performance limits.

Table 6. Performance Results in Ship ETA Prediction Task. Method (used model/approach), Init-Data (Number of initialization data), Example (example Number during inference), Regen (regeneration included: 'w' or excluded: 'wo'), MAE (Mean Absolute Error in hours), DTW (Dynamic Time Warping distance), Correct Rate (The rate of LLM output Correctly).

Method	Init-Data	Example	Regen	MAE(hour)	DTW	Correct Rate(%)
$LLM_{\text{Qwen2.5-7B-Insturct}}$	2	1	wo	30113 (8.36)	52630	77.3
$LLM_{\text{Qwen2.5-7B-Insturct}}$	2	1	w	34824 (9.67)	67219	**99.5**
$LLM_{\text{Qwen2.5-7B-Insturct}}$	1	2	wo	25638 (7.12)	45835	66.6
$LLM_{\text{Qwen2.5-7B-Insturct}}$	2	2	wo	25215 (7.00)	40804	82.3
$LLM_{\text{Qwen2.5-7B-Insturct}}$	3	2	wo	24795 (6.89)	43703	81.1
$LLM_{\text{Qwen2.5-7B-Insturct}}$	50%L	2	wo	**20342 (5.65)**	**26323**	78.6
$LLM_{\text{Qwen2.5-7B-Insturct}}$	2	2	w	28037 (7.79)	49277	99.4
$LLM_{\text{Qwen2.5-7B-Insturct}}$	2	3	wo	25155 (6.99)	41513	83.0
$LLM_{\text{Qwen2.5-7B-Insturct}}$	2	3	w	29140 (8.10)	55506	99.2
$LLM_{\text{Qwen2.5-7B-Insturct}}$	2	4	wo	23981 (6.66)	36738	81.9
$LLM_{\text{Qwen2.5-7B-Insturct}}$	2	4	w	27900 (7.75)	49841	97.3
$GBDT$	–	–	–	207258(57.6)	–	–
$LSTM$	–	–	–	269872(74.96)	–	–

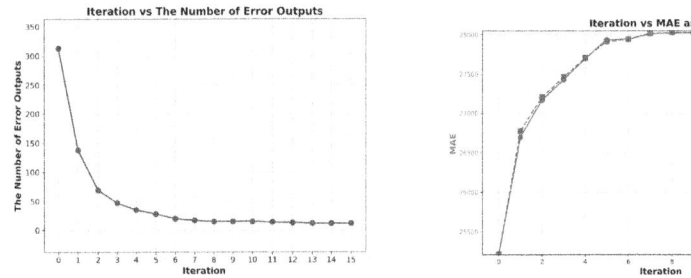
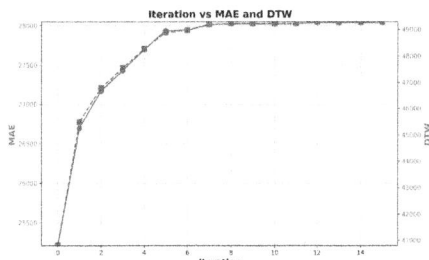

Fig. 9. The Regenerate of 2-shot Qwen2.5-7B-Insturct

7 Analysis

7.1 Path Length

This section explores the interplay between the length of ship trajectories, the prediction accuracy achieved by our method, and the frequency of abnormal outputs generated by the LLM. To conduct this analysis, the MAE of the predicted arrival times (illustrated in Fig. 10) and the average DTW distance (depicted in Fig. 10) of 2-shot Qwen2.5-7B-Instruct case are computed for distinct trajectory length intervals, specifically for lengths ranging from 5–9, 10–14, ..., and 45–49.

Our findings reveal a clear trend: as the length of the ship trajectories increases, both the MAE of arrival times and the DTW distance exhibit a consistent upward trend, indicating a decline in prediction accuracy for longer trajectories. Interestingly, for trajectory lengths exceeding 40, there is an observed decrease in both MAE and DTW. This unexpected behavior is likely due to the sparsity of the test dataset in this length range, which may reduce the representativeness of the data and influence the evaluation results.

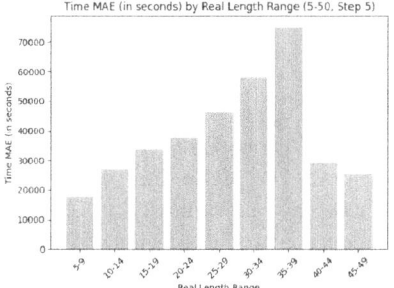
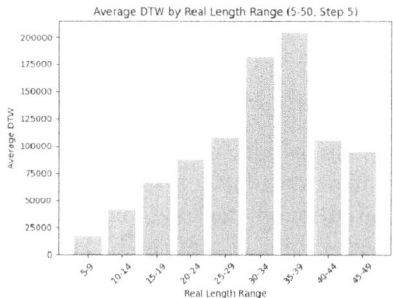

Fig. 10. Compare Different Length's Result

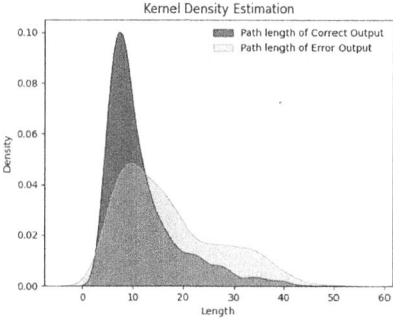

Fig. 11. Compare Length Between Error and Result

Additionally, the analysis uncovers a significant correlation between trajectory length and the probability of abnormal outputs from the LLM. As the trajectory length increases, the likelihood of the LLM producing irregular or anomalous outputs also rises. This relationship is visualized in Fig. 11 using a kernel density estimation (KDE) plot, which highlights the growing risk of anomalies as trajectory complexity and length increase. These findings emphasize the challenges posed by longer trajectories and suggest areas for further improvement in prediction models.

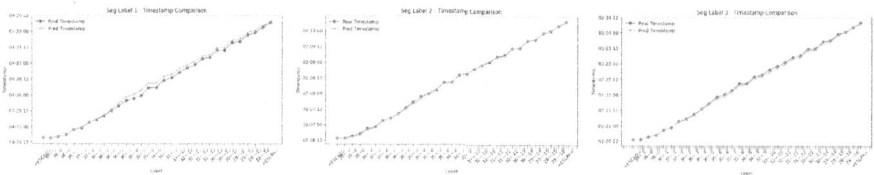

Fig. 12. Case Result

7.2 Case Study

In this section, we focus on all the routes from ESCAD to ESLPA (the specific routes are shown on the map in Fig. 5). We evaluate the prediction results generated by our method and compare them with the actual values (Fig. 12). The results indicate that the LLM provides highly accurate predictions for the arrival times at nearly every position along the route. The MAE for arrival times is impressively low, at just 5249 s, which is less than two hours. This demonstrates the effectiveness of our method in predicting arrival times with high precision.

However, while the arrival time predictions are highly accurate, the predictions for other parameters, such as speed and heading, show significant discrepancies. The accuracy of these predictions is considerably lower, with large errors observed in both speed and heading throughout the route. This discrepancy suggests that while our method excels in predicting arrival times, it faces challenges when it comes to accurately forecasting dynamic ship movement information, such as changes in speed and heading.

8 Conclusion

This study presents a groundbreaking approach to ETA prediction in maritime traffic, utilizing a segmented labeling strategy with Large Language Models (LLMs). By leveraging few-shot in-context learning, structured prompts, and iterative refinement, the proposed framework addresses key challenges in time-series forecasting, including data sparsity and trajectory anomalies. Extensive evaluations on a large-scale dataset validate the effectiveness of this method. The experiments highlight the method's exceptional performance on short-distance routes, where it achieves remarkable accuracy and consistency, and its adaptability across trajectories of varying lengths.

The results underscore the transformative potential of LLMs in maritime applications, particularly through their ability to dynamically integrate spatiotemporal patterns and refine outputs iteratively. The analysis also reveals how iterative feedback mechanisms enhance prediction accuracy and mitigate errors caused by anomalies. This work not only advances the state of the art in ETA prediction but also opens new pathways for applying LLMs to other complex forecasting tasks in intelligent transportation systems. Future research could focus on extending this framework to diverse maritime scenarios, improving scalability, and exploring its application in real-time operational contexts.

References

1. Achiam, J., et al.: Gpt-4 technical report. arXiv preprint arXiv:2303.08774 (2023)
2. Bai, S., Kolter, J.Z., Koltun, V.: An empirical evaluation of generic convolutional and recurrent networks for sequence modeling. arXiv preprint arXiv:1803.01271 (2018)
3. Brown, T., Mann, B., Ryder, N., Subbiah, M., Kaplan, J.D., Dhariwal, P., Neelakantan, A., Shyam, P., Sastry, G., Askell, A., et al.: Language models are few-shot learners. Adv. Neural. Inf. Process. Syst. **33**, 1877–1901 (2020)
4. Cao, D., Jia, F., Arik, S.O., Pfister, T., Zheng, Y., Ye, W., Liu, Y.: Tempo: prompt-based generative pre-trained transformer for time series forecasting. arXiv preprint arXiv:2310.04948 (2023)
5. Chang, C., Wang, W.Y., Peng, W.C., Chen, T.F.: Llm4ts: aligning pre-trained llms as data-efficient time-series forecasters. arXiv preprint arXiv:2308.08469 (2024)
6. Fan, Y., Xu, J., Zhou, R., et al.: Metaer-tte: an adaptive meta-learning model for en route travel time estimation. In: Proceedings of the Thirty-First International Joint Conference on Artificial Intelligence, pp. 2023–2029 (2022)
7. Fang, X., Huang, J., Wang, F., et al.: Constgat: contextual spatial-temporal graph attention network for travel time estimation at baidu maps. In: Proceedings of the 26th ACM SIGKDD International Conference on Knowledge Discovery & Data Mining, pp. 2697–2705 (2020)
8. Fang, X., Huang, J., Wang, F., et al.: SSML: self-supervised meta-learner for en route travel time estimation at baidu maps. In: Proceedings of the 27th ACM SIGKDD Conference on Knowledge Discovery & Data Mining, pp. 2840–2848 (2021)
9. Gruver, N., Finzi, M., Qiu, S., Wilson, A.G.: Large language models are zero-shot time series forecasters. Adv. Neural Inf. Process. Syst. **36** (2024)
10. Hong, H., Lin, Y., Yang, X., et al.: Heteta: heterogeneous information network embedding for estimating time of arrival. In: Proceedings of the 26th ACM SIGKDD International Conference on Knowledge Discovery & Data Mining, pp. 2444–2454 (2020)
11. Jin, G., Wang, M., Zhang, J., et al.: Stgnn-tte: travel time estimation via spatial-temporal graph neural network. Futur. Gener. Comput. Syst. **126**, 70–81 (2022)
12. Jin, M., et al.: Time-llm: time series forecasting by reprogramming large language models. arXiv preprint arXiv:2310.01728 (2023)
13. Li, L., Wang, K., Li, S., Feng, X., Zhang, L.: LST-Net: learning a convolutional neural network with a learnable sparse transform. In: Vedaldi, A., Bischof, H., Brox, T., Frahm, J.-M. (eds.) ECCV 2020. LNCS, vol. 12355, pp. 562–579. Springer, Cham (2020). https://doi.org/10.1007/978-3-030-58607-2_33
14. Messer, C.J., Dudek, C.L., Friebele, J.D.: Method for predicting travel time and other operational measures in real-time during freeway incident conditions. Highway Res. Rec. **461**, 1–16 (1973)
15. Radford, A., Narasimhan, K., Salimans, T., Sutskever, I., et al.: Improving language understanding by generative pre-training (2018)
16. Radford, A., Wu, J., Child, R., Luan, D., Amodei, D., Sutskever, I., et al.: Language models are unsupervised multitask learners. OpenAI blog **1**(8), 9 (2019)
17. Rasul, K., et al.: Lag-llama: towards foundation models for time series forecasting. arXiv preprint arXiv:2310.08278 (2023)
18. Shen, Y., Jin, C., Hua, J., Huang, D.: Ttpnet: a neural network for travel time prediction based on tensor decomposition and graph embedding. IEEE Trans. Knowl. Data Eng. **34**(9), 4514–4526 (2022)

19. Sun, C., Li, Y., Li, H., Hong, S.: Test: text prototype aligned embedding to activate llm's ability for time series. arXiv preprint arXiv:2308.08241 (2023)
20. Touvron, Het al.: Llama: open and efficient foundation language models. arxiv:2302.13971 (2023)
21. Triebe, O., Hewamalage, H., Pilyugina, P., Laptev, N., Bergmeir, C., Rajagopal, R.: Neuralprophet: explainable forecasting at scale. arXiv preprint arXiv:2111.15397 (2021)
22. Wang, C., Zhao, F., Zhang, H., et al.: Fine-grained trajectory-based travel time estimation for multi-city scenarios based on deep meta-learning. IEEE Trans. Intell. Transp. Syst. **23**(9), 15716–15728 (2022)
23. Wang, W., Zhang, J., Cao, W., et al.: When will you arrive? Estimating travel time based on deep neural networks. In: Proceedings of the 32nd AAAI Conference on Artificial Intelligence, pp. 2500–2507 (2018)
24. Wang, Y., Zheng, Y., Xue, Y.: Travel time estimation of a path using sparse trajectories. In: Proceedings of the 20th ACM SIGKDD International Conference on Knowledge Discovery and Data Mining, pp. 25–34 (2014)
25. Zhang, Z., Wang, H., Fan, Z., et al.: GOF-TTE: generative online federated learning framework for travel time estimation. IEEE Internet Things J. **9**(23), 24107–24121 (2022)
26. Zhou, T., Niu, P., Sun, L., Jin, R., et al.: One fits all: Power general time series analysis by pretrained lm. Adv. Neural Inf. Process. Syst. **36** (2024)
27. Zhu, Y., Ye, Y., Liu, Y., Yu, J.J.Q.: Cross-area travel time uncertainty estimation from trajectory data: a federated learning approach. IEEE Trans. Intell. Transp. Syst. **23**(12), 24966–24978 (2022)

HTDiff: Self-Guiding Diffusion Models for Hand Trajectory Prediction

Yu Liu[1], Zipei Fan[1,2(✉)], Tianlv Huang[1], Wei Han[1], and Meiqi Zhou[3]

[1] School of Artificial Intelligence, Jilin University, Changchun 130012, Jilin, China
fanzipei@jlu.edu.cn
[2] LocationMind Inc., Tokyo 100-0004, Japan
[3] School of Computer Science and Technology, Changchun University of Science and Technology, Changchun 130022, Jilin, China

Abstract. Understanding human behavior is pivotal to the development of embodied artificial intelligence. Hand trajectories, as a critical medium of human interaction, offer a valuable lens through which to explore and interpret human actions. In this work, we propose a self-guided diffusion model for hand trajectory prediction (HTDiff). HTDiff consists of two main stages: The unconditional trajectory reconstruction stage learns from existing hand motion data to generate trajectory samples that conform to human motion patterns. In the conditional trajectory prediction stage, historical trajectories serve as contextual information to adaptively guide the pretrained reconstruction model in predicting future hand trajectories. Furthermore, we employ a Transformer architecture as the decoder within the diffusion model to fully exploit its strengths in sequence modeling, enabling the capture of temporal dependencies and complex motion patterns. Experiments conducted on public datasets reveal that HTDiff surpasses existing baseline methods in hand trajectory prediction, achieving the best performance across four evaluation metrics.

Keywords: Hand Trajectory Prediction · Diffusion Models · Conditional Generation

1 Introduction

Embodied artificial intelligence aims to achieve a comprehensive understanding of human behavior, with the ultimate objective of optimizing the performance of autonomous decision-making systems [16]. A fundamental approach to achieving this objective is the extraction of reusable and transferable knowledge from real-world human activities, which is critical for interpreting human intentions and behaviors. This includes a range of tasks, such as action recognition and anticipation [19, 28, 32, 33], temporal action localization [3, 13, 27], gaze prediction [10, 12], object affordance extraction [16, 29], and object interaction anticipation [18, 20].

The hand, as one of the most critical components of human behavioral interaction, has garnered extensive attention in the field of hand trajectory analysis [1,16,22]. However, most publicly available hand trajectory datasets are based on 2D pixel coordinates extracted from video frames. These trajectories represent motion features in the image coordinate system and cannot be directly mapped to the 3D coordinate system of the real world, thus limiting their application in real-world scenarios [1]. In contrast, 3D hand trajectory data captured through motion capture devices, such as RGB-D cameras or inertial measurement units (IMUs), offer higher accuracy and quality. However, due to the high cost of data collection and technical limitations, acquiring large-scale, high-quality datasets remains a significant challenge.

Diffusion Model [6,23], have shown outstanding performance on generative tasks across various domains [4,9,14,15] and have quickly become the framework of choice for generative modeling. Through conditional probability models, diffusion models can also be applied to prediction and imputation tasks [5,21,24]. However, this results in the loss of the ideal unconditional generative ability of the diffusion model [8]. Therefore, the current challenge in hand trajectory analysis is whether it is possible to construct an unconditional probabilistic diffusion model that can simultaneously address unconditional trajectory generation and be applied to conditional downstream tasks such as trajectory generation (i.e., prediction and imputation).

To address the aforementioned problem, we introduce HTDiff, an unconditional diffusion model for hand trajectory conditional generation. Inspired by guiding diffusion models [10], we propose a self-guiding conditional trajectory generation mechanism that allows for model adjustment during inference without the need for auxiliary networks. This enables the unconditional model to be applied to essentially conditional prediction tasks. Specifically, HTDiff optimizes the unconditional probabilistic diffusion model [6] based on Transformer [25] to accommodate unconditional trajectory generation (reconstruction) tasks. Moreover, leveraging the self-guiding mechanism with historical trajectories, HTDiff dynamically adjusts the model during the sampling process by using historical trajectories as conditional constraints, thereby enabling conditional trajectory generation (prediction).

In summary, the main contributions of this work are summarized as follows:

1. HTDiff is an unconditional diffusion model that incorporates a self-guiding mechanism during inference, eliminating the need for auxiliary networks. This enables it to effectively handle tasks that traditionally require conditional generation.
2. This work introduces a novel class of diffusion models by replacing the commonly used U-Net backbone with a Transformer architecture. This enhancement allows for improved capture of spatiotemporal dependencies in hand motion trajectories.
3. Extensive experiments on real-world trajectory datasets demonstrate that HTDiff outperforms existing baselines, producing trajectories with the highest level of plausibility.

2 Problem Statement

Let $\mathbf{X}_{1:\tau} = (x_1, \ldots, x_\tau) \in \mathbb{R}^{\tau \times d}$ denote a time series of hand trajectories observed over τ discrete time steps, where d represents the dimensionality of the trajectory features corresponding to the x, y, and z coordinates. Consider a dataset $\mathcal{D}_A = \{\mathbf{X}_{1:\tau}^i\}_{i=1}^N$ consisting of N such time-series samples. The main objective is to employ a diffusion-based generative model to approximate the underlying distribution of hand trajectories. Specifically, the goal is to learn a mapping function $\hat{\mathbf{X}}_{1:\tau}^i = \mathcal{G}(\mathbf{Z}_i)$, where $\mathcal{G}$ is a diffusion-based generator that transforms Gaussian latent vectors $\mathbf{Z}_i = (z_1^i, \ldots, z_T^i) \in \mathbb{R}^{\tau \times d \times T}$ into generated trajectories $\hat{\mathbf{X}}_{1:\tau}^i$ that closely match those in the dataset $\mathcal{D}_A$. Where, T denotes the total number of diffusion steps involved in the generative process. Subsequently, the self-guiding mechanism leverages the pre-trained generator $\mathcal{G}$ and incorporates historically observed trajectories as conditioning variables $\mathcal{C}$, thereby generating samples from the conditional distribution $p(\cdot \mid \mathcal{C})$.

3 Method

3.1 Overview

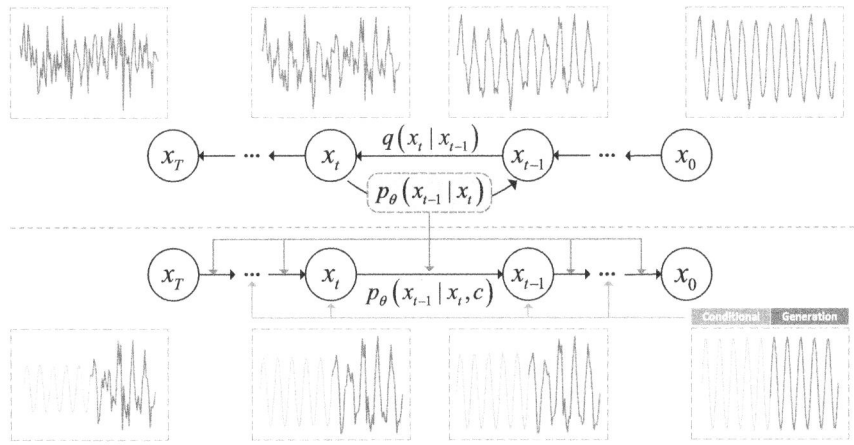

Fig. 1. An overview of the HTDiff Framework. The portion above the dashed line illustrates the forward noise addition and reverse denoising processes of the unconditional diffusion model during the pre-training phase. The portion below the dashed line shows how the self-guiding mechanism fine-tunes the pre-trained model's generation process during the inference phase, based on conditions (historical observation trajectories), enabling the unconditional diffusion model to be applied to conditional generation tasks.

Figure 1 illustrates the overall framework of HTDiff. By integrating the Transformer architecture [26], HTDiff effectively captures the inherent temporal dependencies within hand trajectory data. The framework consists of two main stages. The first stage is unconditional trajectory generation (reconstruction) (Sect. 3.2), where noise $q(x_t|x_{t-1})$ is gradually introduced to simulate the diffusion process of the trajectory. In this stage, the model learns the reverse denoising process $p_\theta(x_{t-1}|x_t)$, iteratively recovering the noisy trajectory and ultimately generating high-quality trajectory data. The second stage is self-guiding trajectory generation (prediction) (Sect. 3.3). The input consists of two components: the historical observation trajectory data as the condition, and the future trajectory to be generated, initialized as Gaussian noise ($x_T \sim \mathcal{N}(0, \mathbf{I})$). During the inference phase, HTDiff utilizes the trajectory reconstruction model, pre-trained in the first stage, to iteratively remove the noise, while the self-guiding mechanism $p_\theta(x_t|x_{t-1}, \mathcal{C})$ further guides the trajectory generation.

3.2 Unconditional Trajectory Generation (Reconstruction)

The diffusion model learns to capture the Markov transition from a simple distribution to the hand trajectory data distribution, generating diverse samples through sequential stochastic transitions, which typically consist of a forward diffusion process and a reverse denoising diffusion process. Specially, a sample $x_0 \sim q(x)$ from the data distribution is progressively corrupted with noise by the forward process, eventually transforming into standard Gaussian noise $x_T \sim \mathcal{N}(0, \mathbf{I})$. The transition of the forward process is parameterized as:

$$q(x_t|x_{t-1}) = \mathcal{N}(x_t; \sqrt{1-\beta_t}x_{t-1}, \beta_t \mathbf{I}), \qquad (1)$$

where $\beta_t \in (0, 1)$ represents the amount of noise added at each diffusion step t. Then neural network learns the reverse process, which iteratively denoises pure Gaussian noise to generate high-quality trajectories:

$$p_\theta(x_{t-1}|x_t) = \mathcal{N}(x_{t-1}; \mu_\theta(x_t, t), \Sigma_\theta(x_t, t)), \qquad (2)$$

where μ_θ represents the mean of the Gaussian distribution computed by a neural network, Σ_θ is the constant variance, and θ denotes the parameters of the network. As demonstrated by [6], the mean can be reparameterized to enable the neural network to directly learn the noise added at each time step t. In this approach, μ_θ can be reparameterized as follows:

$$\mu_\theta(x_t, t) = \frac{1}{\sqrt{\alpha_t}}\left(x_t - \frac{\beta_t}{\sqrt{1-\bar{\alpha}_t}}\epsilon_\theta(x_t, t)\right). \qquad (3)$$

Learning to denoise x_T via the reverse diffusion process can be seen as constructing a surrogate model that parameterizes $\mu_\theta(x_t, t)$ for all t, with the denoising model being trained using a weighted mean squared error loss:

$$\mathcal{L}(x_0) = \sum_{t=1}^{T} \mathbb{E}_{q(x_t|x_0)}\left[\|\mu(x_t, x_0) - \mu_\theta(x_t, t)\|^2\right]. \qquad (4)$$

3.3 Self-Guiding Trajectory Generation (Prediction)

Hand trajectory prediction can be seen as a conditional extension of trajectory reconstruction, where historical trajectory data as the condition $\mathcal{C}$ for generating the future trajectory x_0. Our goal is to leverage a pre-trained trajectory generation model and a self-guiding mechanism to approximate sampling from the posterior distribution:

$$p(x_{0:T} \mid \mathcal{C}) \propto \prod_{t=1}^{T} p(x_{t-1} \mid x_t) \, p(\mathcal{C} \mid x_{t-1}, x_t), \qquad (5)$$

where $p(x_{t-1} \mid x_t)$ denotes the transition probability defined by the pre-trained model, while $p(\mathcal{C} \mid x_{t-1}, x_t)$ represents the conditional transition probability modeled via parameterized self-guiding. This describes the likelihood of the target $\mathcal{C}$ given the states x_{t-1} and x_t.

By applying Bayes' theorem, we perform a gradient update on x_{t-1} to guide the generation process. Specifically, our objective is to optimize x_{t-1} in order to maximize the posterior probability of the generated sample conditioned on $\mathcal{C}$. The gradient update is controlled by the following score function:

$$\nabla_{x_{t-1}} \log p(x_{t-1} \mid x_t, \mathcal{C}) = \nabla_{x_{t-1}} \log p(x_{t-1} \mid x_t) + \nabla_{x_{t-1}} \log p(\mathcal{C} \mid x_{t-1}). \qquad (6)$$

For tasks such as imputation and forecasting of hand trajectories, we propose a method that combines both the conditional history trajectory x_a and the generative trajectory x_b to approximate conditional sampling. This approach can be defined as follows:

$$\tilde{x}_0(x_t, t, \theta) = \hat{x}_0(x_t, t, \theta) + \eta \nabla_{x_t} \left(\|x_a - \hat{x}_a(x_t, t, \theta)\|_2^2 + \gamma \log p(x_{t-1} \mid x_t) \right), \qquad (7)$$

where, γ is a hyperparameter that balances two terms: the first ensures conditional consistency (through the reconstruction of x_a), and the second promotes fluency (through $\log p(x_{t-1} \mid x_t)$). The gradient term can be interpreted as reconstruction-based guidance, with η controlling the strength of the update.

To further improve control over the generation process, we employed a multi-step gradient update strategy at each diffusion step, inspired by [11,30]. This approach helps to enhance the quality of conditional generation, with the pseudocode provided in Algorithm 1. Finally, the generated sample x_{t-1} can be derived using the updated $\tilde{x}_0$, expressed as:

$$\tilde{x}_a(x_t, t, \theta) := \sqrt{\bar{\alpha}_t} x_a + \sqrt{1 - \bar{\alpha}_t} \epsilon. \qquad (8)$$

4 Experiments

4.1 Experimental Settings

Datasets. We evaluated the proposed method on a public dataset [17], which consists of 3D hand motion trajectories captured by motion capture devices. In

Algorithm 1. Self-Guiding Sampling

Input:
Output:
1: $x_T \sim \mathcal{N}(0, \mathbf{I})$
2: **for** all t from T to 1 **do**
3:    **for** all i from $K[t]$ to 1 **do**
4:       $[\hat{x}_a, \hat{x}_b] \leftarrow \hat{x}_0(x_t, t, \theta)$
5:       $L_1 = \|x_a - \hat{x}_a\|_2^2$
6:       $x_{t-1} \leftarrow \mathcal{N}(\mu(\hat{x}_0(x_t, t, \theta), x_t), \Sigma)$
7:       $L_2 = \|x_{t-1} - \mu(\hat{x}_0(x_t, t, \theta), x_t)\|_2^2 / \Sigma$
8:       $x_t = x_t + \eta \nabla_x L_1 + \gamma L_2$
9:    **end for**
10:   $x_{t-1} \leftarrow \mathcal{N}(\mu(\hat{x}_0(x_t, t, \theta), x_t), \Sigma)$
11:   $x_{t-1} \leftarrow \text{Replace}(x_a, x_{t-1}, t)$
12: **end for**

this study, we selected two actions, Moving and Pick Up, as the evaluation targets[1]. Each sample consists of 69 trajectory points. All trajectory points are used to construct an unconditional trajectory reconstruction pretraining model. During inference, the last 30 time steps of the trajectory are masked and predicted, while the remaining points serve as conditions for generation.

Baseline. Hand trajectory data typically exhibit the characteristic of continuous time steps, where the state at each time step is influenced not only by the current input but also by the historical trajectory. To this end, this paper presents a comparison of several baseline time-series modeling methods, including Gated Recurrent Units (GRU) and Long Short-Term Memory (LSTM) networks, both implemented in PyTorch, as well as the Transformer [26] and Dliner [31]. GRU and LSTM are effective in capturing long-term dependencies within sequences, while the Transformer optimizes information transfer through self-attention mechanisms. Dliner, on the other hand, models time-series data using linear transformations. These methods provide distinct strategies for time-series modeling and serve as baseline comparisons for the proposed models. Furthermore, this paper introduces an enhancement to the DDPM [6] model by integrating it with the Transformer framework for unconditional trajectory generation, and demonstrates the effectiveness of the self-guiding mechanism in accurately predicting hand trajectories.

Evaluation Metrics. To validate the performance of the HTDiff model, this study selected four core evaluation metrics to quantitatively assess the quality of the generated hand trajectories. To ensure fairness and comparability, all tests strictly adhered to the evaluation standards outlined in the literature [16]. Specifically, the Average Displacement Error (ADE) was used to measure the

---
[1] https://github.com/ioai-tech/IO-ULTRA-EMBODIMENT-DATASET-DOC.

average deviation between the predicted and ground truth trajectories across the entire time series. The Final Displacement Error (FDE) focused on evaluating the accuracy of the predicted trajectory endpoint, quantifying the discrepancy between the predicted and ground truth endpoints. In addition, the study also employed Root Mean Square Error (RMSE) and standard deviation (STD) to measure the variability of the generated trajectories, thereby further verifying the stability of the model.

Implementing Details. The maximum time step T in HTDiff was set to 1000. Following the design by [2], the variance of the forward process was set to linearly increase from $\beta_1 = 10^{-4}$ to $\beta_T = 0.02$. We employed 4 transformer layers and used 6 attention heads in our model. The Adam optimizer [7] was applied with a learning rate of 1×10^{-5} to optimize the learnable parameters. All experiments were conducted using PyTorch on a single NVIDIA RTX 1060Ti GPU.

4.2 Experiments Results

Comparison with Baseline Model. In this study, we employ the HTDiff model alongside several baseline models for hand trajectory prediction and compare their performance in terms of evaluation metrics such as ADE, FDE, RMSE, and STD. As shown in Table 1, HTDiff outperforms all baseline models across all evaluation metrics. On the Moving dataset, HTDiff achieves improvements of at least 29%, 2%, 35.7%, and 36.3% in ADE, FDE, RMSE, and STD, respectively. On the Pick Up dataset, HTDiff demonstrates enhancements of at least 35.6%, 25.7%, 43.9%, and 46.5% in the same metrics. Additionally, by comparing with the Diff-Transformer model, we further validate the effectiveness of the self-guiding mechanism proposed in this paper for trajectory prediction.

Table 1. Results of hand trajectory prediction. The best and second-best models are shown in **bold** and underlined, respectively.

Method	Moving				Pickup			
	ADE ↓	FDE ↓	RMSE ↓	STD ↓	ADE ↓	FDE ↓	RMSE ↓	STD ↓
GRU	0.0703	0.0737	0.0440	0.0435	0.0697	0.0755	<u>0.0424</u>	<u>0.0418</u>
LSTM	0.0719	0.0786	<u>0.0437</u>	<u>0.0422</u>	0.0681	0.0753	0.0427	0.0426
Transformer	0.0791	0.0841	0.0462	0.0455	0.0786	0.0825	0.0458	0.0458
Dliner	<u>0.0631</u>	0.0660	0.0461	0.0463	<u>0.0596</u>	0.0657	0.0462	0.0552
Diff-Transformer	0.0804	<u>0.0642</u>	0.0480	0.0430	0.0724	<u>0.0626</u>	0.0446	0.0438
HTDiff (Ours)	**0.0448**	**0.0629**	**0.0282**	**0.0269**	**0.0384**	**0.0465**	**0.0238**	**0.0224**

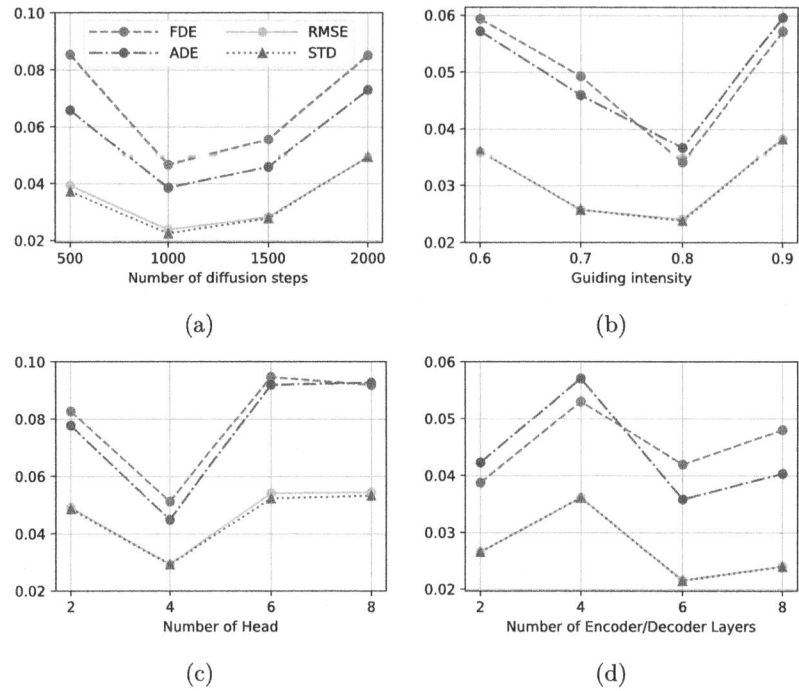

Fig. 2. Ablation study of different components. (a) The effect of diffusion time steps; (b) The impact of guiding strength; (c) The number of attention heads in the Transformer; (d) The number of encoder and decoder layers.

Ablation Study. In order to evaluate the contribution of various components in HTDiff, we performed four ablation experiments, as described below:

1. **Diffusion Step:** We assessed the impact of different diffusion time steps (500, 1000, 1500, 200) on HTDiff's performance. The experimental results, shown in Fig. 2 (a), reveal that the setting with 1000 steps achieves the smallest discrepancies in terms of ADE and FDE, demonstrating the most accurate and stable trajectory generation. This observation is further corroborated by the results from RMSE and STD.
2. **Guiding Intensity:** This study examines the influence of various guiding intensities (0.6, 0.7, 0.8, 0.9) during the self-guiding sampling phase, as described in Eq. 7, on prediction accuracy. The experimental results, presented in Fig. 2, indicate that higher guiding intensities enhance prediction accuracy, thereby validating the effectiveness of the self-guiding mechanism. However, excessively high guiding intensities may impair the model's ability to reconstruct trajectories, potentially leading to overfitting to the conditions.
3. **Transformer:** The Transformer model is utilized to capture complex dependencies in trajectory data through self-attention mechanisms. In this study, we investigate the effects of varying the number of layers in both the encoder

and decoder (2, 4, 6, 8) as well as the number of attention heads (2, 4, 6, 8) on model performance. The results, shown in Figs. 2 (c) and 2 (d), demonstrate that the model performs optimally with 6 layers and 4 attention heads, balancing model complexity and prediction accuracy.

5 Conclusion

In this work, we introduce HTDiff, a self-guiding diffusion model designed to enhance hand trajectory prediction for conditional tasks by adapting an unconditional pre-trained model through a self-guiding mechanism. Experiments on public datasets demonstrate that HTDiff outperforms existing methods, achieving improvements of at least 29%, 2%, 35.7%, and 36.3% in ADE, FDE, RMSE, and STD, respectively. On the Pick Up dataset, HTDiff shows improvements of at least 35.6%, 25.7%, 43.9%, and 46.5% in the same metrics. hese results suggest that HTDiff is a valuable tool for hand trajectory data augmentation and prediction, which can enhance the understanding of human behavior and contribute to the development of embodied intelligence.

Disclosure of Interests. The authors have no competing interests to declare.

References

1. Bao, W., et al.: Uncertainty-aware state space transformer for egocentric 3d hand trajectory forecasting. In: Proceedings of the IEEE/CVF International Conference on Computer Vision, pp. 13702–13711 (2023)
2. Chai, S., Zhuang, L., Yan, F.: Layoutdm: transformer-based diffusion model for layout generation. In: Proceedings of the IEEE/CVF Conference on Computer Vision and Pattern Recognition, pp. 18349–18358 (2023)
3. Chen, M., Gao, J., Xu, C.: Uncertainty-aware dual-evidential learning for weakly-supervised temporal action localization. IEEE Trans. Pattern Anal. Mach. Intell. (2023)
4. Dhariwal, P., Nichol, A.Q.: Diffusion models beat GANs on image synthesis. In: Beygelzimer, A., Dauphin, Y., Liang, P., Vaughan, J.W. (eds.) Advances in Neural Information Processing Systems (2021)
5. Godahewa, R., Bergmeir, C., Webb, G.I., Hyndman, R.J., Montero-Manso, P.: Monash time series forecasting archive. arXiv preprint arXiv:2105.06643 (2021)
6. Ho, J., Jain, A., Abbeel, P.: Denoising diffusion probabilistic models. Adv. Neural. Inf. Process. Syst. **33**, 6840–6851 (2020)
7. Kingma, D.P.: Adam: a method for stochastic optimization. arXiv preprint arXiv:1412.6980 (2014)
8. Kollovieh, M., Ansari, A.F., Bohlke-Schneider, M., Zschiegner, J., Wang, H., Wang, Y.B.: Predict, refine, synthesize: self-guiding diffusion models for probabilistic time series forecasting. Adv. Neural Inf. Process. Syst. **36** (2024)
9. Kong, Z., Ping, W., Huang, J., Zhao, K., Catanzaro, B.: Diffwave: a versatile diffusion model for audio synthesis. arXiv preprint arXiv:2009.09761 (2020)
10. Lai, B., Liu, M., Ryan, F., Rehg, J.M.: In the eye of transformer: global-local correlation for egocentric gaze estimation and beyond. Int. J. Comput. Vision **132**(3), 854–871 (2024)

11. Li, X.L., Thickstun, J., Gulrajani, I., Liang, P., Hashimoto, T.: Diffusion-LM improves controllable text generation. In: Oh, A.H., Agarwal, A., Belgrave, D., Cho, K. (eds.) Advances in Neural Information Processing Systems (2022)
12. Li, Y., Liu, M., Rehg, J.M.: In the eye of beholder: joint learning of gaze and actions in first person video. In: Proceedings of the European conference on computer vision (ECCV), pp. 619–635 (2018)
13. Li, Z., Zhong, Y., Song, R., Li, T., Ma, L., Zhang, W.: Detal: open-vocabulary temporal action localization with decoupled networks. IEEE Trans. Pattern Anal. Mach. Intell. (2024)
14. Lienen, M., Lüdke, D., Hansen-Palmus, J., Günnemann, S.: From zero to turbulence: generative modeling for 3d flow simulation. arXiv preprint arXiv:2306.01776 (2023)
15. Lüdke, D., Biloš, M., Shchur, O., Lienen, M., Günnemann, S.: Add and thin: diffusion for temporal point processes. Adv. Neural. Inf. Process. Syst. **36**, 56784–56801 (2023)
16. Ma, J., Chen, X., Bao, W., Xu, J., Wang, H.: Madiff: motion-aware mamba diffusion models for hand trajectory prediction on egocentric videos. arXiv preprint arXiv:2409.02638 (2024)
17. O'Neill, A., et al.: Open x-embodiment: robotic learning datasets and rt-x models: open x-embodiment collaboration 0. In: 2024 IEEE International Conference on Robotics and Automation (ICRA), pp. 6892–6903. IEEE (2024)
18. Pasca, R.G., et al.: Summarize the past to predict the future: natural language descriptions of context boost multimodal object interaction anticipation. In: Proceedings of the IEEE/CVF Conference on Computer Vision and Pattern Recognition, pp. 18286–18296 (2024)
19. Qi, Z., Wang, S., Zhang, W., Huang, Q.: Uncertainty-boosted robust video activity anticipation. IEEE Trans. Pattern Anal. Mach. Intell. (2024)
20. Ragusa, F., Farinella, G.M., Furnari, A.: Stillfast: an end-to-end approach for short-term object interaction anticipation. In: Proceedings of the IEEE/CVF Conference on Computer Vision and Pattern Recognition, pp. 3636–3645 (2023)
21. Rasul, K., Seward, C., Schuster, I., Vollgraf, R.: Autoregressive denoising diffusion models for multivariate probabilistic time series forecasting. In: International Conference on Machine Learning, pp. 8857–8868. PMLR (2021)
22. Shan, D., Geng, J., Shu, M., Fouhey, D.F.: Understanding human hands in contact at internet scale. In: Proceedings of the IEEE/CVF Conference on Computer Vision and Pattern Recognition, pp. 9869–9878 (2020)
23. Sohl-Dickstein, J., Weiss, E., Maheswaranathan, N., Ganguli, S.: Deep unsupervised learning using nonequilibrium thermodynamics. In: International Conference on Machine Learning, pp. 2256–2265. PMLR (2015)
24. Tashiro, Y., Song, J., Song, Y., Ermon, S.: CSDI: conditional score-based diffusion models for probabilistic time series imputation. Adv. Neural. Inf. Process. Syst. **34**, 24804–24816 (2021)
25. Vaswani, A.: Attention is all you need. Adv. Neural Inf. Process. Syst. (2017)
26. Vaswani, A., et al.: Attention is all you need. In: Proceedings of the 31st International Conference on Neural Information Processing Systems, NIPS'17, pp. 6000–6010. Curran Associates Inc., Red Hook (2017)
27. Wang, B., Zhao, Y., Yang, L., Long, T., Li, X.: Temporal action localization in the deep learning era: a survey. IEEE Trans. Pattern Anal. Mach. Intell. (2023)
28. Wang, X., Zhang, W., Wang, C., Gao, Y., Liu, M.: Dynamic dense graph convolutional network for skeleton-based human motion prediction. IEEE Trans. Image Process. **33**, 1–15 (2023)

29. Ye, Y., et al.: Affordance diffusion: synthesizing hand-object interactions. In: Proceedings of the IEEE/CVF Conference on Computer Vision and Pattern Recognition, pp. 22479–22489 (2023)
30. Yuan, X., Qiao, Y.: Diffusion-TS: interpretable diffusion for general time series generation. In: The Twelfth International Conference on Learning Representations (2024)
31. Zeng, A., Chen, M., Zhang, L., Xu, Q.: Are transformers effective for time series forecasting? In: Proceedings of the Thirty-Seventh AAAI Conference on Artificial Intelligence and Thirty-Fifth Conference on Innovative Applications of Artificial Intelligence and Thirteenth Symposium on Educational Advances in Artificial Intelligence. AAAI'23/IAAI'23/EAAI'23, AAAI Press (2023)
32. Zhang, C., et al.: Object-centric video representation for long-term action anticipation. In: Proceedings of the IEEE/CVF Winter Conference on Applications of Computer Vision, pp. 6751–6761 (2024)
33. Zheng, Y.D., Chen, G., Yuan, M., Lu, T.: MRSN: multi-relation support network for video action detection. In: 2023 IEEE International Conference on Multimedia and Expo (ICME), pp. 1026–1031. IEEE (2023)

A Method for Ship Trajectory Repair Based on Feature Correlation and SHAP Model Interpretability

Lin Ye, Xiaohui Chen[✉], Haiyan Liu, Ran Zhang, Bing Zhang, and Mingqi Zheng

Information Engineering University, Zhengzhou 450000, China
cxh_vis@163.com

Abstract. Aiming at the challenges of data integrity and reliability arising from the sparsity of ship trajectory data, this study proposes a ship sparse trajectory repair method combining feature correlation analysis and the interpretability of the SHapley Additive exPlanations (SHAP) model. Firstly, the methodology involves an analysis of sparse points and outliers within ship trajectory data to identify and address data omissions and anomalies. Subsequently, a comprehensive index of feature correlation is employed to select relevant features to trajectory repair, thereby reducing information redundancy and enhancing the precision of the repair process. Finally, utilizing the interpretability of the SHAP model, an interpretable ship trajectory repair model is constructed on a neural network framework, facilitating trajectory recovery and attribution analysis. The experimental outcomes indicate that the proposed method significantly enhances the accuracy and reliability of trajectory repair. By integrating feature correlation analysis with the interpretability of the SHAP model, this study not only refines the accuracy of ship trajectory repair but also provides a new idea for the interpretability of trajectory data repair models.

Keywords: AIS · Sparse Trajectories · Feature Correlation · SHAP Model · Interpretability Analysis · Trajectory Repair

1 Introduction

Automatic Identification System (AIS) is a widely used navigational aid for maritime safety and communication, and ship trajectory data plays a vital role in many fields such as shipping [1] and traffic monitoring [2, 3]. Obtaining effective ship trajectory data information not only helps to improve the efficiency of maritime traffic management but also enhances the accuracy and safety of ship navigation, thus reducing the occurrence of maritime accidents such as ship collisions [4, 5]. However, the sparsity and incompleteness of ship trajectory data due to equipment failure, environmental interference, and other factors, seriously affect the quality of ship trajectory data and the accuracy of subsequent trajectory analysis [6, 7]. AIS data problems are mainly manifested in the dynamic attribute information in the ship's navigation trajectory data, such as longitude and latitude. Specifically, the error of AIS data mainly consists of two aspects: on the one hand, the wrong data trajectory points appear when the ship's latitude and longitude change suddenly; on the other hand, the trajectory points are lost when the speed is not zero and the latitude, longitude, and heading do not change much. These problems not only seriously affect the ship collision avoidance decision-making and lead to wrong risk judgment, but also the missing trajectory data do not comply with the requirements of maritime supervision [8]. Therefore, there is a need to design a suitable trajectory repair method for improving the quality of raw AIS data, which is of great significance for safeguarding ship navigation and maritime traffic safety.

In the current research, ship trajectory repair methods can be mainly categorized into three aspects, including rule-based methods, interpolation methods, and machine learning methods. The rule-based repair method mainly relies on expert experience, and although the repair results have a certain degree of interpretability, the flexibility and generalization ability of its method is limited, and it is difficult to cope with the diverse ship trajectory repair needs [9]. Interpolation methods mainly include linear interpolation and spline interpolation. Such methods perform numerical calculations by constructing mathematical formulas, which can be used to improve the quality of AIS data, especially in ship trajectory reconstruction. However, the existing interpolation methods are difficult to effectively deal with large-scale missing data or complex trajectory patterns, resulting in unsatisfactory restoration results, and thus have limitations in solving the problem of missing ship trajectory data over long distances [10–12]. With the rapid development of artificial intelligence technology, machine learning methods have gradually become a research hotspot in various fields, especially in the field of intelligent transportation and big data, where data-driven-based methods are widely used. Deep learning models, such as Long Short-Term Memory (LSTM) networks and Gated Recurrent Units (GRU), perform particularly well in the trajectory repair task because of their strong nonlinear fitting ability and efficient processing of complex spatio-temporal dependencies. These models can automatically learn features from massive data and capture long-term dependencies and dynamic change patterns in trajectory data, thus significantly improving the accuracy and robustness of trajectory repair [13–16]. However, these models built on neural network architectures are usually regarded as "black boxes" whose decision-making process lacks transparency, making it difficult for users to understand their internal operation mechanisms. Therefore, increasing the interpretability of the model not only helps people understand the repair logic of the model but also allows for attribution analysis of the model results.

Although existing ship trajectory repair methods have achieved certain results in specific scenarios, they generally face the following challenges: first, when dealing with large-scale missing ship trajectory data, the repair accuracy and robustness of existing methods are often insufficient to cope with complex and changing real-world scenarios; second, the selection of features in the input model has an important impact on the repair accuracy, and there are still limitations of the existing methods in feature screening and optimization; finally, the lack of interpretability limits their wide application in high-security and high-risk fields such as shipping. Secondly, the selection of input model features has an important impact on the restoration accuracy, while the existing methods still have limitations in feature screening and optimization, which may lead to information redundancy or missing key features; finally, the inadequacy of the existing methods in terms of interpretability restricts their wide application in high-security and high-risk fields, such as shipping, and it is difficult to satisfy the demand for model transparency and decision-making credibility in practical applications. Therefore, there is an urgent need for a ship trajectory repair method that can significantly improve the repair accuracy and possesses good interpretability, to cope with the practical needs in complex data environments and provide reliable support for decision-making in related fields.

To address the above challenges, this study proposes a ship sparse trajectory repair method that combines feature correlation and SHAP model interpretability. First, the missing and abnormal data in the data are processed by recognizing the sparse and abnormal points in the ship trajectory data. Second, a comprehensive index of feature relevance is constructed to screen out the features that are closely related to trajectory repair and provide a sufficient number of interpretable training samples for the trajectory repair model. Finally, based on the neural network architecture, a novel ship trajectory repair model is constructed by utilizing the interpretability of the SHAP model. By combining feature correlation analysis with the interpretability of the SHAP model, the model not only achieves high-precision trajectory repair but also calculates the importance of the input variables through attribution analysis and determines the contribution

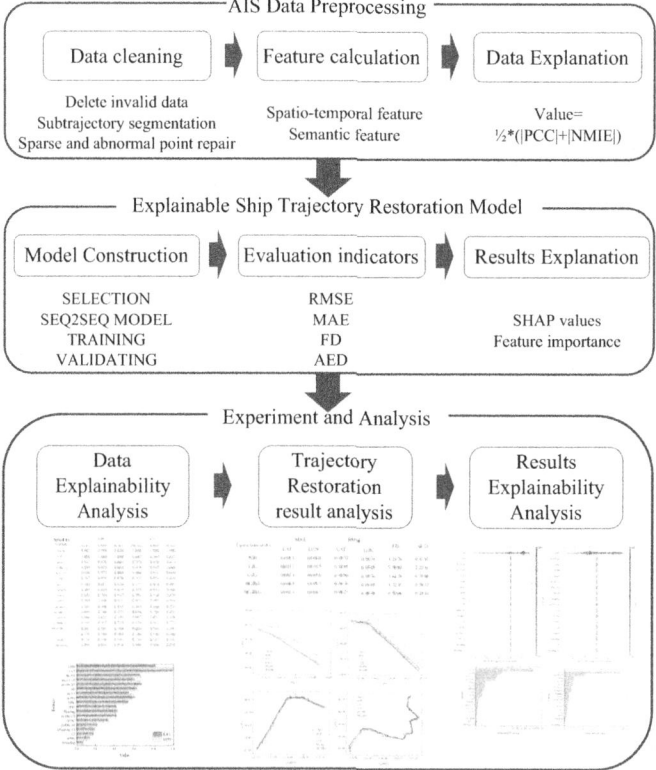

Fig. 1. Overall framework of the ship trajectory repair model

of each input variable to the repaired trajectory, which enhances the credibility of the model. The overall process is shown in Fig. 1.

2 AIS Data Preprocessing

2.1 Data Cleaning

There are often problems such as trajectory data loss, noise, or error in AIS data, which affect the data quality. Aiming at these problems, this study firstly cleans the original trajectory data and eliminates the outliers and noise interference through technical means such as filtering and denoising, to improve the reliability of the trajectory data. Secondly, discontinuous ship trajectories are further eliminated to ensure the continuity of the trajectory data, which lays the data foundation for the subsequent research. Finally, by identifying the sparse and abnormal points and repairing them initially to reduce the impact of missing data on the analysis results, high-quality data is provided for the subsequent feature calculation and model operation.

The steps of AIS data cleaning are as follows: (1) Invalid data deletion. Delete invalid data from AIS data whose MMSI code is not 9 digits, delete data beyond the range of values, and delete time-duplicated records in each category of track points after categorizing track points according to MMSI number. (2) Discontinuous track segmentation. To reduce the discontinuity of AIS data, the trajectory segmentation is processed based on the time threshold method. Based on expert experience, 30 min is selected as the time threshold for segmentation processing, and trajectory segments with less than 30 points are deleted [17]. (3) Sparse and anomaly repair. Based on previous studies [17, 18], 3 min is determined as the interpolation judgment threshold, and if the distance between adjacent points is greater than 2 times the threshold, it indicates that the trajectory segment is sparse, i.e., there is missing data, and marks it as a trajectory restoration point; secondly, based on the default of 24 knots as the maximal COG the maximum sailing theoretical distance is calculated between neighboring trajectory points, and if the actual distance is greater than the theoretical distance, then it is determined as anomalous point and is Marking trajectory anomalies. Three times spline interpolation operation is performed on the labeled sparse and anomalous points to ensure the data quality.

2.2 Feature Calculation

The dynamic information of ship trajectory mainly includes the longitude (LON), latitude (LAT), time, SOG, COG, and Heading of the trajectory points. To facilitate the calculation of the correlation between the ship trajectory points, we introduce fine-grained features. Specifically, we extracted and computed the following 18 features: the LON, LAT, SOG, COG, Heading, time interval (ΔT), longitude variability (ΔLON), latitude variability (ΔLAT), distance variability (ΔD), SOG variability (ΔSOG), COG variability (ΔCOG), and Heading variability ($\Delta Heading$), longitude rate of change ($\Delta LON/\Delta T$), latitude rate of change ($\Delta LAT/\Delta T$), distance rate of change ($\Delta D/\Delta T$), SOG rate of change ($\Delta SOG/\Delta T$), COG rate of change ($\Delta COG/\Delta T$), Heading rate of change ($\Delta Heading/\Delta T$). These spatio-temporal and semantic features of ship trajectories not only have the spatio-temporal information of ship trajectory movement but also cover the dynamic changes of ship trajectories.

2.3 Data Explanation

In the ship trajectory repair task, preprocessing of input data and feature relevance screening are key steps to improve model performance and interpretability. By screening the most relevant features to the ship trajectory, the model inputs can be significantly simplified, redundant information can be reduced, and the interpretability of the model can be enhanced, to provide more accurate and efficient data support for the subsequent trajectory repair.

Feature relevance calculation is the core process of extracting the most relevant features for ship trajectory repair from the original data, and its purpose is to filter out the features that contribute the most to the repair task by quantifying the relationship between the features and the target variables, to optimize the model input and improve the overall performance. In this study, we use Pearson's correlation coefficient and mutual information method to calculate feature relevance. Pearson's correlation coefficient can effectively measure linear relationships, while the mutual information method is suitable for capturing non-linear dependencies. The combination of the two can comprehensively assess the correlation between features and ship trajectories to ensure that the filtered feature set is representative and meets the model's requirements.

(1) Pearson correlation coefficient

The Pearson correlation coefficient (PCC) is used to measure the correlation between the input features and the variable to be repaired (e.g. latitude and longitude of the ship's position). It takes values in the range of $[-1, 1]$, where ± 1 means perfectly positive/negative correlation, and, 0 means no correlation. By calculating the Pearson's correlation coefficient between each input feature and the variable to be repaired, features that are highly correlated with trajectory repair can be filtered out.

$$PCC_{(X,Y)} = \frac{\sum_{i=1}^{n}(X_i - \overline{X})(Y_i - \overline{Y})}{\sqrt{\sum_{i=1}^{n}(X_i - \overline{X})^2}\sqrt{\sum_{i=1}^{n}(Y_i - \overline{Y})^2}} \tag{1}$$

where X and $\overline{X}$ denote the feature values and mean values of the input variables, Y and $\overline{Y}$ denote the feature values and mean values of the surrogate repair variables, respectively.

(2) Mutual information method.

The mutual information method is a statistical method applicable to nonlinear relationships that provides a more comprehensive assessment of the correlation between the input features and the variable to be repaired. Mutual information measures the statistical dependence between two variables, and the larger its value, the stronger the correlation between the feature and the target variable. Compared with Pearson's correlation coefficient, the mutual information method can not only capture linear relationships, but also effectively identify nonlinear dependencies, and therefore has more advantages when dealing with complex trajectory data.

To facilitate the subsequent calculation and analysis, this study adopts the Normalized Mutual Information Entropy (NMIE) to calculate the mutual information between variables. NMIE limits the range of values between [0, 1] by normalizing the values of mutual information, thus facilitating the comparison and screening between different features. The specific calculation formula is as follows:

$$\begin{cases} NMIE_{(X,Y)} = 2\dfrac{MIE_{(X,Y)}}{H(X)+H(Y)} \\ MIE_{(X,Y)} = \sum_{i=1}^{m}\sum_{j=1}^{n} P(X_i, Y_j) \log_2 \dfrac{P(X_i, Y_j)}{P(X_j)P(Y_i)} \\ H(X) = -\sum_{i}^{n} P(X_i) \log(P(X_i)) \end{cases} \quad (2)$$

where, $P(\bullet)$ is edge probability density functions of a variable.

To comprehensively assess the relevance of the input features to the variables to be repaired, the study constructs a composite feature relevance index through weighted summation. The formula is as follows:

$$Value = 1/2 \times (|PCC_{(X,Y)}| + |NMIE_{(X,Y)}|) \quad (3)$$

Among them, to balance the Pearson correlation coefficient and mutual information contribution, the weight is selected as 0.5.

3 Explainable Ship Trajectory Restoration Model

3.1 Model Construction

The core goal of trajectory repair is to minimize the error between the repaired trajectory and the real trajectory through the training data to achieve high-precision trajectory reconstruction. In this study, we adopt the sequence-to-sequence (Seq2Seq) architecture to construct a ship trajectory repair model. Seq2Seq is a generalized encoder-decoder-based framework, which centers on the use of an encoder to extract key spatio-temporal features from ship trajectory data and encode them into a sequence of trajectory states. This sequence can accurately characterize the original trajectory information and provide a reliable basis for inferring the real trajectory. Subsequently, the decoder gradually generates the repaired trajectory sequence based on the feature information extracted by the encoder, thus realizing high-precision repair of missing or abnormal trajectories. The specific framework is shown in Fig. 2. Through this end-to-end learning mechanism, the Seq2Seq architecture is not only able to effectively capture the nonlinear relationships in the trajectory data, but also adapt to repair tasks of different complexity and scale, providing powerful technical support for ship trajectory repair.

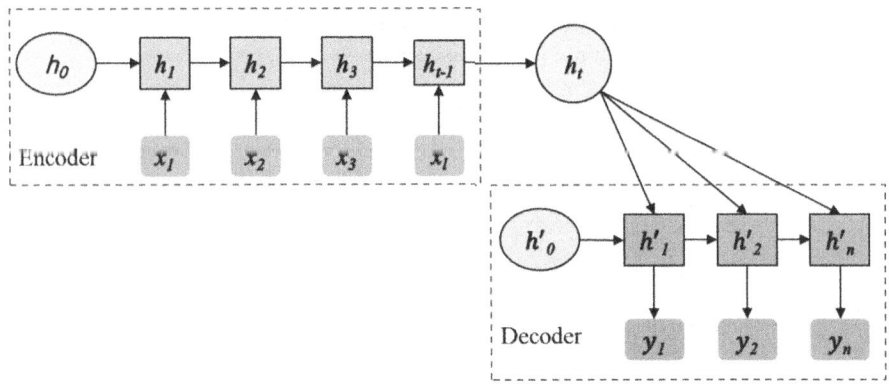

Fig. 2. Model infrastructure diagram

In this study, the partitioned dataset is input into the model. The input sequence $X = \{x_1, x_2, \cdots, x_l\}$ is fed into the encoder, which in turn generates the hidden state vector, and the computational process is represented as:

$$h_t = f_{\text{encoder}}(x_t, h_{t-1}; \theta_{\text{encoder}}) \quad (4)$$

where, f_{encoder} is the network structure of the encoder, θ_{encoder} is the network parameter to be learned by the encoder, h_{t-1} is the hidden state at time step $t-1$, and h_t is the final hidden state vector.

Based on this potential representation h_T, the decoder gradually generates an output sequence of predicted data $Y = \{y_1, y_2, \cdots, y_n\}$, the calculation process is expressed as:

$$y_t = f_{\text{decoder}}(h_t, y_{t-1}; \theta_{\text{decoder}}) \quad (5)$$

where, f_{decoder} is the network structure of the decoder, and θ_{decoder} is the network parameter to be learned by the decoder.

3.2 Results Explanation

SHAP is a game theory-based interpretation method designed to provide an interpretable basis for the model's restoration results. The core idea is to quantify the contribution of each input feature to the repair model output through Shapley values. Therefore, we use the Shapley value to measure the contribution of each input feature to the results of the trajectory repair model. The Shapley value is calculated using the following formula:

$$\phi_i = \sum_{S \subseteq F \setminus \{i\}} \frac{|S|!(|F| - |S| - 1)!}{|F|!} (f(S \cup \{i\}) - f(S)) \quad (6)$$

Among them, ϕ is the Shapley value of the feature i, F is the set of all features, S is a subset of F that does not contain the feature i, and $f(S)$ is the predicted value of the model when the feature subset S is used.

For each repaired track point, SHAP calculates the Shapley value for each input feature (such as longitude, latitude, speed, heading, etc.). These values represent the degree of contribution of features to the restoration results, positive values indicate that features have a positive impact on the restoration results, and negative values indicate a negative impact.

3.3 Evaluation Indicators

In this study, a series of evaluation metrics were used to provide a comprehensive and quantitative assessment of trajectory repair results. These metrics include Root Mean Square Error (RMSE), Mean Absolute Error (MAE), Fréchet Distance (FD), and Average Euclidean Distance (AED). These metrics reflect the accuracy and quality of trajectory repair from different perspectives, providing strong support for the comprehensive assessment of model performance.

RMSE: This metric quantifies the overall accuracy of the repair result by calculating the square root of the mean of the sum of squares of errors between the repaired trajectory and the true trajectory. RMSE is more sensitive to large errors and can effectively reflect the performance of the model when dealing with complex trajectories.

MAE: MAE visually shows the average level of repair error by calculating the average of the absolute value of the error between the repair trajectory and the true trajectory. This metric treats all errors equally, providing a direct view of repair accuracy.

FD: FD is a geometric measure of the similarity of two curves, which reflects the degree to which the repaired trajectory matches the real trajectory in shape. This index not only considers the position information of trajectory points but also takes into account the continuity and overall shape of the trajectory, which can effectively evaluate the model's ability to restore trajectory shape.

AED: The AED reflects the position accuracy of the repaired track point by calculating the average Euclidean distance between the repaired track point and the real track point. This index focuses on the exact location of trajectory points and provides an important reference for evaluating the repair ability of the model in local details.

Its calculation formula is as follows:

$$\begin{cases} \text{RMSE} = \sqrt{\dfrac{1}{n}\sum_{i=1}^{n}(Z_{\text{ture},i} - Z_{\text{re},i})^2} \\ \text{MAE} = \dfrac{1}{n}\sum_{i=1}^{n}|Z_{\text{ture},i} - Z_{\text{re},i}| \\ \text{FD} = \max_{[1,n]}\sqrt{(x_{\text{ture},i} - x_{\text{re},i})^2 + (y_{\text{ture},i} - y_{\text{re},i})^2} \\ \text{AED} = \dfrac{\sum_{i=1}^{n}\sqrt{(x_{\text{ture},i} - x_{\text{re},i})^2 + (y_{\text{ture},i} - y_{\text{re},i})^2}}{n} \end{cases} \quad (7)$$

where, the unit of RMSE value and MAE value are both in degrees, and the common unit of a nautical mile at sea is used as the unit of FD and AED, n is the number of samples,

$Z_{ture,i}$ and $Z_{re,i}$ are the true value of the feature and the repair value, $x_{ture,i}$, $y_{ture,i}$, $x_{re,i}$, and $y_{re,i}$ are the true value of the longitude and latitude after projection and the repair value respectively.

4 Experiment and Analysis

4.1 Experimental Data and Model Parameter Configuration

The ship trajectory data source used in this study is derived from the AIS dataset downloaded from marinecadastre.gov. The original AIS dataset includes both dynamic and static information about the ship, which includes multi-dimensional information such as MMSI, latitude, longitude, and SOG. Following this, the study area was chosen as the eastern oceanic region of North America, which spans the latitude and longitude from 121.75°W to 128.25°W and 40.05°N to 50.35°N.

We used PyTorch to implement the ship trajectory repair model and conducted experiments on the following hardware platforms (CPU: Intel Xeon Gold 6230, GPU: NVIDIA GeForce RTX 3090.) In addition, the parameters of the model experiments were set as follows: the hidden layer unit in the neural network was set to 256, the number of neural network layers was set to 5, the batch size was set to 512, and the number of iterations batch was set to 50. The Mean Square Error (MSE) was chosen as the loss, Adam as the optimizer, the learning rate was initially set to 0.001, the learning rate adjustment multiplier was 0.9, and the loss rate was 0.1.

4.2 Data Explainability Analysis

To assess the importance of each feature in ship trajectory restoration, this study calculates the integrated index value of feature relevance for each ship trajectory, and by calculating its average value as the final index. The specific results are shown in Table 1. It can be seen that the two variables, LAT and LON, have the largest values, indicating that they have extremely high relevance in ship trajectory repair. In addition, the correlations between LAT and LON and other features also show high values, for example, the correlations with $\Delta D/\Delta T$ (are 0.661 and 0.674, respectively, indicating that there is a strong correlation between the change in the ship's position and the change of speed.

Table 1. Feature Correlation Indicator Values

Indicators Values	LAT			LON		
	PPC	NMIE	Value	PPC	NMIE	Value
LON	0.682	0.958	0.820	1.000	1.000	1.000
LAT	1.000	1.000	1.000	0.682	0.959	0.821
$\Delta D/\Delta T$	0.347	0.975	0.661	0.373	0.976	0.674
$\Delta LON/\Delta T$	0.295	0.914	0.604	0.418	0.912	0.665
$\Delta LAT/\Delta T$	0.438	0.922	0.680	0.366	0.925	0.646

(*continued*)

Table 1. (*continued*)

Indicators Values	LAT			LON		
	PPC	NMIE	Value	PPC	NMIE	Value
ΔD	0.282	0.975	0.628	0.314	0.975	0.644
ΔLAT	0.268	0.821	0.545	0.377	0.818	0.597
ΔLON	0.389	0.839	0.614	0.329	0.844	0.586
COG	0.325	0.759	0.542	0.291	0.758	0.525
SOG	0.385	0.456	0.421	0.412	0.454	0.433
Heading	0.383	0.486	0.434	0.363	0.486	0.424
ΔCOG/ΔT	0.059	0.788	0.423	0.058	0.788	0.423
ΔCOG	0.056	0.624	0.340	0.057	0.624	0.340
ΔSOG/ΔT	0.134	0.312	0.223	0.134	0.313	0.223
ΔHeading/ΔT	0.097	0.291	0.194	0.094	0.293	0.193
ΔT	0.179	0.189	0.184	0.184	0.188	0.186
ΔSOG	0.135	0.146	0.141	0.135	0.147	0.141
ΔHeading	0.095	0.044	0.070	0.095	0.046	0.070

Figure 3 further demonstrates the correlation between other features with longitude (LON) and latitude (LAT). As can be seen from the figure, there is a significant correlation between the position change rate features (e.g., ΔLON/ΔT and ΔLAT/ΔT) and LAT and LON, which suggests that these features have a high reference value in trajectory repair tasks. Specifically, ΔLON/ΔT and ΔLAT/ΔT reflect the rate of position change of the ship in the longitude and latitude directions, respectively, which can directly characterize the ship's motion trend, and thus are of great significance in guiding the trajectory repair. In contrast, the dynamic features of heading speed (e.g., COG, SOG, and Heading) have lower correlations with longitude and latitude, indicating that their roles in trajectory repair are relatively weak. Although these features can reflect the ship's navigational state, their direct contribution to position change is limited, and thus they are less important than position change rate features in trajectory repair. In addition, the time-dependent features (e.g., ΔT and ΔHeading/ΔT) are weakly correlated with longitude and latitude, suggesting that they have less impact on trajectory repair. These features mainly describe time intervals and heading change rates, and although they may have an auxiliary role in trajectory repair in some specific scenarios, their overall contribution is relatively limited. In summary, the position change rate features have a high reference value in trajectory repair, while the heading speed dynamic features and time-related features have a relatively weak role.

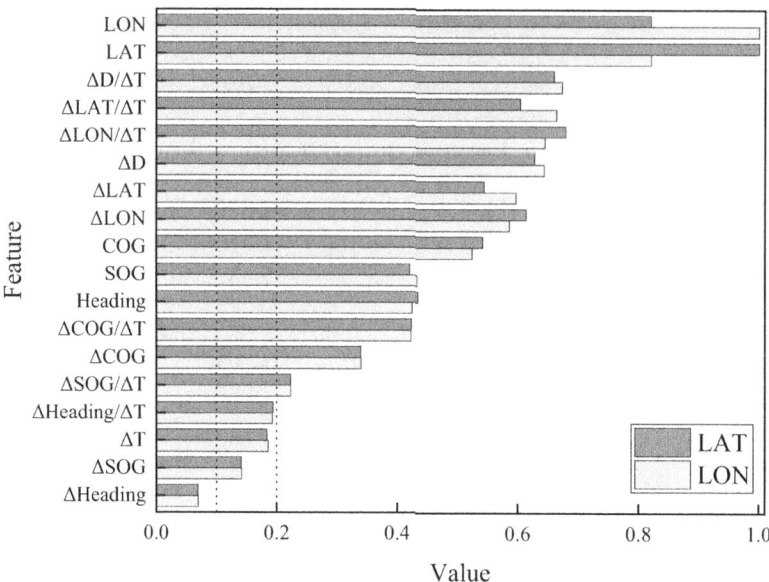

Fig. 3. Correlation results of latitude and longitude features

4.3 Trajectory Restoration Result Analysis

Typical recurrent neural network models (e.g., RNN, LSTM, BILSTM, and GRU) were selected for the study as baseline models for comparison experiments. In the Seq2Seq-based ship trajectory repair model, the structural design of the encoder and decoder has an important impact on the trajectory prediction effect. To comprehensively evaluate and compare the repair performance of different model architectures, multiple Seq2Seq model variants are constructed in this study, including the baseline Seq2Seq (R2R) model, as well as models with LSTM (L2L), BILSTM (BL2BL), GRU (G2G), and BIGRU (BG2BG) units for the encoder and decoder, respectively.

By statistically analyzing the LOSS values of the training data, the changes in the mean square error (MSE) of different models in the training stage can be observed, as shown in Fig. 4. As can be seen from the figure, all models show an overall obvious decreasing trend in the first 10 training rounds, despite the fluctuation of the loss function values, which indicates that the models are in the parameter optimization and learning stage. As the number of training rounds increases, the loss function curve gradually tends to flatten, and the decline is significantly reduced, indicating that the model is close to the convergence state, and the training process tends to be completed. This phenomenon indicates that the model has fully learned the data features and reached a stable performance level.

It is worth noting that the loss function curve tends to stabilize after 30 training rounds, but under the same experimental environment, the model based on the Seq2Seq architecture shows more stable convergence characteristics. Among them, the loss function value of the BG2BG model always stays at the lowest level, indicating its better performance and stronger generalization ability in the trajectory repair task. This result further validates the effectiveness of the Seq2Seq architecture in handling the ship trajectory repair task, especially the advantage of the bidirectional GRU unit in capturing complex spatio-temporal dependencies.

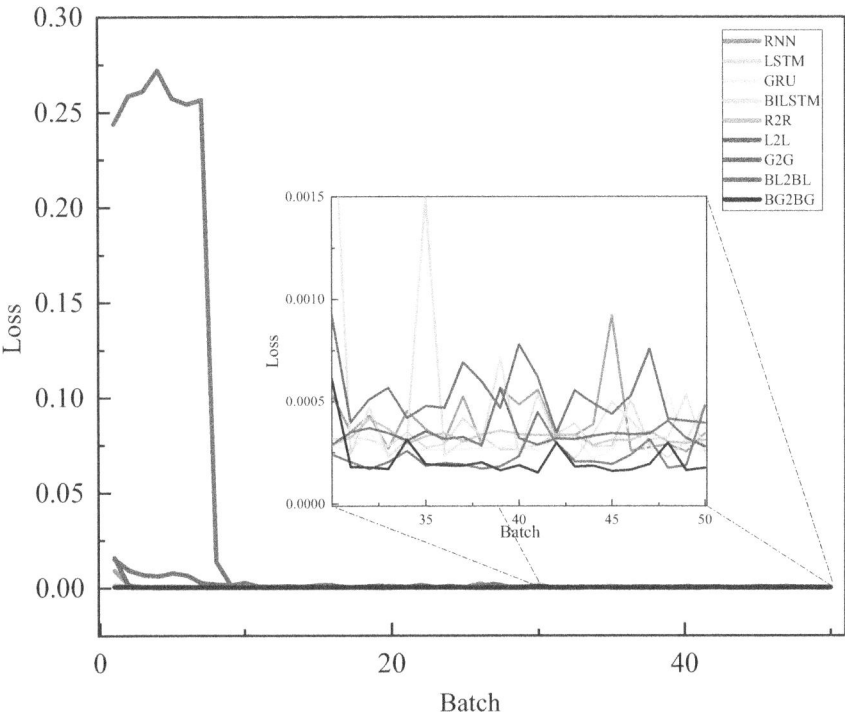

Fig. 4. Comparison of loss functions in different models' training phases

The trained model performed ship trajectory repair on the test set, and the results of the evaluation metrics of repair performance are shown in Table 2. Analyzing Table 2, it can be seen that the BG2BG model exhibits optimal performance in all performance metrics, with the lowest MAE (LAT: 0.0023, LON: 0.0034), RMSE (LAT: 0.0027, LON: 0.0038), FD (0.5066), and AED (0.2114) values, which is significantly better than the other comparative models (such as R2R, L2L, G2G and BL2BL). This result indicates that the BG2BG model has excellent performance in the trajectory repair task, which not only has the highest repair accuracy but also significantly outperforms other models in terms of stability and accuracy of the repair results. In particular, the BG2BG model demonstrates a strong capability in capturing complex spatio-temporal dependencies, thanks to the design of its bidirectional GRU unit, which can utilize both historical and future information for trajectory inference, thus effectively enhancing the repair results. In addition, the low FD and AED values of the BG2BG model further validate its high fidelity in trajectory shape and spatial distribution.

Table 2. Comparison of restoration indicators for different models

Type of networks	MAE		RMSE		FD	AED
	LAT	LON	LAT	LON		
R2R	0.0061	0.0068	0.0072	0.0074	1.2176	0.4797
L2L	0.0157	0.0445	0.0204	0.0505	5.5083	2.2514
G2G	0.0073	0.0070	0.0086	0.0076	1.6278	0.5598
BL2BL	0.0063	0.0095	0.0076	0.0105	1.5235	0.5842
BG2BG	0.0023	0.0034	0.0027	0.0038	0.5066	0.2114

Further comparing the repair effects of different encoder models under the Seq2Seq architecture, we selected 30, 100, 300, and 900 ship trajectory points for repair, and some of the trajectory repair effects are shown in Fig. 5. From the figure, it can be seen that the repaired trajectories of the BG2BG model have the highest similarity to the real trajectories, and its AED is also the smallest, which is significantly better than other models (e.g., R2R, L2L, G2G, and BL2BL). Specifically, the figure shows how the restored trajectories of different models compare in the LAT and LON directions. The true trajectory (TRUE) almost completely overlaps with the restored trajectory of the BG2BG model, indicating that the BG2BG model can more accurately reproduce the true trajectory of the ship. In contrast, the restored trajectories of the other models have different degrees of deviation from the true trajectories, and the restored trajectories of the R2R, L2L, G2G, and BL2BL models have more obvious deviations from the true trajectories.

This result further validates the advantage of the BG2BG model in capturing complex spatio-temporal dependencies. Its bi-directional GRU unit can utilize both historical and future information for trajectory inference, which leads to a more comprehensive learning of the ship's movement patterns. In addition, the multi-level feature extraction mechanism of the BG2BG model also enhances its ability to restore trajectory details, making it significantly better than other models in terms of restoration accuracy and stability. These advantages make the BG2BG model the optimal choice for ship trajectory repair tasks, providing reliable technical support for high-precision trajectory repair.

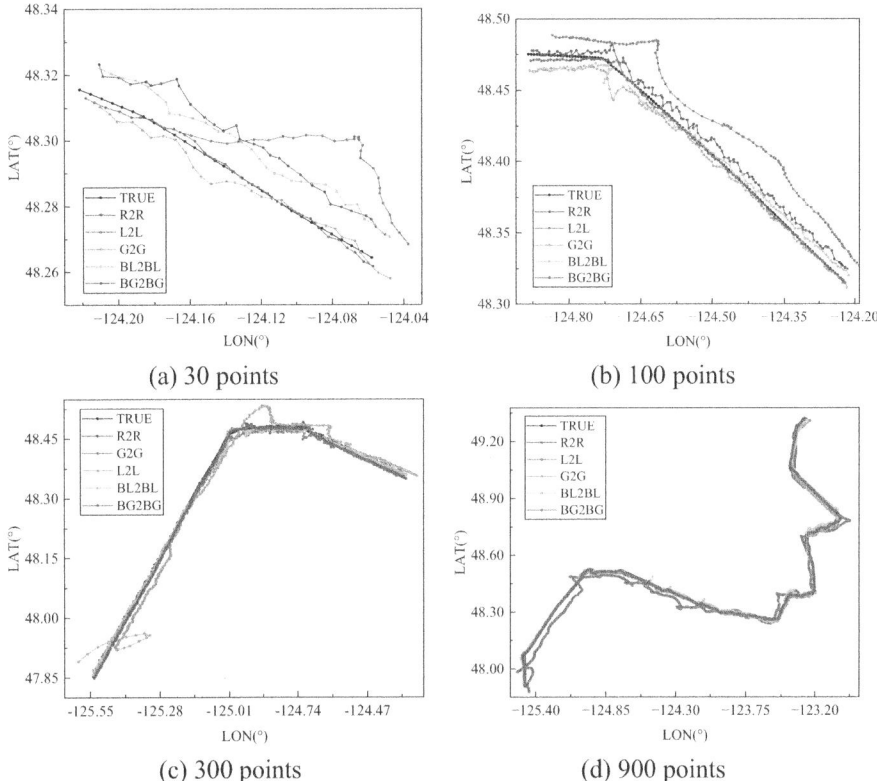

Fig. 5. Comparison of different models' trajectory restoration effects

4.4 Results Explainability Analysis

To gain a deeper understanding of the decision-making process of the ship trajectory repair model, this study analyzed the interpretability of the model using SHAP. SHAP quantifies the contribution of each input feature to the model output by calculating its Shapley value. By visualizing the SHAP values, we can identify which features have the greatest impact on the trajectory repair results, as well as the decision logic of the model when dealing with missing data and outliers.

By visualizing the SHAP values, we made the following key findings: Distribution of Feature Contributions: A plot of the distribution of SHAP values shows how each feature contributes to the model output. For example, features such as the current position of the ship (LON, LAT), SOG, and COG have a large contribution to the repair results, while features such as ΔT have a relatively small contribution. Feature Importance ranking: We ranked the importance of the features based on the mean of the SHAP values. The results show that the current position of the ship (LON, LAT) and other location features, these features have high SHAP values, indicating that they have the most significant impact on the trajectory repair results. Then there are state features such as SOC and COG. It can be observed that features such as ALON/AT and ALAT/AT (positional change rate) also have high SHAP values, indicating that they contribute more to trajectory repair. In contrast, time-dependent features such as ΔT and ΔHeading/ΔT have lower SHAP values, suggesting that they have less impact on the repair results. These findings provide an important basis for feature selection, which can help optimize model inputs and improve the accuracy and efficiency of trajectory repair (Figs. 6 and 7).

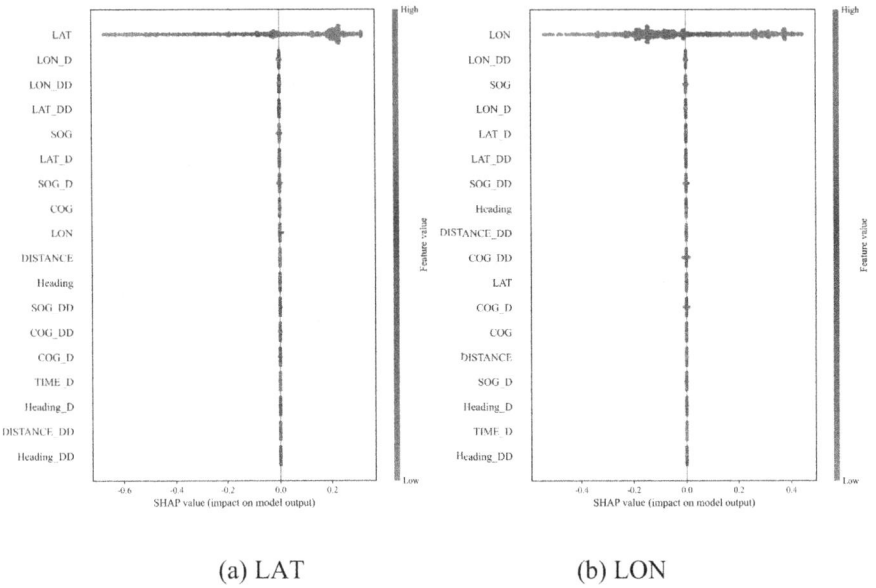

(a) LAT   (b) LON

Fig. 6. Visualization of SHAP model output results

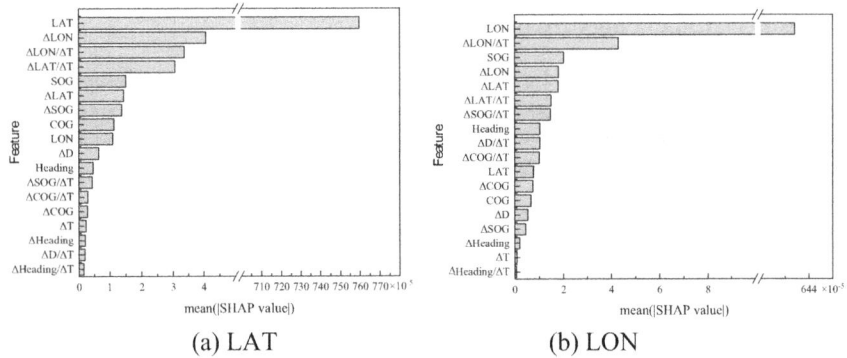

(a) LAT   (b) LON

Fig. 7. Feature importance ranking

5 Conclusion and Future Work

In this study, a sparse ship track repair method based on feature correlation analysis and the interpretability of the SHAP model is proposed. By combining feature correlation analysis and the interpretability of the SHAP model, the accuracy and reliability of ship track repair are significantly improved. The experimental results show that the proposed method is effective and advantageous in trajectory repair tasks. Through comparative experiments, the repair effects of different Seq2Seq architecture models were studied and compared. In addition, by introducing the SHAP model, this study not only demonstrates the high efficiency of the trajectory repair model but also enhances the transparency of the model, making it more operable and trustworthy.

Although this study has made progress in ship trajectory repair, there are still some limitations. Future research work can be carried out from the following aspects: to verify the robustness of the model in more complex navigation environments (such as high-density navigation channels, bad weather conditions, etc.); Introduce more external data (such as weather information, channel limits, sea state, etc.) to further improve the repair accuracy and robustness of the model; Optimize the calculation efficiency of SHAP (such as using Kernel SHAP, Tree SHAP and other approximate calculation methods); Improving the ability to repair latitude data (e.g. introducing more complex feature engineering or improving model architecture); Combine with other advanced models (e.g., reinforcement learning, graph neural networks) to improve the performance and interpretation of trajectory repair; And further explore the role of dynamic features (such as COG and SOG) in specific scenarios (such as complex sea areas or high-density traffic areas) to improve the adaptability and robustness of trajectory repair models.

Acknowledgments. This study was funded by the National Natural Science Foundation of China (grant number 42371438).

References

1. Luin, B., Al-Mansour, F., Perkovič, M.: Optimization of shipping routes with AIS data. Therm. Sci. Eng. Progr. **56**, 103042 (2024). https://doi.org/10.1016/j.tsep.2024.103042
2. Wang, W., et al.: Ship encounter scenario generation for collision avoidance algorithm testing based on AIS data. Ocean Eng. **291**, 116436 (2023). https://doi.org/10.1016/j.oceaneng.2023.116436
3. Chen, W., et al.: Monitoring and evaluation of ship operation congestion status at container ports based on AIS data. Ocean Coast. Manag. **245**, 106836 (2023). https://doi.org/10.1016/j.ocecoaman.2023.106836
4. Zhu, W., et al.: Dynamic multi-period maritime accident susceptibility assessment based on AIS data and random forest model. J. Marine Sci. Eng. **11**(10), 1935 (2023). https://doi.org/10.3390/jmse11101935
5. Liu, Z., Zhang, B., Zhang, M., Wang, H., Fu, X.: A quantitative method for the analysis of ship collision risk using AIS data. Ocean Eng. **272**, 113906 (2023). https://doi.org/10.1016/j.oceaneng.2023.113906
6. Zaman, B., Marijan, D., Kholodna, T.: Interpolation-based inference of vessel trajectory waypoints from sparse AIS data in maritime. J. Marine Sci. Eng. **11**(3), 615 (2023). https://doi.org/10.3390/jmse11030615
7. Bai, X., Ye, K., Xu, X.: Ship trajectory prediction using CNN-BILSTM with sparse attention mechanisms for enhanced maritime safety. Ships Offshore Struct. 1–17 (2024). https://doi.org/10.1080/17445302.2024.2433006

8. Wang, S., Zou, Y., Wang, X.: An intelligent decision-making approach for multi-ship traffic conflict mitigation from the perspective of maritime surveillance. J. Marine Sci. Eng. **12**(10), 1719 (2024). https://doi.org/10.3390/jmse12101719
9. Xiao, G., Yang, D., Xu, L., Li, J., Jiang, Z.: The application of artificial intelligence technology in shipping: a bibliometric review. J. Marine Sci. Eng. **12**(4), 624 (2024). https://doi.org/10.3390/jmse12040624
10. Zhang, L., Meng, Q., Xiao, Z., Fu, X.: A novel ship trajectory reconstruction approach using AIS data. Ocean Eng. **159**, 165–174 (2018). https://doi.org/10.1016/j.oceaneng.2018.03.085
11. Qin, H., Yang, X.: Iterative algorithm for vessel trajectory restoration based on improved linear interpolation. J. Comput.-Aided Design Comput. Graph. **31**(10), 1759–1767 (2019). https://doi.org/10.3724/SP.J.1089.2019.17660
12. He, W., Liu, X., Chu, X., Wang, Z., Fracz, P., Li, Z.: A novel fitting model for practical AIS abnormal data repair in inland river. Elektron. Elektrotech. **27**(1), 60–70 (2021). https://doi.org/10.5755/j02.eie.27661
13. Chen, X., et al.: Ship trajectory reconstruction from AIS sensory data via data quality control and prediction. Math. Probl. Eng. **2020**(1), 7191296 (2019). https://doi.org/10.1155/2020/7191296
14. Zhong, C., Jiang, Z., Chu, X., Liu, L.: Inland ship trajectory restoration by recurrent neural network. J. Navig. **72**(6), 1359–1377 (2019). https://doi.org/10.1017/S0373463319000316
15. Xue, H.: Fractional-order gradient descent with momentum for RBF neural network-based AIS trajectory restoration. Soft. Comput. **25**, 869–882 (2021). https://doi.org/10.1007/s00500-020-05484-5
16. Zhang, W., Jiang, W., Liu, Q., Wang, W.: AIS data repair model based on generative adversarial network. Reliabil. Eng. Syst. Saf. **240**, 109572 (2023). https://doi.org/10.1016/j.ress.2023.109572
17. Ye, L., et al.: A study of multi-step sparse vessel trajectory restoration based on feature correlation. Appl. Sci. **14**(10), 4057 (2023). https://doi.org/10.3390/app14104057
18. Ye, L., Chen, X., Zhang, R., Zhang, B., Liu, H.: An adaptive trajectory segmentation and simplification algorithm based on vessel behavioral features. Ocean Eng. **312**, 119329 (2024). https://doi.org/10.1016/j.oceaneng.2024.119329

A Maritime Route Prediction Method for Large Oil Tankers Based on IMO-MMSI Matching and Encoder-LSTM Model

Xiaohui Chen[1,2], Ran Zhang[2(✉)], Deze Wang[2], Bing Zhang[2], Yunpeng Zhao[2], LinYe[2], and Mingqi Zheng[2]

[1] Key Laboratory of Smart Earth, Beijing 100029, China
[2] Information Engineering University, Zhengzhou 450000, China
zhr_ang@163.com

Abstract. In recent years, with the profound changes in the global energy supply and demand structure, large oil tankers have become key participants in international energy transportation, playing an important role in ensuring the safety and stability of energy transport. Accurate prediction of tanker routes has become a crucial task to guarantee this. However, existing long-distance route prediction methods rarely consider trajectory consistency during data preprocessing, and recursive predictions suffer from error accumulation, leading to low prediction accuracy. To address these issues, our study proposes a new route prediction framework. The framework introduces an IMO and MMSI matching method during data preprocessing to resolve inconsistencies in historical trajectory data caused by changes in MMSI. Furthermore, to better address the issue of continuous position drift in trajectories, this study proposes an outlier cyclic deletion method. After extracting OD trajectory data based on the buffer zone, this study combines the Transformer model with the Long Short-Term Memory (LSTM) network model, leveraging their strong ability to capture long-term dependencies in time-series data. An Encoder-LSTM architecture-based route prediction model is then constructed, alleviating the decline in prediction accuracy caused by error accumulation. Experimental results show that the proposed framework significantly improves the accuracy and reliability of route prediction.

Keywords: Maritime Route Prediction · Encoder-LSTM · AIS

1 Introduction

With the changing global energy supply system, energy security has become an increasingly prominent issue. Energy shipping routes, as a critical link between producing and consuming countries, play a vital role in ensuring the stability and security of the global energy market [1]. Very Large Crude Carrier (VLCC), as the main carriers for international energy transportation, provide key insights into the typical characteristics of cross-border energy transportation routes [2]. Research based on VLCC voyage trajectories for energy route forecasting can help in the early detection of anomalous behavior by vessels, reveal potential risks, and inform contingency plans for critical route points, further enhancing global energy security.

The rapid development of artificial intelligence has significantly accelerated the advancement of big data analytics. Numerous deep learning models have been proposed, among which the Transformer model has gained wide application in natural language processing and time-series prediction tasks due to its ability to capture dependencies across different positions in sequences effectively. Although Transformers perform well in short-term forecasting, challenges remain when generating long-distance routes: (1) how to effectively input trajectory data to support training while preserving both spatiotemporal characteristics and ensuring route continuity, preventing the negative impact of route discontinuities on model performance, thereby enhancing the model's understanding of the temporal sequence of the trajectory. (2) In multi-step forecasting, utilizing prior predictions as input can lead to error accumulation, with early small errors being amplified during the recursive process, ultimately causing significant deviation in the predicted route. Therefore, there is a need to explore effective methods to mitigate this issue and ensure the coherence and accuracy of the predicted routes.

To address these challenges, our study proposes a novel route prediction framework. The framework first introduces the IMO and MMS matching method during the processing of AIS data to resolve inconsistencies caused by MMSI changes in historical AIS trajectories. It also employs an anomaly point loop deletion method to handle continuous drift points in the trajectories. Next, by constructing a buffer zone, the framework extracts the oil tanker's origin-destination (OD) data, and enriches the OD dataset using linear interpolation and anti-transform processing methods. Finally, the framework combines the Transformer model and Long Short-Term Memory (LSTM) network to leverage their capabilities in handling long-range dependencies in time-series data. An Encoder-LSTM architecture is used to construct the route prediction model, which is validated through experiments. Experimental results show that the proposed framework can effectively improve the accuracy and reliability of route predictions. To address these challenges, our study proposes a novel route prediction framework as shown in Fig. 1.

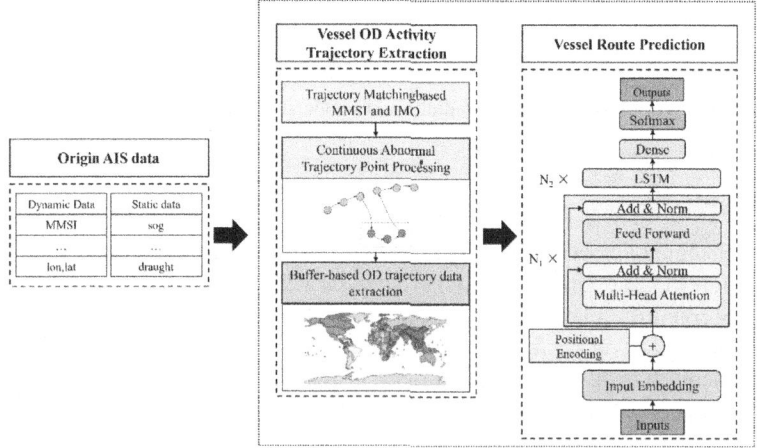

Fig. 1. The route prediction framework of our study.

2 Relate Work

Trajectory prediction aims to predict the long-term development trend of trajectory by capturing the changing law of historical trajectory data. At present, the existing trajectory prediction methods can be divided into three categories: motion based, early intelligent learning algorithm based, and transformer based trajectory prediction method.

2.1 Motion-Based Trajectory Prediction Methods

Motion-based trajectory prediction methods utilize maneuvering parameters and positional calculations to forecast trajectories [3]. Common methods include Gaussian tracking filtering [4], Kalman filtering [5–7], gray prediction [8], vector analysis [9], and inertial positioning principles [10].

Gaussian tracking filtering uses Gaussian functions to provide optimal estimates under uncertain conditions for predicting the target's position. Kalman filtering, based on a linear system dynamics model and sensor noise statistics, provides optimal predictions through recursive estimation. Gray prediction involves building a gray system model for data analysis and forecasting. Vector analysis employs vector operations to analyze trajectories, providing a basis for prediction. Inertial positioning principles use acceleration and angular velocity measurements from an inertial navigation system to predict position and direction of travel.

These physics-based modeling methods can offer good prediction accuracy, but require a comprehensive understanding of performance parameters. When sufficient physical parameters are unavailable, it becomes challenging to improve prediction accuracy.

2.2 Early Intelligent Learning Algorithm Based Trajectory Prediction Methods

Early intelligent learning algorithms primarily include Back Propagation (BP) Neural Network, Support Vector Machines (SVM), Convolutional Neural Networks (CNN), Recurrent Neural Networks (RNN), and Generative Adversarial Networks (GAN).

BP neural networks predict by constructing networks to analyze data patterns, utilizing the approximation of complex functions [11, 12]. However, they are prone to getting stuck in local minima and are difficult to converge, leading to poor performance in long-term predictions. SVM uses kernel functions to establish nonlinear regression functions, identifying the mapping relationship between true and predicted values [13]. The application of differential evolution algorithms on top of SVM effectively improves the model's convergence speed and prediction accuracy. However, SVM can only provide specific predicted values based on historical data, without forecasting data trends. Moreover, the choice of kernel function significantly impacts the prediction accuracy.

CNN predicts by analyzing the patterns of historical data changes using convolutional kernels, followed by processing through pooling layers, which filter and retain key information for output. Li et al. [14] applied this approach by merging time series data into images according to a specific rule and inputting them into CNN for prediction. This method can be trained without feature engineering; however, when the sample dataset is small, it becomes difficult for the model to update its parameters, resulting in poor prediction performance. RNN learns the temporal characteristics of data by associating the output at each time step with historical inputs to make predictions. A limitation of RNNs is that they cannot capture long-term dependencies and are prone to the vanishing gradient problem. Therefore, Long Short-Term Memory (LSTM) networks were introduced by adding three gates to the RNN structure, allowing the model to decide whether to forget or add important information. Some researchers have proposed integrated models that combine LSTM autoencoders, attention mechanisms, and bidirectional LSTM structures [15], along with gated recurrent units (GRU) networks and hybrid neural networks, to predict trajectory sequences. These methods are among the main approaches for trajectory prediction today. However, they require configuring numerous training parameters and large training datasets, and the models still face issues of vanishing and exploding gradients. The fundamental principle of Generative Adversarial Networks (GANs) in trajectory prediction involves a game-theoretic process between a generator (G) and a discriminator (D). The generator's function is to capture the distribution of sample data, with the goal of generating samples that closely resemble real data X by inputting random noise z through a function G(z); whereas the discriminator, a binary classifier, determines whether the generated data is real, with D's output approaching 1 when the generated data is closer to the actual data, and 0 otherwise[16]. The primary advantage of GANs is their ability to capture the distribution patterns and fluctuations of signals more accurately, making the generated data closer to the real situation. However, the issue of vanishing gradients can still arise during usage.

2.3 Transformer Based Trajectory Prediction Method

In 2017, Vaswani et al. introduced the Transformer mode [17], which incorporated the self-attention mechanism to better capture the correlations between different positions when processing multiple input vectors. Additionally, the application of the self-attention module not only reduces the number of parameters but also decreases the computational load under the same conditions, enabling the model to capture long-term dependencies [18] and demonstrating outstanding performance across various sequential tasks [19]. Building on this technology, Google launched the BERT (Bidirectional Encoder Representations from Transformers) model in October 2018 [20]. Furthermore, in 2021, Zhou et al. proposed the Informer model [21], based on the traditional Transformer Encoder-Decoder architecture, effectively addressing the limitations of Transformer-based models in long-sequence time series forecasting tasks.

Existing trajectory prediction methods include linear prediction approaches, which are simple to implement but exhibit limited performance when handling complex data. In contrast, dynamic-based trajectory prediction methods can provide higher accuracy, but they heavily rely on physical parameters, making them highly dependent on specific conditions and limiting their widespread applicability. Moreover, trajectory prediction methods based on early intelligent learning algorithms reduce the dependency on physical parameters; however, their performance is still constrained by the learning capabilities of the individual models (Table 1).

Table 1. Research overview of trajectory prediction methods.

Type of prediction method		disadvantages
Motion-based method		Researchers need to have a full understanding of the vehicle's performance parameters, and it is difficult to improve the prediction accuracy if sufficient physical parameters are not obtained
Early Intelligent Learning Algorithm	BP neural network	It is prone to getting trapped in local minima, making convergence difficult, and tends to perform poorly for long-term predictions.
	SVM	SVM can only provide specific predicted values based on historical data, without being able to predict the underlying trend of changes. Moreover, the choice of kernel function has a significant impact on the prediction accuracy
	CNN	When the sample dataset is small, updating the model parameters becomes challenging, leading to poor prediction performance
	RNN	The model requires a large number of training parameters, demanding extensive training data, and issues such as vanishing and exploding gradients still persist
	GAN	There is an inherent issue of training instability caused by gradient vanishing, and optimizing GAN training remains a challenging task
Transformer Based Method		There is an accumulation of errors when making long-term forecasts

3 AIS Data Preprocessing

In relevant research within the maritime domain, analysts often rely on Automatic Identification System (AIS) data to explore the navigation patterns and related information of oil tankers, in order to identify suspicious vessels and obtain relevant activity insights. However, the large volume, complexity, redundancy, and noise inherent in AIS data pose challenges to the efficiency, accuracy, and reliability of data utilization. Therefore, our study designs a series of data processing strategies, specifically preprocessing the dynamic and static data features of AIS to enhance the data's value density and precision.

3.1 AIS Data Introduction

AIS is a system that tracks vessel movements by exchanging navigation data via transceivers onboard ships, ground stations, or satellites. AIS data includes static and dynamic data. Static data refers to the basic information that describes a vessel's characteristics and typically does not change significantly during a single voyage. Specifically, it includes information about the vessel's type, features, identity, and voyage details. Dynamic data, on the other hand, refers to the data that is continuously transmitted and updated during each voyage, providing detailed descriptions of the vessel's specific sailing conditions. Specifically, it includes identity information, spatiotemporal location, sailing status, and voyage-specific details for each voyage. AIS data offers high positioning accuracy and is not constrained by geographical environment, containing rich information about vessel behavior patterns. Therefore, in the field of maritime traffic engineering, mining and analyzing vessel behavior based on AIS data has become a research hotspot.

The specific contents of the static and dynamic data are shown in the Tables 2 and 3 below.

Table 2. Static data content.

Attribute name	Attribute meaning
Type	Vessel type
Length	Vessel length
Width	Vessel width
Dim_bow	The distance from the vessel's GPS antenna to the bow
Dim_stern	The distance from the vessel's GPS antenna to the stern
Dim_port	The distance from the vessel's GPS antenna to the port side
Dim_starboard	The distance from the vessel's GPS antenna to the starboard side
MMSI	Mobile maritime service identity code
IMO	International maritime organization number
Name	Vessel name
Receive_time	Data reception time
Callsign	Vessel callsign

Table 3. Dynamic data content.

Attribute name	Attribute meaning
MMSI	Mobile maritime service identity code
Receive_time	Data reception time
Nav_status	Navigation status code

(*continued*)

Table 3. (*continued*)

Attribute name	Attribute meaning
Rot	Rate of turn, right turn as positive, left turn as negative
Sog	Speed over ground
Cog	Course over ground
Longitude	Longitude
Latitude	Latitude

3.2 Matching Mechanism for Linking IMO and MMSI

For each oil tanker, the International Maritime Organization number (IMO number) and its physical attributes remain unchanged from construction to decommissioning. However, the Maritime Mobile Service Identity (MMSI) number and the ship's name may change due to different sailing plans or ownership by various companies. To enhance data reliability and eliminate inconsistencies in AIS data caused by MMSI changes, our study designs a matching mechanism that represents the change of MMSI as a specific IMO-numbered vessel using a particular MMSI number during a certain time period, referred to as its lifecycle in our study. In this way, the dynamic trajectory data of the vessel can be uniquely linked to the vessel itself.

Specifically, our study first sorts the AIS static data by time and systematically records and updates the lifecycle of the relationship between the IMO number and MMSI number for each oil tanker. The sorted static data is then traversed, and new IMO-MMSI pairs and their associated attributes are either added or the existing IMO-MMSI lifecycle is expanded. Additionally, the number of times a specific IMO-MMSI pair is detected within the lifecycle is recorded, allowing for further manual assessment of data reliability. When an IMO-MMSI pair appears again after exceeding a predetermined threshold time, it is treated as a new record, and the data processing cycle is restarted to obtain a more accurate mapping between the IMO and MMSI numbers.

3.3 AIS Dynamic Data Processing

Since the AIS data used in our study is obtained from publicly available sources, the dynamic data contains some incomplete trajectories and noisy data. To construct a higher-quality dataset, targeted processing of the AIS data is necessary. As shown in Fig. 2, visualization of the raw data reveals various anomalies, such as trajectory "jumps", trajectory interruptions, and excessively short trajectories. To address these issues, this study has designed a corresponding preprocessing workflow, as illustrated below, which primarily includes trajectory data reduction, outlier handling, and trajectory filtering.

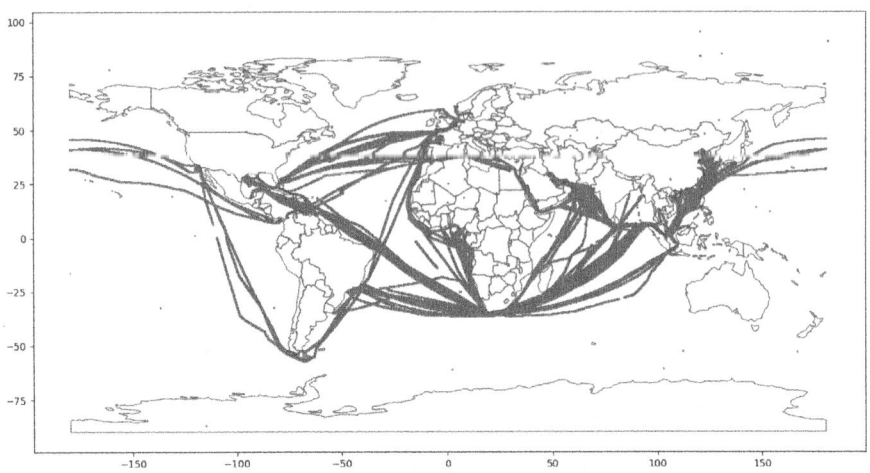

Fig. 2. Visualization of AIS Dynamic Data.

3.3.1 Trajectory Data Simplification

In practical scenarios, oil tankers that are anchored or docked in designated areas are continuously recorded by AIS, leading to redundant data entries. Considering that anchored oil tankers may experience slight drift due to ocean currents, causing distance errors, our study assumes that the drift-induced distance error is approximately 10 m, which corresponds to an error of about 0.0001 degrees in latitude and longitude coordinates. Based on this assumption, our study retains four decimal places when processing latitude and longitude data and applies data deduplication to minimize the impact of data redundancy caused by the anchorage of oil tankers (Table 4).

Table 4. Example of duplicates.

Filestamp	MMSI	Receive_time	Longitude	Latitude
2021-7-25	636014591	1627158096	48.8732	29.6085
2021-7-25	636014591	1627158105	48.8732	29.6085
2021-7-25	636014591	1627158281	48.8734	29.6086
2021-7-25	636014591	1627158282	48.8734	29.6086

3.3.2 Processing of Anomalous Trajectory Data

The processing of anomalous trajectory data primarily involves handling data points, including attribute anomaly processing and spatial anomaly processing. During the AIS data reception process, due to the long distance between the oil tanker and the AIS base station, as well as potential adverse environmental conditions or technical malfunctions, some received data may exhibit significant anomalies. These anomalies typically manifest as sudden changes in attribute values and "jumps" in spatial coordinates, which can have a serious impact on subsequent data operations. Therefore, it is necessary to carry out appropriate processing to address these issues.

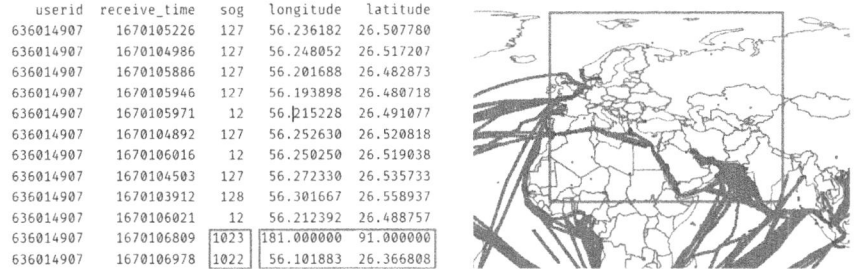

Fig. 3. Examples of anomalous trajectory data. The left is the attribute value anomaly, and the right is the spatial anomaly.

For attribute anomalies, our study uses the interquartile range (IQR) method to detect outliers and fills the detected outliers with the mean of the non-outlier values. The formula for detecting outliers using the interquartile range method is as follows:

$$IQR = Q_{0.75} - Q_{0.25} \tag{1}$$

$$threshold = Q_{0.75} + 1.5 * IQR \tag{2}$$

$$f(x) = \begin{cases} yes, & x \geq threshold \\ no, & x < threshold \end{cases} \tag{3}$$

where $Q_{0.25}$, $Q_{0.75}$ are the first and last quartiles of the selected attribute.

For spatial anomalies, our study performs differential calculations on the longitude and latitude of adjacent trajectory points to obtain the differential values of the coordinates. Considering that the coordinate changes of the collected oil tanker data are very small in the Earth's reference frame, the Euclidean distance between adjacent points can be approximated as the sum of the longitude and latitude differences in such small variations. The formula is shown in Eq. 4. Based on this, and to simplify the calculation, this study uses the interquartile range (IQR) method to detect and identify spatial abnormal values by analyzing the sum of longitude and latitude differences.

$$Dis(i, i-1) = |lon_i - lon_{i-1}| + |lat_i - lat_{i-1}| \tag{4}$$

Our study also improves the IQR method. The conventional IQR method is overly sensitive to outliers, and since the longitude and latitude changes of the oil tanker are generally small over short periods (the time interval recorded by AIS), it may cause some minor variations to be amplified during detection, leading to the removal of data points that should not be removed, thus impacting the results. Therefore, this study proposes a threshold-based improved IQR method, aiming to reduce the sensitivity range for outliers and handle spatial anomalies more accurately. The detection formula for the threshold-based improved IQR method is as follows:

$$IQR = Q_{0.75} - Q_{0.25} \tag{5}$$

$$threshold = threshold\_pre + Q_{0.75} + 1.5 * IQR \tag{6}$$

$$f(x) = \begin{cases} yes, & x \geq threshold \\ no, & x < threshold \end{cases} \tag{7}$$

where $Q_{0.25}$, $Q_{0.75}$ are the first quartile and last quartile, and *threshold_pre* is the initial threshold set manually.

In real-world situations, spatial anomalies may also appear as consecutive adjacent anomalies, as shown in Fig. 4. However, the aforementioned identification method can only remove outlier points that are adjacent to the normal trajectory in the data.

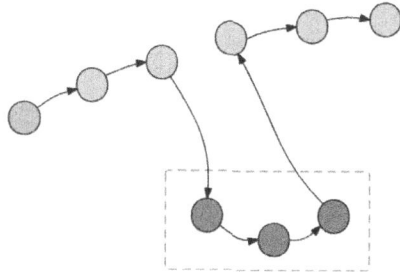

Fig. 4. Example of consecutive multiple anomalies.

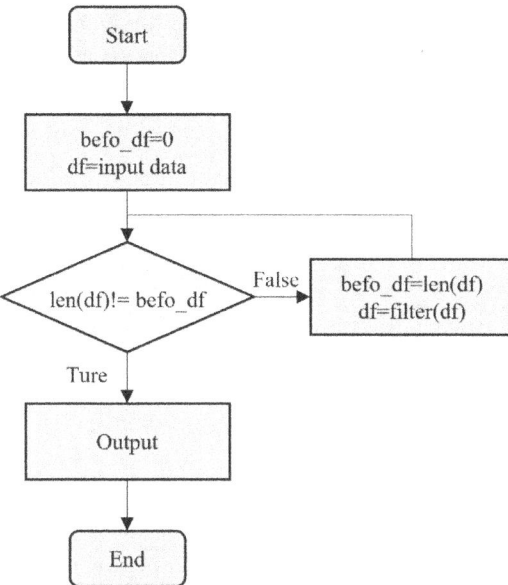

Fig. 5. Example of consecutive multiple anomalies.

To address the case of consecutive spatial anomalies, our study proposes a cyclic deletion algorithm. The algorithm checks whether the length of the data table changes after each processing step to determine whether the deletion process is complete, thus enabling the repeated removal of consecutive anomalies. The flowchart of the algorithm is shown in Fig. 5.

3.3.3 Trajectory Data Filtering

Trajectory data filtering primarily involves short-duration trajectory processing and wandering trajectory processing. Short-duration trajectory processing focuses on identifying and handling trajectories with either a short survival time (the duration during which the trajectory is continuously recorded) or too few recorded data points. These data lack sufficient information and completeness, so removing them reduces computational load and enhances the accuracy of the data. Wandering trajectory processing, on the other hand, aims to identify and eliminate trajectories that oscillate or circle within a small area. While such data may have varying applications in different research contexts, they can interfere with specific studies, such as route generation. Therefore, it is necessary to remove these data to further improve the quality and effectiveness of the dataset.

In practical processing, our study sets thresholds for the duration and number of points in each ship's route per day to filter out short-duration trajectories. For wandering trajectories, the cleaning is performed by setting thresholds for the range of latitude and longitude of each ship's route per day.

After preprocessing, redundant data, outliers, short-duration trajectories, and wandering trajectories that do not contribute to the task are effectively cleaned from the original dataset, thereby enhancing the clarity of the routes. Visualization of the processed dataset reveals significant improvements in both global and local route visual effects, demonstrating the effectiveness of the preprocessing work and laying a foundation for subsequent route prediction tasks.

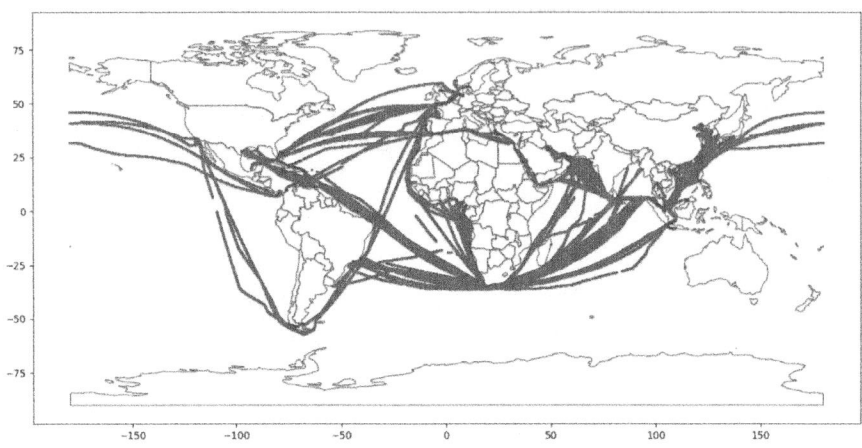

Fig. 6. Preprocessing Results Visualization.

4 Maritime Route Prediction Method Based on Encoder-LSTM Architecture

After matching IMO and MMSI and preprocessing the trajectory data, our study utilizes buffer zone technology to accurately extract route information from the starting point to the destination within a large-scale AIS dataset. Subsequently, the extracted route data is augmented through resampling and reverse processing to expand the effective coverage of the dataset. Finally, an Encoder-LSTM model is constructed for VLCC route prediction.

4.1 OD Route Extraction Based on Buffer Zone

The existing trajectory mining algorithms based on OD are mainly applied in two key areas. First, these algorithms are widely used in the construction of network and graphical structures [22] for spatiotemporal data. By analyzing the interrelations and structural features within the OD data, they can effectively depict the topological structure of complex systems such as transportation networks. This process involves extracting node and edge information from large datasets and modeling them into graphs for further network analysis. Second, OD trajectory mining algorithms play a crucial role in the visual analysis of spatial data [23], especially when combined with Flowmap algorithms for displaying and analyzing spatial flow data. These algorithms can effectively reveal the movement trends of spatial entities, assisting decision-makers and analysts in identifying major flow corridors, assessing spatial connectivity, and discovering abnormal flow patterns.

However, the existing OD-based trajectory mining algorithms are not entirely suitable for this study. The OD-based navigation trajectory recognition algorithm designed in this study is used to extract detailed information between specific origin and destination points from large-scale AIS datasets. Given the relative scarcity of public algorithms targeting such tasks, this study proposes a novel OD data extraction algorithm, whose core steps include effective traversal and fine filtering of AIS data, thus extracting and reconstructing maritime trajectories between two geographical locations.

The algorithm first identifies and traverses the data of each vessel via the MMSI number, analyzing each record sorted by date. It then determines whether the geographical location of these data points lies within the specified range of the concerned region. When the algorithm detects that a vessel sequentially enters two concern region ranges, and the time interval between the corresponding two records meets the user-defined time threshold, it records the relevant voyage information and assigns a unique ID to the voyage trajectory. In this way, the algorithm links the geographic region data on the map with the actual geographic names, achieving a mapping from geographical space text to data. This enables the effective and convenient extraction of required route data from AIS data, providing an accurate data foundation for subsequent route prediction.

Regarding the detection of trajectory data within a specific area, special consideration is given to the bias in the land-sea structure of map data. Tanker navigation typically occurs at sea, whereas existing map data generally focus on land area structures, with relatively scarce data for maritime regions. To address this issue, this study extends the maritime spatial data using a buffering method based on land map data. Specifically, a predetermined width of surrounding space is created around the edges of geographical or geometric entities, in order to cover adjacent maritime areas as much as possible. A schematic diagram of the buffering effect is shown in Fig. 7. In this example, the buffer width is set to 2 to highlight the spatial expansion effect brought by the buffer zone. It is important to note that the buffer zone is established based on latitude and longitude, and due to the spherical nature of the Earth, this method may produce inaccuracies near the poles. However, if the buffer expansion range is kept within a relatively small scale, this method remains practically feasible for most application scenarios.

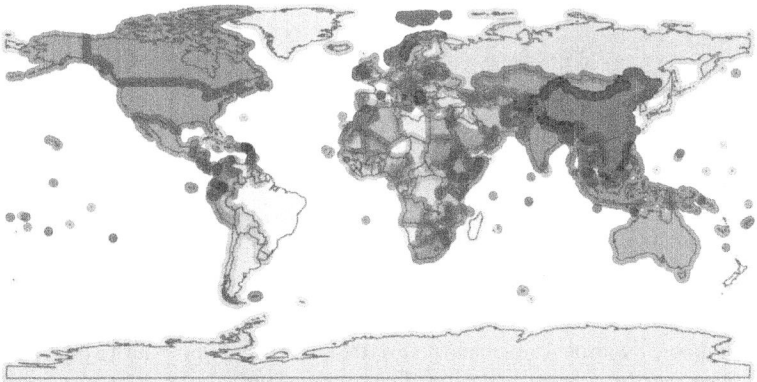

Fig. 7. Example of buffer zone.

4.2 Route Data Augmentation Based on Linear Interpolation

In AIS data, due to factors such as navigation speed and sampling equipment, the interval between records for each trajectory data point may vary significantly. Additionally, considering that the round-trip paths of each route are unlikely to be perfectly identical, our study employs resampling of route data and reverse processing of the route to enhance the route data.

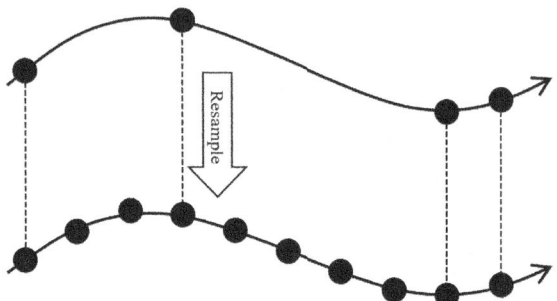

Fig. 8. Example of data resampling.

4.2.1 1Route Resampling Based on Linear Interpolation

Directly resampling the route data may introduce some unreasonable results, such as the resampled route crossing land, as shown in Fig. 9. This occurs because interruptions often happen during actual navigation, causing direct resampling to fail in accurately reflecting the true path of the route.

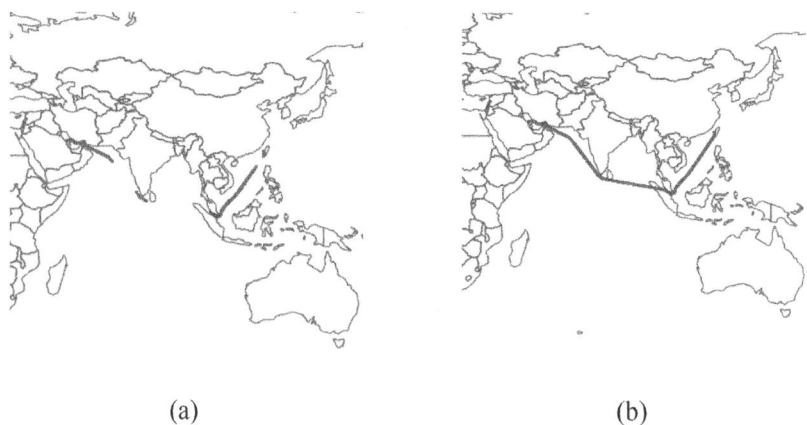

(a)   (b)

Fig. 9. The problem with direct resampling. (a) is the original trajectory with the original presence of interruption, and (b) is the trajectory after linear resampling.

To address this issue, our study proposes an improved route resampling algorithm. The algorithm identifies and detects interruptions in the routes hidden within the data by analyzing the distance between adjacent trajectory points. The specific steps of the improved algorithm are as follows:

① Distance Calculation and Interruption Identification: First, the distance between adjacent trajectory points in each route of the AIS data is calculated to assess the continuity of the route. When the distance between two points exceeds a predefined latitude and longitude threshold, it is considered an interruption, and the interruption location is recorded.
② Route Segmentation: After identifying the potential interruption points, the original route is divided into segments based on the recorded interruption points. Each segment represents a portion of the continuous route.
③ Resampling within Segments: For each continuous segment of each trajectory, separate resampling is performed to generate trajectory feature points that are evenly distributed in the time series.

4.2.2 Route Reversal Processing

In real-world scenarios, the route from point A to point B for an oil tanker is often highly similar to the route from point B back to point A. However, it may also differ due to environmental factors (such as wind direction and ocean currents) and navigation rules. Therefore, for route prediction tasks, by reversing each route, not only can the size and diversity of the dataset be artificially increased, but it also allows the model to learn the bidirectional nature of the routes. This enhances the model's ability to adapt to complex navigational environments, improving prediction accuracy and providing stronger generalization capability.

4.3 Maritime Route Prediction Method Based on Encoder-LSTM Architecture

The maritime route prediction method based on the Transformer model primarily leverages the self-attention mechanism to capture long-range dependencies between waypoints, in order to generate a maritime route from a given starting point to the destination. The model's training objective is not limited to the accuracy of individual waypoint predictions, but more importantly, to predict a continuous and complete maritime route through a multi-step prediction mechanism. However, using the Transformer model for maritime route prediction presents two main limitations:

① Data Input Method: To effectively input data into the model to support the training process, the input method must ensure that it preserves the spatiotemporal characteristics of the ship's trajectory data. At the same time, it should maintain the continuity of the input data while preventing negative impacts on the model's performance caused by interruptions in the voyage data. This is crucial for enhancing the model's understanding of the temporal sequence of the maritime route.
② Recursive Prediction and Error Accumulation: To predict a continuous and complete maritime route, if the model adopts a recursive prediction strategy for multi-step forecasting—i.e., using previously predicted waypoints as inputs for subsequent predictions—it faces the major challenge of error accumulation. Specifically, small errors

in early predictions can progressively amplify during the recursion process, ultimately leading to significant deviations in the predicted route.

Therefore, our study primarily explores ways to mitigate the impact of error accumulation and ensure the coherence and accuracy of the predicted maritime route. To address the issue of error accumulation, this study adopts a multi-output strategy and constructs a maritime route prediction model based on the Encoder-LSTM architecture.

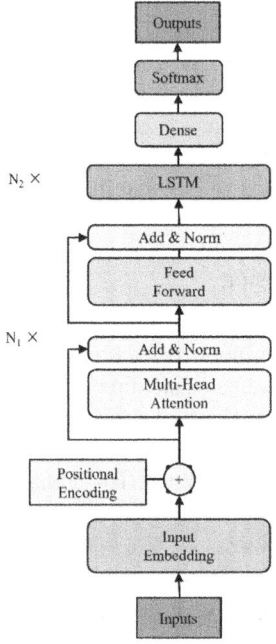

Fig. 10. The Encoder-LSTM maritime route prediction model structure.

The Encoder-LSTM architecture for maritime route prediction starts from a multi-output prediction strategy and is based on the concept of regression. It proposes a maritime route prediction model built on the Transformer base model architecture, aiming to alleviate the issue of error accumulation through multi-output and fewer predictions. This model integrates the Transformer encoder with the decoding ability of LSTM, taking full advantage of Transformer's strength in context feature extraction and LSTM's expertise in temporal feature modeling. In the model design, the classic Transformer decoder is replaced by an LSTM network, with the goal of reducing the errors accumulated through recursive predictions and achieving more accurate long-distance route predictions. The model structure is shown in the figure below: The Encoder-LSTM architecture for maritime route prediction starts from a multi-output prediction strategy and is based on the concept of regression. It proposes a maritime route prediction model built on the Transformer base model architecture, aiming to alleviate the issue of error accumulation through multi-output and fewer predictions. This model integrates the Transformer encoder with the decoding ability of LSTM, taking full advantage of

Transformer's strength in context feature extraction and LSTM's expertise in temporal feature modeling. In the model design, the classic Transformer decoder is replaced by an LSTM network, with the goal of reducing the errors accumulated through recursive predictions and achieving more accurate long-distance route predictions. The model structure is shown in the Fig. 10.

This model takes short-distance trajectory point coordinate sequences as input and utilizes the multi-head self-attention mechanism of the Transformer encoder to capture the spatiotemporal dependencies between trajectory points. The extracted features are then passed to an LSTM network, which models and exploits the temporal characteristics of the features to output long-distance trajectories. The model generates the complete route by iteratively predicting each point along the trajectory.

In the Encoder-Decoder architecture, prediction is a step-by-step process, where only one trajectory point is predicted at a time, and there is a strong dependency between the sequence steps. Each subsequent prediction relies on the output of the previous step as input. This is reflected in the model, where the K and V matrices for the prediction are derived from the output of the Encoder, while the Q matrix comes from the input to the Decoder, which has undergone self-attention computation. During this process, each prediction step involves self-attention computation within the Decoder. As the number of prediction steps increases, the error tends to accumulate in the sequence prediction process, which ultimately affects the quality of the final route.

However, by replacing the standard Decoder with an integrated LSTM, where the feature matrices input to the LSTM come entirely from the Encoder, the model is able to comprehensively analyze the features of the entire input sequence. The prediction process depends on the features generated in the previous step, rather than relying on the output of the previous prediction. The LSTM retains and forgets features of the trajectory, meaning that each step's prediction is based on the accumulated context and the hidden state from the previous step, rather than being dependent on the previous output. The features directly flow through the entire prediction process. Compared to the Decoder, the LSTM reduces the frequent transformation and self-attention computations between the output and features, and can make predictions directly from the input sequence. Thus, each prediction can be viewed as a parallel, synchronous prediction of multiple trajectory points. This not only reduces the risk of error accumulation but also enhances the model's stability and accuracy in long-sequence predictions.

5 Experimental Results Analysis

5.1 Dataset and Study Area

The data set used in our study is the global public AIS data set obtained from the public website from April 2024 to June 2024, and the data size is 16G.

5.2 Prediction Results Analysis

In order to validate the performance of the proposed model in the trajectory prediction task, comparative experiments were conducted between the traditional Transformer and the prediction framework proposed in our study. In the experiment, the data was first segmented according to the flight route IDs. Then, for each flight route, a sliding window method was used to extract point sequences of length (window_length + predict_length), which were used to construct the trajectory dataset for training, as shown in Fig. 11.

Fig. 11. Example of sliding window method.

During the sliding window extraction process, if any interruption in the maritime route is detected (i.e., the difference between adjacent latitude and longitude exceeds a predefined threshold), that segment is removed from the dataset. The following is an analysis of the experimental results for different models under the same training duration.

Figure 12 shows the loss changes for the route prediction model based on the Encoder-Decoder architecture, trained for 30 min with 100 training epochs. The vertical axis "MSE_Loss" represents the mean squared error. From the figure, it can be seen that as the number of training epochs increases, the loss rate of the Encoder-Decoder model decreases and gradually stabilizes, indicating that the model performs well in learning short-distance trajectory prediction tasks on the training dataset.

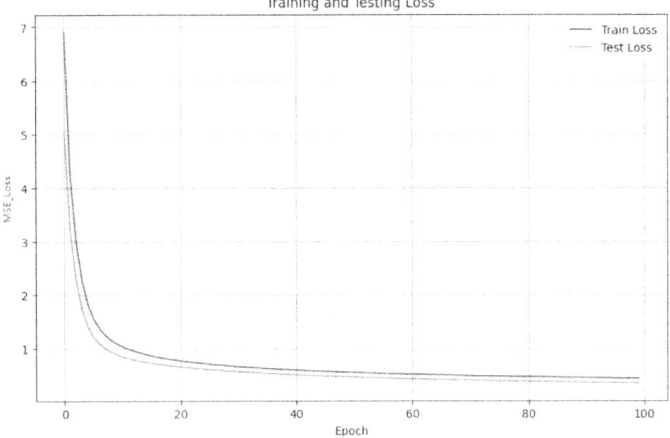

Fig. 12. Training loss for the Encoder-Decoder route prediction model. (Color figure online)

Before training the flight route prediction model based on the Encoder-LSTM architecture, the latitude and longitude data in the dataset were standardized using formulas Eq. 8 and Eq. 9 to improve the model's training accuracy.

$$Lon\_Norm = \frac{lon - \min\_lon}{\max\_lon - \min\_lon} \tag{8}$$

$$Lat\_Norm = \frac{lat - \min\_lat}{\max\_lat - \min\_lat} \tag{9}$$

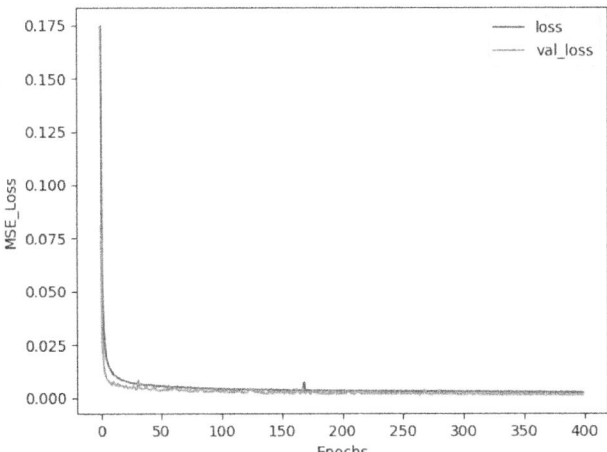

Fig. 13. Training loss for the Encoder-LSTM route prediction model. (Color figure online)

Figure 13 shows the loss function changes for the Encoder-LSTM-based flight route prediction model after training for 30 min with 400 training epochs. The results indicate that as the number of training epochs increases, the loss rate of the Encoder-LSTM model decreases and gradually stabilizes. This suggests that the model also demonstrates good performance in learning short-distance flight route prediction tasks.

Finally, both prediction models were applied to the maritime route prediction task, and the results for 20 identical starting routes were compared. The results are shown in Fig. 14 and Fig. 15. From the figures, it can be seen that the Encoder-LSTM architecture significantly outperforms the Encoder-Decoder architecture in terms of flight route prediction. In Fig. 3–20, the red line represents the original flight route, while the blue line represents the generated flight route. This comparison demonstrates that the Encoder-LSTM model generates more accurate predictions, confirming its superior performance for this task.

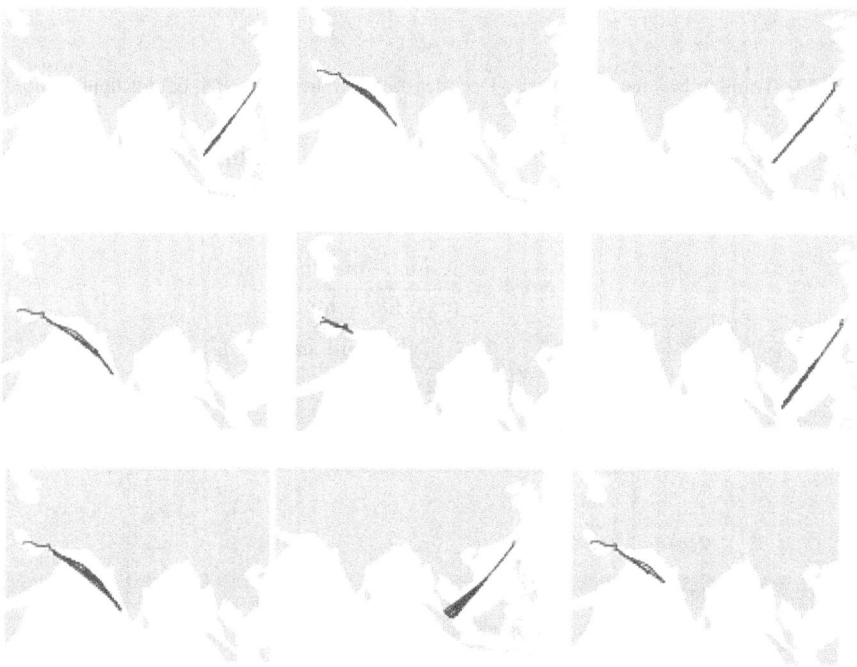

Fig. 14. Generated results of the Encoder-Decoder maritime route prediction model.

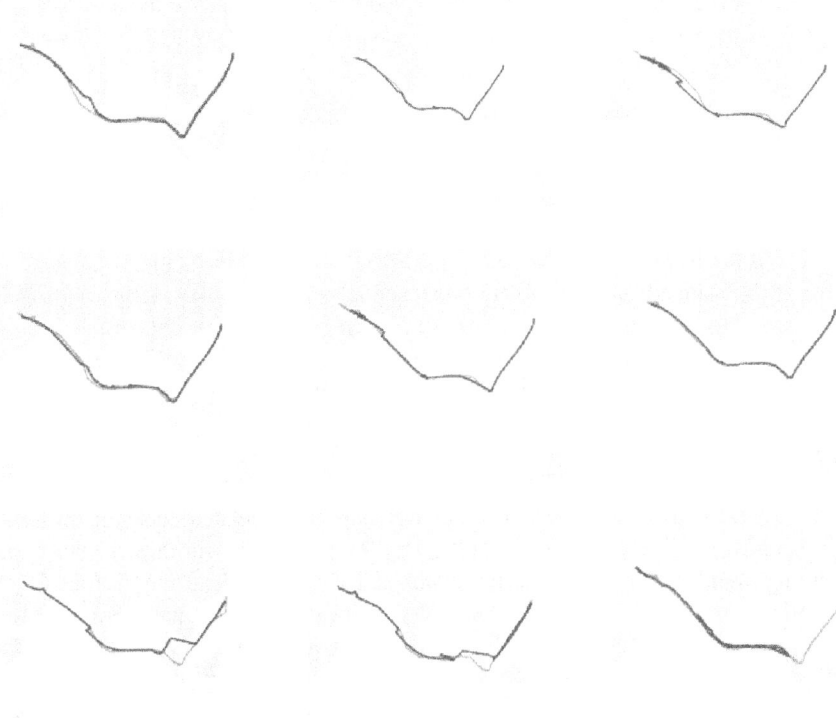

Fig. 15. Generated results of the Encoder-LSTM maritime route prediction model.

After a deeper analysis of the generated maritime routes by both models, it was found that the Encoder-Decoder-based route prediction model essentially stopped predicting the trajectory points towards the end. The main reason for this is that the structure effectively transforms the route prediction task into a classification problem, similar to text generation. In this method, the subsequent choice for each point is modeled as a classification process using a dictionary, with the model selecting the optimal route. Although this method performs well in text processing, it faces challenges when directly applied to trajectory prediction. This is especially true considering the significant difference in training data volume between trajectory and text data. When transformed into a dictionary, an exceptionally sparse matrix is created, which is not conducive to model training. Furthermore, this approach overlooks the geometric distance and location information of the trajectory points, treating all points uniformly in a categorical manner. In such cases, if a prediction error occurs, the model encounters an unknown situation, causing the route prediction to halt.

In contrast, the Encoder-LSTM-based maritime route prediction model preserves the essential spatial characteristics of the data and uses regression analysis for prediction. By generating maritime routes with a multi-output, low-prediction approach, it yields better results overall. However, some unreasonable outcomes still exist. These issues can, to some extent, be attributed to the limitations of the data volume. In the future, increasing the richness and coverage of the data is expected to further improve the accuracy and robustness of the model's predictions.

5.3 Comparison Analysis of Predicted and Truth Trajectories

In the final analysis, our study uses Dynamic Time Warping (DTW) distance as the standard to evaluate the reliability of the flight route prediction results generated by the Encoder-LSTM architecture. DTW distance is used to compare the similarity between the predicted flight routes from the Encoder-LSTM model and the actual test routes.

One of the main advantages of DTW distance is its robustness to inconsistencies in the duration of time series. It can recognize similarities in time series data even when the time axes are not aligned or have different step lengths. This makes DTW particularly suitable for evaluating models in tasks like flight route prediction, where time series data may not always be synchronized, but the overall patterns and trends still need to be compared. By using DTW, this approach allows a more flexible and accurate evaluation of the predicted routes' similarity to the true test routes.

First, the DTW distance for the 20 generated routes is calculated, focusing on the 11 routes that have relatively complete results. The DTW distances for these routes range from a minimum of 582.2984 to a maximum of 1477.6799. Next, the average DTW distance between these available routes and their original counterparts is computed, resulting in a value of 1909.1974. This value serves as a representative threshold for comparing the average similarity between the routes.

It is evident that even the maximum DTW distance is smaller than the average DTW distance between the original routes, which provides preliminary evidence of the reliability of the predicted tanker routes. This result also clearly demonstrates the potential and accuracy of the Encoder-LSTM architecture in the route generation task, validating its feasibility for real-world applications (Table 5).

Table 5. Static data content.

	1	2	3	4	......
1	0	3787.581005	1131.800087	6790.696968	......
2	3787.581005	0	1699.126198	355.0424152	......
3	1131.800087	1699.126198	0	1734.161936	......
4	6790.696968	355.0424152	1734.161936	0	......
...	......	......	......	......	......

6 Conclusion

Our study proposes a new framework for route prediction. In the first stage of handling AIS data, we introduce the IMO and MMS matching method to address the issue of AIS historical trajectory inconsistencies caused by changes in MMSI. Additionally, an anomaly point removal method is employed to solve the problem of continuous drift points in the trajectories. Next, we extract the OD data of the tanker routes by constructing a buffer zone, and enrich the OD dataset using linear interpolation and reverse transformation techniques. Finally, by combining the Transformer model and LSTM network, we leverage their ability to capture long-range dependencies in time-series data to build a route prediction model with the Encoder-LSTM architecture. This framework enables the extraction of vessel route information from large-scale data, from a specified starting point to the destination, and uses this data for training and route prediction. Through comparative experiments, the feasibility and effectiveness of the proposed framework are validated.

However, the framework proposed in this study involves relatively complex steps. The buffer zone method used for route extraction may introduce inaccurate errors in regions near the poles. Additionally, this study only validates the feasibility of the model for route prediction tasks, with the generated results mainly reflecting trends, while the handling of details is not deeply explored. We hope that in future research, other models can be integrated to improve the accuracy of route prediction.

Acknowledgments. This study was funded by the Key Laboratory of Smart Earth (grant number KF2023YB02-10) and the National Natural Science Foundation of China (grant number 42371438).

Disclosure of Interests. The authors have no competing interests to declare that are relevant to the content of this article.

References

1. Yan, Z.J., He, R., Yang, H.: The small world of global marine crude oil trade based on crude oil tanker flows. Regional Stud. Marine Sci. **51**, 102215 (2022). https://doi.org/10.1016/j.rsma.2022.102215
2. Yan, Z., Xiao, Y., Cheng, L., et al.: Analysis of global marine oil trade based on auto-matic identification system (AIS) data. J. Transp. Geogr. **83**, 102637 (2020). https://doi.org/10.1016/j.jtrangeo.2020.102637
3. Alam, M.M., Spadon, G., Etemad, M., Torgo, L., Milios, E.: Enhancing short-term vessel trajectory prediction with clustering for heterogeneous and multi-modal movement patterns. Ocean Eng. **308** (2024)
4. Ristic, B., Scala, B.L., Morelande, M.,et al.: Statistical analysis of motion patterns in AIS data: anomaly detection and motion prediction. IEEE (2008). https://doi.org/10.1109/ICIF.2008.4632190
5. Luo, X., Wang, J., Li, J., Lu, H., Lai, Q., Zhu, X.: Research on ship trajectory prediction using extended Kalman filter and least-squares support vector regression based on AIS data. In: Zhang, Z. (eds.) ICITE 2021. LNEE, vol. 901, pp. 1123–1131. Springer, Singapore (2022). https://doi.org/10.1007/978-981-19-2259-6_99
6. Jiang, B., Guan, J., Zhou, W., et al.: Polynomial Kalman filtering-based ship trajectory prediction algorithm. J. Signal Process. **2019**(5), 6 (2019)
7. Perera, L.P., Oliveira, P., Soares, C.G.: Maritime traffic monitoring based on vessel detection, tracking, state estimation, and trajectory prediction. IEEE Trans. Intell. Transp. Syst. **13**(3), 1188–1200 (2012). https://doi.org/10.1109/TITS.2012.2187282

8. Xiaopeng, T., Xu, C., Lingzhi, S., et al.: Vessel trajectory prediction in curving channel of inland river. In: International Conference on Transportation Information & Safety. IEEE (2015). https://doi.org/10.1109/ICTIS.2015.7232156
9. Luo, W., Zhang, G.: Ship motion trajectory and prediction based on vector analy-sis. J. Coast. Res. **95**(sp1), 1183 (2020). https://doi.org/10.2112/SI95-230.1
10. Li, R.: Ship trajectory prediction based on mathematical model design. Ship Sci. Technol. **42**(8), 17–19 (2020)
11. Wang, S., Cui, Q.: Research on trajectory prediction modeling method based on BP neural network. Ship Electron. Eng. **43**(10), 101–105 (2023)
12. Wu, Z.J., Tian, S., Ma, L.: A 4d trajectory prediction model based on the BP neural network. J. Intell. Syst. **29**(1), 1545–1557 (2019)
13. Liu, J., Shi, G., Yang, X., Zhu, K.: Ship trajectory prediction model based on DE-SVM. J. Shanghai Maritime Univ. **41**(1), 7 (2020)
14. Li, L., Ota, K., Dong, M.: Everything is Image: CNN-based short-term electrical load forecasting for smart grid. In: 2017 14th International Symposium on Pervasive Systems, Algorithms and Networks & 2017 11th International Conference on Frontier of Computer Science and Technology & 2017 Third International Symposium of Creative Computing (ISPAN-FCST-ISCC). IEEE Computer Society (2017). https://doi.org/10.1109/ISPAN-FCST-ISCC.2017.78
15. Wang, W., Yi, Z., Zhao, L., Jia, P., Kuang, H.: Application of switching-input LSTM network for vessel trajectory prediction. Appl. Intell. **55**(4) (2025)
16. Fang, F., Zhang, P., Zhou, B., Qian, K., Gan, Y.: Atten-gan: pedestrian trajec-tory prediction with gan based on attention mechanism. Cogn. Comput. **14**(6), 2296–2305 (2022)
17. Vaswani, A., Shazeer, N., Parmar, N., et al.: Attention is all you need. arXiv (2017). https://doi.org/10.48550/arXiv.1706.03762
18. Wan, J., Xia, N., Yin, Y., Pan, X., Hu, J., Yi, J.: TCDFormer: a transformer framework for non-stationary time series forecasting based on trend and change-point detection. Neural Netw. **173** (2024)
19. Wen, Q., Zhou, T., Zhang, C., et al.: Transformers in time series: a survey (2022). https://doi.org/10.48550/arXiv.2202.07125
20. Devlin, J., Chang, M.W., Lee, K., et al.: BERT: pre-training of deep bidirectional transformers for language understanding (2018). https://doi.org/10.48550/arXiv.1810.04805
21. Zhou, H., Zhang, S., Peng, J., et al.: Informer: beyond efficient transformer for long sequence time-series forecasting (2020). https://doi.org/10.48550/arXiv.2012.07436
22. Liu, H., Wang, Z., Fang, Z.: Integrating hybrid deep learning and path allocation for real-time inbound passenger flow prediction and anomaly detection in urban rail trans-it. Inf. Sci. **692** (2025)
23. Feng, Z., et al.: Trafps: a shapley-based visual analytics approach to interpret traffic. Comput. Vis. Media **10**(6), 1101–1119 (2024)

Learning Sequential Features of Check-Ins for User Relationship Inference

Zhihui Ma[1], Hongmei Chen[1,2(✉)], Lihua Zhou[1,2], and Qing Xiao[1]

[1] School of Information Science and Engineering, Yunnan University, Kunming, China
hmchen@ynu.edu.cn
[2] Yunnan Key Laboratory of Intelligent Systems and Computing, Yunnan University, Kunming, China

Abstract. Location-based social networks (LBSNs) contain a variety of heterogeneous information and are widely used for tasks such as POI recommendation and user relationship inference. However, existing models often overlook the sequential nature of POIs in user check-ins and fail to capture the long-term dependencies of POIs in the check-ins, resulting in suboptimal embedding quality. To address the above issues, this paper proposes a model for learning Sequential Features of check-ins for User Relationship Inference (SFURI), which aims to improve user embeddings. First, we utilize a Bidirectional Long Short-Term Memory network (BiLSTM) to learn the sequential information of POIs in the check-ins, which effectively captures users' dynamical preferences for POIs. Second, we exploit an attention mechanism to learn the long-term dependencies of check-in times in the check-ins and a feedforward neural network (FNN) to optimize the global features of times in the check-ins, which effectively captures users' temporal preferences for POIs. The SFURI model enhances user embeddings, resulting in better user relationship inference. Experimental results show that the SFURI model outperforms the baselines across all the three datasets, demonstrating its effectiveness in learning user embeddings.

Keywords: Location-based social networks · User embedding · Spatial-temporal information · User relationship inference

1 Introduction

With the rapid development of mobile internet and geographic information systems, LBSNs have become an important source of data, capturing not only users' check-in POIs but also their activity patterns and social interactions through the integration of user relationships and check-in information. As a result, LBSNs have been widely applied in tasks such as POI recommendation and user relationship inference.

User relationship inference is particularly significant in LBSNs, as check-in POIs reflect users' behavioral preferences. For instance, if two users frequently visit similar locations but at different times, it may indicate a weak relationship. Conversely, if their check-in sequences are highly similar, it may suggest a strong relationship, such as that of colleagues. Additionally, temporal preferences—such as a habit of visiting coffee shops in the morning versus the evening—can further enhance the inference of user relationships. Recently, MVMN [1] designed a multi-view matching network to learn and fuse specific representations from spatial, temporal, and social views for user relationship inference. HHGNN [2] proposed a heterogeneous hypergraph neural network that models user trajectories and check-in records as hyperedges, integrating an attention mechanism and contrastive learning for social recommendation. However, despite these advancements, existing methods often fail to effectively capture the sequential nature and long-term dependencies of POIs in user check-ins, limiting their accuracy in relationship inference.

To address the above issues, this paper proposes a novel model called learning Sequential Features of check-ins for User Relationship Inference (SFURI), which is inspired by MVMN [1]. The SFURI model aims to capture the sequential nature of POIs in check-ins to understand users' dynamic preferences for POIs and proposes a sequential embedding of POIs. In addition, the SFURI model also learns the long-term dependency of check-in times in check-ins to capture users' temporal preferences for POIs and proposes a dependency embedding of times. The main contributions of this paper are as follows:

(1) Presenting a method for sequential embedding of POIs in the check-ins. This method uses a Bidirectional Long Short-Term Memory network (BiLSTM) to learn the sequential information of POIs in the check-ins, which effectively captures users' dynamical preferences for POIs.
(2) Presenting a method for dependency embedding of check-in times in the check-ins. This method uses an attention mechanism to learn the long-term dependencies of times in the check-ins and a feedforward neural network (FNN) to optimize the global features of times in the check-ins, which effectively captures users' temporal preferences for POIs.
(3) Experimental results show that the SFURI model outperforms the baselines across all the three datasets, demonstrating its effectiveness in learning user embeddings.

2 Related Work

2.1 User Embedding Based on Sequence

Sequence-based methods focus on capturing the order and temporal constraints of user check-ins. Commonly used models, such as BiLSTM [3], generate embedding representations of user dynamic preferences. LBSN2Vec++ [4] leverages hypergraph structures to learn features, while MVMN [1] multi-view matching network integrates spatial and temporal information for reasoning. HHGNN [2] uses hypergraph neural networks to model user trajectories and optimizes embeddings through attention and contrastive learning. TimesNet [5] decomposes complex time series variations into different periods and achieves unified modeling of intra-period and inter-period changes by mapping one-dimensional time series into a two-dimensional space. SCINet [6] captures local temporal patterns through sample convolution and combines a sample interaction mechanism to model global dependencies between time steps. The obtained features reflect users' activity habits and social tendencies.

2.2 User Embedding Based on Graph

Graph-based methods capture user relationships and learn embeddings by constructing user relationship graphs or heterogeneous graphs. For instance, GCN [7] performs convolution operations on adjacent nodes in the graph to aggregate information and generate user embeddings. Similarly, Walk2friends [8] employs graph embedding techniques, using random walks on user-location bipartite graphs to infer user relationships. CMGE [9] introduces category-aware multi-bipartite graph embedding, which simultaneously captures users' interest point neighborhood similarities and activity category similarities. MSC-LBSN [10] captures high-level, dynamic, and multi-role contexts in LBSN hypergraphs through multiple representations for user relationship inference and POI recommendation. HMGCL [11] uses multiple graphs and attention mechanisms for social recommendations. SRINet [12] integrates multiple types of information through user interaction graphs and graph structure learning to effectively infer user relationships. MR-GAN [13] captures the influence and relationship importance between users from multi-relationship graphs.

Distinct from the above methods, the proposed SFURI model not only takes into account the sequential information of POIs in check-ins, but also addresses the long-term dependency of times in check-ins, thereby optimizing user embeddings and improving user relationship inference.

3 Problem Definition

Definition 1. Location-Based Social Network. A location-based social network (LBSN) is a heterogeneous graph $G = (V = U \cup L, E = S \cup C)$, where the node set V includes two types of nodes: user nodes U and POI nodes L, whose corresponding sets are U and L. The edge set E contains two types of edges: user-user relations S and user-POI check-in records C, whose sets are S and C. The POI is represented by $l_i = (x, y) \in L$, where x and y are the geographic coordinates of the POI, the relationship between users $u_i \in U$ and $u_j \in U$ is denoted by $s = (u_i, u_j) \in S$, and the check-in record between user $u_i \in U$ and POI $l_j \in L$ is denoted by $c = (u_i, l_j, t_k) \in C$, where t_k represents the check-in time.

Definition 2. User Check-in Trajectories. The check-in trajectory of user $u_i \in U$ refers to the sequence of all check-in records between user u_i and POIs arranged by check-in times $tr^{u_i} = \{(u_i, l_{i1}, t_{i1}), (u_i, l_{i2}, t_{i2}), \ldots, (u_i, l_{i|tr^{u_i}|}, t_{i|tr^{u_i}|})\} = \{c_1^{u_i}, c_2^{u_i}, \ldots, c_{|tr^{u_i}|}^{u_i}\}$, where $t_{i1} < t_{i2} < \ldots < t_{i|tr^{u_i}|}$.

This paper studies the node embedding of LBSNs and uses the embeddings of user nodes to infer relationships between users. The problem can be formally described as follows:

Problem Description: Given a LBSN $G = (V = U \cup L, E = S \cup C)$, we aim to learn an embedding function $\Phi : U \to \mathbb{R}^d (d \ll |U|)$ by capturing the spatial and temporal information from user check-in trajectories. The learned embeddings $\Phi(u_i)$ and $\Phi(u_j)$ are then used to infer the relationship between users u_i and u_j.

4 The SFURI Model

This paper extracts spatial and temporal information of the POIs from user check-in trajectories, learns user embeddings, and designs the SFURI model as shown in Fig. 1. Specifically, the SFURI model consists of the following three modules: a sequential embedding layer of check-in POIs, a dependency embedding layer of check-in times, and an information fusion layer. The sequential embedding layer of check-in POIs captures the users' dynamic preferences for POIs by learning the sequential information of POIs in user check-ins. The dependency embedding layer of check-in times captures the users' temporal preferences for POIs by learning the long-term dependencies of times in the check-ins. Finally, the information fusion layer integrates the above information to infer the relationships between users.

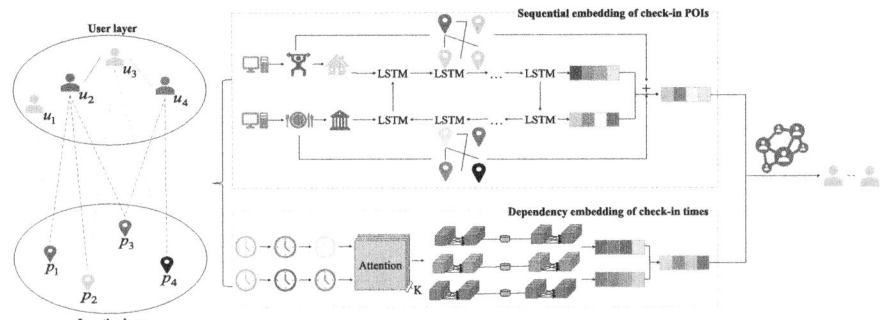

Fig. 1. The framework of SFURI

4.1 Sequential Embedding of Check-In POIs

The POI sequence in a user check-in trajectory reflects the sequential information and reveals the user's dynamic preference for POIs to a certain extent. Therefore, this paper captures the user's dynamic preference for POIs from the perspective of the check-in POI sequence.

For the user check-in trajectory tr^{u_i} of each user u_i, we extract the POI sequence $L^{u_i} = \{l_{i1}, l_{i2}, \ldots, l_{i|tr^{u_i}|}\}$ of user u_i. Based on this POI sequence, we learn the sequential embedding of check-in POIs.

First, a BiLSTM is employed to calculate the forward and backward representations $\overrightarrow{h_m^{u_i}} \in \mathbb{R}^d$ and $\overleftarrow{h_m^{u_i}} \in \mathbb{R}^d$ of the POI sequence of user u_i respectively, the calculation formula is shown in Eq. (1).

$$\begin{cases} \overrightarrow{h_m^{u_i}} = LSTM\left(\overrightarrow{h_{m-1}^{u_i}}, e_m\right) \\ \overleftarrow{h_m^{u_i}} = LSTM\left(\overleftarrow{h_{m+1}^{u_i}}, e_m\right) \end{cases} \quad (1)$$

Here, e_m represents the one-hot encoding of the POI $l_m \in L^{u_i}$.

Secondly, the forward and backward representations of POI are concatenated to generate the POI feature vector $h_m^{u_i} \in \mathbb{R}^{2d}$, the calculation formula is provided in Eq. (2). All feature vectors eventually form the POI sequence feature matrix $H^{u_i} \in \mathbb{R}^{|L^{u_i}| \times 2d}$ of user u_i.

$$h_m^{u_i} = \overrightarrow{h_m^{u_i}} || \overleftarrow{h_m^{u_i}} \tag{2}$$

Finally, the similarity between the POI sequence feature matrices H^{u_i} and H^{u_j} of users u_i and u_j is calculated to obtain the similarity vector si^{u_i,u_j} for the user pair (u_i, u_j) based on the POI order, the calculation formula is shown in Eq. (3).

$$si^{u_i,u_j} = (W \cdot \sum_{m=1}^{|L^{u_i}|} \alpha_m^{u_i} H_m^{u_i}) \odot (W \cdot \sum_{n=1}^{|L^{u_j}|} \alpha_n^{u_j} H_n^{u_j}) \tag{3}$$

Here, $W \in \mathbb{R}^{d \times 2d}$ is a learned matrix.

Additionally, considering the influence of distance, the Haversine formula [14] is used to calculate the geographical distance between POIs, while the Gaussian kernel function is utilized to construct the proximity matrix. Specifically, the top k POIs with the highest counts visited by user u_i are selected. Then, the top k closest POIs to each of these are identified to generate the top-k proximity matrix $PR_{top-k}^{u_i} \in \mathbb{R}^{k \times |L^{u_i}|}$. Next, the features of these POIs are aggregated using a two-layer GCN to create a POI feature matrix $PR_{new}^{u_i} \in \mathbb{R}^{k \times d}$ based on the top-k proximity matrix, the calculation formula is shown in (4). Subsequently, the rows and columns of the POI feature matrix $PR_{new}^{u_i}$ are max-pooled, and the results are concatenated into a feature vector $pr^{u_i} \in \mathbb{R}^{k+d}$ of user u_i based on geographic proximity, the calculation formula is shown in (5). Finally, the cosine similarity between the feature vectors pr^{u_i} and pr^{u_j} of users u_i and u_j is calculated to obtain the similarity score pr^{u_i,u_j} for the user pair (u_i, u_j) based on geographic proximity, the calculation formula is shown in (6).

$$PR_{new}^{u_i} = GCN(PR_{top-k}^{u_i}, E^{u_i}) \tag{4}$$

$$pr^{u_i} = \max_{a=1}^{d} PR_{new}^{u_i}[m, a] || \max_{b=1}^{k} PR_{new}^{u_i}[b, n] \tag{5}$$

$$pr^{u_i,u_j} = \cos(pr^{u_i}, pr^{u_j}) \tag{6}$$

Here, $E^{u_i} \in \mathbb{R}^{|L^{u_i}| \times d}$ represents the one-hot encoding matrix of POIs in L^{u_i}.

To learn users' dynamic preferences for POIs, the similarity vector si^{u_i,u_j} and the similarity score pr^{u_i,u_j} of the user pair (u_i, u_j) are linearly fused to generate the user pair embeddings $Z_L^{u_i,u_j} \in \mathbb{R}^d$ based on the POI sequence, the calculation formula is shown in (7).

$$Z_L^{u_i,u_j} = \alpha \cdot si^{u_i,u_j} + (1-\alpha)(pr^{u_i,u_j} \cdot 1_d) \tag{7}$$

Here, α is the weight hyperparameter, 1_d is a d − dimension all-ones vector.

4.2 Dependency Embedding of Check-In Times

The check-in times at POIs reflect the long-term dependency and reveal the user's temporal preference for POIs. Therefore, this paper captures the user's temporal preference for POIs by analyzing the check-in time sequence.

Given the user check-in trajectories tr^{u_i} of a user u_i, the check-in time sequence $T^{u_i} = \{t_{i1}, t_{i2}, \cdots, t_{i|tr^{u_i}|}\}$ of u_i is extracted. Based on this time sequence, this paper learns the dependency embedding of check-in times.

First, the check-in times in the user time sequence are converted into corresponding time intervals: [0, 2), [2, 4), [4, 7), [7, 12), [12, 20), [20, 24). These time intervals are then mapped to embedding vectors in a manner similar to positional encoding [15], generating the check-in time embedding matrix $TT^{u_i} \in \mathbb{R}^{|T^{u_i}| \times d}$.

To learn the long-term dependencies of times in the sequence, we apply an attention mechanism to learn the check-in time embedding matrix TT^{u_i}, the calculation formula is shown in (8).

$$TT_{att}^{u_i} = soft\max(\frac{TT^{u_i} \cdot W_Q (TT^{u_i} \cdot W_K)^T}{\sqrt{d_k}}) \cdot (TT^{u_i} \cdot W_V) \tag{8}$$

Here, W_Q, W_K and $W_V \in \mathbb{R}^{d \times d_k}$ are the weight matrices of query, key and value.

Finally, the output time embedding matrix $TT_{att}^{u_i} \in \mathbb{R}^{|T^{u_i}| \times d_k}$ is normalized and then passed through a FNN to obtain the temporal feature matrix $TT_{new}^{u_i} \in \mathbb{R}^{|T^{u_i}| \times d}$ which is then normalized again to obtain the final temporal embedding matrix $TT_{final}^{u_i} \in \mathbb{R}^{|T^{u_i}| \times d}$, the calculation formula is shown in (9).

$$\begin{cases} TT_{new}u_i = FFN(\frac{TT_{att}^{u_i} - Mean(TT_{att}^{u_i})}{\sqrt{Var(TT_{att}^{u_i})}}) \\ TT_{final}^{u_i} = LayerNorm(TT_{new}^{u_i} + TT_{att}^{u_i}) \end{cases} \tag{9}$$

To calculate the temporal embedding between the two users, we compute the Hadamard product of their average pooled temporal embeddings and obtain the temporal dependency embedding $Z_T^{u_i, u_j} \in \mathbb{R}^d$ as shown in (10).

$$Z_T^{u_i, u_j} = MeanPool(TT_{final}^{u_i}) \odot MeanPool(TT_{final}^{u_j}) \tag{10}$$

4.3 User Relationship Inference Based on Information Fusion

The information fusion layer combines the above information to infer the relationships between users.

To obtain the user relationship representation, the adjacency matrices $A_{UU}, A_{UUU}, A_{UPU} \in \mathbb{R}^{|U| \times |U|}$ based on meta-paths U - U, U-U-U, U-P-U are first fused to form a new adjacency matrix. Next, based on the new adjacency matrix, user neighbors are identified, and their features are aggregated using GCN to generate the user embedding matrix $Y_{new} \in \mathbb{R}^{|U| \times d}$, the calculation formula is shown in (11). Finally, the Hadamard product of the embeddings of users u_i and u_j is calculated to measure the relationship strength $Z_S^{u_i,u_j} \in \mathbb{R}^d$ the user pair (u_i, u_j), the calculation formula is shown in (12).

$$Y_{new} = GCN(A_{UUU} + A_{UPU} + A_{UU}, Y) \tag{11}$$

$$Z_S^{u_i,u_j} = Y_{new}^{u_i} \odot Y_{new}^{u_j} \tag{12}$$

Here, $Y \in \mathbb{R}^{|U| \times d}$ is the user feature matrix initiated randomly.

Then, the relationship strength of the user pair is combined with their embeddings based the sequential embedding of check-in POIs and the dependency embedding of check-in times to compute the probability of their relationship, the calculation formula is provided in (13).

$$\hat{P}_{ij} = sigmoid(FC(Z_L^{u_i,u_j} || Z_T^{u_i,u_j} || Z_S^{u_i,u_j})) \tag{13}$$

Here, $FC(\cdot)$ represents a fully connected layer.

Finally, the cross-entropy loss function is used to train the SFURI model. The calculation formula is given in (14).

$$\mathcal{L} = -(P_{ij} \log \hat{P}_{ij} + (1 - P_{ij}) \log(1 - \hat{P}_{ij})) \tag{14}$$

Here, P_{ij} is the real connection between users u_i and u_j, that is $A_{UU}[i,j]$.

5 Experiments

5.1 Experiment Setup

Datasets. In the experiment, we selected three datasets from LBSNs: Gowalla, BrightKite, and FourSquare. We removed users and POIs with fewer than 20, 15, and 15 check-ins in the three datasets, respectively.

Baselines. We compare the proposed SFURI model with the following baseline models.

GCN[7]: This model regards users as nodes and social relationships as edges, aggregates information from neighbors through convolution, and generates user embeddings.

BiLSTM[3]: This model generates user embeddings by learning the representations of POI sequences in both forward and backward directions.

MVMN[1]: This model learns view-specific representations from spatial, temporal, and social views and fuses them for final link inference.

MSC-LBSN[10]: The model is a hypergraph embedding model that simultaneously learns friend edges, check-in hyperedges, and node roles. In the experiment, node role learning was removed to adapt to the problem in this paper.

HHGNN[2]: This model uses hypergraph neural networks to model user trajectories and optimizes embeddings through attention and contrastive learning.

HMGCL[11]: The model models LBSNs through heterogeneous multi-graphs and captures the spatiotemporal and semantic information of user check-in trajectories using a hierarchical information fusion mechanism.

Metrics. This paper employs the area under the ROC curve (ROCAUC), recall, precision, and mean reciprocal rank (MRR) as evaluation metrics for user relationship inference.

Settings. This paper utilizes 60% of the existing user relationships in the dataset as the training set, 5% as the validation set, and 35% as the testing set.

For the baselines, we use the source codes released by the authors. The parameters of the proposed SFURI model are set as follows: the weight parameter α is 0.6, the embedding dimension d is 128, the number of POIs k is 75, and the learning rate is gradually adjusted from 0.0001 to 0.01.

5.2 User Relationship Inference

The results of user relationship inference are shown in Table 1. The SFURI model outperforms the baselines across all datasets. Compared with GCN, which relies solely on graph structure, and BiLSTM, which is based only on sequential information, the models incorporating multi-dimensional information achieves better performance, indicating that multi-dimensional information fusion can more effectively capture user features. Furthermore, compared with other models utilizing multi-dimensional information, SFURI improves four evaluation metrics by 2.33%–4.86%, 1.7%–5.8%, 1.61%–5.29%, and 1.06%–5.75% on the Gowalla dataset, by 2%–5.9%, 2.03%–5.72%, 1.1%–5.24%, and 1.49%–5.36% on the BrightKite dataset, and by 1.71%–6.37%, 1.54%–4.36%, 1.82%–3.8%, and 1.23%–5.23% on the FourSquare dataset. This demonstrates that the proposed SFURI model can better capture user features and enhance user relationship inference by learning the sequential information of POIs and long-term dependencies of times in the check-ins.

Table 1. Experiment results of user relationship inference

Datasets	Metrics	GCN	BiLSTM	MVMN	MSC-LBSN	HHGNN	HMGCL	SFURI
Gowalla	ROCAUC	0.6208	0.6433	0.6943	0.7052	0.7123	0.7196	**0.7429**
	R@10	0.5234	0.5777	0.6274	0.6437	0.6563	0.6684	**0.6854**
	P@10	0.3997	0.4445	0.5169	0.5395	0.5498	0.5537	**0.5698**
	MRR	0.6467	0.7214	0.7926	0.8195	0.8314	0.8395	**0.8501**
BrightKite	ROCAUC	0.6239	0.6725	0.7599	0.7683	0.7808	0.7989	**0.8189**
	R@10	0.6037	0.6537	0.7096	0.7285	0.7306	0.7465	**0.7668**
	P@10	0.4692	0.5074	0.5574	0.5788	0.5857	0.5988	**0.6098**
	MRR	0.7395	0.8105	0.8739	0.8945	0.9082	0.9126	**0.9275**
FourSquare	ROCAUC	0.6227	0.6216	0.7326	0.7544	0.7685	0.7792	**0.7963**
	R@10	0.5626	0.5784	0.6676	0.6801	0.6834	0.6958	**0.7112**
	P@10	0.4387	0.4496	0.5274	0.5293	0.5363	0.5472	**0.5654**
	MRR	0.7238	0.7424	0.8564	0.8673	0.8885	0.8964	**0.9087**

5.3 Ablation Study

To evaluate the impact of the two main modules in the proposed SFURI model, we design two variants: SFURI_1 and SFURI_2. SFURI_1 replaces BiLSTM in the sequential embedding layer of check-in POIs with a max-pooling operation, while SFURI_2 replaces the dependency embedding layer of check-in times with an LSTM. The results of the ablation experiments on the three datasets are shown in Table 2.

Table 2. Experiment results of ablation study

Datasets	Metrics	SFURI_1	SFURI_2	SFURI
Gowalla	ROCAUC	0.6944	0.6965	**0.7429**
	R@10	0.6305	0.6375	**0.6854**
	P@10	0.5441	0.5356	**0.5698**
	MRR	0.8156	0.8188	**0.8501**
BrightKite	ROCAUC	0.7366	0.7546	**0.8189**
	R@10	0.6952	0.7038	**0.7668**
	P@10	0.5724	0.5781	**0.6098**
	MRR	0.8716	0.8866	**0.9275**
FourSquare	ROCAUC	0.7258	0.7378	**0.7963**
	R@10	0.6483	0.6564	**0.7112**
	P@10	0.5349	0.5228	**0.5654**
	MRR	0.8413	0.8409	**0.9087**

As shown in Table 2, SFURI consistently outperforms its two variants across all three datasets. The four metrics of SFURI_1 on the three datasets decrease by 4.85%–8.23%, 5.49%–7.16%, 2.57%–3.74%, and 3.45%–6.74%, respectively, indicating that BiLSTM plays a crucial role in capturing the sequential information of POIs in check-ins. Similarly, the four metrics of SFURI_2 on the three datasets decrease by 4.64%–6.43%, 4.79%–6.3%, 3.17%–4.26%, and 3.13%–6.78%, respectively, demonstrating that SFURI effectively captures the long-term dependencies of times in check-ins, thereby enhancing inference performance.

5.4 Hyperparameter Analysis

This section analyzes the impact of the weight parameter α, the number of selected POIs k, and the embedding dimension d in the SFURI model on the model's performance.

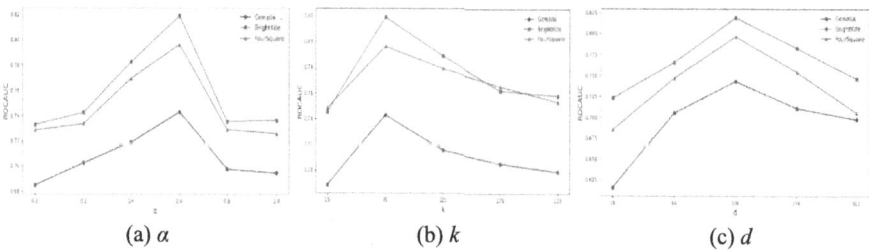

Fig. 2. Effect of Hyperparameters on SFURI

Effect of α. When the weight parameter α changes from 0 to 1 with a step size of 0.2, the ROCAUC of the model on the three datasets is shown in Fig. 2(a). As α increases, the ROCAUC value initially rises and then falls. When α is small, the model mainly learns geographical features and neglects its sequentiality. When α is large, SFURI primarily learns dynamic preferences from sequentiality but fails to effectively capture the geographical features of users' check-in POIs, resulting in a lower ROCAUC value. When $\alpha = 0.6$, SFURI achieves a better balance between sequentiality and geographical features, the ROCAUC value reaches its peak.

Effect of k. The number of POIs k varies from 25 to 225 with a step size of 50. The results on the three datasets are shown in Fig. 2(b). As k increases, ROCAUC first increases and then slowly decreases. When k is small, the proximity matrix is too sparse to capture the geographic proximity of the check-in POIs; as k increases, the sparsity gradually eases; it reaches a peak at $k = 75$; then as k increases, irrelevant POIs may be introduced, resulting in performance degradation.

Effect of d. The embedding dimension d is set to 16, 64, 128, 256, and 512, respectively. The inference results on the three datasets are shown in Fig. 2(c). As d increases, the ROCAUC value first increases and then decreases slightly. The larger d is, the stronger the expressive power of the embedded features is, and the better it can capture users' preferences for POIs. The performance is best when $d = 128$. As d continues to increase, overfitting may occur, resulting in a decrease in generalization performance.

6 Conclusion

This paper proposes a user relationship inference model, SFURI, which captures the users' dynamic and temporal preferences for POIs by learning from the check-in POIs and times. The SFURI model leverages the sequential and long-term dependencies of POIs in check-ins to learn the embeddings of users, thus optimizing user relationship inference. Experimental results across three datasets demonstrate that SFURI outperforms the baseline models, validating its effectiveness.

Acknowledgments. This work is supported by the National Natural Science Foundation of China (62266050, 62276227), the Program for Young and Middle-aged Academic and Technical Reserve Leaders of Yunnan Province (202205AC160033), Yunnan Fundamental Research

Projects (202501AT070227), the Program of Yunnan Key Laboratory of Intelligent Systems and Computing (202405AV340009).

References

1. Zhang, W., Lai, X., Wang, J.: Social link inference via multiview matching network from spatiotemporal trajectories. IEEE Trans. Neural Netw. Learn. Syst. (99), 1–12 (2020)
2. Li, Y., Fan, Z., Zhang, J., et al.: Heterogeneous hypergraph neural network for friend recommendation with human mobility. In: CIKM 2022, pp. 4209–4213. ACM, New York (2022)
3. Siami-Namini, S., Tavakoli, N., Namin, A.S.: The performance of LSTM and BiLSTM in forecasting time series. In: 2019 IEEE International Conference on Big Data (Big Data), pp. 3285–3292. IEEE, New York (2019)
4. Yang, D., Qu, B., Yang, J., et al.: LBSN2Vec++: Heterogeneous hypergraph embedding for location-based social networks. IEEE Trans. Knowl. Data Eng. **34**(4), 1843–1855 (2020)
5. Wu, H., Hu, T., Liu, Y., et al.: TimesNet: temporal 2D-variation modeling for general time series analysis. arXiv preprint arXiv:2210.02186 (2022)
6. Liu, M., Zeng, A., Chen, M., et al.: SCINet: time series modeling and forecasting with sample convolution and interaction. Adv. Neural. Inf. Process. Syst. **35**, 5816–5828 (2022)
7. Kipf, T.N., Welling, M.: Semi-supervised classification with graph convolutional networks. In: Proceedings of the International Conference on Learning Representations (ICLR), pp. 1–X (2017)
8. Backes, M., Humbert, M., Pang, J., et al.: walk2friends: inferring social links from mobility profiles. In: Proceedings of the 2017 ACM SIGSAC Conference on Computer and Communications Security (CCS 2017), pp. 1943–1957. ACM, New York (2017)
9. Ren, L., Hu, R., Li, D., et al.: Cross-regional friendship inference via category-aware multi-bipartite graph embedding. In: 2022 IEEE 47th Conference on Local Computer Networks (LCN), pp. 73–80. IEEE, New York (2022)
10. Trung, H., Vinh, T., Nguyen, T., et al.: MSC-LBSN: multi-social context-aware hypergraph representation learning for LBSNs, vol., 2, no. 26964.07048 (2022). https://doi.org/10.1109/TKDE.2022.3150792
11. Li, Y., Fan, Z., Yin, D., et al.: HMGCL: Heterogeneous multi-graph contrastive learning for LBSN friend recommendation. World Wide Web **26**(4), 1625–1648 (2022)
12. Qin, G., Song, L., Yu, Y., et al.: Graph structure learning on user mobility data for social relationship inference. In: Proceedings of the AAAI Conference on Artificial Intelligence, pp. 4578–4586. AAAI, New York (2023)
13. Qin, G., Qi, J., Wang, B., Jiang, G., Yu, Y., Dong, J.: Multi-relational graph attention network for social relationship inference from human mobility data. In: Larson, K. (ed.) Proceedings of the 33rd International Joint Conference on Artificial Intelligence (IJCAI-24), pp. 2315–2323. International Joint Conferences on Artificial Intelligence Organization, New York (2024)
14. Maria, E., Budiman, E., Taruk, M.: Measure distance locating nearest public facilities using Haversine and Euclidean methods. In: Journal of Physics: Conference Series, 24–25 October 2019, Bali, Indonesia, p. 012080 (2020)
15. Vaswani, A., Shazeer, N., Parmar, N., et al.: Attention is all you need. Adv. Neural Inf. Process. Syst. **30** (2017)

Spatial Optimization of Fire Stations in Beijing Based on Multi-factor Fire Risk Analysis and Covering Problem Model

Chang Liu[1,2], Shaohua Wang[1,2(✉)] [iD], Cheng Su[1,2], Xiao Li[3], Yang Zhong[4], Junyuan Zhou[3], Dachuan Xu[3], Haojian Liang[1], and Jiayi Zheng[1]

[1] Aerospace Information Research Institute, Chinese Academy of Sciences, Beijing 100094, China
{liuchang248,sucheng23}@mails.ucas.ac.cn, {wangshaohua,lianghj, zhengjiayi}@aircas.ac.cn
[2] University of Chinese Academy of Sciences, Beijing 100101, China
[3] Faculty of Geomatics, Lanzhou Jiaotong University, Lanzhou 730070, China
{11220869,11220851,12232104}@stu.lzjtu.edu.cn
[4] School of Information Systems and Technology, Claremont Graduate University, Claremont, CA 91711, USA
yang.zhong@cgu.edu

Abstract. This study utilizes population, road, building, community and Point of Interest (POI) data to conduct spatial distribution analysis and network analysis of Beijing's fire stations. Geodetector is employed to analyze the explanatory power of various factors on fire risk. Based on the spatial analysis results, replacing the traditional Euclidean distance coverage radius by network travel time, the Location Set Covering Problem (LSCP) model is used to add new fire stations, and the Maximal Covering Location Problem (MCLP) model is applied to select key fire station locations, thereby optimizing the spatial distribution of Beijing's fire stations. On the basis of setting $p_1 = 100$ for the first MCLP model solution, we set $p_2 = 50$ and conducted the second model solution to explore the secondary coverage of the model. The results show that our research can cover the demand points in the study area well, and the distribution among all Rings is more balanced, which has guiding significance for the layout of large fire stations.

Keywords: Fire station · Spatial optimization · LSCP · MCLP · Beijing

1 Introduction

Today, with more than half of the world's population living in cities, sustainable urban development has become the focus of global attention. A significant goal of the United Nations Sustainable Development Agenda is to build inclusive, safe, resilient and sustainable cities and human settlements [1]. Cities are also facing various urban safety problems in the process of increasing population density and accelerating urbanization, especially urban fire safety. Asia has a large population and many cities, with the most densely populated cities in the world, and the urban situation is more complex. In 2000, a huge fire broke out in Dongdu commercial building in the old city of Luoyang. In 2015, a dangerous goods warehouse exploded in Tianjin Binhai New Area. In April 2023, the construction work of Beijing Changfeng Hospital caused a fire in the east building of the inpatient department. In November 2023, a fire broke out in the commercial street of Changqing University Town in Jinan, during which abandoned liquefied gas tanks exploded; In May 2024, the 90-year-old auditorium of Henan University, a key cultural relic protection unit, caught fire during renovation. Every year, hundreds of thousands of fires occur in China, causing many casualties.

In recent years, many countries have formulated local disaster risk reduction strategies, making the resolution of urban emergency disaster issues an urgent task [2]. Fire stations are critical for rescue efforts following fires and serve as an essential public infrastructure facility, effectively preventing the spread of fires. According to China's "Fifteen-Minute Fire Response Time" regulation, the time from dispatch to the arrival of fire trucks should be within 5 min. On February 16, 2019, a large fire occurred in Qingyuan City, but the fire station was 21 km away from the scene, and it took 35 min from receiving the alarm to the fire truck arriving at the scene. Therefore, the layout of fire stations is a crucial element in urban fire prevention and disaster mitigation efforts, holding significant practical importance in addressing urban fire issues. This study intends to explore the spatial distribution pattern of the existing fire stations in Beijing by combining multiple geospatial data, using spatial analysis and spatial optimization methods, so as to find the dense areas and weak locations of the spatial distribution of fire stations in Beijing, optimize the spatial configuration of fire stations in big cities, and make the future fire station construction more scientific and urban fire service more efficient.

2 Related Work

Early fire protection issues were mainly studied from the perspective of policies. The Great Fire of London in 1666 prompted authorities to pay greater attention to fire prevention and establish relevant building fire regulations, which can be considered the first planning effort addressing fire safety issues [3]. As mathematical Problem, the facilities location models such as *P*-median Problem, Covering problem (including the Location Set Covering Problem (LSCP) and the Maximal Covering Location Problem (MCLP)), and P-center have also appeared in fire facilities location for a long time [4]. In 1977, Plane and Hendrick applied the Location Set Covering Problem (LSCP) theory to fire station siting, with a maximum response time of two minutes as the standard, aiming to cover the fire service area with the fewest fire stations while maximizing the use of existing stations [5]. Reilly and Mirchandani, in 1985, proposed selecting p fire stations from m candidates such that the time for the first two stations to reach the fire unit is minimized [6]. Bo Jia et al. used the minimal facility number model and the maximal coverage range model to determine the optimal number of fire stations [7]. Murray took California as an example and used the Maximal Covering Location Problem (MCLP) model to study how to weigh between rebuilding fire stations and retaining and maintaining existing fire stations [8].

In recent years, there are more and more researches on the use of various data and methods to assist the site selection of fire stations, as well as the improvement of various models and the optimization of algorithms. Qiang Niu et al. took the fire station layout of Baocheng District in Baoan, Shenzhen as an example to conduct a preliminary exploration of the facility optimization layout model based on road network [9]. Qingbin He et al. divided fire units and optimized the layout of fire stations with GIS network analysis method [10]. Kiran extended the MCLP model by utilizing small area population forecasts to determine the number and locations of future fire stations in Brisbane, Australia [11]. Yuehong Chen et al. developed a multi-objective optimization model considering traffic conditions and actual fire service demand to optimize fire stations in Nanjing [12]. Kaixin Zhu et al. considered spatial constraints of fire station jurisdictions and the variability of urban traffic conditions, proposing a real-time traffic-supported urban fire station coverage evaluation model and analyzing the coverage rates of fire stations in Nanjing under different response times [13]. Church et al. proposed a comprehensive approach integrating network search, GIS, and spatial optimization, comparing actual fire station deployment with ideal scenarios to estimate the spatial efficiency of fire services in Los Angeles [14]. Nyimbili et al. took Istanbul, Turkey as an example and determined the weights of six fire station location factors by using the fuzzy extension simulation expert evaluation of multi-criteria decision-making method in analytic hierarchy process [15]. Rodriguez et al., taking Concepcion, Chile as an example, proposed a site selection for emergency facilities with maximum expected demand coverage, comprehensively considered multiple regions, demand types, vehicle types and scheduling rules, and used the hypercube queuing model to calculate vehicle utilization [16]. Yi Deng et al. used a major city as an example to compare the traditional "circle method" fire station layout model with a GIS-based network analysis model, identifying blind spots and heavily overlapping areas in the fire station layout [17]. Jing Yao et al. proposed a bi-objective spatial optimization model combining coverage and median objectives, along with a constraint-based solution procedure to generate Pareto boundaries, identifying candidate sites for fire stations in the main urban area of Nanjing [18]. Bolouri et al. compared the results of solving spatial optimization problems using Simulated Annealing (SA) and Genetic Algorithms (GA), evaluating fire stations in Tehran's District 11, Iran [19]. Jingwen Guo proposed a Fire-station Location Planning model based on Genetic Algorithm (GAFLP) for large-scale fire station siting problems, which provides better site selection strategies given the same number of fire stations [20].

Although existing research on urban fire station site optimization is relatively mature, each city has its unique characteristics due to geographical spatial heterogeneity and political-economic factors. With the rapid development of Nanjing, the fire risk in urban villages, warehouses, underground transportation and high-rise buildings is very high, while the construction of fire stations lags far behind the urban development [18]. As the hub of central China, new communities and regions are constantly emerging in Wuhan, and various functional areas are mixed together [21]. As an important transportation hub in the Central Plains, there are many old buildings, ancient streets and uneven distribution of fire stations in Zhengzhou [22]. For Beijing, the massive urban scale results in high public service demands and challenging fire safety issues. Education and medical places concentrated, fire safety hazards; the height of the building is uneven, and the difficulty of fire rescue is high; the old residential area is densely built, and the fire escape is missing. As the national capital and a historical and cultural city, Beijing holds significant social status and numerous national key cultural relics, making fire safety extremely important [23]. Therefore, this study selects Beijing's fire stations as the research object, comprehensively utilizing various spatial analysis methods to reveal the distribution pattern of fire stations and optimize their spatial configuration. The aim is to provide scientific methods and reference bases for sustainable urban development.

3 Preliminaries

3.1 Study Area

Beijing is located in northern China, on the northern part of the North China Plain. The terrain is high in the northwest and low in the southeast, with mountains surrounding the western, northern, and northeastern parts. The city center is situated at 116°20' E longitude and 39°56' N latitude. To the southeast is Tianjin, while the rest of the city is bordered by Hebei Province. Beijing administers 16 districts, which can be divided into central urban areas, suburban areas, and outer suburban areas, covering a total area of 16,411 square kilometers. By the end of 2022, the permanent population was 21.843 million, with 10.945 million residing in the six central districts (Dongcheng, Xicheng, Chaoyang, Haidian, Fengtai and Shijingshan), and the regional GDP was 4,161.09 billion yuan. Beijing is a famous ancient capital and a modern international city, home to numerous historical sites and cultural landscapes, and it has the most UNESCO World Heritage sites of any city in the world. This study focuses on the Beijing area. To facilitate the spatial optimization of fire stations, the area within the Sixth Ring Road of Beijing is selected for the study, as shown in Fig. 1.

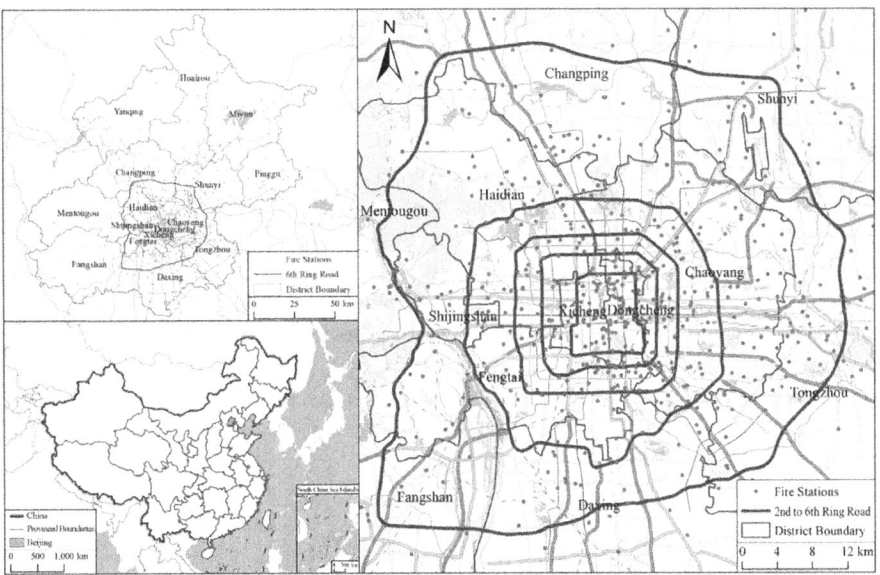

Fig. 1. Study Area

3.2 Data Sources

The road data for this study is obtained from OpenStreetMap (https://www.openstreetmap.org), and all carriageways are selected for analysis, namely motorway, trunk road, primary road, secondary road, tertiary road, and the link corresponding to five types of roads, plus residential road and unclassified road, totaling 12 types of roads. The fire station POI data is integrated from Amap and Baidu Maps, primarily using Amap data supplemented by Baidu Maps data. POI data for hospitals and schools is also obtained through the Amap API. The collected hospital data mainly includes tertiary hospitals and other general hospitals, while school data covers universities, middle schools, primary schools, and kindergartens. The building footprint data came from open-source data in an article by Sun et al. [24], which utilized Beijing-3A and Beijing-3B satellite imagery with a resolution of 0.5–0.8 m to generate detailed 3D building models. Population density raster data has a resolution of 100 m and is sourced from a study by Chen et al. [25], with a dataset $R^2 = 0.8936$ (R^2 is Coefficient of determination), outperforming the existing WorldPop ($R^2 = 0.7427$) and LandScan ($R^2 = 0.7165$) datasets for China. The community data comes from Lianjia website (https://bj.lianjia.com/xiaoqu/), including the name, longitude and latitude coordinates, number of households, number of buildings, greening rate, floor area ratio, average price and other attribute information. The Cultural Heritage data in Beijing is obtained from the National Integrated Online Government Service Platform and National Cultural Heritage Administration Comprehensive Administrative Management Platform, totaling 141 records. After removing line data such as the Great Wall, the Grand Canal, and the Jingzhang Railway, and splitting some records, there are 151 point locations.

3.3 Methods

This study takes Beijing as an example to analyze the spatial distribution and accessibility of existing fire stations and assess key areas with potentially high fire risks. Based on this analysis, the spatial optimization of Beijing's fire stations will be carried out to improve urban firefighting efficiency and more effectively reduce urban fire risks. Firstly, multi-source data acquisition and processing will be conducted, collecting data including fire station POIs, densely populated places (hospitals and schools), road networks, population density, high-rise buildings, and cultural heritages. The obtained point data undergo coordinate system conversion, data cleaning and integration; road data is segmented and used to create a network topology; building data repairs geometry and convert to raster; the community data excludes points where the number of buildings is greater than the number of households and the floor area ratio is greater than the number of households divided by the number of units. The acquired data will be subjected to spatial analysis, including statistical analysis, density analysis, and directional analysis of fire stations and related risk factors. Road data will be processed to create a network dataset, and network analysis will be used to determine the spatial accessibility of fire stations using the closest facility analysis. Based on GIS network analysis, the coverage areas of the existing fire stations were determined, and the weakly covered areas were identified, resulting in a risk visualization map [26]. Multi-source data will then be used to assess the potential fire risk of each factor and normalized. The comprehensive fire risk will be calculated using a Geodetector to obtain model weights (demand) [27]. Finally, a spatial optimization problem will be solved using the LSCP and MCLP models, and the Gurobi solver will be utilized to optimize the spatial distribution of Beijing's fire stations, as illustrated in the Fig. 2.

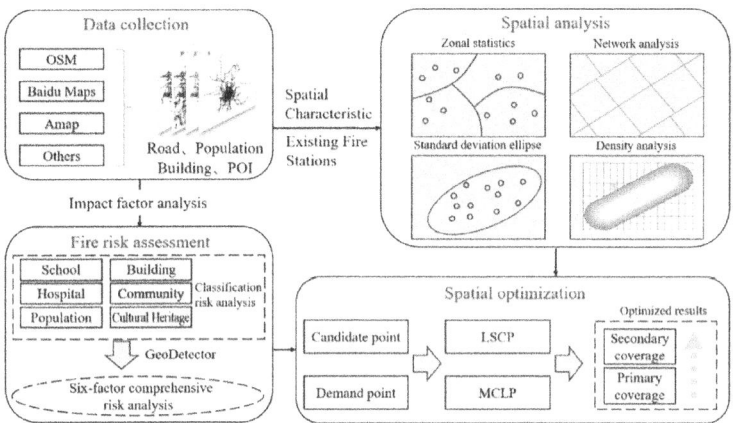

Fig. 2. Framework

4 Results

4.1 Spatial Analysis of Fire Station

To study the distribution range and direction of fire stations in Beijing, a standard deviation ellipse analysis was conducted using a one-standard-deviation ellipse. The visualization result overlaid with Beijing's ring roads is shown in Fig. 3. The overall distribution of fire stations in Beijing follows a northeast-southwest orientation. The one-standard-deviation ellipse roughly corresponds to the extent of the Sixth Ring Road in the southeast and northwest directions, slightly lessens the Sixth Ring Road in the southwest direction, and significantly exceeds the Sixth Ring Road in the northeast direction. The entire distribution shifts towards the northeast of the city, with the mean center located between the Third and Fourth Ring Roads near Taiyanggong. Out of the 743 fire stations in Beijing, 561 fall within the ellipse, accounting for 75.50% of the total.

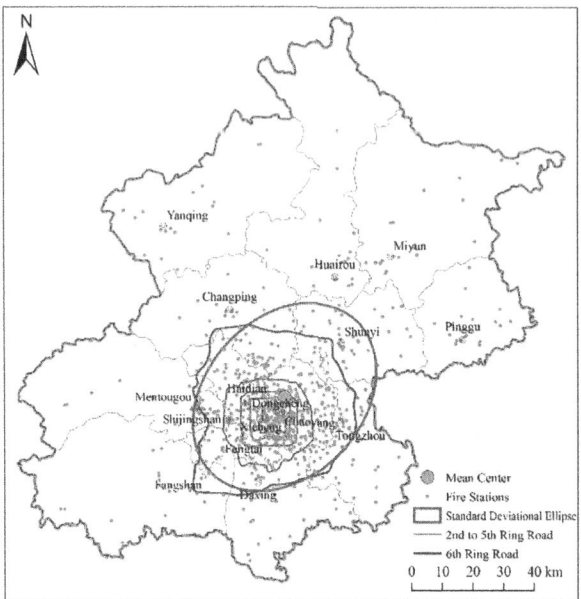

Fig. 3. Fire Station Standard Deviation Ellipse

A kernel density analysis was conducted on the fire stations in Beijing, with the results shown in Fig. 4, representing the number of fire stations per square meter. The highest density of fire stations is concentrated in the city center, with the number increasing from the outskirts towards the center. The closer to the city center, the denser the distribution of fire stations, particularly around the core areas of Dongcheng District, Xicheng District, and the western side of Chaoyang District. Other densely populated urban areas include the eastern part of Chaoyang District, Haidian District, Fengtai District, and Shijingshan District, followed by parts of Tongzhou in the east, Daxing in the south, Mentougou in the west, and Shunyi in the northeast, as well as the southern part of Changping.

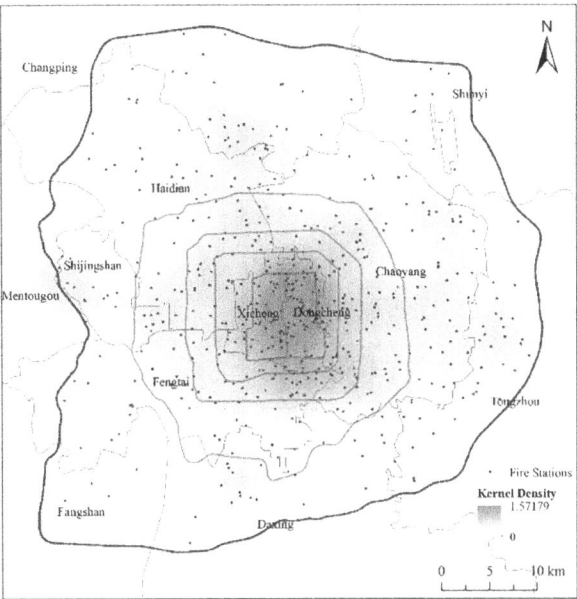

Fig. 4. Fire Station Kernel Density

This study uses the time to reach the nearest fire station from grid points as an indicator of fire station accessibility. Considering that some facility points and incident points are relatively far from the road network, especially in the northwestern mountainous areas where incident points are farther from the road network, it theoretically takes longer for fire trucks to reach these areas. To obtain more accurate results, we need to account for this additional travel time. The distance from facility points and incident points to the nearest road is calculated and converted into time based on a speed of 30 km/h, which is then added to the network analysis results. Additionally, the straight-line distance between the nearest fire station and the incident point is calculated. If this distance is shorter than the minimum distance of either to the road network, the time converted from this distance is used directly. Figure 5(a) shows that the spatial accessibility of fire stations in Beijing generally decreases from the city center outward. The city center has the best accessibility, with most areas in Dongcheng and Xicheng districts reachable within 1.5 min; areas within the Fifth Ring Road generally have good accessibility, with most reachable within 5 min; most areas within the Sixth Ring Road can reach the nearest fire station within 10 min, with only a few areas exceeding 10 min. Overall, 7494 out of 9069 incident points (82.63%) have a travel time of less than 5 min. To explore secondary coverage by existing fire stations, we analyze the time for the second nearest fire station to reach incident points. As shown in Fig. 5(b), 5890 points have a time of less than 5 min (64.95%). The second fire station can reach most areas within the Fifth Ring Road within 5 min, while areas near the Sixth Ring Road take longer. The weak coverage areas within the Sixth Ring Road are mainly around mountainous areas, water bodies, and road sections, while the city center has better accessibility.

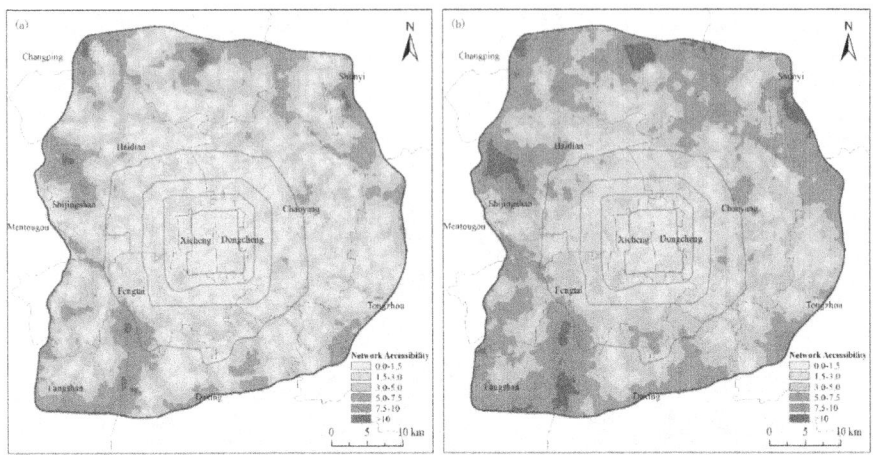

Fig. 5. Network Accessibility Result. (a) Primary Coverage (b) Secondary Coverage

4.2 Fire Risk Calculation

This study assesses potential fire risks. Six potential factors were hospital, school, population, high-rise building, community and cultural heritage, in which X1, X2 and X6 correspond to the core density of this type of POI, X3 is the population density, X4 corresponds to the highest building height, and X5 is the spatial interpolation of the floor area ratio of the community. The six fire risk factors are normalized, and the classified fire risk obtained is shown in Fig. 6. With the grid of 500 m as the minimum analysis unit and the center point as the demand point, the fire risk value of each type of factor is extracted to the demand point as the independent variable X. The value of the core density of the fire station is also extracted to the point, which is used as the dependent variable Y. Factor analysis was carried out with Geodetector, corresponding q values of the six factors were calculated, and the values of the six factors were normalized to obtain q_n, so that the sum of the weight values of the six factors was 1, as shown in Table 1. The comprehensive fire risk of each pixel is calculated according to the value of q_n, and the result is shown in Fig. 7. The potential comprehensive fire risk is roughly symmetrical, with the highest areas around the Second Ring Road, gradually decreasing towards the outskirts along the Third, Fourth, and Fifth Ring Roads. The risk extends to Tongzhou on the east side and Shijingshan on the west side, slightly higher near Tiantongyuan and Huilongguan in the north, and higher in Fangshan and Daxing in the south.

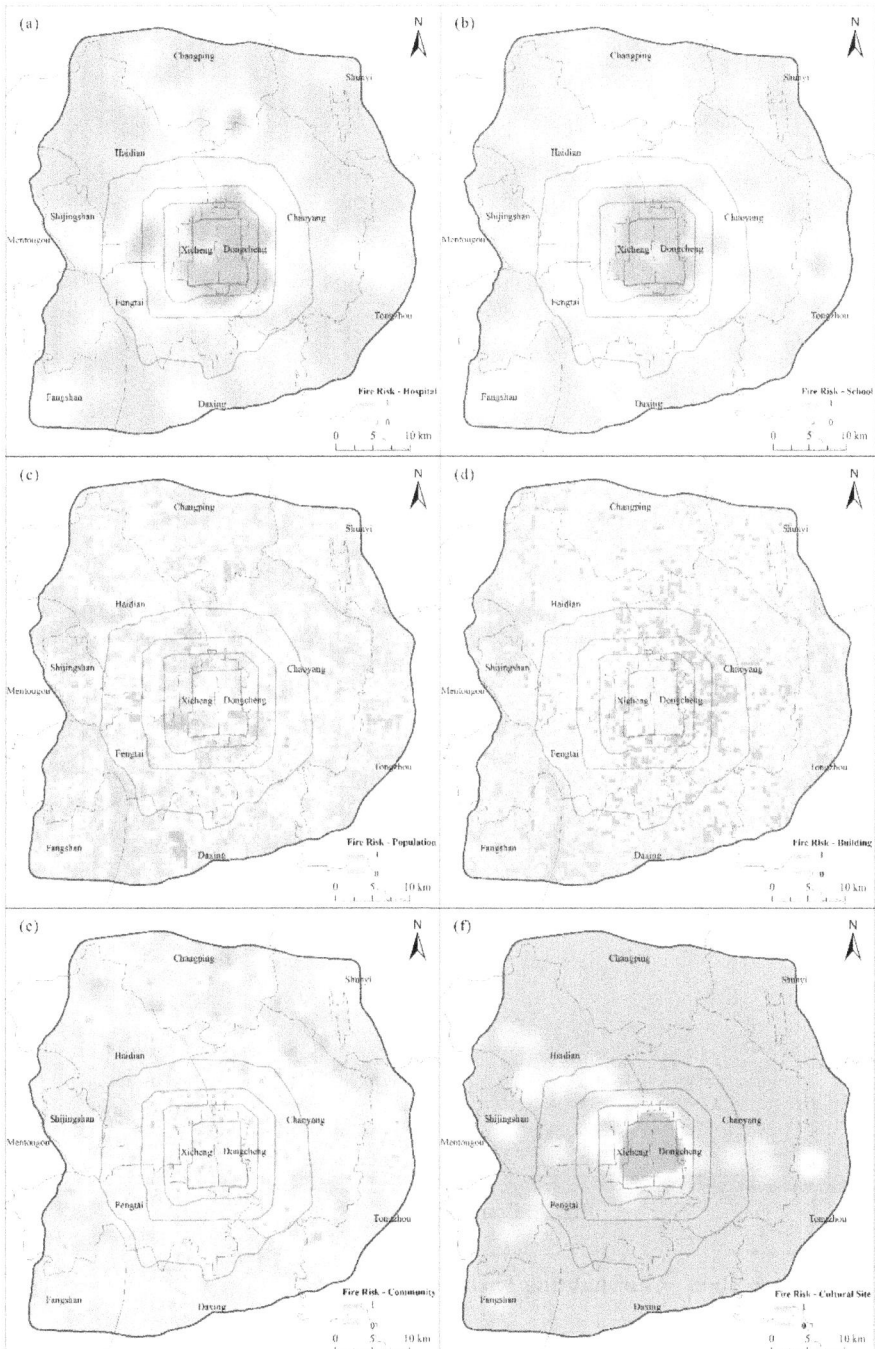

Fig. 6. Classified Fire Risk. (a) Hospital (b) School (c) Population (d) Buildings (e) Community (f) Cultural Heritage

Table 1. Geodetector Results

Factor	Classification	q	q_n
X1	Hospital	0.685	0.272
X2	School	0.719	0.286
X3	Population	0.284	0.113
X4	Building	0.178	0.071
X5	Community	0.128	0.051
X6	Cultural Heritage	0.523	0.208

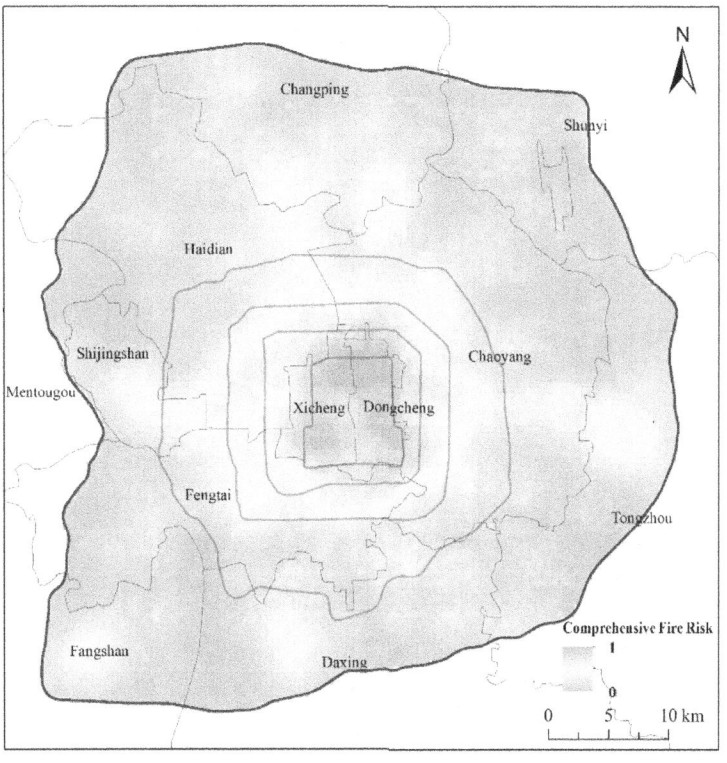

Fig. 7. Comprehensive Fire Risk

4.3 Optimization of Firefighting Facilities

Based on whether a fire station can reach within 5 min, demand points are first classified into two categories. The LSCP model is used to cover areas not currently covered by fire stations, without considering demand point weights. Both demand points and candidate points are set as 500-m grid points. Through network analysis, the network passing time between all the points is calculated as the standard to judge whether it can be covered. Using the Gurobi solver to solve the LSCP model. Figure 8 shows the LSCP results, selecting the minimum number of facilities from 1575 uncovered points, resulting in 119 locations. The results indicate that areas like Shahe, Future Science City, east of the airport in the north, Yizhuang in the southeast, Daxing in the southwest, Dongba, Xishan, and Yongding River banks are weak links in the current fire station coverage, requiring additional fire stations for complete coverage. Some originally uncovered points can be approximately covered by nearby fire stations.

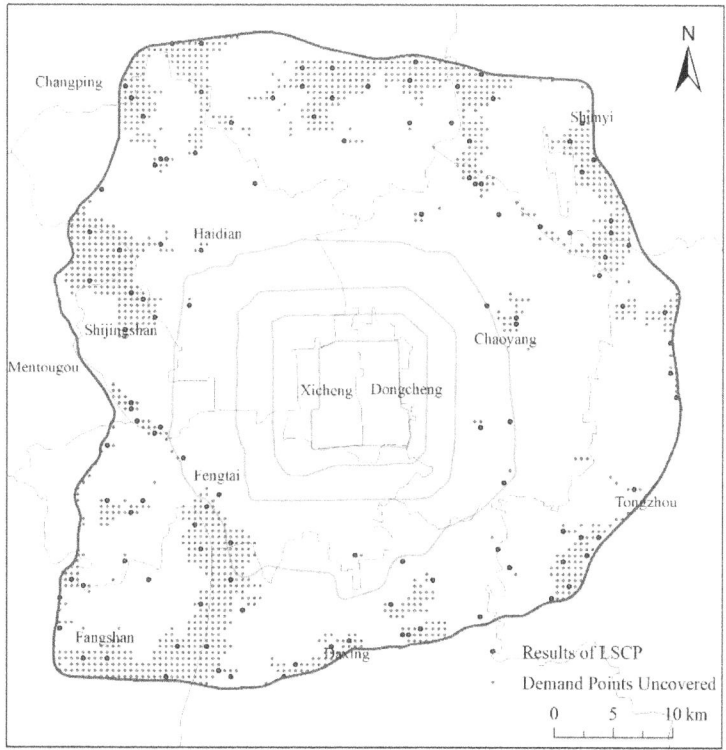

Fig. 8. The Solution of LSCP

The MCLP model optimizes existing fire stations using 528 current stations within the Sixth Ring Road as candidate points, as well as 119 LSCP results, totaling $M_1 = 647$ points. Demand points are 500-m grid points, totaling $N = 9069$ points, with demand point weights as comprehensive fire risk values. The network travel time between candidate points and demand points is calculated as the reference of whether it can be covered, with a 5-min threshold, solving the MCLP model. The first solution sets $p_1 = 100$, with results in Fig. 9(a), showing a fairly even distribution of fire stations covering the entire study area. To achieve secondary coverage for key areas, the MCLP model is used again to select $p_2 = 50$ fire stations from the remaining $M_2 = 547$

candidate points. As shown in Fig. 9(b), due to the smaller number of selected points, it can be clearly seen that the result of this selection is more inclined to select the area with higher comprehensive fire risk. The location of fire stations in these places turned out to be more dense, with higher secondary coverage. The two rounds of solutions total 150 points, as shown in Fig. 10.

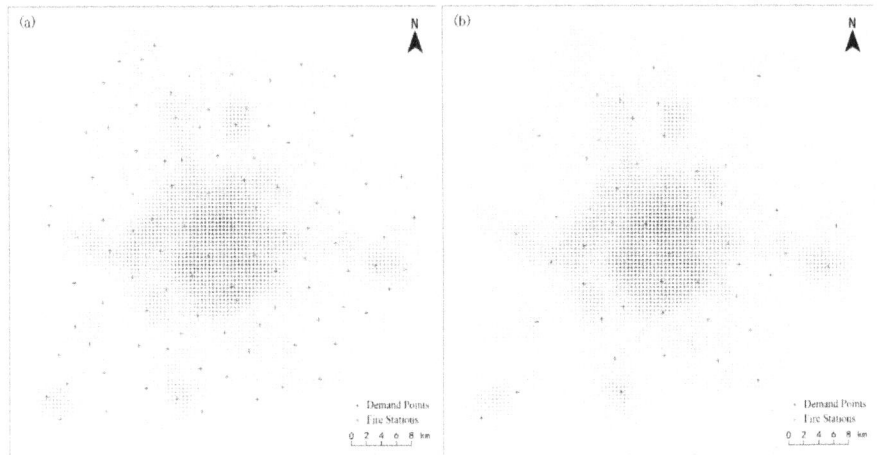

Fig. 9. The Solution of MCLP. (a) Initial Solution $p_1 = 100$ (b) Secondary Solution $p_2 = 50$

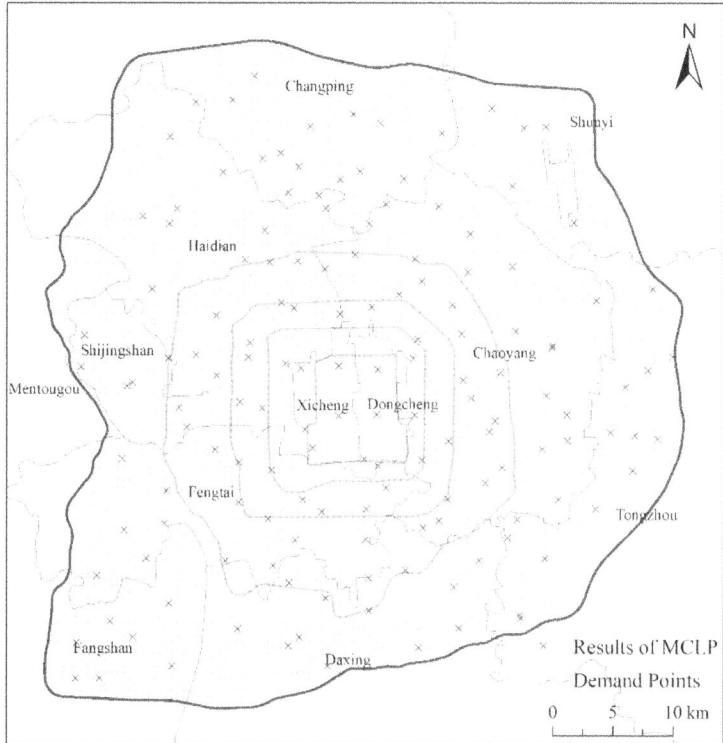

Fig. 10. The All Solution of MCLP

In order to better display our solution results, we calculated the distribution of the result points among various ring roads in Beijing, as shown in Table 2. Compared with the existing fire stations, it can be seen that our solution results are not only limited to the urban center area, but are more balanced among various ring roads, and the gap between the density of regional fire stations in the third to fifth ring road and the urban center area is narrowed, and these areas are also the areas where the population is gradually dense with the development of the city.

Table 2. Quantity statistics of fire stations between each ring road

Region	Area (km^2)	Number of existing fire stations (unit)	Number per unit area (unit/km^2)	Number of resulting fire stations (unit)	Number per unit area (unit/km^2)
Within the 2nd Ring	63	82	1.30	6	0.10
2nd Ring – 3rd Ring	96	58	0.60	8	0.08

(*continued*)

Table 2. (*continued*)

Region	Area (km²)	Number of existing fire stations (unit)	Number per unit area (unit/km²)	Number of resulting fire stations (unit)	Number per unit area (unit/km²)
3rd Ring – 4th Ring	144	80	0.56	14	0.10
4th Ring – 5th Ring	365	98	0.27	34	0.09
5th Ring – 6th Ring	1601	210	0.13	88	0.05

The accessibility of MCLP optimization results was calculated using the same method, and the accessibility of the nearest facility and the secondary facility were shown in Fig. 11. The Fig. 11 reveals that in most areas of the study area, the nearest fire station can be reached within 5 min, and the network accessibility of most areas near the site selection results is within 3 min, while only a few areas in the mountain area, reservoir, airport and other places exceed 10 min. The secondary coverage of the areas within the fifth ring road is good, especially the areas within the fourth ring road hardly exceed 5 min, and most areas within the sixth ring road are also within 10 min. In addition, the originally uncovered Fangshan and other areas with large demand have also been basically covered by better fire stations.

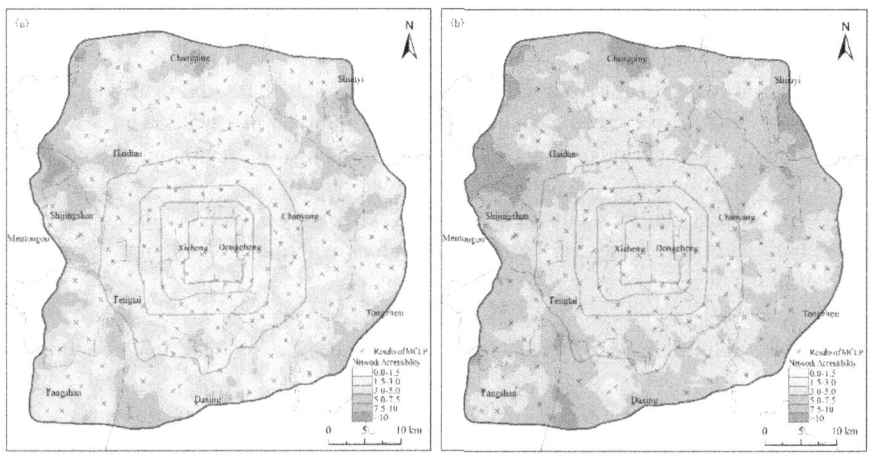

Fig. 11. Network Accessibility of MCLP Result. (a) Primary Coverage (b) Secondary Coverage

5 Conclusion

Beijing's existing fire stations vary in scale, including large, small, and micro stations. According to spatial analysis and accessibility results, the densest area of fire stations is around the Second Ring Road, where stations can generally reach within 1.5 min; the fire stations are relatively dense in the outskirts of the central area, and the overall number of fire stations in urban areas is sufficient, with good accessibility; beyond the Fifth Ring Road, the number of fire stations significantly decreases. Due to the relatively regular coverage in the central area, once the coverage is saturated, facility selection shifts outward. The peripheral areas, however, cannot be covered as regularly, resulting in more overlapping areas and a higher density of fire stations compared to the central area. Therefore, after selecting 100 facility points, another 50 facility points were selected for secondary coverage. Using the MCLP model, this study selected 150 important fire station locations, mainly based on existing stations, without requiring extensive new construction except for some peripheral points. This study considers multiple influencing factors, including population, building, community and cultural heritage, combining spatial analysis methods with optimization solvers to propose innovative ideas for multiple coverage and secondary optimization, improving optimization efficiency. It provides new methods for urban firefighting facility location research. However, there are some limitations. This study only selected some important points as the preferred location of large fire stations, but not consider to classify and grade the fire stations, and did not give the optimization of small fire stations. In addition, affected by urban road network conditions and real-time traffic conditions, different fire stations have varying service ranges, response times and response frequencies at different times, which were not considered. This may lead to insufficient allocation of firefighting resources in some areas, and comparative experiments with similar methods were not conducted.

Acknowledgments. This study was financially supported by the National Key R&D Program of China (Grant No. 2021YFB1407002), Talent introduction Program Youth Project of the Chinese Academy of Sciences (E2Z10501), innovation group project of the Key Laboratory of Remote Sensing and Digital Earth Chinese Academy of Sciences (E33D0201-5), Henan Zhongmu County Research Project (E3C1050101), CBAS project 2023, Remote Sensing Big Data Analystics Project (E3E2051401), and the Beijing Chaoyang District Collaborative Innovation Project (E2DZ050100).

Disclosure of Interests. The authors have no competing interests to declare that are relevant to the content of this article.

References

1. Vaidya, H., Chatterji, T.: SDG 11 sustainable cities and communities: SDG 11 and the new urban agenda: global sustainability frameworks for local action. In: Actioning the Global Goals for Local Impact: Towards Sustainability Science, Policy, Education and Practice, pp. 173–185 (2020)
2. Xu, Z., Zhou, L., Lan, T., Wang, Z., Sun, L., Wu, R.: Spatial optimization of mega-city fire station distribution based on Point of Interest data: a case study within the 5th Ring Road in Beijing. Prog. Geogr. **37**(4), 535–546 (2018)
3. Garrioch, D.: 1666 and London's fire history: a re-evaluation. Hist. J. **59**(2), 319–338 (2016)
4. Owen, S., Daskin, M.: Strategic facility location: a review. Eur. J. Oper. Res. **111**(3), 423–447 (1998)
5. Plane, D., Hendrick, T.: Mathematical programming and the location of fire companies for the Denver fire department. Oper. Res. **25**(4), 563–578 (1977)

6. Reilly, J., Mirchandani, P.: Development and application of a fire station placement model. Fire Technol. **21**(3), 181–198 (1985)
7. Jia, B., Zhao, H., Xu, H.: A study on the optimization of fire station layout in ancient towns based on GIS. Constr. Sci. Technol. 67–68 (2018)
8. Murray, T.: Optimising the spatial location of urban fire stations. Fire Saf. J. 6264–6271 (2013)
9. Qiang, N., Chong, P.: Preliminary study on optimal layout model of public and municipal utilities based on real road network. Comput. Commun. **05**, 49–53 (2004)
10. He, Q., Ma, J., Duan, J., Liu, J.: Determination of fire station site selection and layout analysis based on GIS network analysis method. Value Eng. **42**(21), 7–9 (2023)
11. Kiran, K., Corcoran,J., Chhetri, P.: Spatial optimisation of fire service coverage: a case study of Brisbane, Australia. Geogr. Res. **56**(3), 270–284 (2018)
12. Chen, Y., Wu, G., Chen, Y., Xia, Z.: Spatial location optimization of fire stations with traffic status and urban functional areas. Appl. Spat. Anal. Policy **16**(2) (2023)
13. Zhu, K., Zhang, F., Li, Y., Chen, Y.: Spatiotemporal pattern analysis of fire service coverage rate in nanjing from real-time road conditions. J. Geo-inf. Sci. **23**(12), 2201–2214 (2021)
14. Church, R., Li, W.: Estimating spatial efficiency using cyber search, GIS, and spatial optimization: a case study of fire service deployment in Los Angeles County. Int. J. Geogr. Inf. Sci. **30**(3) (2016)
15. Nyimbili, H., Erden, T.: GIS-based fuzzy multi-criteria approach for optimal site selection of fire stations in Istanbul, Turkey. Socio-Econ. Plan. Sci. **71** (2020)
16. Rodriguez, A., Fuente, L., Aguayo, M.: A facility location and equipment emplacement technique model with expected coverage for the location of fire stations in the Concepción province, Chile. Comput. Ind. Eng. **147** (2020)
17. Deng, Y., Li, A., Dou, W.: A comparative analysis of the models in urban fire station layout planning. J. Geo-inf. Sci. **10**(2), 242–246 (2008)
18. Tao, J., Zhang, X., Murray, T.: Location optimization of urban fire stations: access and service coverage. Comput. Environ. Urban Syst. **73** (2017)
19. Bolouri, S., Vafaeinejad, A., Alesheikh, A., Aghamohammadi, H.: The ordered capacitated multi-objective location-allocation problem for fire stations using spatial optimization. ISPRS Int. J. Geo Inf. **7**(2), 44 (2018)
20. Guo, J., Zhao, P., Ni, J.: Fire station location planning model based on genetic algorithm. J. Comput. Appl. **40**(S1), 41–44 (2020)
21. Jiang, Y., Lv, A., Yan, Z., Yang, Z.: A GIS-based multi-criterion decision-making method to select city fire brigade: a case study of Wuhan, China. ISPRS Int. J. Geo-Inf. **10**(11), 777 (2021)
22. Chen, M., Wang, K., Yuan, Y., Yang, C.: A POIs based method for location optimization of urban fire station: a case study in Zhengzhou City. Fire **6**(2), 58 (2023)
23. Wang, W., Xu, Z., Sun, D., Lan, T.: Spatial optimization of mega-city fire stations based on multi-source geospatial data: a case study in Beijing. ISPRS Int. J. Geo-Inf. **10**(5) (2021)
24. Sun, X., Huang, X., Mao, Y., et al.: GABLE: a first fine-grained 3D building model of China on a national scale from very high resolution satellite imagery. Remote Sens. Environ. **305**, 114057 (2024)
25. Chen, Y., Xu, C., Ge, Y., Zhang, X., Zhou, Y.: A 100-m gridded population dataset of China's seventh census using ensemble learning and geospatial big data. Earth Syst. Sci. Data Discuss. **2024**, 1–19 (2024)
26. Zhong, E.: Deep mapping—a critical engagement of cartography with neuroscience. Geom. Inf. Sci. Wuhan Univ. **47**(12), 1988–2002 (2022)
27. Wang, J., Xu, C.: Geodetector: principle and prospective. Acta Geogr. Sin. **72**(01), 116–134 (2017)

A Location Label Optimization Method for Crowdsourcing Trajectory Data

Kehong Xiao, Xiang Li(✉), Fang Ren, and Jiaqi Li

Institute of Geospatial Information, Information Engineering University, Zhengzhou 450001, China
ryolx13@126.com

Abstract. With the vigorous development of mobile internet technology and the widespread use of smart devices represented by mobile phones, crowdsourcing mobile trajectory collection has emerged as a significant means of data acquisition due to its efficiency, flexibility, data diversity, and low cost. However, variations in the types of intelligent terminals and user habits have led to inconsistent quality in the crowdsourcing data obtained. Especially in complex environments with signal shielding, the reliability of location precision is low, making it difficult to meet the application needs. Addressing these issues, this paper analyzes and extracts multiple features from crowdsourcing multi-source observation data collected by various models of intelligent terminals (such as Xiaomi and HUAWEI). In open scenarios, it employs multi-source fusion methods based on trajectory segmentation and clustering for data processing. In shaded environments, it utilizes map-matching algorithms to correct errors, thereby enhancing positional accuracy. Field tests and validations have demonstrated that the positioning accuracy of crowdsourcing data has been improved by the algorithm proposed in this paper. This proves the feasibility and effectiveness of this method, which can provide assistance in the analysis and processing of crowdsourcing data.

Keywords: Crowdsourcing data · location label · trajectory clustering · map-matching · error correction

1 Introduction

With the popularization of mobile Internet and intelligent terminals, crowdsourcing collection of mobile trajectories has become a key means of data acquisition [1–3] because of its advantages of high efficiency and flexibility, rich and diverse data, and low cost [4, 5]. It is widely used in traffic planning, geographic information update, commercial site selection, and other fields [6, 7].

However, there are certain differences in the performance of positioning modules across different acquisition devices, and the acquisition strategy conditions are not uniform. For example, low sampling frequency and insufficient sampling time can lead to insufficient data accuracy and integrity [8]. Particularly in indoor or signal shielding environments, satellite signals of mobile terminal is severely blocked, reducing the accuracy of crowdsourcing trajectory data. This results in unreliable location information and limits the advantages of crowdsourcing collection [9, 10].

Based on the above problems, this paper proposes a location label optimization algorithm for crowdsourcing trajectory data. The algorithm employs multiple optimization strategies, including multi-source fusion processing and map matching. In environments with good satellite signals, the initial trajectory data extracted through feature analysis undergo trajectory segmentation based on carrier movement direction, trajectory clustering processing based on distance, and optimization based on road centerlines. In environments with signal denial, the map matching algorithms are further optimized. To address the limitations of the hidden Markov model (HMM), such as insufficient utilization of historical trajectory information and over-reliance on prior knowledge, the Markov model algorithm is improved. This improvement involves calculating the emission probability using comprehensive distance and direction factors, introducing reliable points for trajectory segmentation, reducing the computation of transition probabilities, and minimizing the output delay of matching results. These enhancements ensure the accuracy and time efficiency of the algorithm. Finally, the feasibility of the algorithm is verified by experiments.

2 Related Work

2.1 Research Status of Positioning Technology of Crowdsourcing Data

To ensure the accuracy of the extraction, the acquired crowdsourcing trajectories need to be preprocessed, i.e. segmentation and clustering. There are several approaches to trajectory clustering, including distance-based, identifier-based, and map-based solutions. In distance-based solutions, the Euclidean distance is a common measure of trajectory similarity, but it only assesses partial similarity [11]. To obtain the global similarity, other metrics such as vertical distance, parallel distance, or angular distance are employed. However, these methods incur significant computational overhead since three metrics must be computed for each pair of trajectories [12]. In the identifier-based method, each participant is required to negotiate the road identifier in advance and autonomously delineate their trajectory. This approach may introduce additional communication and computational overhead for both the system and its participants [13]. Map-based solutions have also been extensively researched, facilitating trajectory clustering by aligning benchmark maps with intermediate representations of trajectories. However, due to the inherent complexity of road maps, achieving high clustering accuracy continues to pose significant challenges [14] (Table 1).

Table 1. Research status of clustering algorithm

Algorithm Type	Peculiarity	Shortcoming
Based on distance	Euclidean distances are usually employed, and algorithms that use vertical distances, parallel distances, or angular distances exist	Only partial similarity can be assessed using Euclidean distance, and using other distance measures yields larger calculations Overhead
Identifier based	Each participant is required to upload their own trajectory and its associated identifier	Would impose additional communication and computational overhead on the system and participants
Map-based	Clustering by intermediate representation matching of datum maps and trajectories	Requires a map and has poor accuracy due to the complexity of the map

2.2 Research Status of Map Matching Technology

Since the acquisition carrier is driving on the road, the high-precision reference map can provide accurate position information without being affected by the signal source. Therefore, the map matching method can be used to further optimize the accuracy of the acquisition data. At present, the research of map matching methods mainly includes the following categories:

Most researchers utilize various filtering techniques to address errors in positioning data. This approach is fundamentally straightforward, presents low operational complexity, and is well-suited for batch data processing. However, its interpretability is limited, and verifying its processing accuracy poses challenges—particularly for intelligent terminal data with constrained initial precision. As a result, the optimization effect remains restricted [15].

Early map matching research focused on real-time or online matching of high sampling rate positioning data, which is typically suitable for of good satellite signals. Geometric analysis and topology analysis algorithms are typical representatives of this approach [16]. However, in actual driving scenarios, due to limitations of in equipment performance, environmental interference and sampling rate, it is challenge to ensure that the acquisition terminal provides continuous and reliable positioning information. This leads to mismatching problems such as multi-path selection and topology search failures, complicating efforts to achieve requisite accuracy.

Machine learning-based artificial intelligence algorithms enhance map matching accuracy by establishing more comprehensive models and optimizing map matching algorithms, demonstrating strong accuracy and adaptability. However, this type of algorithm requires a large amount of labeled data to train model parameters, while obtaining labeled training data can be challenging; Furthermore, the design of path selection models, prediction models or neural networks involves substantial computational demands, which require high performance and cost of hardware resources [17].

Advanced matching algorithms based on optimization models focus on positioning data with low sampling rates and large positioning errors. These algorithms demonstrate greater stability and reliability compared to other methods [18]. While they perform well in general scenarios, their effectiveness can be compromised by various factors. For instance, autonomous navigation tasks may fail in special or complex environments.

Additionally, road network maps are not always accurate due to measurement errors or untimely updates, and methods relying on additional sensors cannot effectively address these errors (Table 2).

Table 2. Research status of map matching

Algorithm Type	Representative algorithm	Algorithm features
Filtering algorithm	Kalman filter and so on	Simple principle, high efficiency, suitable for large batch data processing
Geometry/topology information algorithm	Projection algorithms, simple/weighted topology algorithms, etc.	It is suitable for good satellite signal environment (high sampling rate and small positioning error), simple calculation and fast matching speed
Machine learning algorithms	Deep - MM algorithms, ranking learning-based algorithms, and more	Large training data requirements, but strong matching accuracy and adaptability
Advanced matching algorithm	HMM (Implicit Markov) algorithm, fuzzy logic model, etc.	Comprehensive consideration of comprehensive information, high stability and reliability

3 Technical Route

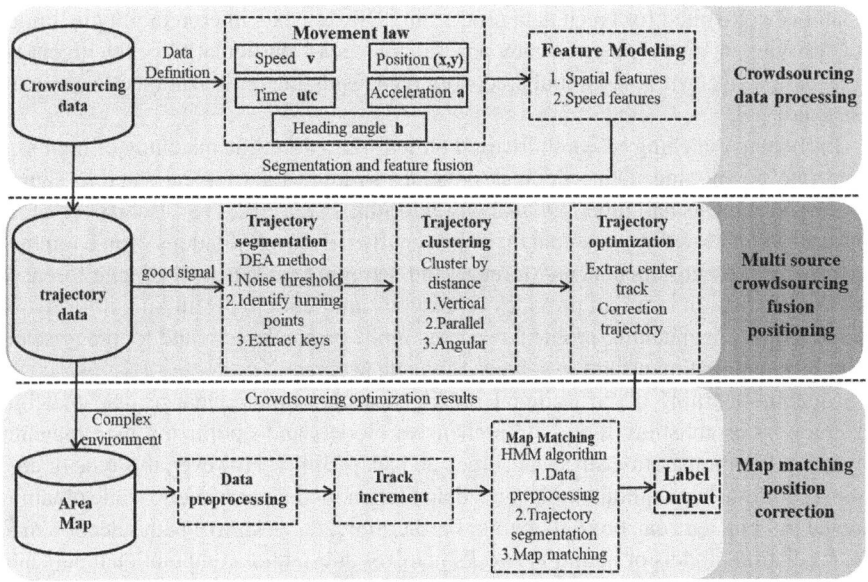

Fig. 1. Technical route

There are abundant sources of crowdsourcing trajectory data. However, due to differences in mobile phone brands and performance, the data varies, making trajectory feature extraction challenging (Fig. 1).

Firstly, crowdsourcing trajectory data is influenced by environmental constraints and the dynamics of vehicle movement, exhibiting spatial and velocity characteristics. Spatial characteristics include turning behavior, U-turn behavior, lane change behavior, and straight-ahead behavior. Speed characteristics typically fall into two categories: one is the strong constraints of traffic rules on fixed road sections, and the other is sudden changes due to real-time situations. By identifying key behaviors, relevant parameters are selected to extract trajectory features. These features should be modeled, and the original data is integrated for segmentation and feature fusion, thereby completing the feature extraction of the trajectory data.

Secondly, optimizing multi-source trajectory data involves several steps. Firstly, sub-trajectories are segmented based on motion direction using the DEA method, with data processing guided by the direction extension and motion characteristics of the carrier. Secondly, a composite distance-based trajectory clustering method is employed to preserve the geometric integrity of crowdsourcing trajectory data. Thirdly, lane centerline optimization is applied, where trajectories with significant errors are corrected using the lane centerline to achieve optimization.

Finally, a improved hidden Markov model (HMM) algorithm is used for map matching. Emission probabilities are calculated by integrating distance and direction factors. By introducing reliable points for trajectory segmentation, this approach reduces transition probability calculations and minimizes output delays in matching results, thereby enhancing the refinement of location labels.

4 Motion Feature Analysis for Crowdsourcing Trajectory Data

When a vehicle is driving on the road, its trajectory is influenced by the road environment, primarily reflected in behavioral changes. Vehicle movement patterns indicate that crowdsourcing trajectory data exhibits spatial behavior characteristics and speed variation characteristics [19].

4.1 Spatial Behavior Characteristics

(see Fig. 2).

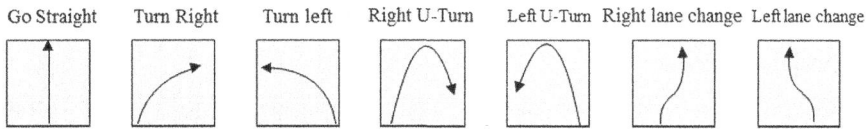

Fig. 2. Classification of spatial behavior characteristics

The spatial behavior characteristics include turning behavior, U-turn behavior, lane change behavior, and straight-going behaviour [20]. The spatial behavior characteristics of trajectories are primarily reflected in changes in trajectory curvature, which can be characterized using heading angle, coordinates, and time parameters. Assuming the vehicle's position at time t is $(x1, y1)$ and at time $t + \Delta t$ is $(x2, y2)$, the heading angle θ can be calculated using the following formula:

$$\theta = \arctan2(y2 - y1, x2 - x1) \tag{1}$$

Calculate the difference between the target heading angle and the initial heading angle, denoted as $\Delta\theta$. The formula is:

$$\Delta\theta = target\ heading\ angle - initial\ heading\ angle \tag{2}$$

A. Characteristics of turning behavior

In terms of turning behavior, it is primarily categorized into left and right turns. After a turn, the trajectory's heading angle θ changes, and the rate of change of θ reflects the turning amplitude of the vehicle. A larger change rate of the heading angle indicates a greater turning amplitude.

If $\Delta\theta$ is between $-90°$ and $0°$, the vehicle trajectory is a right turn.

If $\Delta\theta$ is between $0°$ and $90°$, the vehicle trajectory is a left turn.

B. Characteristics of U-turn behavior

U-turn behavior involves the carrier changing its direction of movement, which can be either a left U-turn or a right U-turn. Unlike regular turns, U-turns involve more pronounced curvature changes, with the heading angle θ changing by nearly 180°, resulting in movement in the opposite direction.

If $\Delta\theta$ is between $-90°$ and $-180°$, the vehicle trajectory is a right U-turn.

If $\Delta\theta$ is between $90°$ and $180°$, the vehicle trajectory is a left turn.

C. Characteristics of lane change behavior

Lane change behavior refers to the lane changes made by a moving carrier, which can be categorized as left or right lane changes. The heading angle remains constant before and after a lane change, and the direction of the lane change can be determined by the change in the heading angle θ.

If, within a time interval Δt, the heading angle θ is $\Delta\theta = 0$ at both the start and end of the interval, and $\Delta\theta$ initially changes between approximately $0°$ and $-45°$, then the vehicle trajectory indicates a right lane change. Conversely, if $\Delta\theta$ initially changes between approximately $0°$ and $45°$ within the time interval, the vehicle trajectory indicates a left lane change.

D. Straight behavior

Straight behavior refers to the continuous movement of a carrier in a specific direction, with both trajectory curvature and heading angle θ remaining constant.

If the heading angle difference $\Delta\theta$ consistently remains 0 over the time interval Δt, the vehicle's trajectory is considered straight.

4.2 Speed Change Characteristics

There are typically two scenarios regarding speed change characteristics: one is the strong constraints imposed by traffic rules on fixed road sections, such as high-speed limit signs on expressways [21]. In such cases, the vehicle maintains a constant speed over a period, resulting in zero acceleration and closely spaced trajectory points, which is reflected in the speed, acceleration, and position parameters of the trajectory data. The other scenario involves sudden changes due to real-time situations, such as yielding to pedestrians on sidewalks, traffic congestion, or signal light changes. In these cases, the vehicle may stop, causing the track point position to remain unchanged and the speed to drop to zero.

The velocity change characteristics of the trajectory can be analyzed by examining velocity, acceleration, and position parameters:

A. Characteristics of traffic rule identification with strong constraints on fixed road sections

In this case, the vehicle is subject to compliance with traffic rules, such as highway speed limit signs, which cause the vehicle to maintain a constant speed for a period of time. In this scenario, the velocity v remains constant, the acceleration a is zero, and the interval between trajectory points Δs is relatively small.

The track point interval can be calculated using the formula $\Delta s = v \cdot \Delta t$, where Δt represents the time interval.

B. Sudden changes according to the actual situation

In this case, the vehicle's speed may change abruptly due to real-time situations (such as yielding to pedestrians, traffic congestion, temporary parking, or signal light changes) [22, 23]. During such events, the velocity v can suddenly drop to zero or undergo a significant change. The acceleration a may become negative (indicating deceleration) or positive (indicating acceleration), with a large magnitude of change.

Speed:

$$v(t) = \begin{cases} v_0, & \text{Before the change} \\ 0 \text{ or } v_1, & \text{After the change} \end{cases} \quad (3)$$

where v0 is the speed before the change and v1 is the speed after the change (if the vehicle starts to move).

Acceleration:

$$a = \frac{dv}{dt} = \begin{cases} 0, & \text{when chaging} \\ \text{Larger values,} & \text{Before the change} \end{cases} \quad (4)$$

Track Point Location:

$$s(t) = \begin{cases} S_0 + v_0 t, & \text{Before the change} \\ S_0, & \text{If parking (with constant speed)} \\ S_0 + \int_{t_0}^{t} v(\tau) d\tau, & \text{After the change, (if the speed changes)} \end{cases} \quad (5)$$

where s0 is the position before the change and t0 is the time when the change began.

From the feature analysis discussed above, several issues have been identified. For instance, long trajectory segments may encompass multiple features, which can negatively impact subsequent clustering analysis results. Furthermore, since the movement direction of crowdsourcing trajectories on the same road section is typically consistent (or directly opposite), trajectory segmentation based on movement direction is essential. Additionally, the sub-trajectories resulting from segmentation often belong to different road sections and lane groupings. Accurate trajectory clustering ensures that sub-trajectories within the same group are located in the same lane, thereby guaranteeing the accuracy of subsequent trajectory optimization algorithms [24].

5 Segmentation and Clustering of Crowdsourcing Trajectory Data

5.1 Trajectory Segmentation Based on Carrier Motion Direction

The Data Envelopment Analysis (DEA) method is based on the directional extension of the carrier's motion, with data processing tailored to the carrier's movement characteristics [25]. In the DEA algorithm, trajectory points are categorized into three types: abnormal points, feature points, and turning points. Abnormal points are those that significantly deviate from the normal trajectory. Feature points are significant or representative points in the trajectory data, often indicating key locations such as starts, ends, or turning points. Turning points specifically refer to locations where the moving object changes direction, typically found at trajectory bends and reflecting changes in the object's motion state [26] (Fig. 3).

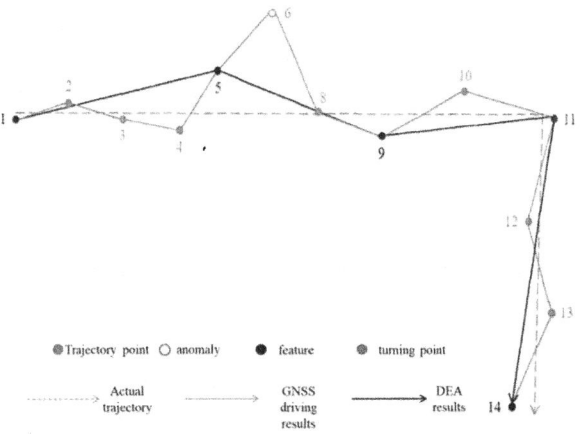

Fig. 3. DEA Method schematic (Color figure online)

The principle of the DEA method is illustrated in the figure above. In the figure, the vehicle trajectory is represented by a green solid line. Starting from the initial point $p$start, a simple line segment L is formed with the subsequent trajectory point pj as the endpoint. The distance from each trajectory point to the line segment L is calculated as d_j.

If d_j If it is less than the distance threshold d, the point is regarded as the trajectory redundancy point.

If d_j Larger than the distance threshold d, judging the trajectory point p_j With neighborhood points (p_{j-1}, p_{j+1}) distance of d_{j-1} And d_{j+1} Relationship with d.

If $d_{j-1} < d$ And $d_{j+1} < d$ represents a point p_j If a point is inconsistent with the direction of its neighboring points, it is treated as an outlier, such as point p6. Otherwise, the point is considered a feature point (KeyPoint). By analyzing the segments (p_{j-1}, p_j) with (p_j, p_{j+1}) along with the movement time interval, we can determine whether the carrier changes direction at this point or stops at an intersection.

Finally, the trajectory is simplified as {p1, p5, p9, p11, p14}, where p11 is the turning point. According to the principle of DEA method, the trajectory segmentation is expressed as (Fig. 4):

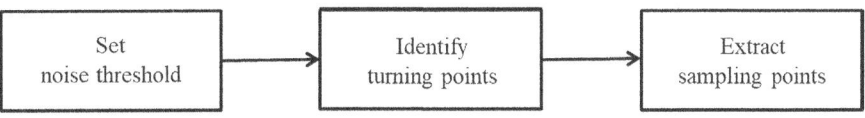

Fig. 4. Trajectory segmentation technical route

Firstly, during trajectory processing, a noise threshold for sampling points is set. This helps identify and eliminate trajectory noise, thereby enhancing the reliability of the geometric quality of trajectory data. Secondly, the impact of data heterogeneity from turning points and reduced sampling rates on road characteristics is analyzed, and the robustness of the road network construction method is improved. Finally, key sampling points are extracted from the trajectory data and used as feature points. The vehicle trajectory data is simplified using as few feature points as possible to minimize data redundancy.

5.2 Trajectory Clustering Based on Composite Distance

Once trajectory segmentation is complete, most trajectory features can be preserved within each segment. To further enhance processing efficiency, a clustering algorithm is necessary. Considering the need to maintain the geometric features of crowdsourcing trajectories and improve optimization accuracy, this paper adopts a trajectory clustering method based on composite distance [27].

When clustering point sets, a common approach is to determine whether points belong to the same class based on the Euclidean distance between them. However, when clustering line segments, the distance function comprises three components: vertical distance, parallel distance, and angular distance. Parallel distance refers to the distance between two tracks in parallel directions. Vertical distance is the perpendicular distance from a track point to another track. Angular distance measures the directional difference between two trajectories, typically represented by the angle between them (Fig. 5).

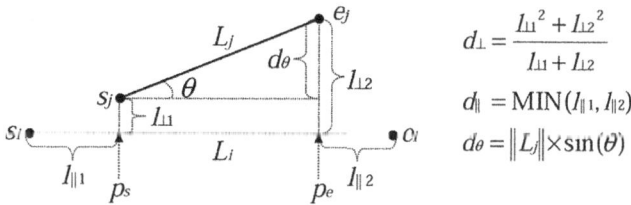

Fig. 5. 1c diagram of trajectory distance

The vertical point calculation formula is as follows:

$$p_s = s_i + u_1 \cdot \overrightarrow{s_i e_i}, \quad p_e = s_i + u_2 \cdot \overrightarrow{s_i e_i}, \tag{6}$$

$$\text{where } u_1 = \frac{\overrightarrow{s_i s_j} \cdot \overrightarrow{s_i e_i}}{\|\overrightarrow{s_i e_i}\|^2}, \quad u_2 = \frac{\overrightarrow{s_i e_j} \cdot \overrightarrow{s_i e_i}}{\|\overrightarrow{s_i e_i}\|^2} \tag{7}$$

$$\cos(\theta) = \frac{\overrightarrow{s_i e_i} \cdot \overrightarrow{s_j e_j}}{\|\overrightarrow{s_i e_i}\| \|\overrightarrow{s_j e_j}\|} \tag{8}$$

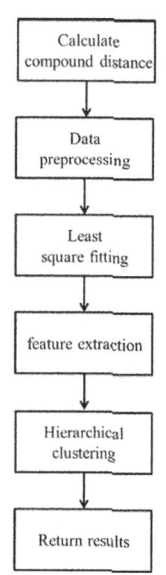

Fig. 6. Trajectory clustering technical route

Firstly, according to the above method, the segmented trajectory distance is calculated by weighting. Based on the traditional DBSCAN method, this approach considers the number of trajectory clusters generated from a single cluster to prevent sub-trajectories of the same trajectory from being misclassified into the same cluster. Secondly, the collected trajectory data is preprocessed, which includes removing noise points, deduplicating points, and eliminating outliers. Thirdly, least squares fitting is performed on each preprocessed trajectory to obtain the fitted trajectory straight line. Fourthly, features are extracted from both the fitted trajectory straight line and the original trajectory, yielding feature values such as trajectory feature points and trajectory directions. Fifthly, a hierarchical clustering method is employed to cluster the trajectories based on their feature values. Finally, the trajectory clustering results are sequentially returned (Fig. 6).

$$p_s = s_i + u_1 \cdot \overrightarrow{s_i e_i}, p_e = s_i + u_2 \cdot \overrightarrow{s_i e_i}, \tag{9}$$

$$\text{where } u_1 = \frac{\overrightarrow{s_i s_j} \cdot \overrightarrow{s_i e_i}}{\left\| \overrightarrow{s_i e_i} \right\|^2}, u_2 = \frac{\overrightarrow{s_i e_j} \cdot \overrightarrow{s_i e_i}}{\left\| \overrightarrow{s_i e_i} \right\|^2} \tag{10}$$

$$\cos(\theta) = \frac{\overrightarrow{s_i e_i} \cdot \overrightarrow{s_j e_j}}{\left\| \overrightarrow{s_i e_i} \right\| \left\| \overrightarrow{s_j e_j} \right\|} \tag{11}$$

6 Crowdsourcing Trajectory Optimization Method Based on Lane Centerline

After cluster analysis, most trajectories have been reasonably fitted. However, some trajectories exhibit significant deviation from the road. To address this, the method leverages lane-level sub-trajectory grouping obtained from the previous trajectory clustering step. By extracting the lane centerline, trajectories that deviate significantly from the lane are corrected back toward the lane, thereby enhancing the positioning accuracy of the trajectory [15].

Crowdsourcing trajectory optimization involves obtaining the trajectory cluster on the same lane within an L-meter road section after segmentation and clustering. The central trajectory is extracted from this cluster, and all trajectories within the cluster are adjusted to align with this central trajectory (Fig. 7).

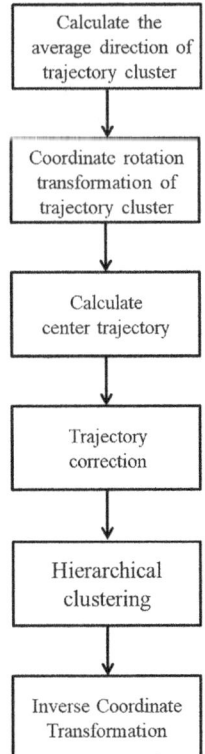

Fig. 7. Trajectory optimization technical route

A. Calculate the average direction of the trajectory cluster

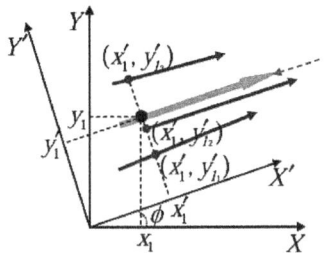

Fig. 8. Trajectory cluster coordinate system (Color figure online)

The input consists of trajectory clusters on the same lane within an L-meter road section, with the assumption that these sub-trajectories are moving in the same lane direction. By connecting the start and end points of these sub-trajectories, directional vectors $v1, v2, v3,\ldots,vn$ are formed, as indicated by the blue vectors in the figure above. The average directional vector is calculated using the formula V, where $|V|$ represents the number of sub-trajectories within a trajectory cluster (Fig. 8).

$$\vec{V} = \frac{\vec{v_1} + \vec{v_2} + \vec{v_3} + \cdots + \vec{v_n}}{|\mathcal{V}|} \quad (12)$$

B. Trajectory cluster coordinate rotation transformation

The angle ϕ between the average direction vector and the x-axis can be calculated. To facilitate subsequent calculations, the coordinates of the original trajectory cluster are transformed into a new coordinate system, which is rotated by ϕ in the positive direction of the original coordinate system. As shown in the figure, the average direction vector is parallel to the X'-axis of the new coordinate system. The coordinate transformation formula is as follows:

$$\begin{bmatrix} x' \\ y' \end{bmatrix} = \begin{bmatrix} \cos\phi & \sin\phi \\ -\sin\phi & \cos\phi \end{bmatrix} \begin{bmatrix} x \\ y \end{bmatrix} \quad (13)$$

C. Calculate the center trajectory

After the above coordinate transformation, the central trajectory is parallel to the X'-axis. Therefore, it is only necessary to calculate the coordinates of the intersection points with the Y'-axis. The calculation formula is as follows:

$$y'_1 = \left(\sum_{i=1}^{n} \sum_{j=1}^{m_i} y'_{ij} \right) / num \quad (14)$$

Among them, n is the number of trajectories in the trajectory cluster, mi is the number of trajectory points for the i-th trajectory, yij' represents the y-coordinate of the j-th track point of the i-th trajectory in the new coordinate system, and num is the total number of track points in the trajectory cluster.

D. Trajectory correction

All of track points' coordinates set to y'_1 in the new coordinate system y.

E. Inverse coordinate transformation

Transforms the coordinates of all track points in the new coordinate system back to the original coordinate system.

7 Map Matching Algorithm Based on Hidden Markov Model (HMM)

The segmentation and clustering of trajectory data, as well as the optimization of road trajectory data, are primarily based on open environments. In contrast, in sheltered environments, the original data accuracy is often low, and the reliability of processing results is compromised [28]. To address the significant location deviations in signal-shielded areas and the challenges in ensuring both the accuracy and time efficiency of traditional map-matching algorithms, this paper proposes an enhanced map-matching algorithm based on a Hidden Markov Model (HMM). This algorithm integrates distance and direction factors to calculate emission probabilities and introduces reliable points for trajectory segmentation. These improvements reduce the computational load of transition probabilities and minimize the output delay of matching results, thereby accurately identifying the corresponding road sections for trajectory points. Reliable points are trajectory points with high reliability and quality, which, after preprocessing, can more accurately reflect the true position and motion state of the moving object [29].

The HMM-based map-matching algorithm comprises three main components: data preprocessing, trajectory segmentation, and map matching. The algorithm is illustrated in the figure below. Data preprocessing involves constructing a road network directed graph and generating a grid index. The purpose of trajectory segmentation is to generate trajectory increments, and the key steps include obtaining the candidate set of trajectory points, calculating emission probabilities, and identifying reliable points. Map matching focuses on calculating transition probabilities, solving the Viterbi algorithm, and outputting the optimal path (Figs. 9 and 10).

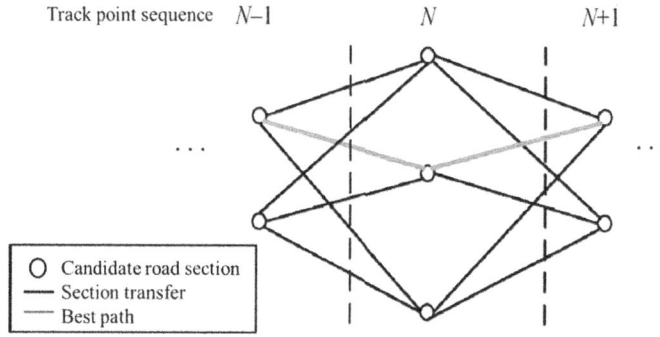

Fig. 9. Application of HMM in map matching

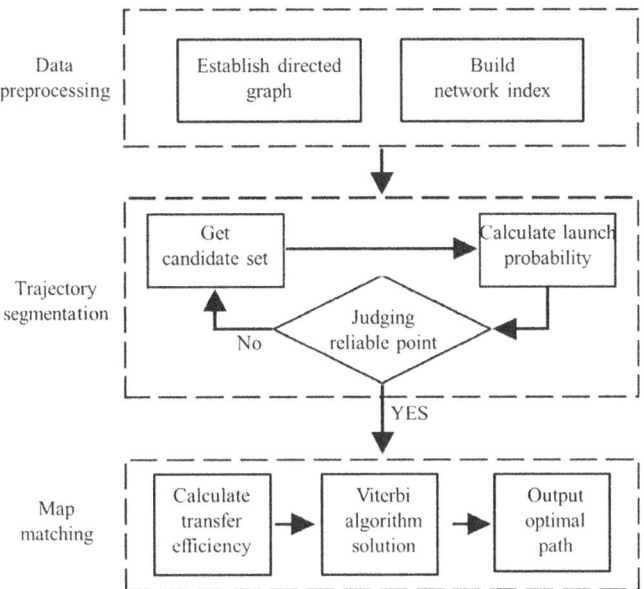

Fig. 10. Map matching algorithm flow

The data preprocessing part involves two main steps: establishing the road network directed graph and generating the grid index. Road network data is typically stored in shapefile format. By reading this file, relevant information is extracted to construct the directed graph of the road network. Given the sparse nature of traffic networks and the memory efficiency of adjacency linked lists, this paper employs an adjacency linked list to represent the directed graph. During map matching, candidate road sections for track points must be identified. Introducing a grid index allows for rapid retrieval of candidate road segments. In this study, the entire map is partitioned into a 1000 × 1000 grid system. As shown in the figure below, the grid index is linked to segment data through segment IDs.

The concept of grid indexing involves dividing the entire map into an M × N grid structure. Using an inclusion analysis algorithm, road segments that intersect each grid are pre-calculated. In this study, the map is partitioned into a 1000 × 1000 grid system. The in-memory structure of the grid index is depicted in the figure below. The grid index correlates with road segment data through the use of road segment IDs (Fig. 11).

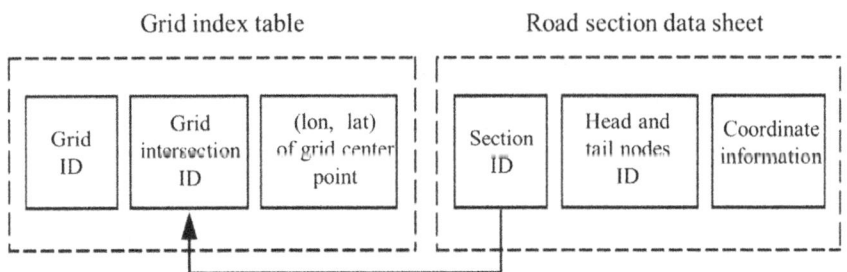

Fig. 11. Grid index structure

The trajectory segmentation part consists of three parts: candidate set acquisition, emission probability calculation and reliable point judgment. Firstly, a buffer zone with radius R is set for the track point, the grid where the track point is located is determined based on the grid index, and several road sections closest to the track point in the grid centered on the grid are queried as candidate road sections.

Secondly, the emission probability is calculated. The emission probability is the probability of obtaining a certain observation value in a certain implicit state. The calculation of emission probability is mainly divided into two parts, which consider the influence of distance factor and direction factor respectively.

Finally, judge the reliable point. The reliable point is defined as follows: for the trajectory point p_i and its candidate road section set, if the size of the road section set is 1, pi is considered to be a reliable point; The transmission probabilities of the candidate road sections are sorted to obtain the sum of the candidate road sections with the first two transmission probabilities l_i^m and l_i^n, and the corresponding l_i^m transmission probabilities are larger. If the transmission probabilities of the two road sections satisfy the following formula, it is considered that pi is also a reliable point, and the road sections other than the road sections corresponding to the maximum transmission probability in its candidate road sections are deleted, thus reducing the uncertainty of the algorithm and the calculation amount of state transition probability.

$$\frac{P(p_i|l_i^m)}{P(p_i|l_i^n)} > \lambda \qquad (15)$$

Here, the reliable point parameter λ is an empirical parameter used to identify reliable points. Reliable points enhance the traditional point-to-line map-matching algorithm. In the traditional approach, a weight function based on distance and direction factors determines the matching point by selecting the point with the highest weight, achieving high accuracy. In contrast, reliable points are identified by setting a threshold λ, which ensures matching accuracy based on data statistics and processing experience. The selection of λ values will be analyzed in the experimental section.

Map matching section. Finding the optimal matching path using a hidden Markov model (HMM) is a prediction problem, typically solved by the Viterbi algorithm. Commonly applied in speech recognition and computational linguistics, the Viterbi algorithm incrementally computes the joint probability of states based on transition and observation probabilities. It records the previous state of the current implied state, ultimately determining the optimal path's endpoint. The entire optimal path is then derived through backtracking using the recorded state information.

8 Experiment

8.1 Overview of Test Data

The data acquisition equipment comprises test data collection devices and benchmark data collection devices. The quantity of test data collection devices and the data collected in Zhengzhou are listed in the table below. The benchmark data collection equipment consists of one TS5Pro GNSS receiver. This benchmark device employs RTK positioning, achieving a planar positioning accuracy of better than 8 mm (Table 3).

Table 3. Mobile phone model and number of data pieces

Mobile phone model	Number of data strips
HUAWEI Mate60	30
Xiaomi14	30
Honor magic6pro	30
HUAWEI nova12	30

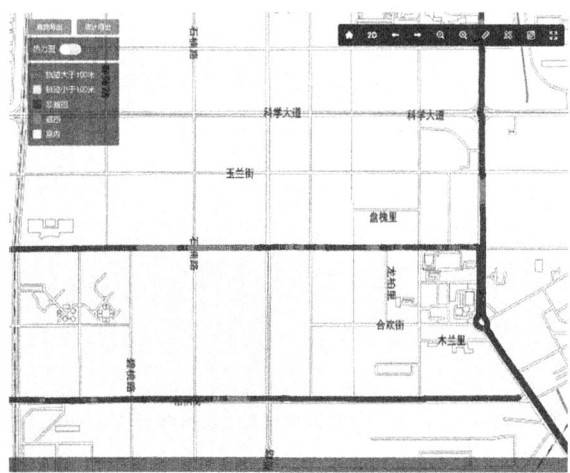

Fig. 12. Obstruction of Test Area (Color figure online)

The entire data collection area, situated in a specific part of the Zhengzhou High-tech Industrial Development Zone in Henan Province, resembles a parallelogram. Bounded by Science Avenue, West Third Ring Road, West Fourth Ring Road, and Zhengshang

Road, this region forms a closed route network. As depicted in Fig. 12, orange dots indicate occluded scenes, while blue dots represent non-occluded scenes. Spanning approximately 44 km^2, the experimental area encompasses a road network of about 52 km, with urban canyon and basement scene data accounting for roughly 20%. This diverse terrain includes open areas, elevated roads, and urban canyons, making it a representative urban area that reflects typical urban landscapes and traffic conditions. The data's diversity renders it suitable for analyses across various environments and terrains (Tables 4 and 5).

Table 4. Statistical table of accuracy of different mobile phone positioning in open environment (unit: meters)

Mobile phone model	Road segment scenario	Position accuracy (RMS)
HUAWEI Mate60		3.52
HUAWEI Nova12		5.19
Xiaomi 14		4.31
Honor Magic6pro		5.01

Table 5. Statistical table of accuracy of different mobile phone positioning occlusion environments (unit: meters)

Mobile phone model	Road segment scenario	Positioning accuracy (RMS)
HUAWEI Mate60		4.87
HUAWEI Nova12		8.19
Xiaomi 14		5.09
Honor Magic6pro		5.19

As shown in the table above, the positioning accuracy varies significantly among different mobile phones in the same environment and for the same mobile phone across different environments. The scene section also illustrates the trajectories of four mobile phones and benchmark data, where red indicates HUAWEI Mate60, yellow represents Xiaomi 14, brown corresponds to Honor Magic6pro, and blue denotes HUAWEI Nova12. From this dataset, it is evident that the positioning accuracy of some mobile phones (e.g., HUAWEI Nova12 and Honor Magic6pro) exceeds 5 m in open environments. In obstructed environments, such as those with bilateral buildings, the positioning accuracy of most mobile phones surpasses 5 m, underscoring the necessity for refining positioning results.

8.2 Open Environment Segmentation and Clustering and Trajectory Optimization Experiments

A. Trajectory segmentation and clustering verification

Firstly, the collected crowdsourcing data undergoes preprocessing steps such as time alignment and completeness screening. Trajectories within the same spatiotemporal period are subsequently classified and clustered. The trajectory segmentation results for certain data collected in Zhengzhou are presented below, with different colors indicating trajectories resulting from segmentation. As shown in the figure, complete trajectories can be segmented into smaller segments based on turning points (Fig. 13).

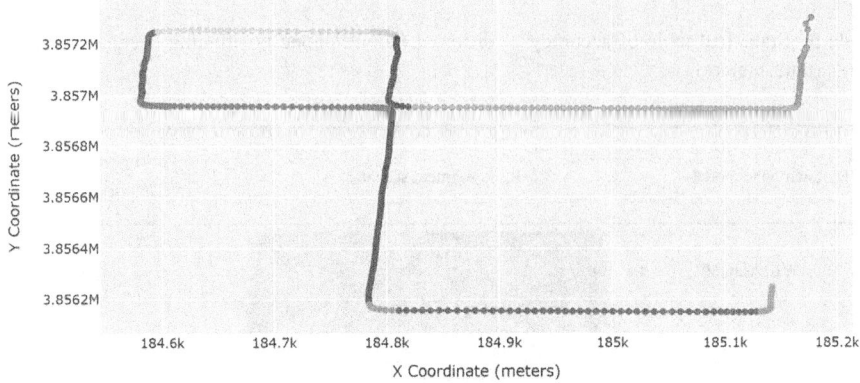

Fig. 13. Trajectory segmentation sample (Color figure online)

Different colors denote distinct trajectory segments. Given a set of trajectory inputs, the algorithm must output a cluster of sub-trajectories. A cluster comprises sub-trajectories where line segments within the same cluster are similar based on trajectory characteristics (Fig. 14).

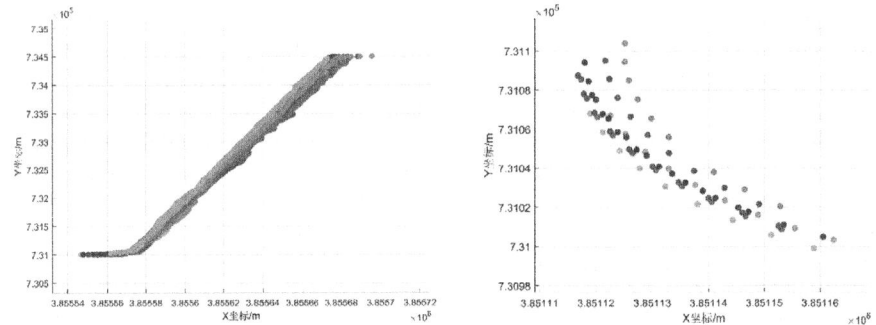

Fig. 14. Analysis of trajectory clustering results after Zhengzhou area segmentation (Color figure online)

B. Trajectory optimization verification

After completing feature-based trajectory segmentation, the optimization algorithm for extracting the road center line proposed in this paper is applied to obtain the trajectory processing results for the same road section. The results are shown in the figure below. The figure illustrates the trajectories (red) and reference trajectories (green) of four mobile phones on the same road section. It is evident from the original trajectories that the trajectory accuracy of Honor Magic6 is significantly lower than that of the other three mobile phones. After performing trajectory segmentation and clustering, we obtain four sub-trajectories for this road section (Fig. 15).

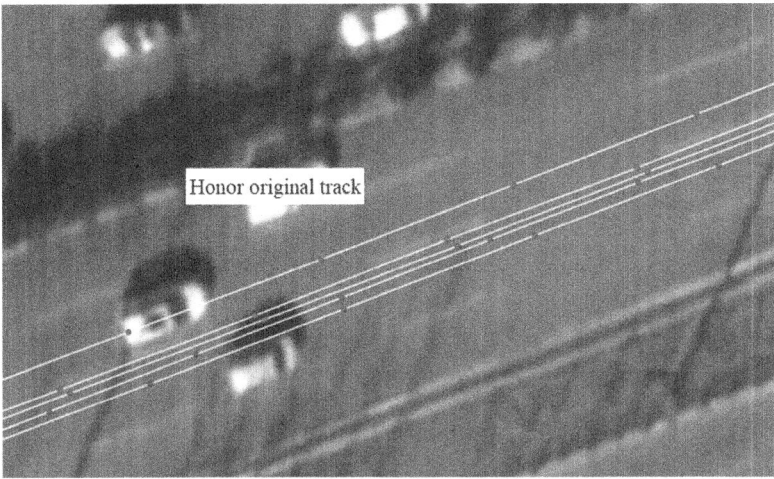

Fig. 15. Original results of trajectory (Color figure online)

After trajectory optimization, the accuracy of refined trajectory points is optimized from 3.64 m to 2.78 m, and the refined trajectory is as follows (Fig. 16):

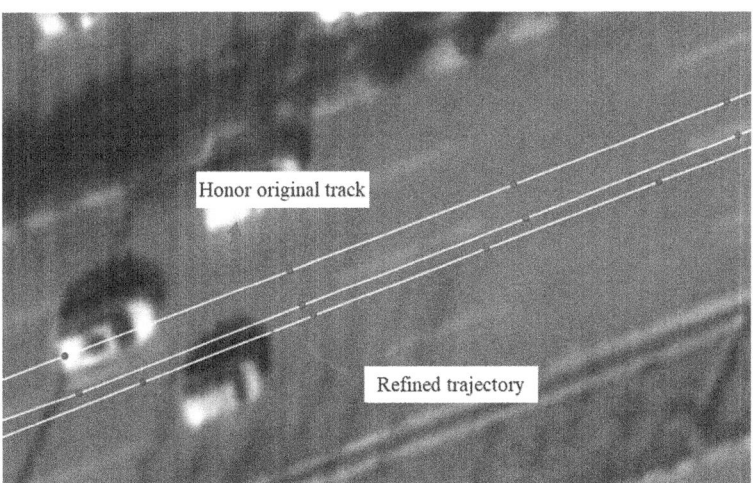

Fig. 16. Trajectory correction results (Color figure online)

In the experimental area, data from the HUAWEI Mate60 and Xiaomi 14 mobile phones are used, with both the benchmark and test data collected simultaneously to ensure the accuracy of positional comparisons. The benchmark results, matched by the closest timestamp, are compared with the test results to calculate the root mean square error (RMSE). The experimental results for several complex scenarios are as follows: green trajectories represent reference results, blue trajectories indicate refined results, and red trajectories show the original results (Fig. 17 and Table 6).

a) occlude the scene b) open the scene

c) Partially occluded scene

Fig. 17. Multi-scene location refinement results (Color figure online)

Table 6. Statistical table of multi-scene position refinement results (unit: m)

Scene	Raw Result Error (RMSE)	Error after refinement (RMSE)
Occlude the scene	8.30	4.98
Open scene	6.12	4.31
Partial occlusion	7.45	4.70

As shown in the figure above, after fusing multi-source crowdsourcing data, the blue (refined) trajectory closely aligns with the green (reference) trajectory. Consequently, the position error is significantly reduced after fusing trajectories from the HUAWEI Mate60 and Xiaomi 14 mobile phones. Specifically, in occluded environments, the error is reduced from 8.30 m to 4.98 m, reflecting a 40% improvement. In open scenes, the error decreases from 6.12 m to 4.31 m, indicating a 30% enhancement. For partially occluded scenes, the error is optimized from 7.45 m to 4.70 m, corresponding to a 37% improvement (Table 7).

Table 7. Statistical Error Table (unit: m)

Mobile phone model	HUAWEI Mate60	Xiaomi 14	Honor Magic6	HUAWEI Nova12
First time	3.73	3.37	3.34	3.76
Second time	3.46	7.05	2.18	2.12
Third time	1.89	1.18	2.6	1.07

Numerous experiments across various acquisition devices demonstrate that position accuracy is generally enhanced. However, due to varying initial errors among devices, optimization outcomes differ. The algorithm proposed in this paper effectively improves positional accuracy across different devices.

8.3 Experiment of Map Matching Method for Occluded Scenes

The self-collected dataset covers the Zhengzhou High-tech Development Zone in Henan Province and includes vector road traffic network data in .shp format with an accuracy of 0.1 m. The dataset comprises 137 road sections and 13,336 trajectory points, recorded at a original time interval of 1 s. Since the data lacks heading information, the emission probability corresponding to the direction factor for all candidate points was set to a fixed value of 1 during the experiment. The improved hidden Markov model (HMM) algorithm proposed in this paper was used for matching and correction, with results presented below.

Matching accuracy is calculated as the number of correctly matched trajectory points divided by the total number of trajectory points. Using this formula, the achieved matching accuracy exceeds 90%, with a positioning accuracy of approximately 2.85 m. Comparisons with the traditional HMM algorithm demonstrate that the hidden Markov algorithm proposed in this paper is both effective and feasible (Figs. 18 and 19 and Table 8).

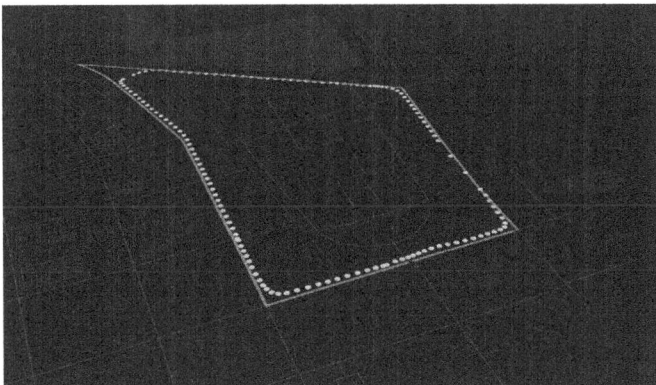

Fig. 18. Map matching trajectory result diagram

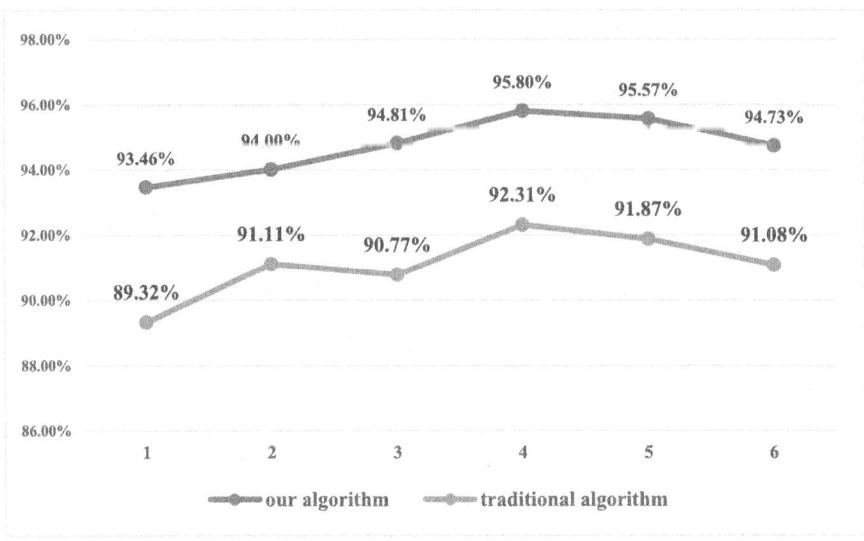

Fig. 19. Comparison chart of map matching accuracy

Table 8. Comparison table of map matching accuracy

Number of experiments	Total number of track points	The algorithm in this paper			Traditional algorithm		
		Total number of correct matches	Matching accuracy	RMS (m)	Total number of correct matches	Matching accuracy	RMS (m)
1	2126	1987	93.46%	4.51	1899	89.32%	6.49
2	967	909	94.00%	3.16	881	91.11%	4.55
3	1214	1151	94.81%	2.87	1102	90.77%	4.13
4	429	411	95.80%	2.83	396	92.31%	4.08
5	812	776	95.57%	4.12	746	91.87%	5.93
Average	1109.6	1046.8	94.73%	3.50	1004.8	91.08%	5.04

Sum Up

To address the issue of limited accuracy in crowdsourcing trajectory data collection by intelligent terminals in complex environments, this paper proposes a label optimization method for crowdsourcing trajectory data. This method, based on feature-extracted trajectory data, combines multi-source fusion techniques—including trajectory segmentation, clustering, optimization, and map matching—to enhance the label accuracy of crowdsourcing trajectory data. Experimental verification shows that this method improves the accuracy to a certain extent, demonstrating its feasibility and effectiveness compared to other methods. While this study primarily focuses on areas with regional maps, future research should consider raw data selection for large-scale data volumes and trajectory processing in map-less environments, such as underground garages and spaces. Additionally, integrating deep learning algorithms could further optimize these processes, thereby expanding the applicability and reliability of label refinement methods for crowdsourcing trajectory data.

Acknowledgments. This study was funded by National Natural Science Foundation of China (grant No. 42201493).

References

1. Yang,Tang, Ren, et al.: Pedestrian network generation based on crowdsourcing tracking data. Int. J. Geogr. Inf. Sci. (34), 1051–1074 (2020)
2. Zhang, C., Li, Y., Xiang, L., Jiao, F., Wu, C., Li, S.: Generating road networks for old downtown areas based on crowd sourced vehicle trajectories. Sensors **21**(1), 235 (2021)
3. Huang, J., Zhang, Y., Deng, M.,et al.: Mining crowdsourcing trajectory and geo-tagged data for spatial-semantic road map construction. Trans. GIS (2021)
4. Wang, S.: Lane-level map building and privacy protection in crowdsourcing. Harbin Institute of Technology (2020)
5. Ren, C., Tang, L., Yang, X., et al.: Mapping grade-separated junctions in detail using crowdsourcing trajectory data. IEEE Trans. Intell. Transp. Syst. (99), 1–10 (2021)
6. Ruan, S., Xiong, K., Wang, S., et al.: A survey of urban geographic information inference driven by crowd-sourced spatio-temporal data. Acta Eletronica Sinica **51**(08), 2238–2259 (2023)
7. Badran, A., El-Geneidy, A., Miranda-Moreno, L.:Intersection movements delay modelling based on crowd-sensed global positioning system trajectory data. Can. J. Civil Eng. **51**(9) (2024)
8. Ga, L.: Location sensor data analysis and application research based on Android smartphone. Southeast University (2023)
9. Meng, S.: Research on low-cost indoor and outdoor seamless positioning technology based on multi-sensor fusion. Hunan University of Science and Technology (2023)
10. Bao, S.: Research on indoor and outdoor positioning system combining GNSS/UWB and IMU. Shanghai Normal University(2023)
11. Shi, Z., Li, J., Liu, C., et al.: Research on crowd sourced map road factor fusion discriminant clustering method. Sci. Surv. Mapp. **49**(4), 196–207 (2024)
12. Wang, N., Gao, S., Peng, X., Wang, M.: Research on fast and parallel clustering method for trajectory data. In: Proceedings of the IEEE 24th International Conference on Parallel Distributed System (ICPADS), no. 12, pp.252–258 (2018)
13. Niu, X., Chen, T., Wu, C.Q., et al.: Label-based trajectory clustering in complex road networks. IEEE Trans. Intell. Transp. Syst. (21), 4098–4110 (2020)
14. Guo, Y.: Key information extraction and model construction of high definition map based on crowdsourcing vehicle data. Wuhan University (2021)
15. Wang, S., Bao, Z., Culpepper, J.S., et al.: Fast large scale trajectory clustering. Proc. VLDB Endow. (13), 29–42 (2019)
16. Wang, H., Liu, Y., Li, S., et al.: Matching the high sampled trajectory with road networks based on path increment. Acta Geodaetica et Cartographica Sinica **52**(2), 329–340 (2023)

17. Yang, X., Yu, J., Zheng, X., et al.: Improved hidden Markov model map matching method and device: CN202210017516.1. CN202210017516.1 (2025)
18. Chen, S., Li, P., Yan, C., et al.: Lane-scale map matching based on hidden Markov model. Comput. Sci. Appl. **13**(7), 1438–1446 (2023)
19. Sijie, R., Cheng, L., Jie, B., et al.: Learning to generate maps from trajectories. In: Proceedings of the AAAI Conference on Artificial Intelligence, no. 34, pp. 890–897 (2020)
20. Pan, Z., Zhang, W., Liang, Y., et al.: Spatio-temporal meta learning for urban traffic prediction. IEEE Trans. Knowl. Data Eng. (99), 1 (2020)
21. Lyu, H., Pfoser, D., Sheng, Y.: Movement-aware map construction. Int. J. Geogr. Inf. Sci. (6), 1065–1093 (2021)
22. Wang, W.F., Hu, J.H., He, Y., et al.: Synchronized trajectory analysis of multi-sources tracking data from taxi drivers. J. Univ. Chin. Acad. Sci. **40**(3), 313–321 (2023)
23. Zheng, Z., Rasouli, S., Timmermans, H.: Modeling taxi driver search behavior under uncertainty. Travel Behav. Soc. (22), 207–218 (2021)
24. Deng, M., Luo, B., Tang, J., et al.: Extracting road intersections from vehicle trajectory data in the face of trace density disparity. Acta Geodaetica et Cartographica Sinica **52**(6), 1000–1009 (2023)
25. Yang, X., Tang, L., Zhang, X., Li, Q.: A data cleaning method for big trace data using movement consistency. Sensors (18), 824 (2018)
26. Chen, X., Xiang, L., Jiao, F., et al.: Detecting turning relationships and time restrictions of OSM road intersections from crowdsourcing trajectories. ISPRS Int. J. Geo-Inf. **12**(9) (2023)
27. Zhou, X., Miao, F., Ma, H., et al.: A trajectory regression clustering technique combining a novel fuzzy c-means clustering algorithm with the least squares method. ISPRS Int. J. Geo-Inf. (7), 164 (2018)
28. Wang, Y., Kang, Z., Liu, J., et al.: An improved map matching algorithm based on hidden Markov model. Inf. Technol. Informationization (03), 103–106 (2021)
29. Fu, C., Huang, S., Tang, Y., et al.: A real-time map matching method for road network using driving scenario classification. Acta Geodaetica et Cartographica Sinica **50**(11), 1617–1627 (2021)

Leveraging Data Augmentation Through Contrastive Self-supervised Learning for Next Point-of-Interest Recommendation

Limin Guo, Weijia Liu, Zhi Cai[✉], and Xing Su

Beijing University of Technology, Beijing 100020, China
caiz@bjut.edu.cn

Abstract. In recent years, point-of-interest (POI) recommendation has been extensively studied, with existing methods typically modeling user preferences through the integration of multi-factor information (e.g., temporal, spatial, and categorical features) and capturing the periodicity and discontinuity of user check-in sequences. However, these approaches struggle with data sparsity, missing data, and noisy data, leading to suboptimal user representations. To effectively mitigate the above problems, we utilize contrastive self-supervised learning techniques to achieve data augmentation and apply them to the next POI recommendation task. Specifically, we propose DACL (Data Augmentation through Contrastive Self-supervised Learning), a novel framework that unifies next POI recommendation and contrastive self-supervised learning (SSL) via a multi-task strategy. Furthermore, DACL introduces five tailored data augmentation operations to generate high-quality contrastive views, mitigating data limitations while enhancing robustness. Extensive experiments on two real-world datasets (NYC and TKY) demonstrate that DACL significantly outperforms state-of-the-art baselines, achieving 14.3% and 4.3% improvements in $Recall@10$ and $NDCG@5$, respectively, while maintaining superior robustness against noisy and sparse scenarios.

Keywords: Point-of-Interest · Recommendation · Spatio-temporal · Contrastive Learning

1 Introduction

In recent years, the mobile Internet has expanded exponentially. Users on social networking platforms increasingly share their daily lives, which has given rise to location-based service platforms including Foursquare, Gowalla, and Yelp. These platforms enable users to share their locations and experiences with friends by checking in at points of interest (POIs), such as restaurants and shopping malls. With the accumulation of vast spatio-temporal check-in data, a solid foundation has been established for POI recommendation research [9,24,31,33]. POI recommendations can not only help users better explore their surroundings, but also help merchants improve their advertising strategies [12,27].

In next POI recommendation, the goal is to predict the next POI that a user will visit based on their current and historical check-in records, which has been extensively studied by researchers [27]. In the early stages, models primarily focused on learning implicit user and POI features (e.g., via matrix factorization [14]) and sequential transitions (e.g., using Markov chains [26]). With the rapid development of deep learning, researchers leveraged the powerful sequential modeling capabilities of RNNs to propose models for inferring correlations within trajectories [20,36]. With recent breakthroughs in natural language processing brought about by Transformers [29], researchers have started to leverage self-attention mechanisms [22] to capture the importance of items during sequence encoding.

Although considerable advancements have been achieved in existing studies, there are still several key challenges and questions that require deeper investigation. (1) *Data Sparsity*. The inherent sparsity of user check-in data limits Transformer-based models' capacity to capture POI correlations within sequences. Although existing methods alleviate the data sparsity issue by taking into account factors such as categories, periodicity, and discontinuity, they perform poorly on short sequences and may lead to model overfitting. (2) *Missing Data*. As check-ins rely on voluntary user actions, incomplete trajectories frequently arise from forgotten records. Such missing data hinder the model's understanding of behavioral context, thereby reducing the accuracy of the recommendation. (3) *Noisy Data*. POI sequences often contain noise caused by promotional events or redundant check-ins (e.g. repeated visits to the same location). Figure 1 quantifies repeated check-ins in two benchmark datasets (NYC and TKY). Our analysis reveals that 26% and 22% of user trajectories in NYC and TKY, respectively, contain 10%–20% redundant POIs, confirming widespread noisy data. These noisy sequences degrade the model's capability to learn authentic user preferences.

Self-supervised learning (SSL) techniques have achieved significant breakthroughs in computer vision (CV) and natural language processing (NLP) [2, 3,6,15], prompting researchers to explore their application to sequential recommendation [5,21,30]. For instance, Xie et al. [30] proposed a contrastive SSL framework with stochastic augmentation operations, demonstrating promising results in sequential recommendation tasks. However, the geographical dependencies inherent to POI trajectories (e.g., spatial proximity and category clustering) limit the direct applicability of generic sequential recommendation methods. Specifically, the POI recommendation requires modeling complex spatial patterns and user mobility constraints, which are often overlooked in standard sequential approaches. To address the aforementioned challenges in POI recommendation, we propose DACL, a novel framework that integrates contrastive SSL with tailored data augmentation. DACL comprises three core components: (1) Five customized augmentation operations that address data sparsity, missing data, and noisy data. (2) A contrastive SSL objective aiming to maximize the agreement of positive views of sequences. (3) A recommendation module based on Transformer, which offers robust sequence modeling capabilities. Specifically, we propose five novel data augmentation operations, including Geo-Insert,

Geo-Substitute, Delete, Reorder and Mask. The Geo-Insert and Geo-Substitute operations leverage trajectory graphs integrated with geographical factors to construct semantically consistent positive views, generating high-quality positive pairs. The Geo-Insert operation addresses missing data, while the Geo-Substitute operation enhances model generalization and facilitates the recommendation of novel locations. The Delete operation removes noisy data points, while all proposed augmentation methods collectively mitigate data sparsity through complementary strategies. Extensive experiments on two real-world datasets demonstrate the superior performance of DACL, with ablation studies validating the contribution of each component.

In summary, our contributions are summarized as follows:

(1) We propose a novel data augmentation framework based on contrastive SSL, namely DACL, which effectively mitigates the issues of data sparsity, missing data, and noisy data.
(2) We put forward data augmentation operations, that is Geo-Insert and Geo-Substitute, based on trajectory graphs and geographical factors.
(3) We propose a novel operation termed Delete and introduce an operation termed Reorder which is incorporating the cyclic pattern of sequences.
(4) The experimental results on two real-world datasets show that DACL significantly outperforms state-of-the-art baselines, achieving 14.3% and 4.3% improvements in $Recall@10$ and $NDCG@5$, respectively.

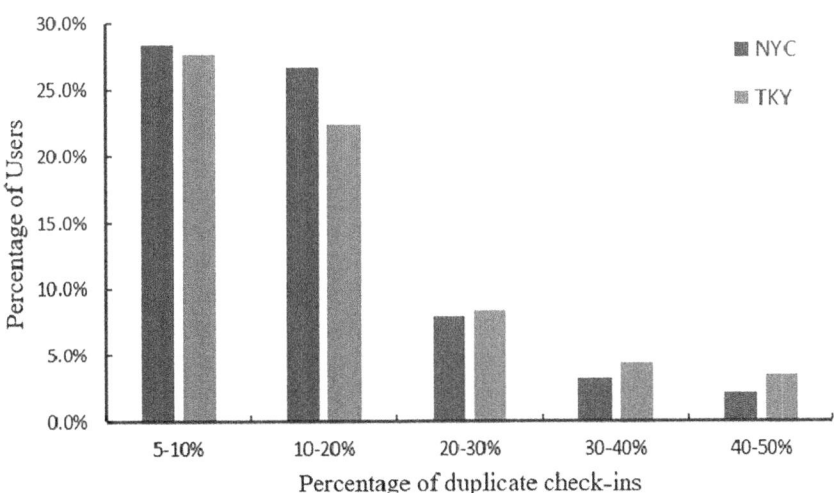

Fig. 1. The x-axis represents the repeated-check-in ratio (R), defined as the number of duplicated check-ins in a user sequence divided by the sequence length. The y-axis indicates the user proportion distribution, calculated as the number of users within each R interval divided by the total user count. The statistical data originate from the real-world datasets, NYC and TKY.

2 Related Work

2.1 POI Recommendation

Early research on POI recommendation primarily comprised techniques based on Collaborative Filtering (CF) [34] and Markov Chains (MC) [10,26]. Collaborative filtering operates on the basis of user or item similarity to make recommendations, with many researchers employing Matrix Factorization (MF) technology to implement POI recommendation [4,18,26]. For instance, Ye et al. [34] proposed a collaborative recommendation algorithm that integrates geographical influence and combines user preference, social influence, and geographic influence within a unified framework for POI recommendation. A series of research studies on next POI recommendation operate on the assumption that users' subsequent check-in behavior is strongly influenced by their recent visits. Consequently, a category of Markov chains-based methods has been introduced to capture the transition probabilities between consecutive check-ins. FPMC [26] utilized a Matrix Factorization technique to understand the general taste of users, followed by employing a Markov Chain-based approach to capture short-term sequential behaviors. By predicting the next action based on the user's recent actions, FPMC emerged as the most advanced method during that period.

Motivated by the achievements of RNN in modeling sequential data [11,20,38], techniques built upon RNN and its variants have gained considerable popularity within the domain of next POI recommendation. STRNN [20] employs a time-specific transition matrix and a distance-specific transition matrix to model local temporal and spatial contexts effectively. STGN [37] incorporates two sets of time gates and distance gates to regulate the update of short-term and long-term interests respectively, thus capturing the spatio-temporal relationship between consecutive check-ins. LSTPM [28] uses a geo-dilated RNN to comprehend the geographical relation of non-consecutive check-ins.

With the significant advancements brought about by the Transformer [29] model in natural language processing, researchers have been exploring the application of the attention mechanism in next POI recommendation tasks [16,22,28,35]. This is done to effectively capture and model the user's static and dynamic preferences, leveraging the superior long-term sequence modeling capability of the attention mechanism over RNN and its variations. Zhang et al. [35] designed a future preference extractor to learn multi-step future preferences from historical trajectory data by considering the impact of future actions on next POI recommendations. Luo et al. [22] proposes a spatio-temporal bi-attention model named STAN that captures spatio-temporal correlations between non-adjacent locations and non-contiguous visits.

2.2 Data Augmentation for Sequential Recommendation

So far, research on data augmentation for POI recommendation tasks has been scarce, with only a few research findings [17,39]. Li et al. [17] pioneered the application of data augmentation to achieve recommendation in the field of next

POI recommendation. They designed a content-aware attention framework and a multi-layer bi-directional LSTM network architecture to compensate for the missing data and attained good prediction results. Recently, data augmentation based on contrastive learning has been widely studied in the field of sequential recommendation [5,21,23,30]. Qi et al. [23] proposed the use of counterfactual data augmentation to generate positive and negative user sequences and combined it with contrastive learning to boost the accuracy of recommendation. Xie et al. [30] introduced three random data augmentation operations and integrated them with contrastive SSL techniques to achieve promising prediction accuracy. Based on this, Liu et al. [21] proposed item-based similarity-based data augmentation operations, effectively alleviating the data sparsity problem. Dang et al. [5] posited that sequences with uniform time intervals are helpful for the model to better learn user preferences. However, these methods are only applicable to general sequential recommendation tasks. As a special case of sequential recommendation, POI recommendation has unique geographical location attributes and irregular behaviors. Therefore, the above-mentioned data augmentation operations are not applicable to POI recommendation tasks.

3 Problem Description

Let $U = \{u_1, u_2, \ldots, u_{|U|}\}$ denote a set of users. Let $L = \{l_1, l_2, \ldots, l_{|L|}\}$ be a set of POIs. Here, $|U|$ and $|L|$ denote the total number of users and POIs respectively. Each user $u \in U$ has a check-in sequence sorted by time, denoted as $S_u = \{l_1, l_2, \ldots, l_n\}$, along with the corresponding time sequence $T_u = \{t_1, t_2, \ldots, t_n\}$.

Given the check-in sequence S_u of user u, our goal is to recommend a location l_{n+1} from the candidate location set L for user u to visit at the next timestamp t_{n+1}, with the current timestamp t_n. Formally, the prediction target for user u at time t_{n+1} is denoted as $\hat{l}_{n+1}$, and the prediction task is expressed as:

$$\hat{l}_{n+1} = argmax_{l \in L} Pr(l \mid S_u, T_u) \quad (1)$$

where $Pr(l \mid S_u, T_u)$ enotes the probability of visiting the next location, given the historical sequences S_u and T_u.

4 Model

In this section, we introduce our DACL model, as shown in Fig. 2. We first present the overall architecture of our model. Then we will elaborate on the five data augmentation operations. We will also explain the rationale behind these operations. Finally, we will introduce the detailed architecture of the model.

4.1 Data Augmentation Module

Our data augmentation module transforms raw check-in sequences into augmented variants through five tailored operations. For each user sequence, we

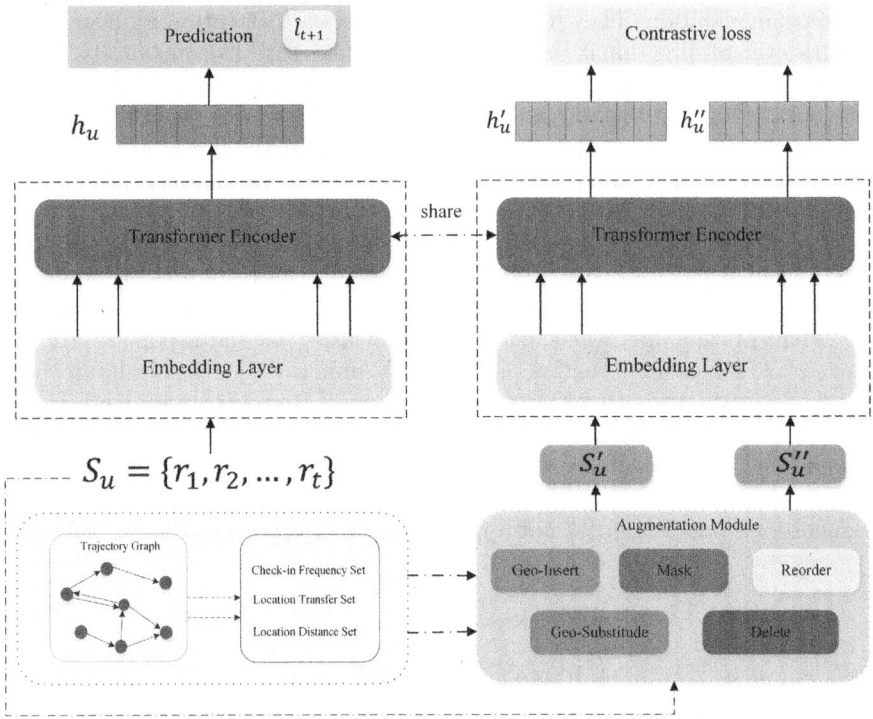

Fig. 2. Overall Architecture of the Model. In the bottom layer, on the left is the trajectory graph we proposed, which is applied in the Geo-Insert and Geo-Substitute data augmentation operations. On the right are five data augmentation modules. The middle part consists of the embedding module for the check-in sequence and the Transformer-based encoding module. The parameters for encoding the augmented sequence and the original sequence are shared. The top layer includes the next POI recommendation module and the contrastive SSL module.

stochastically select two distinct operations (e.g., Geo-Insert + Delete) to generate positive pairs, while sequences from different users form negative pairs. Firstly, we present two data augmentation operations that integrate trajectory graphs and geographical factors, namely Geo-Insert and Geo-Substitute. Subsequently, we introduce the Delete augmentation aimed at reducing data noise and the Reorder augmentation operation based on sequence cyclic patterns. Finally, we introduce the Mask augmentation operation based on random methods. The five data augmentation algorithms proposed by us effectively mitigate the issue of data sparsity.

Geo-Insert and Geo-Substitute Augmentation. The Geo-Insert operation addresses missing data by inserting geographically feasible POIs into incomplete trajectories, while Geo-Substitute improves generalization by replacing existing POIs with contextually relevant alternatives. Unlike generic sequence augmentation relying on item similarity [21], our method prioritizes spatial coherence through trajectory graph mining. This geographic-aware strategy overcomes the limitations of similarity-based approaches in next POI recommendation.

Geo-Insert (GI). To identify potential missing check-ins, we adopt a spatio-temporal interval ranking inspired by [5]. For a check-in sequence $S_u = [l_1, \ldots, l_n]$, we compute intervals between consecutive POIs as:

$$\Delta^i_{(t,d)} = \gamma \frac{t_{i+1} - t_i}{t_{max}} + (1-\gamma) \frac{||l_{i+1} - l_i||}{d_{max}}, \qquad (2)$$

where t_{max} and d_{max} normalize time (hours) and distance (km) across the dataset. Larger $\Delta^i_{(t,d)}$ indicates higher missing likelihood. We select top-k positions $\{idx_j\}$ with $k = \lfloor \alpha n \rfloor$ ($\alpha \in [0, 1]$ via grid search). Subsequently, locations generated from the trajectory graph and geographical factors are inserted at these positions. Formally, the sequence after insertion is:

$$S_u^{GI} = GeoInsert(S_u) = [l_1, l_2, \ldots, \hat{l}_{idx_i}, \ldots, l_{n+k}] \qquad (3)$$

where $i \in \{1, 2, \ldots, k\}$ and $\hat{l}_{idx_i}$ is the inserted location. The length of the augmented sequence becomes $n+k$. We will introduce how to select the locations to be inserted based on the trajectory graph and geographical factors in the following.

Geo-Substitute (GS). We randomly select k distinct indices $\{idx_1, idx_2, \ldots, idx_k\}$. The number of substitution positions is governed by the hyper parameter $\beta \in [0, 1]$, such that $k = \beta n$. Subsequently, the elements at these positions are replaced using information from the trajectory graph and geographical data. The sequence after substitution is:

$$S_u^{GS} = GeoSubstitute(S_u) = [l_1, l_2, \ldots, \hat{l}_{idx_i}, \ldots, l_n] \qquad (4)$$

where $i \in \{1, 2, \ldots, k\}$ and $\hat{l}_{idx_i}$ is the location replaced using the trajectory graph and geographical factors.

Trajectory Graphs and Geographical Factors. We utilize the check-in sequences of all users to construct a trajectory graph, and count the check-in frequency of each location and the geographical distances between them. As shown in Fig. 3, we illustrate some node instances of a trajectory graph. We provide the following two definitions:

Definition 1. *Prefix Set: The prefix set of a node contains all the nodes that point to it. For example, the prefix set of node T is $\{l_3, l_4, l_5\}$.*

Definition 2. *Suffix Set: The suffix set of a node includes all the nodes that it directly points to. For example, the suffix set of node P is $\{l_3, l_4\}$.*

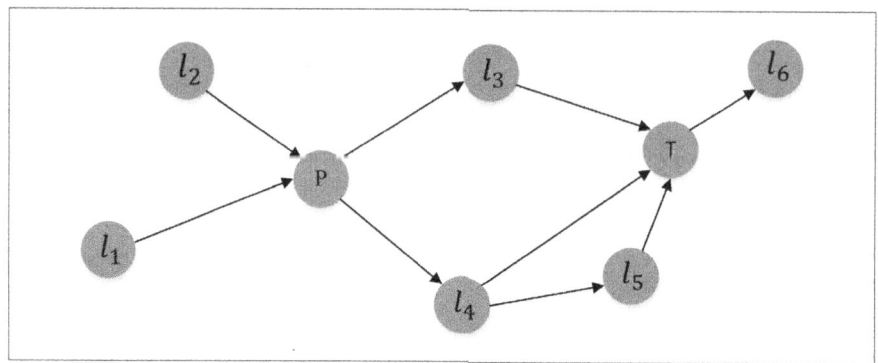

Fig. 3. Trajectory Graph Composed of Check-in Sequences of Some Users.

Geo-Insert with Trajectory Graph For a location $l_i \in \{idx_1, idx_2, \ldots, idx_k\}$ to be inserted. The objective is to insert a location subsequent to l_i. Initially, through querying the trajectory graph, we retrieve the suffix set S_f of location l_i such that $\{l_i, l_{i+1}\} \notin S_f$, and the prefix set S_p of location l_{i+1} such that $\{l_i, l_{i+1}\} \notin S_p$. Subsequently, we obtain the candidate location set $S_c = S_f \cap S_p$. We consider the locations within the candidate set as those for potential insertion or substitution. Given its simplicity and effectiveness, we propose a method to measure the score of a location to be inserted based on check-in frequency and geographical distance. Formally, the scoring function for candidate locations is defined as:

$$avg(l_d) = \frac{H(l_i, l_d) + H(l_{i+1}, l_d)}{2} \qquad (5)$$

$$score = e^{-(\frac{avg(l_d)-\eta)^2}{2\sigma^2})} + \delta log(1 + f_{l_d}) \qquad (6)$$

where $l_d \in S_c$ represents a candidate location. H denotes the *Haversine* formula, which is widely employed to compute the distance between two locations. $avg(l_d)$ represents the average distance between the candidate location l_d and the locations l_i, l_{i+1}. The score of a candidate location is computed based on geographical proximity and check-in frequency. A Gaussian function is utilized to compute the distance score. The control parameter σ determines the attenuation rate, and η represents the expected value of the distance. The check-in frequency f_{l_d} of location l_d is used to calculate the frequency score. δ is the adjustment coefficient for the frequency weight.

Geo-Substitute with Trajectory Graph. The Geo-Substitute operation can also identify candidate replacement locations based on the trajectory graph and geographical factors. For an index $j \in \{idx_1, idx_2, \ldots, dix_k\}$, we first locate the locations l_{j-1} and l_{j+1}. Then, by querying the suffix set of l_{j-1} and the prefix set of l_{j+1}. After that, we can calculate the scores according to Eqs. 5 and 6.

Delete Augmentation. As illustrated in Fig. 1, noisy check-ins (e.g., repeated consecutive visits) compromise the quality of check-in sequence. Direct removal risks aggravating data sparsity and information loss. To address this, we propose a constrained deletion operation:

$$S_u^D = Delete(S_u) = [l_1, l_2, \ldots, l_i] \tag{7}$$

where the length of the original sequence is n, and the length of the sequence after deletion is i. The operation triggers only when consecutive identical POIs exceed one, preserving essential transitions while eliminating redundancies. To mitigate the impact of deletion operations, the number of elements to be removed $n-i$ was constrained to satisfy $n-i \leq k \cdot n$. Grid search validation demonstrated that setting $k = 0.2$ achieved optimal recommendation performance.

Reorder Augmentation. The Reorder operation enhances model generalization and mitigates data sparsity by generating plausible trajectory variations. While prior work employs random swaps [30], such stochasticity disrupts critical spatio-temporal transitions between POIs. To preserve transition coherence, we propose a reordering strategy. A cyclic pattern occurs if a subsequence starts and ends at the same POI (e.g., $l_i \rightarrow l_{i+1} \rightarrow l_i$ in Fig. 4). Formally, given trajectory $S_u = [l_1, l_2, \ldots, l_n]$, a cyclic subsequence satisfies:

$$\exists [l_i, \ldots, l_j] \subseteq S_u \quad \text{where } l_i = l_j \ (1 \leq i < j \leq n) \tag{8}$$

Upon detecting such cycles, we reverse the subsequence to create augmented variants while preserving transition dependencies:

$$S_u^R = \text{Reorder}(S_u) = [l_1, \ldots, \underbrace{l_j, l_{j-1}, \ldots, l_i}_{\text{reversed cycle}}, \ldots, l_n]. \tag{9}$$

This approach captures real-world backtracking behaviors (Fig. 4) without introducing implausible transitions from random swaps. The experiments in Sect. 5.6 show the effectiveness of our proposed reordering operation based on cyclic patterns.

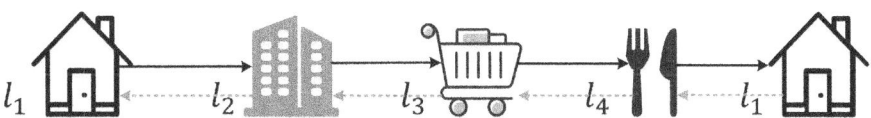

Fig. 4. An example of Cyclic Pattern.

Mask Augmentation. In line with the approach of Xie et al. [30], we implement augmentation through a random masking operation. Specifically, we randomly mask $l = \mu n$ locations within the original sequence. Formally, this can be represented as:

$$S_u^M = Mask(S_u) = [l_1', l_2', \ldots, l_n'] \tag{10}$$

where l_i' will be set to the value of zero if l_i' is selected for masking, otherwise, $l_i' = l_i$. l is controlled by a hyper parameter μ, where $0 \leq \mu \leq 1$.

4.2 Recommendation Module

Embedding Layer. Given a user's check-in trajectory S_u, we learn the latent embedding of the check-in behavior. Since the recommended next location is highly correlated with the user and the check-in time, we respectively learn a dense vector representation for the user, location, and time. Specifically, the embedding representation of each check-in behavior $r = (l, u, t)$ is:

$$\mathbf{e}_{r_i} = \mathbf{l} + \mathbf{u} + \mathbf{t} + \mathbf{p} \tag{11}$$

where + symbol represents the summation of vector dimensions; $\mathbf{l}, \mathbf{u}, \mathbf{t}, \mathbf{p}$ represents POI, user, timestamp and position encoding respectively. Thus, for a user u, the embedding representation of their check-in trajectory is $E_{S_u} = [\mathbf{e}_{r_1}, \mathbf{e}_{r_2}, \ldots, \mathbf{e}_{r_{|S_u|}}]$.

Transformer Encoder. Since user check-in trajectories are lengthy and sparse, and POIs visited by users are affected by various contexts (e.g., temporal, spatial), it becomes difficult to learn accurate user preferences. Transformer [29] is a powerful approach for encoding sequences. Compared with traditional models, Transformer has higher computational efficiency and excellent performance, and is widely used in image classification [7], time series analysis [19] and other fields [1,13]. It consists of two key components: a multi-head self-attention module and a position-wise Feed-Forward Network (FNN). We formulate the encoding process as:

$$h_u = TransEncoder(E_{S_u}) \tag{12}$$

where $h_u = [h_u^1, h_u^2, \ldots, h_u^t]$ represents the encoded hidden representation of the user's check-in sequence S_u. We adopt the negative log likelihood with sampled $SoftMax$ as the recommendation loss for each user u at each time step $t+1$ as:

$$L_{rec}(h_u^t) = -\log \frac{exp((h_u^t)^T l_{t+1}^+)}{exp((h_u^t)^T l_{t+1}^+) + \sum_{l_{t+1} \in L} exp((h_u^t)^T l_{t+1}^-)} \tag{13}$$

where $h_u^t, l_{t+1}^+, l_{t+1}^-$ indicate the hidden representation of the user sequence, the location which user u interacts, and the randomly sampled negative position at the time step $t+1$, respectively.

4.3 Contrastive Self-supervision Module

Recently, some studies have started to apply contrastive learning in sequential recommendation to improve the performance of models. Contrastive SSL optimizes the encoder by maximizing the consistency between positive pairs, where positive pairs refer to two different augmentations from the same sequence. Specifically, given a batch of sequences $\{S_u\}_{u=1}^n$, we randomly assign two different augmentation operations to each sequence S_u. Eventually, we obtain $2N$ augmented sequences:

$$\{S'_1, S'_2, \ldots, S'_{2u-1}, S'_{2u}, \ldots, S'_{2N-1}, S'_{2N}\} \tag{14}$$

where $u \in \{1, 2, \ldots, N\}$. Each adjacent pair (S'_{2u-1}, S'_{2u}) is regarded as a positive pair, and the remaining pairs are regarded as negative samples. These augmented sequences, like the original sequences, pass through the embedding layer to obtain embedding representations, which are then fed into a shared sequence encoder for sequence encoding. For each adjacent pair (S'_{2u-1}, S'_{2u}), their encoded representations are (h'_{2u-1}, h'_{2u}). We adopt the NT-Xent loss for optimization as follows:

$$L_{cls}(h'_{2u-1}, h'_{2u}) = -\log \frac{exp(sim(h'_{2u-1}, h'_{2u}))}{\sum_{m=1}^{2N} exp(sim(h'_{2u-1}, h'_m))[m \neq 2u-1]} \tag{15}$$

where $sim(\cdot)$ is a dot product to measure the similarity between two augmented sequences.

4.4 Multi-task Training

Similar to Xie et al. [30], we adopt a multi-task learning strategy, and the total loss is a linear weighted sum, as shown below:

$$L = L_{rec} + \lambda L_{csl} \tag{16}$$

where λ is a hyper parameter that controls the influence intensity of contrastive SSL. L_{csl} represents the loss of the contrastive learning module, and L_{rec} represents the loss of the recommendation module.

5 Experiments

In this section, we evaluate our proposed model on a real-world dataset and show experimental results.

5.1 Datasets

We evaluate our model on public Foursquare check-in datasets collected from New York City (NYC) and Tokyo (TKY) [32], which have been widely used in POI recommendation research papers [22,28,35]. The check-in records are collected from April 2012 to February 2013. Each record contains user ID, POI ID, GPS and timestamp. For each user, we sort the sequence in timestamp order to obtain a sequence of user interactions. To ensure that each user has enough interactions and to demonstrate the ability of our model to cope with data sparsity, we only discard users with less than 5 check-ins. The statistical results of the two datasets after preprocessing are shown in Table 1.

Table 1. Dataset statistics (after preprocessing).

Dataset	# User	# POI	# Check-in	Sparsity
NYC	1083	38333	227428	99.45%
TKY	2293	61858	573703	99.60%

5.2 Evaluation Metrics

To evaluate the performance of each method for next POI recommendation, we use two common evaluation metrics from previous works [22,28]: $Recall@K$ and Normalized Discounted Cumulative Gain ($NDCG@K$). $Recall@K$ checks if the correct POI is among the top-K ranking list. That is, with the same number of correct recommendations, a higher-ranked POI gives a higher score. In this paper, we choose $K = \{5, 10, 20\}$ for evaluation. Overall, the larger the value of the metric, the better the performance of the recommendation.

5.3 Baselines

We compare out DACL with the following baselines:

(1) BPR-MF [25]: a personalized recommendation model combining Bayesian Personalized Ranking (BPR) and Matrix Factorization (MF).
(2) DeepMove [8]: a model based on attention mechanism and RNN captures the multi-level periodic patterns of human mobility.
(3) LSTPM [28]: a state-of-the-art model, which propose a geo-dilated RNN to fully exploit the geographical relations among non-consecutive POIs.
(4) TiSASRec [16]: a sequential model, which models both the absolute positions of items as well as time intervals between them. They believe that the size of the time interval will have different effects on the next item.
(5) CL4SRec [30]: a sequence recommendation model applying contrast learning which proposes three randomized enhancement operations. However, the randomization operations destroy the correlation of items between sequences.
(6) CoSeRec [21]: the authors propose two data augmentation operations, content-based correlation and model-based correlation, based on CL4SRec and applied them to sequence recommendation tasks. However, it's not applicable to the next POI recommendation tasks.

(7) TiCoSeRec [5]: the authors concluded that sequences with uniform time intervals are more conducive to performance improvement than sequences with highly variable time intervals, and improved on CoSeRec.

5.4 Parameter Settings

For all baseline models, we use their publicly available implementations. Following [5], we set the dimension of embeddings and the hidden states to 128 for all deep learning based methods. The rest parameters of each method are searched as suggested by the original papers. For DACL, we implement it with *Pytorch*, and the model is optimized by Adam optimizer with a learning rate of 0.001 and batch size of 128. Follow [30], we set the number of the self-attention blocks and attention heads as 2. We tune α, β, μ, λ and the maximum sequence length within the range of $[0.1, 0.9]$, $[0.1, 0.9]$, $[0.1, 0.9]$, $\{0.1, 0.2, 0.3, 0.4, 0.5\}$, $\{20, 40, 60, 80, 100\}$ respectively.

5.5 Results and Analysis

Table 2 compares the performance of DACL with baseline methods on NYC and TKY datasets. In each column, the best result is highlighted in boldface and the second best is underlined. Based on the experiment results, we can observe that:

(1) The MF-based model, BPR-MF, performs worse than other deep learning-based models, especially in the TKY dataset. This shows the importance of deep learning for recommender systems. Moreover, most of the current models that achieve state-of-the-art performance are based on RNNs and attention mechanisms.
(2) DeepMove, LSTPM is designed to complete the next POI recommendation task by considering the periodicity and discontinuity of the user's moving trajectory, respectively. TiSASRec is designed with an interval-aware self-attention model for the sequence recommendation. However, we can observe that the performance of TiSASRec is relatively poorer than that of LSTPM. This may be because the TiSASRec model is designed for sequential recommendation tasks, and in the POI recommendation task, due to its special geographical location attributes, the performance of TiSASRec is inferior.
(3) CL4SRec, CoSeRec, TiCoSeRec are all data augmentation models proposed based on comparative learning and applied in sequence recommendation tasks. We observe that CL4SRec, as the first proposed model, outperforms CoSeRec and TiCoSeRec instead, which may be due to the fact that the data augmentation operation based on the similarity of items is not applicable to the POI recommendation, which leads to constructing false positive samples and impairs the performance of the model. In addition, the performance of the TiCoSeRec model outperforms CoSeRec in almost all metrics, which suggests that the uniformly distributed time intervals proposed by Dang et al. [5] contribute to the improved model performance.

(4) The proposed DACL consistently outperforms other models across all datasets and evaluation metrics. Compared to the best baseline, DACL achieves improvements ranging from 2.21% to 19.09% in terms of *Recall* and *NDCG*. These results demonstrate the effectiveness of employing contrastive SSL techniques in next POI recommendation tasks.

Table 2. Recommendation performance comparision with baselines

Datasets	Methods	Recall@5	Recall@10	Recall@20	NDCG@5	NDCG@10	NDCG@20
NYC	BPR-MF	0.2017	0.2703	0.3354	0.1369	0.1950	0.2146
	DeepMove	0.1967	0.2423	0.2843	0.1435	0.1583	0.1689
	TiSASRec	0.3000	0.3352	0.3800	0.2423	0.2536	0.2649
	LSTPM	0.3094	0.3784	0.4389	0.2322	0.2545	0.2700
	CL4SRec	0.3352	0.3721	0.4035	0.2497	0.2620	0.2700
	CoSeRec	0.2761	0.3241	0.3592	0.2027	0.2183	0.2271
	TiCoSeRec	0.2789	0.3389	0.4007	0.2024	0.2222	0.2377
	DACL(Ours)	**0.3703**	**0.4257**	**0.4765**	**0.2659**	**0.2840**	**0.2967**
	Improvement	10.47%	12.50%	8.57%	6.49%	8.40%	9.89%
TKY	BPR-MF	0.1190	0.1712	0.2187	0.0787	0.0961	0.1205
	DeepMove	0.2652	0.3175	0.3668	0.1978	0.2147	0.2271
	TiSASRec	0.2800	0.3200	0.3750	0.2262	0.2393	0.2536
	LSTPM	0.3009	0.3669	0.4233	0.2252	0.2466	0.2609
	CL4SRec	0.2560	0.3162	0.3799	0.1930	0.2124	0.2286
	CoSeRec	0.1832	0.2176	0.2573	0.1446	0.1559	0.1660
	TiCoSeRec	0.2250	0.2813	0.3406	0.1703	0.1886	0.2036
	DACL	**0.3354**	**0.4261**	**0.5041**	**0.2312**	**0.2576**	**0.2796**
	Improvement	11.46%	16.13%	19.09%	2.21%	4.46%	7.17%

5.6 Ablation Study

In this paper, we include five augmentation operators for the contrastive SSL. To study the impact of these augmentation operations, we carried out two sets of ablation experiments on the NYC and TKY datasets. The first set of experiments is to remove only one augmentation operation at a time from the augmentation set $\{GS, GI, M, R, D\}$. The second set of experiments is to use only one augmentation operation at a time.

Remove One. The results of the experiments where only one enhancement operation is removed are presented in Fig. 5 and compared to 'w/o A', which uses only the recommendation module. We observe that the models applying data augmentation all outperform the models using only recommendations. This proves the superiority of our proposed data augmentation operation. In addition, we observe that both datasets perform worse in the absence of 'GI' or 'GS' operations, a phenomenon that implies the effectiveness of our proposed 'GI' and 'GS' operations based on trajectory maps and geographic factors.

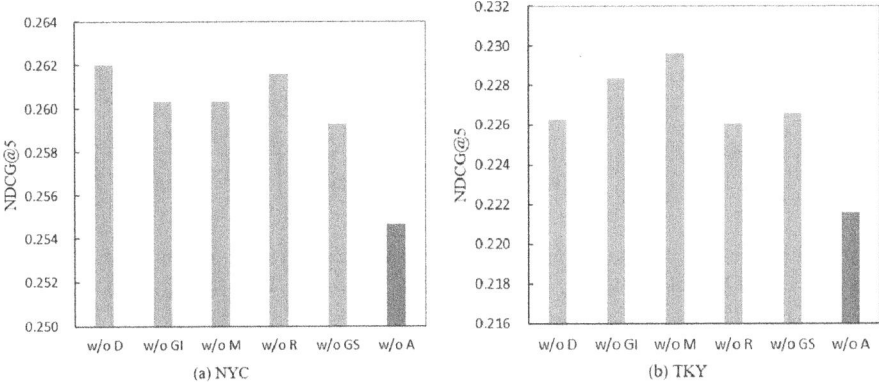

Fig. 5. Performance comparison (in $NDCG@5$) w.r.t. different augmentation sets on NYC and TKY datasets. 'w/o' indicates one type is removed from the full augmentation set $\{GS, GI, M, R, D\}$. 'w/o A' represents the removal of all augmentation operations, i.e. using only the recommendation module.

One Augmentation. Figure 6 shows the experimental results using only one augmentation operation and compares it with the model 'w/o A'. We can observe:

(1) The performance of the models applying only one augmentation operation all outperform 'w/o A', which indicates that each of our proposed augmentation operations is effective.
(2) In both datasets, $\{GI, GS, M\}$ shows the most performance improvement because $\{GI, GS\}$ applying trajectory maps and geographic factors effectively mitigates the data sparsity problem and is able to provide more confident positive pairs in contrastive learning. While the 'M' operation by random masking, which is similar to next POI recommendation, enables the model to infer location information masked between sequences.
(3) In both datasets, the performance improvement of $\{D, R\}$ is not significant. A possible reason is that these two operations provide relatively less information.

5.7 Robustness Study

In POI recommendation, the problem of data sparsity is commonly encountered, which is also a prevalent issue in recommendation systems. To simulate

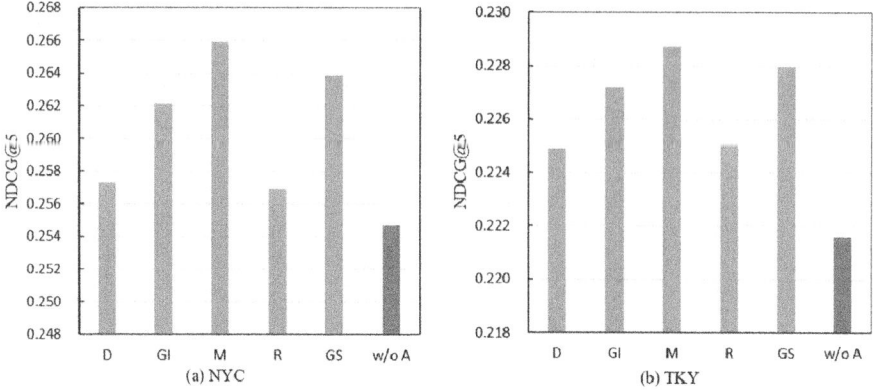

Fig. 6. Performance comparison (in $NDCG@5$) w.r.t. different augmentation operation on NYC and TKY datasets.

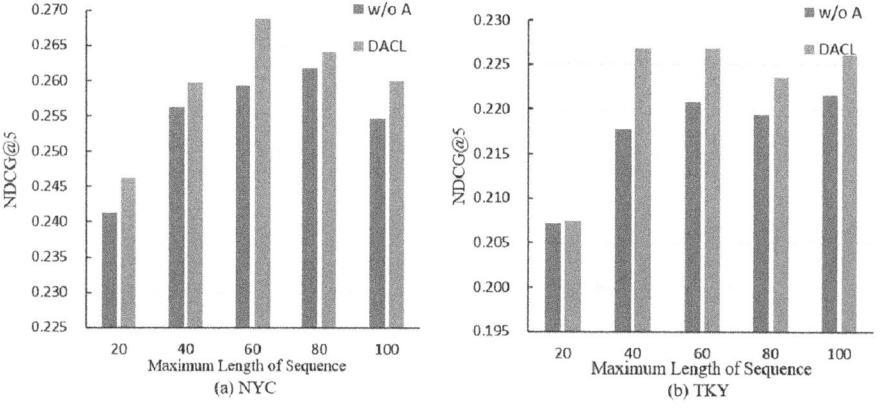

Fig. 7. Performance comparison w.r.t. sparsity ratio.

the performance of our model under data-sparse conditions, we adjust the maximum sequence length of the sequences to $(20, 40, 60, 80, 100)$ while keeping other hyperparameters the same.

Figure 7 shows the performance of our model DACL under different maximum sequence lengths and compares it with the model 'w/o A' that only uses the recommendation module. We observe the following:

(1) Our model outperforms 'w/o A' at any maximum sequence lengths.
(2) The performance of our model when the maximum sequence length is 40 has already surpassed that of 'w/o A' in most cases. This indicates that our model can effectively alleviate the problem of data sparsity.
(3) Our model still maintains a high accuracy when the maximum sequence length is 20, i.e., in the case of short sequences. Therefore, it can also mitigate the cold-start problem.

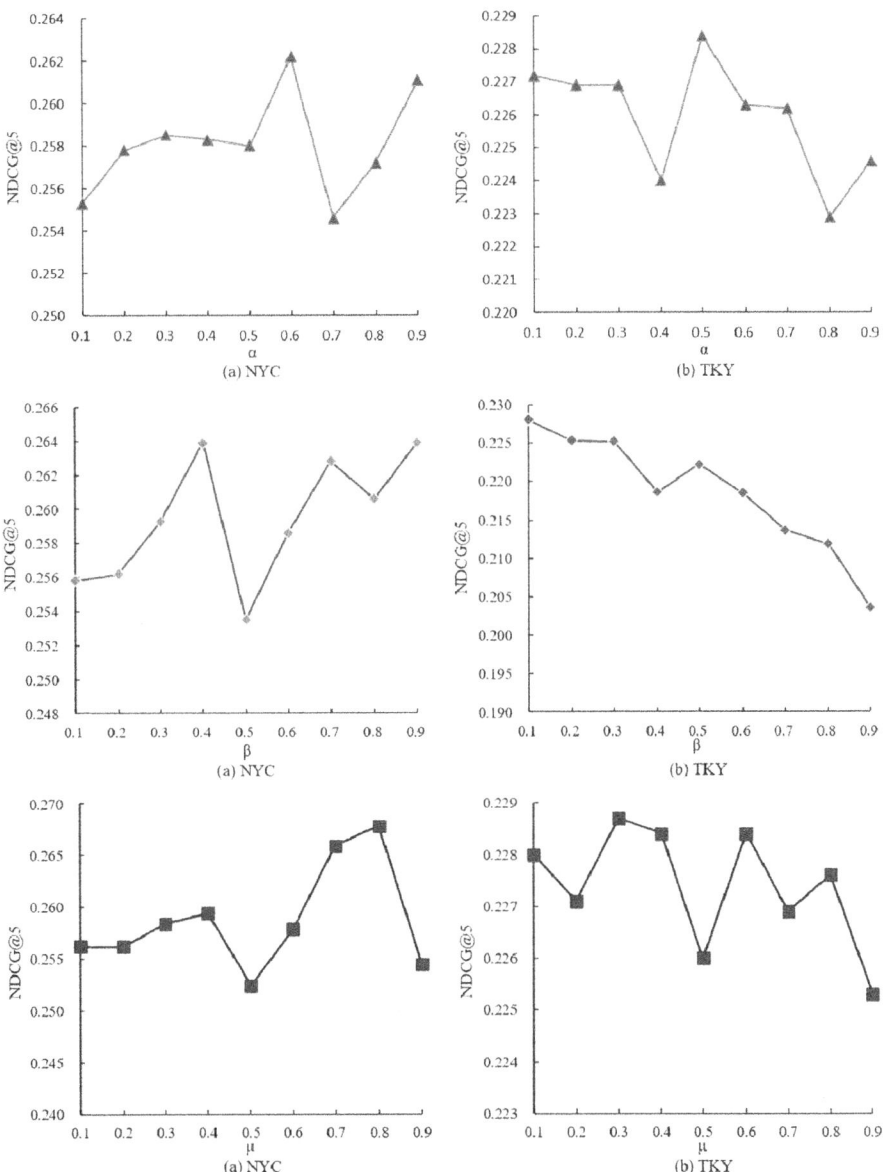

Fig. 8. Performance comparison of DACL w.r.t. different α, β, μ on NYC and TKY datasets.

5.8 Study of DACL

In this section we verify the impact of the key hyperparameters of DACL, we explore the effects of hyperparameters α, β, μ, λ in DACL, which control the 'insert' ratio, 'substitute' rate, 'mask' rate and the intensity of contrastive SSL,

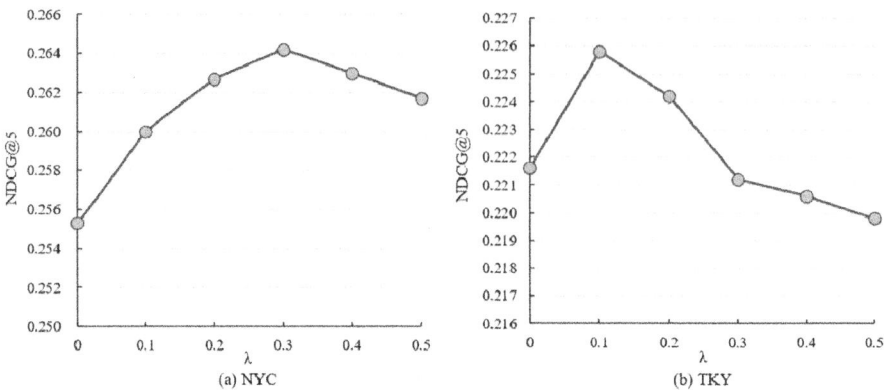

Fig. 9. Performance comparison of DACL w.r.t. different λ on NYC and TKY datasets.

respectively. In particular, when a particular hyperparameter is studied, all other hyperparameters are set to optimally adjusted values.

(1) By observing Fig. 8, we can discern that in both datasets, the models show different performance under the three data augmentation operations. In the NYC dataset, a general pattern is that the performance increases then decreases and finally increases again, while the TKY dataset shows an overall decreasing trend. In addition, a common thread in both datasets is the ability to achieve better results when the ratio is less than 0.4, due to the fact that the augmentation sequence provides a positive view for comparison learning. We also observe that in the TKY dataset, as the ratio increases too high, it leads to more severe corruption, which in turn builds negative samples to compromise the SLL. On the contrary, in the NYC dataset, higher ratios still achieve better results, and a possible reason for this is that its smaller data size allows the model to have enough parameters to learn higher-order user representations.

(2) From the Fig. 9, we can see that applying comparative SSL in the next POI recommendation task is effective. In the NYC and TKY datasets, DACL improves 3.5% and 1.9% over using only the recommendation module (i.e., $\lambda = 0$) on $NDCG@5$, respectively. We also observe a trend of increasing and then decreasing model performance as λ increases. When λ is large, the performance starts to deteriorate, which implies that the contrastive SSL signal serves as a complementary element rather than a dominant factor in the learning objective, especially within the context of next POI recommendation.

6 Conclusion and Future Work

In this paper, we put forward a novel model, abbreviated as DACL, for next POI recommendation. Specifically, we apply contrastive SSL techniques to data augmentation and conduct multi-task training in combination with the next POI recommendation task. Moreover, we introduce five innovative data augmentation operations, namely Geo-Insert, Geo-Substitute, Delete, Reorder and Mask operations, to construct high-quality views for contrastive learning. In the experimental section, we carried out comprehensive comparison experiments, ablation studies, and stability studies. The experimental results demonstrate that, compared with state-of-the-art methods, our proposed method significantly improves the recommendation accuracy. Future work will explore data augmentation techniques that integrate additional features (e.g., POI categories and temporal periodicity) to further alleviate data sparsity.

References

1. Bi, K., Ai, Q., Croft, W.B.: A transformer-based embedding model for personalized product search. In: Proceedings of the 43rd International ACM SIGIR Conference on Research and Development in Information Retrieval, pp. 1521–1524 (2020)
2. Chen, R.J., et al.: Scaling vision transformers to gigapixel images via hierarchical self-supervised learning. In: 2022 IEEE/CVF Conference on Computer Vision and Pattern Recognition (CVPR), pp. 16123–16134 (2022). https://doi.org/10.1109/CVPR52688.2022.01567
3. Chen, T., Kornblith, S., Norouzi, M., Hinton, G.E.: A simple framework for contrastive learning of visual representations. In: Proceedings of the 37th International Conference on Machine Learning, ICML 2020, 13–18 July 2020, Virtual Event. Proceedings of Machine Learning Research, vol. 119, pp. 1597–1607. PMLR (2020), http://proceedings.mlr.press/v119/chen20j.html
4. Cheng, C., Yang, H., Lyu, M.R., King, I.: Where you like to go next: successive point-of-interest recommendation. In: Twenty-Third International Joint Conference on Artificial Intelligence (2013)
5. Dang, Y., et al.: Uniform sequence better: Time interval aware data augmentation for sequential recommendation. In: Williams, B., Chen, Y., Neville, J. (eds.) Thirty-Seventh AAAI Conference on Artificial Intelligence, AAAI 2023, Thirty-Fifth Conference on Innovative Applications of Artificial Intelligence, IAAI 2023, Thirteenth Symposium on Educational Advances in Artificial Intelligence, EAAI 2023, Washington, DC, USA, 7–14 February 2023, pp. 4225–4232. AAAI Press (2023). https://doi.org/10.1609/AAAI.V37I4.25540
6. Devlin, J., Chang, M., Lee, K., Toutanova, K.: BERT: pre-training of deep bidirectional transformers for language understanding. In: Burstein, J., Doran, C., Solorio, T. (eds.) Proceedings of the 2019 Conference of the North American Chapter of the Association for Computational Linguistics: Human Language Technologies, NAACL-HLT 2019, Minneapolis, MN, USA, 2–7 June 2019, Volume 1 (Long and Short Papers), pp. 4171–4186. Association for Computational Linguistics (2019). https://doi.org/10.18653/V1/N19-1423
7. Dosovitskiy, A., et al.: An image is worth 16×16 words: transformers for image recognition at scale. arXiv preprint arXiv:2010.11929 (2020)
8. Feng, J., et al.: DeepMove: predicting human mobility with attentional recurrent networks. In: Champin, P., Gandon, F., Lalmas, M., Ipeirotis, P.G. (eds.) Proceedings of the 2018 World Wide Web Conference on World Wide Web, WWW 2018, Lyon, France, 23–27 April 2018, pp. 1459–1468. ACM (2018). https://doi.org/10.1145/3178876.3186058

9. Feng, S., Li, X., Zeng, Y., Cong, G., Chee, Y.M., Yuan, Q.: Personalized ranking metric embedding for next new POI recommendation. In: Yang, Q., Wooldridge, M.J. (eds.) Proceedings of the Twenty-Fourth International Joint Conference on Artificial Intelligence, IJCAI 2015, Buenos Aires, Argentina, 25–31 July 2015, pp. 2069–2075. AAAI Press (2015). http://ijcai.org/Abstract/15/293
10. He, J., Li, X., Liao, L., Song, D., Cheung, W.K.: Inferring a personalized next point-of-interest recommendation model with latent behavior patterns. In: Schuurmans, D., Wellman, M.P. (eds.) Proceedings of the Thirtieth AAAI Conference on Artificial Intelligence, 12–17 February2016, Phoenix, Arizona, USA, pp. 137–143. AAAI Press (2016). https://doi.org/10.1609/AAAI.V30I1.9994
11. Huang, J., Zhao, W.X., Dou, H., Wen, J., Chang, E.Y.: Improving sequential recommendation with knowledge-enhanced memory networks. In: Collins-Thompson, K., Mei, Q., Davison, B.D., Liu, Y., Yilmaz, E. (eds.) The 41st International ACM SIGIR Conference on Research & Development in Information Retrieval, SIGIR 2018, Ann Arbor, MI, USA, 08–12 July 2018, pp. 505–514. ACM (2018). https://doi.org/10.1145/3209978.3210017
12. Jiang, S., Qian, X., Shen, J., Fu, Y., Mei, T.: Author topic model-based collaborative filtering for personalized poi recommendations. IEEE Trans. Multimedia **17**(6), 907–918 (2015)
13. Jin, T., Huang, S., Chen, M., Li, Y., Zhang, Z.: SBAT: video captioning with sparse boundary-aware transformer. arXiv preprint arXiv:2007.11888 (2020)
14. Koren, Y., Bell, R., Volinsky, C.: Matrix factorization techniques for recommender systems. Computer **42**(8), 30–37 (2009)
15. Lan, Z., Chen, M., Goodman, S., Gimpel, K., Sharma, P., Soricut, R.: ALBERT: a lite BERT for self-supervised learning of language representations. In: 8th International Conference on Learning Representations, ICLR 2020, Addis Ababa, Ethiopia, 26–30 April 2020. OpenReview.net (2020). https://openreview.net/forum?id=H1eA7AEtvS
16. Li, J., Wang, Y., McAuley, J.J.: Time interval aware self-attention for sequential recommendation. In: Caverlee, J., Hu, X.B., Lalmas, M., Wang, W. (eds.) WSDM 2020: The Thirteenth ACM International Conference on Web Search and Data Mining, Houston, TX, USA, 3–7 February 2020, pp. 322–330. ACM (2020). https://doi.org/10.1145/3336191.3371786
17. Li, Y., Luo, Y., Zhang, Z., Sadiq, S., Cui, P.: Context-aware attention-based data augmentation for POI recommendation. In: 35th IEEE International Conference on Data Engineering Workshops, ICDE Workshops 2019, Macao, China, 8–12 April 2019, pp. 177–184. IEEE (2019). https://doi.org/10.1109/ICDEW.2019.00-14
18. Lian, D., Zhao, C., Xie, X., Sun, G., Chen, E., Rui, Y.: GeoMF: joint geographical modeling and matrix factorization for point-of-interest recommendation. In: Proceedings of the 20th ACM SIGKDD International Conference on Knowledge Discovery and Data Mining, pp. 831–840 (2014)
19. Lim, B., Arık, S.Ö., Loeff, N., Pfister, T.: Temporal fusion transformers for interpretable multi-horizon time series forecasting. Int. J. Forecast. **37**(4), 1748–1764 (2021)
20. Liu, Q., Wu, S., Wang, L., Tan, T.: Predicting the next location: a recurrent model with spatial and temporal contexts. In: Schuurmans, D., Wellman, M.P. (eds.) Proceedings of the Thirtieth AAAI Conference on Artificial Intelligence, 12–17 February 2016, Phoenix, Arizona, USA, pp. 194–200. AAAI Press (2016). https://doi.org/10.1609/AAAI.V30I1.9971

21. Liu, Z., Chen, Y., Li, J., Yu, P.S., McAuley, J.J., Xiong, C.: Contrastive self-supervised sequential recommendation with robust augmentation. CoRR abs/2108.06479 (2021). https://arxiv.org/abs/2108.06479
22. Luo, Y., Liu, Q., Liu, Z.: STAN: spatio-temporal attention network for next location recommendation. In: Proceedings of the Web Conference 2021, pp. 2177–2185 (2021)
23. Qi, L., et al.: Counterfactual user sequence synthesis augmented with continuous time dynamic preference modeling for sequential POI recommendation. In: Proceedings of the Thirty-Third International Joint Conference on Artificial Intelligence, IJCAI 2024, Jeju, South Korea, 3 9 August 2024, pp. 2306 2314. ijcai.org (2024). https://www.ijcai.org/proceedings/2024/255
24. Qin, Y., et al.: Disentangling geographical effect for point-of-interest recommendation. IEEE Trans. Knowl. Data Eng. **35**(8), 7883–7897 (2023). https://doi.org/10.1109/TKDE.2022.3221873
25. Rendle, S., Freudenthaler, C., Gantner, Z., Schmidt-Thieme, L.: BPR: bayesian personalized ranking from implicit feedback. In: Bilmes, J.A., Ng, A.Y. (eds.) UAI 2009, Proceedings of the Twenty-Fifth Conference on Uncertainty in Artificial Intelligence, Montreal, QC, Canada, 18–21 June 2009, pp. 452–461. AUAI Press (2009), https://www.auai.org/uai2009/papers/UAI2009_0139_48141db02b9f0b02bc7158819ebfa2c7.pdf
26. Rendle, S., Freudenthaler, C., Schmidt-Thieme, L.: Factorizing personalized Markov chains for next-basket recommendation. In: Proceedings of the 19th International Conference on World Wide Web, pp. 811–820 (2010)
27. Sánchez, P., Bellogín, A.: Point-of-interest recommender systems based on location-based social networks: a survey from an experimental perspective. ACM Comput. Surv. (CSUR) **54**(11s), 1–37 (2022)
28. Sun, K., Qian, T., Chen, T., Liang, Y., Nguyen, Q.V.H., Yin, H.: Where to go next: modeling long- and short-term user preferences for point-of-interest recommendation. In: The Thirty-Fourth AAAI Conference on Artificial Intelligence, AAAI 2020, The Thirty-Second Innovative Applications of Artificial Intelligence Conference, IAAI 2020, The Tenth AAAI Symposium on Educational Advances in Artificial Intelligence, EAAI 2020, New York, NY, USA, 7–12 February 2020, pp. 214–221. AAAI Press (2020). https://doi.org/10.1609/AAAI.V34I01.5353
29. Vaswani, A., et al.: Attention is all you need. In: Advances in Neural Information Processing Systems, vol. 30 (2017)
30. Xie, X., Sun, F., Liu, Z., Gao, J., Ding, B., Cui, B.: Contrastive pre-training for sequential recommendation. CoRR abs/2010.14395 (2020). https://arxiv.org/abs/2010.14395
31. Yang, D., Fankhauser, B., Rosso, P., Cudre-Mauroux, P.: Location prediction over sparse user mobility traces using RNNs. In: Proceedings of the Twenty-Ninth International Joint Conference on Artificial Intelligence, pp. 2184–2190 (2020)
32. Yang, D., Zhang, D., Qu, B.: Participatory cultural mapping based on collective behavior data in location-based social networks. ACM Trans. Intell. Syst. Technol. (TIST) **7**(3), 1–23 (2016)
33. Yang, D., Zhang, D., Zheng, V.W., Yu, Z.: Modeling user activity preference by leveraging user spatial temporal characteristics in LBSNs. IEEE Trans. Syst. Man Cybern.: Syst. **45**(1), 129–142 (2014)
34. Ye, M., Yin, P., Lee, W.C., Lee, D.L.: Exploiting geographical influence for collaborative point-of-interest recommendation. In: Proceedings of the 34th international ACM SIGIR Conference on Research and Development in Information Retrieval, pp. 325–334 (2011)

35. Zhang, L., Sun, Z., Wu, Z., Zhang, J., Ong, Y.S., Qu, X.: Next point-of-interest recommendation with inferring multi-step future preferences. In: Raedt, L.D. (ed.) Proceedings of the Thirty-First International Joint Conference on Artificial Intelligence, IJCAI 2022, Vienna, Austria, 23–29 July 2022, pp. 3751–3757. ijcai.org (2022). https://doi.org/10.24963/IJCAI.2022/521
36. Zhao, P., et al.: Where to go next: a spatio-temporal gated network for next POI recommendation. IEEE Trans. Knowl. Data Eng. **34**(5), 2512–2524 (2020)
37. Zhao, P., et al.: Where to go next: a spatio-temporal gated network for next poi recommendation. IEEE Trans. Knowl. Data Eng. **34**(5), 2512–2524 (2020)
38. Zhu, Y., et al.: What to do next: Modeling user behaviors by time-LSTM. In: Sierra, C. (ed.) Proceedings of the Twenty-Sixth International Joint Conference on Artificial Intelligence, IJCAI 2017, Melbourne, Australia, 19–25 August 2017, pp. 3602–3608. ijcai.org (2017). https://doi.org/10.24963/IJCAI.2017/504
39. Zhuang, Z., Wei, T., Liu, L., Qi, H., Shen, Y., Yin, B.: TAU: trajectory data augmentation with uncertainty for next POI recommendation. In: Wooldridge, M.J., Dy, J.G., Natarajan, S. (eds.) Thirty-Eighth AAAI Conference on Artificial Intelligence, AAAI 2024, Thirty-Sixth Conference on Innovative Applications of Artificial Intelligence, IAAI 2024, Fourteenth Symposium on Educational Advances in Artificial Intelligence, EAAI 2014, 20–27 February 2024, Vancouver, Canada, pp. 22565–22573. AAAI Press (2024). https://doi.org/10.1609/AAAI.V38I20.30265

Deductive Inference of How Urbanization Shaped by Governmental Policy in Beijing from 2005 to 2022

Zhi Cai[1(✉)], Hanming Fan[1], Sheng Li[2], Hanwen Liao[3], and Haiyan Gao[3]

[1] College of Computer Science, Beijing University of Technology, Beijing 100124, China
caiz@bjut.edu.cn, 390041682@qq.com
[2] Department of Sociology, Beijing University of Technology, Beijing 100124, China
lisheng@bjut.edu.cn
[3] Department of Architecture, Beijing University of Technology, Beijing 100124, China
{h.liao,gaohaiyan}@bjut.edu.cn

Abstract. The driving forces of urbanization research in previous studies are socio-economic, environmental and technological development. We argue that government policies play an important role in shaping urbanization, especially in Socialist countries. In the past two decades, many super cities have emerged in China, and their size and spatial patterns are constantly changing. This paper aims to develop a deductive method to reveal the development patterns of Beijing under the influence of governmental policies and predict the future development of the city. Specifically, we first propose the concept of road network-based urban texture to describe the level of urbanization. Second, we use linear functions and neural networks to learn the spatio-temporal development patterns from Beijing's survey and mapping data from 2005 to 2015. Finally, we validate the proposed method using the survey and mapping data of 2022. The experimental results confirm that our hypothesis in findings reasonable and the proposed method is able to predict the future development of cities.

Keywords: Urbanization · Government policies · Spatio-temporal development

1 Introduction

Despite its small land coverage, urban land and its expansion have exhibited profound impacts on global environments [1]. Urbanization has left a significant mark on global environments. As urban areas expand, they inevitably give rise to substantial socioeconomic disparities [2]. Recognized as a vital catalyst for social and economic progress, urbanization drives multifaceted advancements in human life [3]. The phenomenon of urbanization owes itself to shifting lifestyles, improvements in infrastructure, heightened mobility, and a flourishing economy, resulting in the proliferation of high-density, fragmented urban developments across various regions worldwide [4].

Urbanization stands as a cornerstone of modernization and economic growth, representing an inevitable trend in human societal development [5]. Cities, meanwhile, have emerged as crucial arenas for promoting a more sustainable future for human society [6]. Pro-urban policies facilitating rural-urban migration and the flow of rural resources into urban areas have accelerated urbanization [7]. With over half of the world's population residing in urban areas, a figure expected to reach 66% by 2050 and with the number of cities in developing countries projected to triple by 2030, rapid urbanization presents significant challenges to sustainable development [8,9]. Addressing issues of social equity and justice has become imperative [10], particularly concerning peri-urbanization in developing countries, which presents both opportunities and challenges [11].

China has experienced rapid urbanization and extensive urban expansion in recent decades. China's high-speed economic development over the past four decades has closely paralleled this process, guided by evolving central government policies in pursuing high quality development [12]. In recent years, the Chinese government has embarked on a new phase of urbanization to tackle the environmental and social costs of previous decades' tumultuous growth [13]. The impact of China's epic transition from a rural to an urban society is propelled by its economic ambitions [14]. The significance of the future of cities in China has extended beyond domestic borders to global arenas [15]. Indeed, "the urbanism" has emerged as a paramount ideological realm in contemporary China as its urbanization rate has reached 66.16% by 2023 [16].

Urbanization is a process related to economic growth and spatial of the core metropolitan city towards regional urban cluster [17]. Urbanization has long been associated with human development and progress [18] and Urbanization is one of the most impactful human activities across the world today affecting the quality of urban life and its sustainable development [19]. China's urbanization with increasing intensity and quickening pace has always been central to debates over the past few decades [21]. Urban land sprawl and rural-urban migration have caused rapid global urbanization over the past several decades [15]. The Chicago School pioneered the human ecological approach to urban studies, employing theoretical frameworks and methodologies from ecology to examine the relationship between humans and cities, and to elucidate patterns of urban development. And theorists of the Chicago School of Urban Sociology were concerned with the consequences of increasing urbanization on social processes and people's place-based behaviour [22]. They posited that cities are manifestations of human social relations determined by spatial distribution characteristics. Therefore, studying the spatial distribution features of cities becomes particularly important. As the world's largest developing country, China has made a target to achieve a comprehensive level of modernization by 2035 and to reach catch up the major developed countries by the mid-21st century. China is continuously expanding urban development in accordance with its planned trajectory.

Cities are closely connected socially, economically, and technologically [23]. Urban social spatial differentiation and evolution typically refer to the temporal disparities in economic, industrial, and cultural structures across the entire urban framework, as urban areas expand and develop, and populations fluctuate. China has been haunted by a variety of issues related to uncoordinated urban-rural interaction in recent decades and is in the midst of a critical stage faced with great challenges and opportunities as well in realizing urban-rural integration [24]. The capital city Beijing, for example, is still in the process of transitioning from fast development to the stage of maturity. This trend will continue until the mid-2030s [25]. The patterns of urban development differ between developed and developing countries. Taking China and the United States as examples, in terms of urban evolution trends and resident income distribution, the United States exhibits a "high-income exterior, low-income interior" social spatial pattern, which is starkly contrasted with the typical "high-income interior, low-income exterior" pattern observed in Chinese cities.

Spatial planning refers to the long-term planning and overall arrangement of land resources and space layout under the jurisdiction of a country or region government [26]. Regarding the development of Beijing, urban developing remains characterized by issues such as disorderly sprawl, exacerbation of social stratification and differentiation in residential spaces, and imbalanced spatial distribution of urban public service facilities. More immigrants have settled outside the city and are known as an urban sprawling phenomenon [27]. Urban sprawl has become a global phenomenon resulting in many critical social and environmental problems [28]. In most cities, urban growth follows a sprawl pattern [29]. Recent studies have also highlighted the sprawl issues in Beijing's development. As urban development continues, existing literature on Beijing's development may overestimate the impact of policies aimed at addressing these issues. Additionally, there is still limited research evaluating the influence of policies on Beijing's development process and studying scenarios and countermeasures for urban development.

This study focuses on the research and prediction of the development of Beijing, China. Unlike the Chicago School's human ecological perspective on urban studies, we approach urban development from a policy standpoint. The analysis of big data is deemed to define a new era in urban research, planning, and policy [30], so we employ neural networks and linear prediction methods (see "Methods" for details) to evaluate the impact of policies on the development of Beijing, while also establishing models for scenario analysis and countermeasures for urban development. We introduce the concept of urban texture to construct "snapshots" of cities at different stages of development. The multi-head attention mechanism and stacking layers enable the transformer to learn dynamic and hierarchical features in sequential data [31]. So, we utilize Transformer neural network models to learn and predict changes in urban road networks. We find that urban planning policies in China exert significant regulatory effects, influencing the scale, speed, and morphology of urban development. Different policies have varying degrees of impact on different regions of the city, and even adjacent areas may exhibit divergent development trends due to policy disparities. Currently, Beijing's central area has been well developed comparing to the outskirts and is relatively stable in terms of built environmental transition. Looking ahead to 2035, Beijing's urban development will enter a new stage.

2 Methods

In this study, an urban texture generation method was applied to investigate the development levels of different regions in Beijing. The road development levels of various regions in Beijing were obtained from the urban texture generation method. Then, road lengths in three different years - 2005, 2015, and 2022 - were predicted using a combination of linear function models and neural network models to identify areas influenced by policies. Finally, a function prediction model was constructed to predict the future development outcomes of the city.

2.1 Urban Texture Generation Method

To investigate urban development planning, the study focuses on the analysis of road changes. Three sets of road data from Beijing in the years of 2005, 2015, and 2022 were selected for this study (Fig. 1).

The emphasis is to identify the impact of policies on urban development through changes in road infrastructure. Considering China's goal to significantly enhance its economic and technological prowess, comprehensive national strength, and the living standards of its people by 2035, Beijing, as the capital of China, is poised to epitomize the development trajectory of a centrally governed socialist nation.

Traditional data can be categorized into macro, meso, and micro levels. Macro data typically involves statistical and descriptive data on an overall, large-scale, and comprehensive basis, covering diverse fields and extensive information. Such data often manifest in forms like national, regional, or global GDP and population figures. In urban development, concerning roads, micro-level data typically include information such as road geometry, width, length, location, type, and classification. These details hold significant reference value for traffic planning and urban spatial layout, providing fundamental support for urban development and traffic management. When discussing the connection between macro and micro data, we find ourselves at the intersection of data levels, where macro data represents abstract overall aspects, while micro data presents detailed individual elements. In this context, meso-level data act as vital connectors, bridging the macro and micro data levels. Therefore, we propose the method of generating urban texture, aiming to treat urban texture as meso-level data, closely connecting macro and micro data.

Urban texture refers to the traces and scale formed by the historical development of a city, as well as the organizational methods and characteristics displayed in its urban landscape. Analogous to tree rings, it showcases features such as the

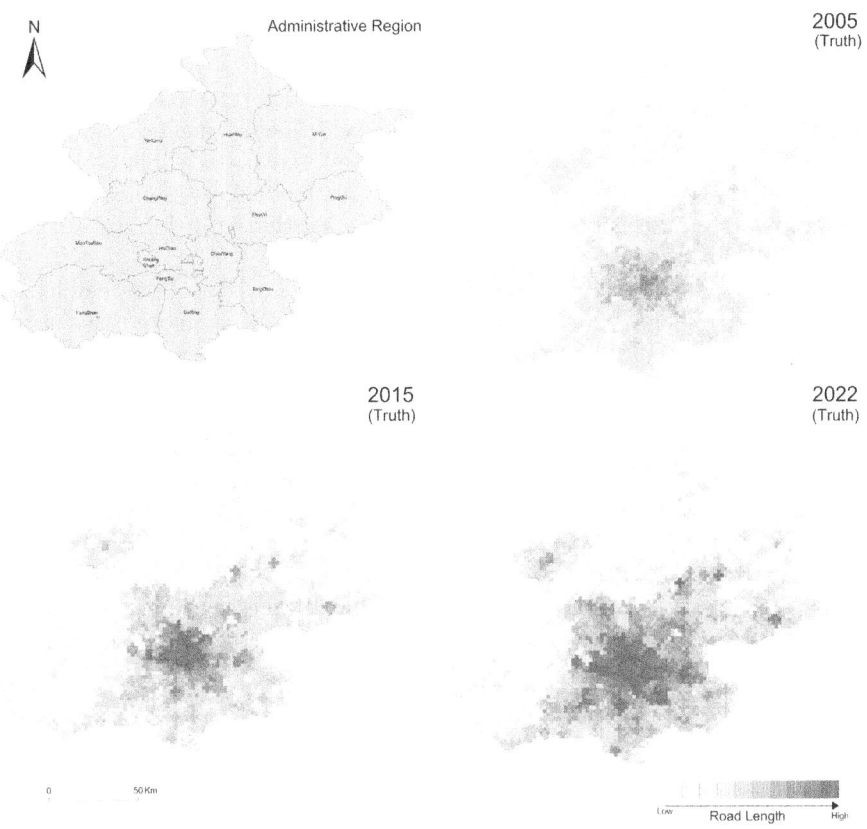

Fig. 1. | Beijing Road Data for 2005, 2015, and 2022 Presented in Full.

city's historical evolution, architectural styles, neighborhood layouts, and distribution of green spaces. We adopted a method of map rasterization for generating urban texture, wherein it's crucial to determine the size of the map grid. The mismatch between the grid size and the city area may lead to a loss of urban information. Additionally, the grid size plays a vital role in data analysis and computation. After continuous experimentation, we settled on a grid size of 2 km x 2 km. This choice was made to simplify data processing and ensure an appropriate spatial resolution for spatial analysis, enabling the capture of internal road networks and road distribution characteristics within the city. Furthermore, to facilitate data integration, statistical analysis, data mining, and prediction, we assigned a unique identifier to each region for spatial identification and indexing.

Firstly, we imported the road network data into the system and conducted rigorous topological analysis using the built-in network analysis tools in ArcGIS Pro. This critical step involved establishing topological rules, such as the mutual correlation of nodes and the connectivity of road edges, to ensure the integrity and coherence of the overall road network. During the topological repair process, we continuously documented and corrected detected topological errors to ensure the accuracy and completeness of the data.

Next, we proceeded with the detailed segmentation of the road network. This step aimed to decompose the road network into distinct segments, ensuring that each segment was clearly labeled with start and end nodes while maintaining the overall continuity of the road network. This meticulous segmentation laid a solid foundation for subsequent road length statistics, providing reliable data support for our research.

Finally, we conducted a comprehensive statistical analysis of the road lengths within each grid. This process aimed to comprehend the characteristics of road networks in different areas, providing crucial data for urban texture and development patterns. It offered vital information for further spatial analysis and urban planning initiatives.

Thus far, we have treated the city as a canvas, dividing it into regular grids. Similar to observing tree rings, each grid represents a scale of urban development, recording the growth, evolution, and transformations of the city. By rasterizing maps and calculating road lengths within each grid, we have imprinted the "annual rings" of the city for each period. These imprints are not merely numbers; they serve as clues to urban development, reflecting varying degrees of transportation development in different regions, distinctive urban layouts, and development trends over different periods.

2.2 Urban Development and Reconstruction

At the strategic level of urban development, it is essential to clearly define the city's vision and long-term goals. This includes envisioning and aspiring to the city's future overall, encompassing its positioning, development direction, and future image. Additionally, in terms of land use and urban planning, it is necessary to accurately define the city's expansion direction and the planning and distribution of various functional areas. This involves the layout of areas such as green spaces, residential areas, commercial districts, and industrial zones to achieve the orderliness and sustainability of urban development. Furthermore, it involves determining economic development strategies, environmental protection, and sustainable development strategies. These strategic decisions will provide long-term guidance and goals for urban planning and development, assisting urban planners and decision-makers in comprehensive planning to promote more orderly, efficient, and sustainable urban development. Therefore, predictive analysis of future urban development is particularly important.

For computer science, the most mainstream approach currently is to utilize neural networks for prediction. When referring to neural networks, we mean a computational model that simulates the structure and functionality of the human brain's neural system. It consists of a large number of artificial neurons that transmit information through connections. Neural networks are typically divided into multiple layers, including the input layer, hidden layers, and output layer. Each neuron receives input from the neurons in the previous layer and produces output through weighted summation and activation functions, which is then passed to the neurons in the next layer. By learning patterns and features from large amounts of data, neural networks can perform tasks such as prediction, classification, and recognition

Transformer is a neural network architecture based on attention mechanisms. It mainly consists of an encoder and a decoder, utilizing self-attention mechanisms to handle input sequences and capture correlations between different positions in the sequence. The emergence of the Transformer architecture has changed the way many sequence tasks are processed, thanks to its parallel computing capabilities and its ability to capture long-range dependencies, making it perform exceptionally well in handling sequence data. Therefore, we adopt the Transformer approach to simulate the development of city roads. The data for the neural network prediction model comes from the road network data of Beijing in 2005 and 2015. The structure of this model includes an encoder and a decoder. The encoder accepts sequences (road data from different regions of Beijing) and encodes the input sequence using self-attention mechanisms. The decoder is responsible for generating output sequences. It learns and predicts by receiving the output of the encoder and combining it with the target sequence (predicting the future development of Beijing). Additionally, we include positional encoding by adding specific positional information to elements in the sequence, helping the model understand the sequential relationships between elements. We employ Transformer to simulate the development of roads in Beijing, and we use the Mean Squared Error (MSE) calculation method to measure the difference between predicted values and true values.

$$\text{MSE} = \frac{1}{n}\sum_{i=1}^{n}(y_i - \hat{y}_i)^2 \tag{1}$$

Afterwards, we continuously utilize the Adam optimizer to update the model parameters. During the training process, the model iteratively processes the training data and adjusts the model weights by minimizing the loss function to improve the model's predictive accuracy on the training dataset. Subsequently, we employ the trained Transformer model to predict unknown data. We retrieve the data to be predicted from the existing dataset, which consists of new samples that our model has not encountered before. Then, we load the best model saved during the training process and make predictions on the test set. Simultaneously, we establish a linear function aiming to predict how our city roads will look like without intervention, based on the input data from 2005 and 2015. By comparing the actual 2022 data with the predictions generated by the Transformer model, considering an error margin of thirty percent, we identify areas in Beijing's development that are subject to human intervention.

$$y = mx + c \tag{2}$$

Finally, through the comprehensive application of the difference formula and in conjunction with the prediction section, we have successfully identified the areas in Beijing's development process that are influenced by policies. This achievement has laid a solid foundation for us to establish subsequent predictive function models and to more accurately understand and forecast the future development trends of Beijing.

$$\Delta R_{\text{dif1}} = R_{\text{transformer}} - R_{\text{true}} \tag{3}$$

(Prediction difference 1 = Transformer prediction - True prediction)

$$\Delta R_{\text{dif2}} = R_{\text{linear}} - R_{\text{true}} \tag{4}$$

(Prediction difference 2 = Linear prediction - True prediction)

2.3 Predictive Function Model

Based on previous studies, the road network in the central urban area is relatively well-developed. These roads have been adequately planned and constructed over the years, resulting in a high level of infrastructure. Furthermore, after years of urban planning and development, the road network in the central urban area has remained stable. Additionally, land use in the central urban area is restricted, making it difficult to carry out large-scale road widening or construction. Therefore, we believe that the road network in the central urban area of Beijing (within the Fourth Ring Road) has reached a mature stage of development and is unlikely to undergo significant changes.

Given this, we have adopted the Manhattan distance formula and designated the developed area within the central urban area as a reference to set a development threshold for the peripheral urban areas. This threshold is used to limit development in the peripheral urban areas, with each grid cell's development not exceeding the set threshold. The Manhattan distance formula is as follows:

$$d = |x_1 - x_2| + |y_1 - y_2| \tag{5}$$

This formula calculates the Manhattan distance between two points based on their coordinates (x_1, y_1) and (x_2, y_2).

This approach, based on the use of the central urban area as a reference point to limit the development of peripheral urban areas, contributes to guiding urban development towards a more rational and sustainable direction, avoiding excessive development and waste of resources. Setting thresholds also helps reduce uncertainty in the urban development process, contributing to stabilizing overall urban development. Moreover, it enhances the accuracy of our predictive function model, as this approach takes into account real-world constraints and trends in urban development.

Moving forward, with rigorous data preparation and preprocessing as the premise, we will employ a quadratic polynomial model for surface fitting, used to describe the changing trends in data:

$$y = ax_1^2 + bx_2 + ct \tag{6}$$

In this equation, a, b, and c are coefficients, x_1 and x_2 are input data from the first and second years respectively, and t is the time interval description from the first year to the prediction year.

This fitting formula integrates the influences of three variables: x_1, x_2, and time t. Each part considers the impact of different variables on the result y. Through the coefficients a, b, and c, this model can more accurately describe the relationships between the data, enabling better prediction of future development trends.

Ultimately, we integrated time and input data from previous years. Based on observations of the mature development of the road network in the central urban area (within the Fourth Ring Road of Beijing), we used the Manhattan distance formula to set development thresholds for peripheral urban areas. This is aimed at guiding urban development towards a more rational and sustainable direction, avoiding excessive development and resource wastage. By utilizing a quadratic polynomial model for surface fitting and considering real-world constraints and urban development trends, we have provided a more accurate and reliable model for future predictions. This integrated approach considers the relationships between data, providing more practical and sustainable guidance for urban planning and prediction.

3 Results

3.1 The Predictive Effectiveness

Firstly, we segmented the city data based on Transformer model and linear functions. We found that while our model demonstrated predictability in urban area data, the prediction efficacy was less satisfactory for mountainous areas. Hence, we decided to only forecast the urban areas. It's worth noting that data from mountainous regions may be influenced by factors such as topography and thus were excluded from our prediction scope. For the prediction of city road data, we employed different prediction functions for the outskirts and inner city areas. In the model construction process, we integrated data from 2005 and 2015, and predicted the changes in city road data for 2022 based on the constructed function models. Our combined approach of using Transformer model and linear functions enabled us to capture the trends in city road changes more accurately.

To assess the prediction accuracy, we set the comparative error at 30% for comparison with actual data. Our analysis revealed that for the outskirts, our prediction accuracy reached 88%, while for the inner city areas, it was 85%. These results indicate that our model achieved high accuracy in predicting city road data (Fig. 2).

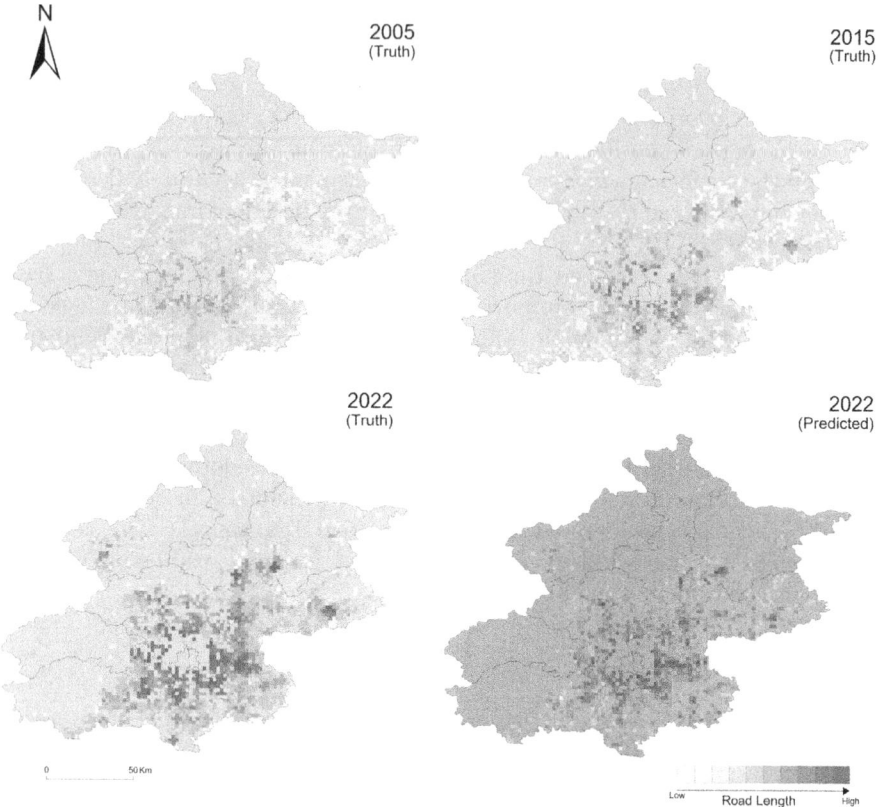

Fig. 2. | Comparison Between Real Road Data and Predicted Road Data in Beijing Municipality. The chart with a pink background represents the actual road data for Beijing over the years, while the one with a red background represents the predicted road data for Beijing in 2022.

Building upon previous research and considering the maturity of the central urban area (within the Fourth Ring Road) and the current policy context, we conducted a forecast for Beijing's data in 2030. Based on the current policy framework and development trends, we observe a pattern of urban expansion in Beijing. The forecast indicates that over time, the peripheral urban areas will experience rapid development. In this evolving process, we will adopt a more scholarly approach, combining theoretical frameworks with Geographic Information System (GIS) technology to conduct in-depth research on the dynamics of urban expansion.

Our research aims to delve into the urban expansion process of Beijing in 2030, exploring its driving factors and impacts on various geographic elements within the region. By analyzing historical data and predicting future trends, we will utilize spatial analysis methods to examine land use changes, population distribution shifts, and infrastructure development in the peripheral urban areas.

This will provide theoretical support and scientific guidance for future urban planning and sustainable development (Fig. 3).

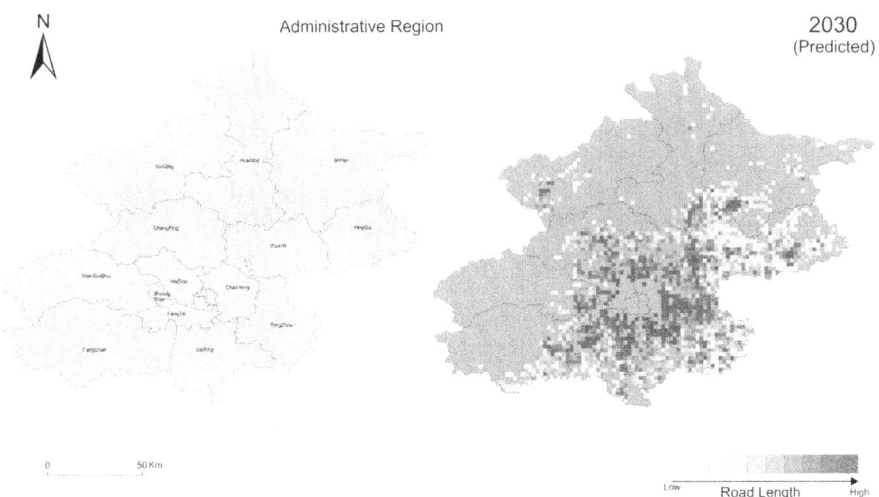

Fig. 3. | The predicted road lengths for different regions of Beijing in 2030.

Furthermore, we will comprehensively consider factors from multiple dimensions such as social, economic, and environmental aspects, to fully understand the potential impacts of urban expansion on urban ecosystems, social structures, and residents' livelihoods. Our research seeks to provide policymakers with profound insights to help formulate future urban development strategies and offer scientific support for urban planning and management.

Thus far, we have successfully established a functional model aimed at predicting the developmental trends of cities under different policy frameworks and their resulting development outcomes.

4 Discussion

4.1 Urban Texture

The urban spatial structure reflects the organization of urban land use [32]. This study introduces the concept of urban texture, which refers to the traces and scale formed by the historical development of a city, as well as the organizational methods and features manifested in the urban landscape. Analogous to tree rings, it illustrates features such as the historical evolution of the city, architectural styles, neighborhood layouts, and distribution of green spaces.

Spatio temporal data are critical inputs to mobility studies for urban management purposes [33] and the current digital technology age has a drastic impact on city strategies [34]. In urban research, various data sources such as Point of Interest (POI) data and road network data are utilized, with road network data playing a pivotal role in studying urban development and planning. Road network is the core component of urban transportation, and it is widely useful in various traffic-related systems and applications [35]. These datasets serve not only as the foundation of urban planning but also as crucial clues for interpreting the city's structure, understanding its morphology and functionality, and predicting future developments. Through the analysis of road networks, we can glimpse into the vitality and changes within cities, revealing the connections and disparities between different regions. This understanding is essential not only for managing traffic flow effectively but also for promoting balanced urban development, enhancing residents' quality of life, and constructing more inclusive and sustainable urban environments. Therefore, the application of road network data in urban planning and development not only provides decision-makers with data support but also paves the way for the sustainable development of cities in the future.

Study of a city could exploit the synergies between city planning and three techno-scientific domains including Big Data, Geographic Information Science and Systems, and Data Science [36]. Big data analytics and artificial intelligence, paired with blockchain technology, the Internet of Things, and other emerging technologies, are poised to revolutionise urban management [37]. It can be seen that data plays an important role in urban planning. Three layers of data simultaneously influence urban development: macro data, meso data, and micro data. Macro data typically refers to data collected at a larger scale, often used to describe overall trends, patterns, or general characteristics. They usually cover a wide geographic area or a large population. In urban studies, macro data may include indicators such as the total population and GDP of a city. Meso data falls between macro and micro levels, being more specific and localized. It typically describes specific parts or groups within a moderate scale or range, providing more detailed information than macro data. In urban research, meso data may include the number of Points of Interest (POIs) in a specific area, road lengths, and similar data. Micro data is more detailed and specific, often describing individual or local subtle features and details. In urban studies, micro data may involve specific road shapes and other detailed data. We utilize meso data as a bridge between macro and micro data. It combines the general summaries of macro data with the specific details of micro data, providing a deeper level of analysis.

This study considers three scenarios, represented by road data from Beijing in 2005, 2015, and 2022, respectively, and incorporates urban development planning policies and goals. Urban development is visually reflected in road construction. To support sustainable urban growth, effective transportation infrastructure construction is essential. In 2005, the total length of roads in Beijing was approximately 40,089 km. With the increase in traffic volume and the influence of policies such as the Olympic Games, by 2015, the total road length in Beijing had increased to approximately 54,526 km, representing a growth of approximately 30%. Furthermore, driven by policies such as "Village to Village Connectivity", the Winter Olympics, Rural Revitalization, and the Beijing Municipality's Urban Area Decongestion and Promotion, by 2022, the total road length in Beijing reached approximately 95,380 km, an increase of approximately 75% compared to 2015. This development process highlights the positive role of urban planning and policy guidance in road construction (Fig. 4).

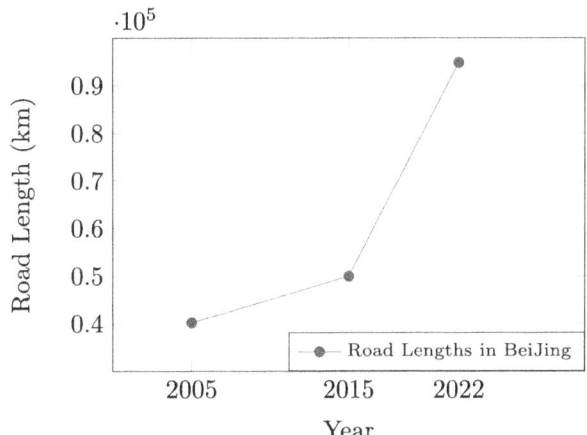

Fig. 4. Evolution of Road Lengths in Beijing: 2005-2022. The figure illustrates the changes in road lengths in Beijing for the years 2005, 2015, and 2022, with corresponding lengths of 40,163 km, 50,002 km, and 94,784 km respectively. This reflects a significant increase over the period, indicative of ongoing urban development and expansion.

By 2035, it is anticipated that the total length of roads in Beijing will further increase to meet the future demands of urban development. However, by this time, there may be challenges associated with reaching a saturation point in development.

4.2 The Impact of Policies on Urban Development

As a spatial carrier of high-intensity social activities and economic development, the relationship between cities and people is complicated, and the population, socio-economic, resource, and environmental problems are intertwined with the process of urban development [38]. In countries with neo-liberal economy, urban development is primarily market-driven, with less government intervention, allowing cities to more flexibly adapt to market demands. Conversely, in centrally planned socialist developing countries, policy has much stronger influences the development trends of cities. We believe that these trends can be quantified, even though they belong to the realm of economics, and we consider that their positive or negative impacts on urban development can be evaluated through quantitative indicators. Our research indicates that policies directly regulate the development of Beijing, with different policies having significant variations in their impacts on urban planning and development, specifically affecting regional planning, technology, and culture, collectively shaping our urban texture.

China has experienced rapid urbanization over the past four decades, which has profoundly transformed the physical and governance landscapes of peri-urban areas [39]. First, policies influence which areas within the city will receive priority for development opportunities. These policies may specify key development areas through the formulation of specific development plans and consciously direct resources and investments towards regions with relatively underdeveloped economies, weak technological capabilities, or lacking cultural resources, in order to achieve more balanced urban development.

In 2004, Beijing's masterplan proposed the urban planning concept of "Two Axes, Two Belts, and Multiple Centers". "Two Axes" specifically refers to the east-west axis along Chang'an Street and the north-south axis of the traditional central axis. Meanwhile, "Two Belts" denote the eastern development belt and the western development belt. This planning concept emphasizes the "Multiple Centers" idea, aiming to create multiple urban functional centers serving the nation and the international affairs within the city's jurisdiction, in order to enhance the core functions and overall competitiveness of the city. The concept aims to specify the key areas of urban development, namely the historical and cultural core areas, the ecological and cultural leisure belts, and the innovative science and technology belts. It also guides resources and investments towards these key areas to promote the balance of urban development. This planning prioritizes optimizing the urban spatial structure, emphasizing the protection of historical and cultural heritage, promoting ecological conservation and cultural activities, and supporting the development of scientific and technological innovation and modern service industries. Its goal is to construct a more diverse and complementary urban development model.

In 2016, Beijing's new masterplan proposed the urban development concept of "One Core, One Main, One Sub-center, Two Axes, Multiple Points, and One Zone". "One Core" represents the core functional area of the capital, "One Main" refers to the central urban area of Beijing, and "One Sub-center" serves as an important auxiliary center outside the main urban area. This policy aims to optimize the urban spatial structure, highlight the importance of the central urban area, develop sub-centers to alleviate pressure and construct two central axes in the east-west and north-south directions, while nurturing multiple development nodes. Additionally, this policy also emphasizes the development of specific areas around the sub-center, aiming to establish a multi-center development pattern, guide the transfer of urban resources to the periphery, and promote more balanced and sustainable urban development.

Urban green belts (UGBs), an important green infrastructure of cities, have the function of constraining urban sprawl, which is of great significance to urban green, resilient and sustainable development [40]. Beijing has gradually formed and improved the green belt policy in urban planning and long-term practices of ecological environment protection. The purpose is to prevent "piecemeal" development of the city, and disorderly sprawl. The green belt area, in addition to bearing the mission of the urban ecological barrier of Beijing, is also the main front to safeguard the future development of the capital and prevent the disorderly sprawl of the city.

Furthermore, policies influence urban development through various means in the field of science and technology. These include providing tax incentives, establishing science and technology parks, supporting incubators for startups, etc., to encourage technology companies to root or expand in specific areas. The government also promotes technological innovation and research and development, supports the training of scientific and technological talents, and provides infrastructure construction and technical support to transform certain areas into become core areas of technological innovation.

Present day Beijing developed on the urban layout of the capital city of Ming Dynasty which was constructed in the 15th century [41]. Beijing is also deeply influenced by traditional Feng Shui (Chinese geomancy) concepts in sitting of cities and houses for auspiciousness. The mostly applied Feng shui principle is to locate the city on a site that is surrounded by mountains and embraced by a water course so that vital energy can be gathered. Another principle emphasizes the importance of the central axis of urban spaces and buildings in pursuing a perfect order. These traditional concepts have left a profound imprint on the development of Beijing.

At the same time, Beijing has been continuously committed to inheriting and protecting famous historical sites in cultural protection. In terms of modern material culture, especially in the industrial aspects of the Olympics held in 2008 and 2022, Beijing attaches importance to their development. In addition, cultural and creative industries such as the 798 Art District are also strongly supported by the Beijing municipal government, becoming an important part of cultural development. This diversified cultural development strategy reflects Beijing's dual focus on cultural inheritance and innovation in the evolving urban development.

These policy factors collectively shape the scale, speed, and form of urban development. We apply these policies to the concept of urban texture to deeply understand and quantify the impact of policies on urban development.

4.3 The Central Urban Area (within the Fourth Ring Road)

Beijing's the Fourth Ring Road was competed in 1999 as the link between suburban districts. During the past 20 years it has been gradually seen as the boundary of the central urban area and become stable in terms of landscape transformation. Initially, we compared the road network changes of this particular area for the years 2005, 2015, and 2022, and found that the central area has indeed been steadily growing. Subsequently, utilizing transformer neural network prediction methods based on data from 2005 and 2015, we forecasted the road length data for Beijing in 2022, while also conducting linear predictions. We set the road growth error at 30% and compared the predicted data with the actual road data length to identify areas that do not conform to the error range. We believe these areas are influenced and regulated by policies.

When comparing dataset of different years, we found that the central urban area of Beijing (within the Fourth Ring Road) has consistently followed a normal development pattern and has not been classified as a "development anomaly area." Therefore, we believe that similar to the development of many cities in developed countries, the central urban area of Beijing (within the Fourth Ring Road) has demonstrated a mature development status and is unlikely to undergo significant development changes in the present or future (Fig. 5).

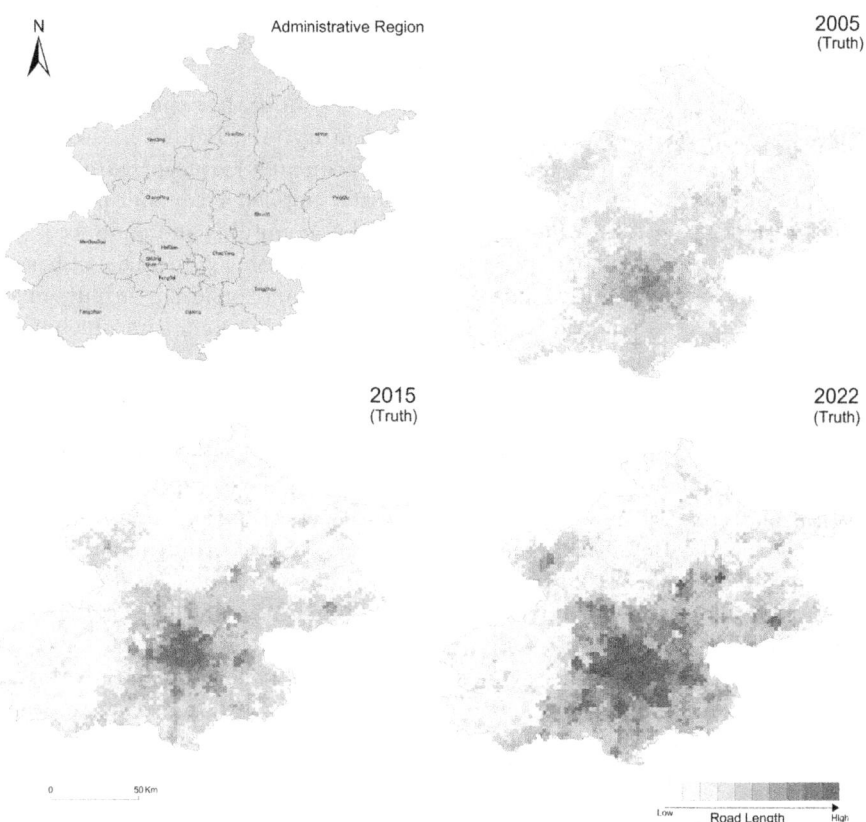

Fig. 5. | Visualization of Beijing's Urban Road Lengths in 2005, 2015, and 2022

In contrast, urban development and expansions concentrated in the areas outside the Fourth Ring Road, especially the outer regions of the city such as Fengtai District, Changping District, Shunyi District, Tongzhou District, and others, exhibit sprawling expansion and the development model of satellite cities. In the development process of Beijing, the remote areas of Beijing are providing more housing options for people to alleviate the pressure of population density and resource scarcity in the central city area. These remote areas benefit from a series of policies and economic advantages of Beijing, while the population in the central city area gradually shifts to these remote areas. Compared to the central urban area of Beijing, these areas benefit from the tailor made urban planning policies such as decentralization of overcrowded population, manufacturing industry and other functions irrelavant to the capital city. These policies aim to achieve coordinated development between Beijing and its surrounding areas, improve the overall development level of the entire region, and thereby enhance the living environment and public service level of the capital region. We used Transformer and linear prediction results to construct the development curve and based on this to delineate the regions to determine the development areas affected by policy control. The graphical results show that apart from the central urban area, most areas exhibit an exponential development curve (Fig. 6).

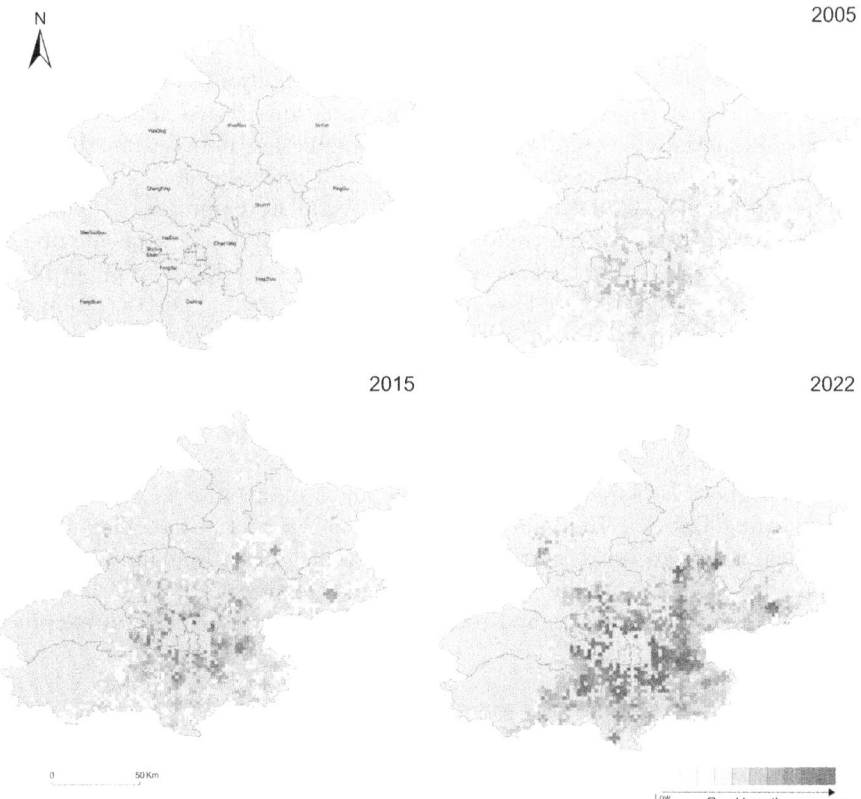

Fig. 6. | The delineated regions. The areas delineated in the figure represent the development zones identified based on the development curves constructed using Transformer and linear prediction results, guided by which policy-regulated development regions were determined.

In contrast, areas outside the central urban zone (within the Fourth Ring Road of Beijing), especially the peripheral regions such as Fengtai District, Changping District, Shunyi District, Tongzhou District, and others, are experiencing rapid development trends. In response to this situation, we employed Manhattan distance to group the peripheral areas and utilized the road length of the matured central urban zone as a constraint. We believe that selecting the peak based on the road data of the inner city can serve as a significant indicator to constrain the development of outer city roads.

Using rasterization technology and the Manhattan distance method, we set length peaks for each grid to plan urban development. We consider the development of the inner city area to be of great significance to the development of the peripheral areas. Therefore, we use the peak of inner city road development as a constraint for outer city development and combine it with function models to predict the future development of the city.

4.4 The Diversity of Policy Intensity: A Case Study of Beijing

In the context of urban development, the implementation of different policies exhibits significant regional and hierarchical variations. These differences manifest in the spatial coverage of policies, the distinction between northern and southern regions, as well as at individual street or micro-levels.

Under the policy regulation in Beijing, the overall development of road length shows an exponential growth trend. However, this growth trend can be divided into two main parts. First, there is the relatively rapid development of peripheral areas, including but not limited to Fangshan District, Daxing District, Tongzhou District, Shunyi District, Pinggu District, Huairou District, Miyun District, etc., collectively referred to as the urban peripheral areas. The main reasons for the formation of urban peripheral areas lie in the development of village connectivity and the construction of large-scale infrastructure, a process largely driven by the extensive construction of roads and other infrastructure.

Second, there is the relatively slow development of inner areas, mainly including Chaoyang District, Haidian District, Fengtai District, Changping District, Shijingshan District, etc., described as urban inner areas. Is mainly attributed to a number of reasons, including a more advanced hence stable uran landscape, historical blocks conservation and recent policy of decentralization development (Fig. 7 and 8).

Fig. 7. | The urban periphery areas of Beijing.

The development of urban periphery areas is often heavily influenced by policy emphasis. Taking the Daxing District as an example, the rapid rise of surrounding areas due to the construction of Daxing Airport has spurred rapid development within the district itself. Similarly, Tongzhou District, positioned as the sub-center of Beijing, has experienced a surge in development opportunities with its elevated geographic and political status, striving to establish itself as a district-level central area, thus driving its rapid development to a certain extent.

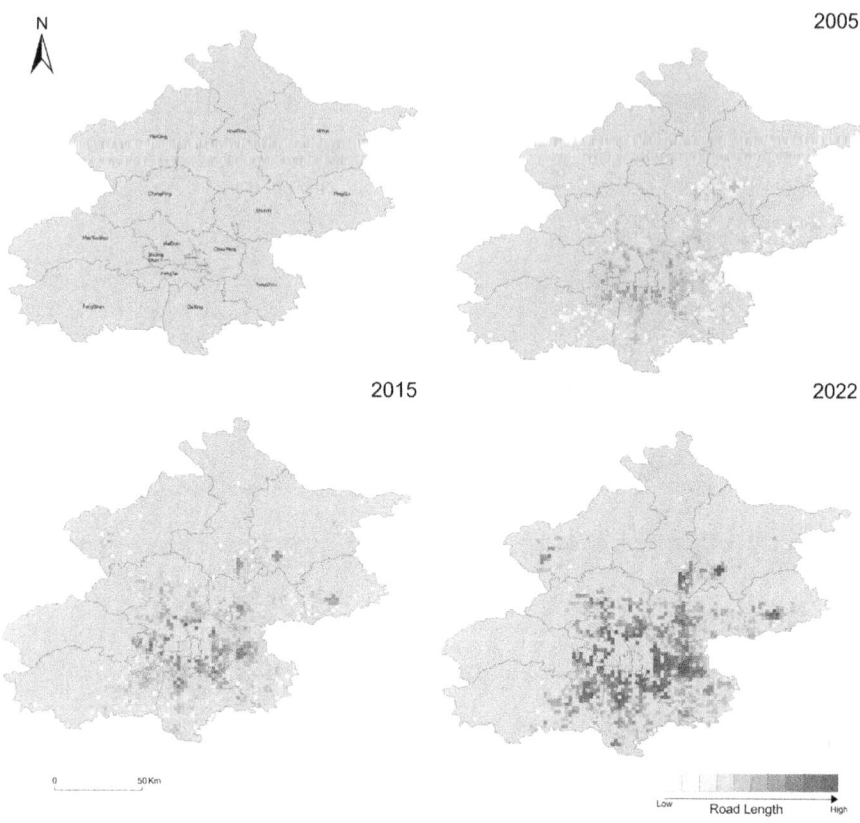

Fig. 8. | The inner-city areas of Beijing.

We have established different development curves for different regions. The outer urban areas of Beijing correspond to the blue curve, while the inner urban areas correspond to the orange curve. Both curves exhibit exponential growth trends. In contrast, the central urban area of Beijing (within the Fourth Ring Road) corresponds to the green curve, indicating saturation in development (Fig. 9).

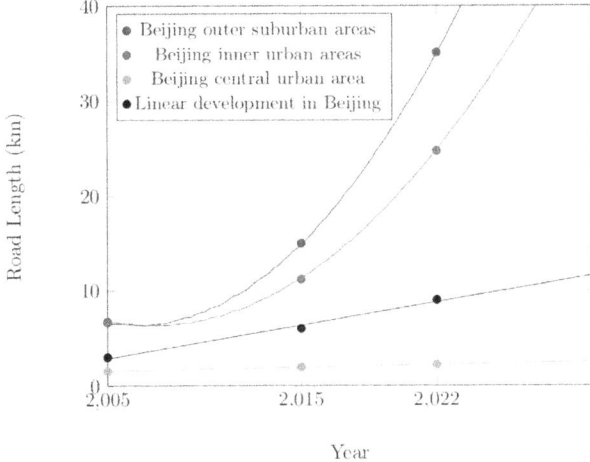

Fig. 9. | The road data development curve.

New towns or new urban function centers were built in urban planning, and polycentric spatial strategies have played an important role in guiding future urban space development [42]. With regard to policy granularity, we have subdivided policies into national, municipal (Beijing), and street levels to conduct a fine-grained study on the impact of policies on urban development over the past 20 years.

At the national level, the 2008 Beijing Olympics Games was the first Olympic event held in Beijing's history, bringing tremendous development opportunities to the city. To host this event, Beijing carried out large-scale infrastructure construction, including the construction of modern sports venues, transportation infrastructure, and urban public facilities. These measures not only enhanced Beijing's urban image but also greatly improved the quality of life for its residents, laying a solid foundation for the city's future development. The Olympics improved infrastructure in the Chaoyang and Datun sub-distric of Beijing, promoted commercial and economic development, enhanced residents' quality of life, and improved the city's image, with profound implications (Fig. 10).

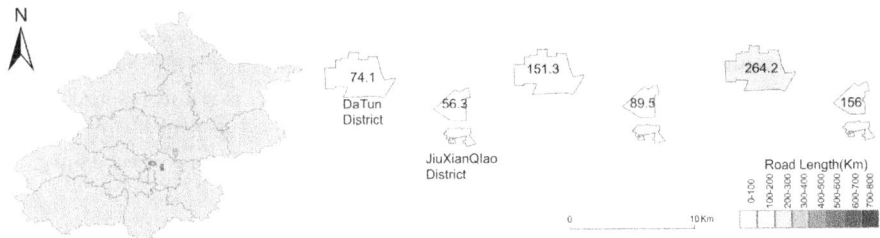

Fig. 10. | Comparison of road lengths in Jiuxianqiao Street(left) and Datun sub-distric(right) in 2005, 2015 and 2022.

The 2022 Winter Olympics further solidified Beijing's status as a global city. Before and after the Winter Olympics, Beijing underwent further urban renewal and transformation, strengthening the construction of winter sports facilities and committing to enhancing the city's level of sustainable development. The Winter Olympics not only injected new vitality into Beijing but also elevated its influence and status on the international stage, further advancing the city's process of internationalization. In Yanqing Town, renovations were made to the Winter Olympics Village, improving transportation and infrastructure, while also promoting economic development and growth in the area. Meanwhile, Zhangshanying Town, serving as the venue for the Winter Olympics' alpine skiing, bobsleigh, and skeleton events, not only spurred its economic development and growth but also stimulated the development of the tourism industry (Fig. 11).

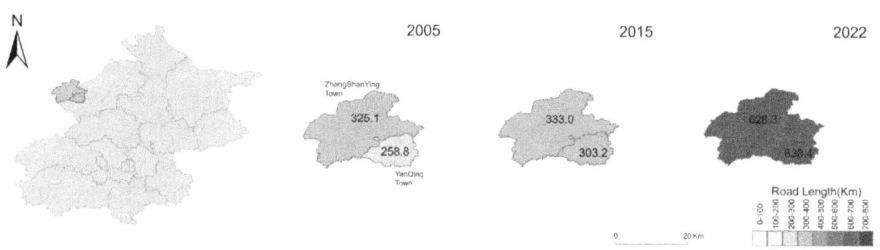

Fig. 11. | Comparison of road lengths in Zhangshanying Town (left) and Yanqing Town (right) in 2005, 2015, and 2022.

Furthermore, as the national central administrative region, areas such as the Yizhuang Sub-district Office, Beijing Economic-Technological Development Area, Yuqiao Sub-district, Yongshun Sub-district Office, and Majuqiao Town are also deeply influenced by these policies.

Additionally, Beijing, as the national central administrative region, fulfills essential functions such as being the political center, technological innovation hub, and cultural heritage guardian. Among them, the Yizhuang Sub-district Office, as one of Beijing's significant economic development zones, focuses on high-tech industries and technological innovation, conducive to driving innovation and industrial development. The Beijing Economic-Technological Development Area, as a national-level development zone, encompasses various vital industries while also concentrating on technological innovation and research and development, attracting both domestic and foreign enterprises and research institutions. Similarly, the Changping Future Science City, located in Beiqijia Town in Changping District, is an emerging technological and innovation center in Beijing, providing new momentum for the city's development (Fig. 12).

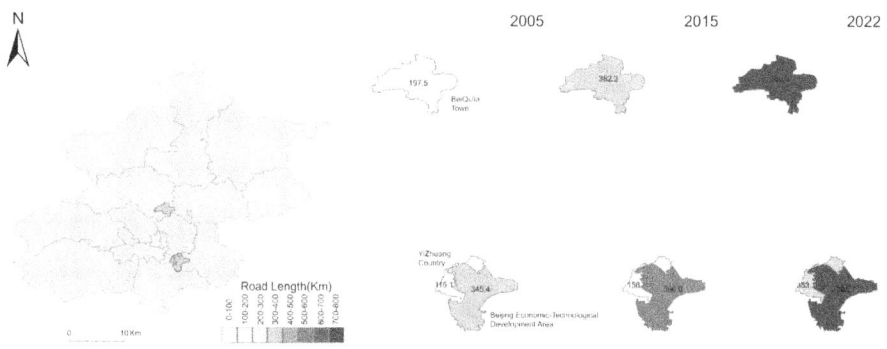

Fig. 12. | Comparison of road lengths in Yizhuang Sub-district Office (left), Beijing Economic-Technological Development Area (center), and Changping Future Science City (Beiqijia Town) (right) in 2005, 2015, and 2022.

At the municipal level in Beijing, the implementation of the Green Separation Policy aims to increase green area, improve the ecological environment, enhance urban quality, and carry out greening and ecological restoration in the city.

Meanwhile, Tongzhou District assumes the role of the city sub-center, attracting a large number of government agencies, corporate headquarters, and financial institutions to relocate to this area. The sub-center role has led to large-scale infrastructure construction in Tongzhou District, including improvements in transportation, education, and healthcare. The development of the city sub-center has also attracted a large influx of population, including many high-quality talents. At the same time, Tongzhou District undertakes more urban functions and responsibilities such as administrative function undertaking, cultural education, and medical services.

Among them, Majuqiao Town, as an important administrative area of Tongzhou District, mainly undertakes functions such as infrastructure construction and planning, economic industry layout, and development guidance. The Liyuan Sub-district Office focuses on urban renewal and environmental improvement projects in the area while providing community services for residents. Additionally, the Yongshun Sub-district Office is responsible for the implementation of key projects in the region, participating in the promotion of infrastructure construction in the region, and providing grassroots community services (Fig. 13).

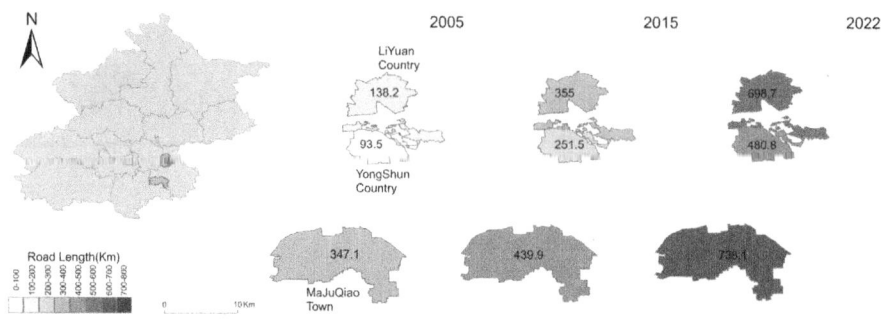

Fig. 13. | Yongshun Sub-district (top), Liyuan Sub-district Office (middle), and Majuqiao Town (bottom) road length comparison in 2005, 2015 and 2022.

It is worth noting that, at the sub-district level, between inner city neighborhoods and suburban towns. We conducted a study on six pairs of sub-district in Chaoyang District, Haidian District, and Fengtai District, and found these micro-level development disparities. This may be due to unequal policy and resource allocation. Specifically, some sub-district may receive more government investment and policy support, leading to rapid development, while others face resource constraints or policy restrictions, resulting in relatively slow development. This inconsistent development trend reflects the characteristics of centrally-planned urban planning and development in socialist developing countries. Even neighboring areas may present different development outlooks due to policy reasons. In general, policies play a leading role in the urban development process (Fig. 14).

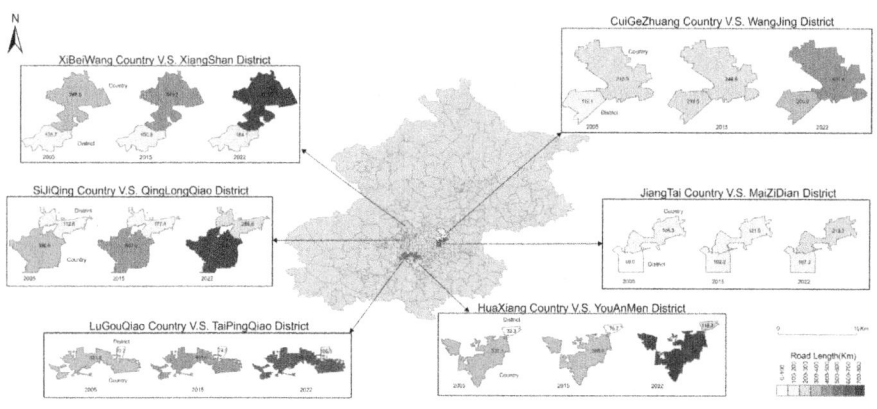

Fig. 14. | Comparison of district and country in Chaoyang District, Fengtai District, and Haidian District in Beijing in 2005, 2015, and 2022.

These observations reflect the profound influence of different policies on various levels and regions of the city, showing geographical and hierarchical differences.

5 Conclusion

This study has explored the impact of governmental policies on the urbanization process in Beijing from 2005 to 2022, using a deductive method that integrates urban texture analysis, neural networks, and linear prediction models. The findings reveal that government policies have played a pivotal role in shaping the urban development patterns in Beijing, with distinct spatio-temporal characteristics observed across different regions.

The concept of urban texture, analogous to tree rings, has been effectively utilized to capture the historical evolution and spatial characteristics of Beijing's urban development. Through the analysis of road network data, we identified significant policy-driven changes, particularly in the peripheral areas, where rapid development has been influenced by initiatives such as the "Village to Village Connectivity" and the construction of new urban functional centers. In contrast, the central urban area within the Fourth Ring Road has demonstrated a mature development status, with relatively stable and saturated growth patterns.

Our predictive models, combining Transformer neural networks and linear functions, have shown high accuracy in forecasting urban road development, achieving an accuracy rate of 88% for the outskirts and 85% for the inner city areas. This highlights the effectiveness of our methodology in capturing the complex dynamics of urban growth under policy influence. The application of the Manhattan distance formula and the quadratic polynomial model further enhanced our ability to set development thresholds and predict future trends, providing valuable insights for sustainable urban planning.

The study also underscores the diversity of policy intensity and its granular impact on urban development at various levels, from national to municipal and sub-district levels. For instance, major events like the 2008 Beijing Olympics and the 2022 Winter Olympics have significantly propelled infrastructure development and urban renewal in specific areas. Meanwhile, policies such as the Green Separation Policy and the designation of Tongzhou District as a sub-center have driven regional development and population redistribution.

In conclusion, this study demonstrates that government policies are crucial drivers of urbanization, particularly in centrally planned socialist countries like China. The findings emphasize the need for balanced and sustainable urban development strategies that consider both the central urban areas and the peripheral regions. Future research could further explore the long-term environmental and social impacts of these policies, as well as the potential for adaptive and resilient urban planning in the face of rapid urbanization and global challenges.

References

1. Chen, G., et al.: Global projections of future urban land expansion under shared socioeconomic pathways. Nat. Commun. **11**, 537 (2020)
2. Asghar Pilehvar, A.: Spatial-geographical analysis of urbanization in iran· humanities and social Sci. Commun. **8**, 1–12 (2021)
3. Ouyang, X., Tang, L., Wei, X., Li, Y.: Spatial interaction between urbanization and ecosystem services in Chinese urban agglomerations. Land Use Policy **109**, 105587 (2021)
4. Shaw, B.J., van Vliet, J., Verburg, P.H.: The peri-urbanization of Europe: a systematic review of a multifaceted process. Landsc. Urban Plan. **196**, 103733 (2020)
5. Guo, J., Yu, Z., Ma, Z., Xu, D., Cao, S.: What factors have driven urbanization in china? Environ. Dev. Sustain. **24**, 6508–6526 (2022)
6. Chen, M., Chen, L., Li, Y., Xian, Y.: Developing computable sustainable urbanization science: interdisciplinary perspective. Comput. Urban Sci. **2**, 17 (2022)
7. Jiang, Y., et al.: Modes and practices of rural vitalisation promoted by land consolidation in a rapidly urbanising china: a perspective of multifunctionality. Habitat Int. **121**, 102514 (2022)
8. Xu, H., Pittock, J., Daniell, K.A.: China: a new trajectory prioritizing rural rather than urban development?.Land **10**, 514 (2021)
9. Zhang, C., Zhou, W.: New direction of sustainable urbanization: the impact of digital technologies and policies on china's in situ urbanization. Buildings **12**, 882 (2022)
10. Chang, M., et al.: A challenge of sustainable urbanization: Mapping the equity of urban public facilities in multiple dimensions in zhengzhou, china. Land **12**, 1545 (2023)
11. Christiawan, P.I., Nguyen, T.P.L.: Peri-urbanization in populous developing Asian countries: a systematic review. Int. J. Sustain. Develop. Plann. **19** (2024)
12. Bian, H., Gao, J., Liu, Y., Yang, D., Wu, J.: China's safe and just space during 40 years of rapid urbanization and changing policies. Landscape Ecol. **39**, 74 (2024)
13. Verdini, G., Zhang, L.: Urban China: the tortuous path towards sustainability. Plann. Theory Practice **21**, 330–336 (2020)
14. Wang, G., Salman, M.: The driving influence of multidimensional urbanization on green total factor productivity in China: evidence from spatiotemporal analysis. Environ. Sci. Pollut. Res. **30**, 52026–52048 (2023)
15. Hamnett, C.: Is chinese urbanisation unique?Urban Stud. **57**, 690–700 (2020)
16. Oakes, T.: In China's urban ideology: new towns, creation cities, and contested landscapes of memory, pp. 60–81 Routledge (2021)
17. Surya, B., Ahmad, D.N.A., Sakti, H.H., Sahban, H.: Land use change, spatial interaction, and sustainable development in the metropolitan urban areas, south sulawesi province, Indonesia. Land **9**, 95 (2020)
18. Kuddus, M.A., Tynan, E., McBryde, E.: Urbanization: a problem for the rich and the poor? Pub. Heal. Rev. **41**, 1–4 (2020)
19. Gao, J., O'Neill, B.C.: Mapping global urban land for the 21st century with data-driven simulations and shared socioeconomic pathways. Nat. Commun. **11**, 2302 (2020)
20. Jiang, H., et al.: Projections of urban built-up area expansion and urbanization sustainability in china's cities through 2030. J. Clean. Prod. **367**, 133086 (2022)
21. Xia, C., Yeh, A.G.-O., Zhang, A.: Analyzing spatial relationships between urban land use intensity and urban vitality at street block level: a case study of five Chinese megacities. Landsc. Urban Plan. **193**, 103669 (2020)

22. Buchecker, M., Frick, J.: The implications of urbanization for inhabitants' relationship to their residential environment. Sustainability **12**, 1624 (2020)
23. Xia, C., Zhang, A., Wang, H., Zhang, B., Zhang, Y.: Bidirectional urban flows in rapidly urbanizing metropolitan areas and their macro and micro impacts on urban growth: a case study of the yangtze river middle reaches megalopolis, China. Land Use Policy **82**, 158–168 (2019)
24. Yang, Y., Bao, W., Wang, Y., Liu, Y.: Measurement of urban-rural integration level and its spatial differentiation in china in the new century. Habitat Int. **117**, 102420 (2021)
25. Hu, R., Zhang, C.: Research on urban evolution in china from an ecological perspective: a case of Beijing. J. Urban Plann. Develop. **149**, 05022047 (2023)
26. Liu, Y., Zhou, Y.: Territory spatial planning and national governance system in China. Land Use Policy **102**, 105288 (2021)
27. Ammapa, J., Visuttiporn, P., Klaylee, J., Chayphong, S., Iamtrakul, P.: Using GIS-based spatial analysis: comparing pattern of urbanization and transportation networks, pp. 17–21. IEEE (2022)
28. Jia, M., Zhang, H., Yang, Z.: Compactness or sprawl: multi-dimensional approach to understanding the urban growth patterns in Beijing-Tianjin-hebei region, china. Ecol. Ind. **138**, 108816 (2022)
29. Rahnama, M.R., Wyatt, R., Shaddel, L.: A spatial-temporal analysis of urban growth in Melbourne; were local government areas moving toward compact or sprawl from 2001–2016? Appl. Geogr. **124**, 102318 (2020)
30. Kandt, J., Batty, M.: Smart cities, big data and urban policy: towards urban analytics for the long run. Cities **109**, 102992 (2021)
31. Yan, H., Ma, X., Pu, Z.: Learning dynamic and hierarchical traffic spatiotemporal features with transformer. IEEE Trans. Intell. Transp. Syst. **23**, 22386–22399 (2021)
32. Dong, R., Yan, F.: Revealing characteristics of the spatial structure of megacities at multiple scales with jobs-housing big data: a case study of Tianjin, China. Land **10**, 1144 (2021)
33. Fekih, M., et al.: A data-driven approach for origin-destination matrix construction from cellular network signalling data: a case study of Lyon region (France). Transportation **48**, 1671–1702 (2021)
34. Kourtit, K.: City intelligence for enhancing urban performance value: a conceptual study on data decomposition in smart cities. Asia-Pacific J. Regional Sci. **5**(1), 191–222 (2021). https://doi.org/10.1007/s41685-021-00193-9
35. Wu, N., Zhao, X.W., Wang, J., Pan, D.: Learning effective road network representation with hierarchical graph neural networks, pp. 6–14 (2020)
36. Mortaheb, R., Jankowski, P.: Smart city re-imagined: city planning and geoai in the age of big data. J. Urban Manage. **12**, 4–15 (2023)
37. Engin, Z., et al.: Data-driven urban management: mapping the landscape. J. Urban Manage. **9**, 140–150 (2020)
38. Yang, Z., Yang, H., Wang, H.: Evaluating urban sustainability under different development pathways: a case study of the Beijing-Tianjin-Hebei region. Sustain. Cities Soc. **61**, 102226 (2020)
39. Dai, Y., Wang, Z., Huan, M.: Shifts in governance modes in village redevelopment: a case study of Beijing Lugouqiao township. Habitat Int. **135**, 102795 (2023)
40. Zhou, L., Gong, Y., López-Carr, D., Huang, C.: A critical role of the capital green belt in constraining urban sprawl and its fragmentation measurement. Land Use Policy **141**, 107148 (2024)

41. Baratta, N.C., Magli, G.: The role of astronomy and Feng Shui in the planning of Ming Beijing. Nexus Netw. J. **23**, 767–787 (2021)
42. Lv, Y., Zhou, L., Yao, G., Zheng, X.: Detecting the true urban polycentric pattern of Chinese cities in morphological dimensions: a multiscale analysis based on geospatial big data. Cities **116**, 103298 (2021)

LERI Evaluation and Driving Mechanism Analysis via GWRF Model

Chenfeng Xu[1], Zhihao Kang[1], Min Li[2], Yike Hu[1(✉)], Zhengyang Zou[1], Xing Geng[3], Haolan Huang[4], Zibo Zhu[5], Fenglei Chen[6], Ziruo Feng[7], and Yan Cheng[8]

[1] School of Architecture, Tianjin University, Tianjin 300072, China
xcf2024@tju.edu.cn
[2] College of Landscape Architecture, Nanjing Forestry University, Nanjing 210037, Jiangsu, China
[3] The Bartlett School of Environment, Energy and Resources, University College London, London NW1 9HZ, UK
[4] School of Arts, Southeast University, Nanjing 210096, Jiangsu, China
[5] College of Horticulture and Forestry Sciences, Huazhong Agricultural University, Hubei 430070, China
[6] School of Architecture and Environment, Sichuan University, Chengdu 610065, Sichuan, China
[7] School of Architecture and Urban Planning, Chongqing University, Chongqing 400030, China
[8] School of Architecture, Tsinghua University, Beijing 100084, China

Abstract. Evaluating the landscape ecological risk index (LERI) at the landscape level and identifying its driving mechanism is crucial for ensuring regional ecological stability. Firstly, we developed an LERI evaluation model to comprehensively evaluate its spatial-temporal evolution in the Nanjing Metropolitan Area from 2000 to 2020. Secondly, we applied the geographically weighted random forest model to explore the driving mechanisms of different factors on LERI. Finally, we analyzed the correlations between various driving factors. The results indicated that: (1) the spatial distribution pattern of LERI remained stable, with a general "high in the north, low in the south" pattern. The area of medium-risk zones decreased by 1.25×10^3 km^2 (a decline of 5.76%), while the area of high-risk zones increased by 0.39×10^3 km^2 (a rise of 8.11%), with the areas of extremely low, low, and extremely high-risk zones changing relatively steadily; (2) the normalized difference vegetation index (NDVI), annual average precipitation (AAP), and net primary productivity (NPP) are the main driving factors of LERI evolution, with population density (PD) playing a secondary role. The effects of annual average temperature (AAT) and nighttime lights (NTL) are relatively small, and the spatial distribution of factor importance varies significantly; (3) there is a consistently strong positive correlation between driving factors such as AAP, NDVI, NPP, and AAT. These findings aim to provide scientific support for regional landscape ecological risk management.

Keywords: Landscape ecological risk evaluation · geographically weighted random forest model · driving mechanism · Nanjing Metropolitan Area

1 Introduction

Maintaining the stability of ecosystem structure and function is a core objective for achieving sustainable development (Luo, et al. 2018). However, the accelerating pace of global urbanization has led to more complex and far-reaching impacts of urban spatial expansion, industrial restructuring, and rapid population mobility on the natural environment, triggering a series of ecological issues. Among these, the dramatic changes in land use patterns have resulted in land fragmentation, pollution spread, biodiversity loss, and ecosystem services degradation, all of which have become major challenges to urban sustainable development (Bryan, et al. 2018; Peng, et al. 2024; Ran, et al. 2022). In this context, constructing a scientific and precise ecological risk evaluation system to identify the key driving factors affecting regional ecological sustainability and effectively mitigate potential risks has become an important research topic.

Unlike traditional ecological risk evaluation methods, Landscape Ecological Risk Index (LERI) evaluation focuses more on analyzing the impact of ecosystem changes on overall landscape patterns at different spatial and temporal scales (Cao, et al. 2019). This approach takes a landscape perspective, systematically evaluating the degree of human-induced disturbances on ecosystems and analyzing the large-scale ecological risks and their impacts caused by dynamic changes in regional land use. It comprehensively measures the robustness and sustainability of regional ecosystems (Li, et al. 2024c). Meanwhile, the driving factors of LERI often exhibit significant spatial heterogeneity, meaning that the importance of the same factor may vary across different geographical areas. However, existing studies mainly focus on the quantitative evaluation of ecological risk and have not sufficiently analyzed its spatial heterogeneity. For instance, traditional regression models such as Ordinary Least Squares (OLS), Partial Least Squares Structural Equation Modeling (PLS-SEM), Random Forest (RF), and Boosted Regression Trees (BRT) can reveal the overall impact of driving factors on ecological risk (Li, et al. 2024b; Wang, et al. 2023), but they neglect the local spatial variability of driving factors, which could lead to the homogenization of optimization strategies (Wang, et al. 2025b). Furthermore, while Geographically Weighted Regression (GWR) model can account for spatial heterogeneity, its explanatory and generalization capabilities are limited when faced with multicollinearity among variables (Xu, et al. 2024; Zhang, et al. 2025). Therefore, how to incorporate more accurate spatial analysis methods into LERI evaluation to enhance the understanding of ecological risk driving mechanisms and provide scientific support for efficient ecological protection and sustainable land use planning has become a key issue in current research that requires urgent breakthrough.

A metropolitan area is an urban functional spatial unit centered around one or more core cities, supported by a highly developed transportation network and closely interconnected social-economic ties, consisting of the core city and its surrounding closely related areas (Li, et al. 2022). As an important platform for driving national economic growth, promoting regional coordinated development, and enhancing international competitiveness, metropolitan areas play a crucial role in the modernization process. By 2024, China has planned 14 national-level metropolitan areas, including the Nanjing Metropolitan Area, Fuzhou Metropolitan Area, and Chengdu Metropolitan Area (Li, et al. 2022; Peng, et al. 2024). Against the backdrop of rapid development, metropolitan areas are facing numerous existing or potential ecological risks, which significantly impact their sustainable development. However, existing studies on LERI mainly focus on regions defined by natural geographic units such as mountains and watersheds (Li, et al. 2024b; Li, et al. 2024c; Liu and Tang 2024; Zeng, et al. 2024), while research on the complex urban spatial type of metropolitan areas remains relatively scarce.

The Nanjing Metropolitan Area is China's first planned and constructed interprovincial metropolitan area, and it is currently the most mature and typical example of such development, holding significant strategic importance and demonstrative value (Liu, et al. 2023). In the context of the accelerating urbanization process, scientifically evaluating the spatial-temporal evolution of LERI and its driving mechanisms in the Nanjing Metropolitan Area is of great theoretical and practical significance for maintaining regional ecological security, optimizing land use, and formulating sustainable development policies. Based on this, the present study takes the Nanjing Metropolitan Area as the research object and introduces the Geographically Weighted Random Forest (GWRF) model to explore in depth the spatial-temporal evolution patterns of LERI and the spatial heterogeneity of its driving factors. The study focuses on the following core scientific questions: (1) What are the spatial-temporal evolution characteristics of LERI in the Nanjing Metropolitan Area? (2) What are the integrated impact mechanisms and functional characteristics of different driving factors on LERI? (3) What are the spatial-temporal variations in the importance distribution of different driving factors across geographic space?

2 Study Area and Data Sources

2.1 Study Area

The Nanjing Metropolitan Area is an economic region centered around Nanjing, located in the developed coastal region of eastern China. It lies at the core of the Yangtze River Delta city cluster, spanning the middle and lower reaches of the Yangtze River, and covers both Jiangsu and Anhui provinces. As China's first planned and constructed interprovincial metropolitan area, its spatial layout and economic functions hold significant strategic importance for the integrated development of the Yangtze River Delta. The Nanjing Metropolitan Area includes core cities such as Nanjing, Zhenjiang, Yangzhou, Huaian, Chuzhou, Wuhu, Ma'anshan, and Xuancheng, as well as Liyang and Jintan in Changzhou. It comprises a total of 33 urban districts, 11 county-level cities, and 16 counties, with a total area of approximately 66,000 km^2 (Liu, et al. 2023). Its geographic location is shown in Fig. 1. With its favorable location, well-developed infrastructure network, and strong industrial synergies, the metropolitan area has become an important growth pole driving the integration of the Yangtze River Delta, promoting regional coordinated development, and enhancing international competitiveness.

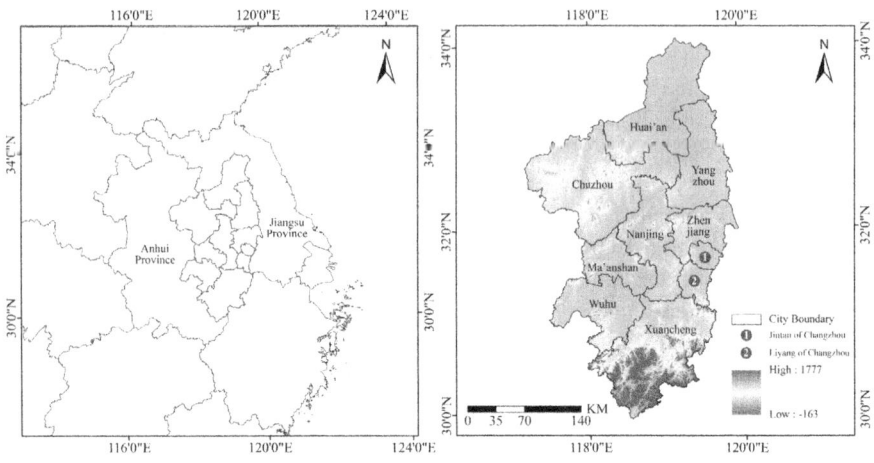

Fig. 1. Location map of the study area

2.2 Data Sources

(1) Basic data: This study used the national land cover dataset released by Wuhan University as the foundational data for the study area. The dataset includes seven major land use types within the study area: cropland, forest, shrub, grassland, water, barren (i.e., unused land), and impervious (i.e., construction land). Additionally, the dataset covers five time points: 2000, 2005, 2010, 2015, and 2020, which allows for a systematic reflection of the land use evolution characteristics in the Nanjing Metropolitan Area, providing high-quality data support for the LERI evaluation.

(2) Driving factor data: Drawing on existing research (Wang, et al. 2025b), this study selected six key natural and social-economic factors as the driving factors for LERI, which comprehensively reflected the regional climate, vegetation, and social-economic conditions. Specifically, these include Annual Average Precipitation (AAP), Annual Average Temperature (AAT), Normalized Difference Vegetation Index (NDVI), Net Primary Productivity (NPP), Population Density (PD), and Nighttime Lights (NTL) (Table 1).

Table 1. Data sources.

Type	Data format	Temporal resolution	Spatial resolution	Source
AAP	Raster	Year	1000 m	National Tibetan Plateau Data Center (https://data.tpdc.ac.cn/home)
AAT			1000 m	National Tibetan Plateau Data Center (https://data.tpdc.ac.cn/home)

(continued)

Table 1. (*continued*)

Type	Data format	Temporal resolution	Spatial resolution	Source
NDVI			250 m	The data is sourced from the MOD13A2 V6.1 product of the MODIS. This product utilizes an algorithm to select the best available pixel from all acquisitions within a 16-day period, prioritizing images with lower cloud cover, lower viewing angles, and the highest NDVI values. Using the GEE platform, NDVI data from the 16-day cycles were processed with JavaScript to generate annual NDVI datasets.
NPP			500 m	https://lpdaac.usgs.gov/products/mod17a3hgfv061/
PD			1000 m	https://landscan.ornl.gov/
NTL			500 m	Resource and Environmental Science Data Platform (https://www.resdc.cn/)

3 Research Methods

3.1 LERI Evaluation Model

LERI Risk Zone Division

To achieve a spatial representation of LERI, it is necessary to systematically sample the entire study area into risk zones. In delineating these risk zones, factors such as the scale characteristics of regional landscape patches, spatial differentiation patterns, and the study area boundaries were comprehensively considered. Using ArcGIS 10.8 software, square grids of 5 km × 5 km were constructed, and an equidistant sampling net operation was applied. A total of 2,831 landscape ecological risk zones were identified. Subsequently, the LERI values for each risk zone were evaluated to ensure accurate representation of the spatial pattern of LERI.

LERI Evaluation

(1) Landscape Disturbance Index (LDI): The LDI is used to quantify the degree of external disturbance experienced by ecosystems represented by different landscape types. The higher the value, the greater the disturbance that the regional ecosystem endures, and correspondingly, the higher the ecological risk. The evaluation formula is as follows (Wang, et al. 2025a):

$$E_i = aC_i + bN_i + cD_i \tag{1}$$

$$C_i = \frac{n_i}{A_i} \tag{2}$$

$$N_i = \frac{A}{2A_i}\sqrt{\frac{n_i}{A}} \tag{3}$$

$$D_i = \frac{Q_i + M_i}{4} + \frac{L_i}{2} \tag{4}$$

where E_i is LDI; C_i is Landscape Fragmentation Index; N_i is Landscape Separation Index; D_i is Landscape Dominance Index; n_i is the number of patches of landscape type i; A_i is the total area of the landscape type i; Q_i = The number of sample plots where patch i appears/Total number of sample plots; M_i = The number of patches of type i/Total number of patches; L_i = Sample plot area of patch i/Total sample plot area; a, b, and c represent the weights of C_i, N_i, and D_i, respectively, and a + b + c = 1. Based on relevant literature (Li, et al. 2024b) and expert opinions, the weights for a, b, and c were assigned as 0.5, 0.3, and 0.2, respectively.

(2) Landscape Fragility Index (LFI): The LFI (F_i) measures the vulnerability of ecosystems represented by different landscape types in terms of their structural sensitivity, reflecting their resistance to external disturbances. Based on the ecological characteristics of the study area and drawing on existing research (Li, et al. 2024a), the final corresponding index values were as follows: unused land (0.2500), water (0.2143), cropland (0.1786), grassland (0.1429), shrub (0.1071), forest (0.0714), and construction land (0.0357).

(3) Landscape Loss Index (LLI): The LLI (R_i) is constructed by overlaying different indices to measure the degree of degradation in the natural attributes of ecosystems represented by different landscape types when subjected to both natural and anthropogenic disturbances simultaneously. The evaluation formula is as follows (Du, et al. 2023):

$$R_i = E_i \times F_i \tag{5}$$

(4) LERI: The final evaluation formula for the LERI is as follows (Guo, et al. 2024):

$$LERI_k = \sum_{i=1}^{N} \frac{A_{ki}}{A_k} R_i \tag{6}$$

where $LERI_j$ is the LERI of the risk zone k; A_{ki} is the area of the landscape type i in the risk zone j; A_k is the area of the risk zone k; R_i is the LLI of the landscape type i.

3.2 GWRF Model

We introduced the GWRF model from the R package SpatialIML to explore the spatial-temporal evolution patterns of LERI and the spatial heterogeneity of its driving factors. GWRF is a spatial extension of the Random Forest (RF) model, decomposing the overall model into local models made up of multiple sub-models. GWRF allows for the training of RF using multivariate vector information and computes Local RF for each spatial location i. A distance-based weighting function is used to adjust the data sampling probability, while simultaneously modeling the spatial relationships between adjacent observations, effectively capturing spatial heterogeneity and spatial autocorrelation. By integrating the spatial location information of feature variables and combining the predictions from all local RF models, GWRF ultimately uses a voting mechanism to output the predicted values, enhancing the spatial adaptability and interpretability of the model (Zhang, et al. 2025).

3.3 Pearson Correlation Analysis

Additionally, we employed Pearson correlation analysis to quantitatively measure the linear relationships between the driving factors, in order to evaluate the strength and direction of the correlations between variables (Yang, et al. 2024b). The analysis results indicate that the p-values for all variables were less than 0.05, reaching a significance level, suggesting that there were statistically significant correlations between the different driving factors.

4 Results

4.1 Spatial-Temporal Evolution Characteristics of LERI

As shown in Table 2, between 2000 and 2020, the areas of different LERI levels exhibited certain dynamic changes. Specifically, the area of the very low-risk zones slightly increased in 2005, followed by a decreasing trend, reaching its lowest point in 2015 (8.69×10^3 km^2), and then rebounded close to the initial value in 2020 (9.22×10^3 km^2). The area of the low-risk zones initially decreased (from 26.60×10^3 km^2 in 2000 to 24.01×10^3 km^2 in 2010), then showed an increasing trend (reaching 27.03×10^3 km^2 in 2020), remaining relatively stable overall. The area of the medium-risk zones showed a growth trend between 2000 and 2010 (increasing from 21.72×10^3 km^2 to 23.89×10^3 km^2), but has continuously decreased since 2010 (dropping to 20.47×10^3 km^2 in 2020). The area of the high-risk zones exhibited a relatively small change, maintaining between 3.00×10^3 km^2 and 3.49×10^3 km^2 throughout the study period, with the most significant increase occurring in 2020 (an increase of 0.49×10^3 km^2). In contrast, the area of the very high-risk zones displayed more volatility, experiencing a slight decrease from 2000 to 2010 (from 4.81×10^3 km^2 to 4.39×10^3 km^2), but increased significantly after 2015 (reaching 5.20×10^3 km^2 in 2020).

Table 2. Area changes of different LERI levels (Unit: 10^3 km^2).

Level	Value range	Year				
		2000	2005	2010	2015	2020
Very low	0.000–0.020	9.29	9.84	9.57	8.69	9.22
Low	0.021–0.030	26.60	24.54	24.01	26.02	27.03
Medium	0.031–0.040	21.72	23.18	23.89	22.55	20.47
High	0.041–0.050	3.00	3.47	3.60	3.63	3.49
Very high	>0.051	4.81	4.39	4.34	4.53	5.20

Between 2000 and 2020, the spatial distribution pattern of LERI remained generally stable, with an overall "high in the north and low in the south" trend (Fig. 2). The very high-risk zones were mainly concentrated in the northern part of the study area, including Hongze Lake, Gaoyou Lake, the Yangtze River basin, as well as in the southern regions around Shijiu Lake and Nanyi Lake. Notably, the fragmented distribution in the southern part gradually evolved into more cohesive patches. High-risk zones typically surrounded the very high-risk zones, presenting a transitional feature. The middle and low-risk zones occupied a larger proportion of the study area, with an interwoven distribution pattern, appearing either as continuous areas or isolated patches. The very low-risk zones were mainly concentrated in the southern part of the study area, with only sparse distributions in other regions.

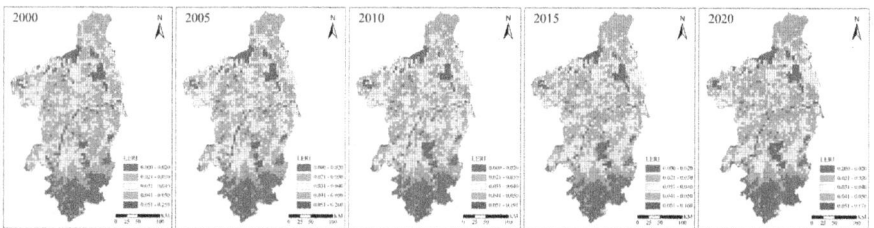

Fig. 2. Spatial distribution changes of different LERI levels

4.2 Comprehensive Spatial-Temporal Evolution Characteristics of LERI Driving Factors

The average importance of each driving factor on LERI exhibited significant differences and dynamic evolution characteristics over the time series (Table 3). Among them, NPP had the highest local importance mean in 2000, 2015, and 2020, while NDVI was highest in 2005 and 2010. AAP generally ranked second or third. From an overall trend, both climate factors (AAP, AAT) and vegetation factors (NPP, NDVI) showed an increasing trend in their average importance for LERI, though at different rates. Among these, the influence weight of NDVI increased the most significantly, rising from 1.55 in 2000 to 7.61 in 2020. NPP, while peaking in 2015 at 4.11, declined to 2.32 in 2020. AAP also gradually increased year by year, particularly accelerating after 2010. In contrast, while AAT showed some rise, its overall value remained low (with a maximum of 1.34). Regarding human activity factors, the influence of PD increased overall (from 1.17 to 2.36), while the influence of NTL, despite a rise in 2015 (0.41), remained low overall (0.37 in 2020).

Table 3. Local importance mean of each driving factor in the GWRF model.

Driving factor type	Year				
	2000	2005	2010	2015	2020
AAP	1.33	1.28	2.30	2.99	3.78
AAT	0.47	0.70	1.04	1.27	1.34
NDVI	1.42	2.06	3.31	4.11	2.32
NPP	1.55	1.94	3.06	4.84	7.61
PD	1.17	1.07	1.55	1.53	2.36
NTL	0.02	0.02	0.15	0.41	0.37

As shown in Fig. 3, there are significant differences in the spatial distribution and variation trends of the most important driving factors in the same spatial area. The influence of AAP was primarily concentrated in the southern and northwestern regions, showing an overall decreasing trend from 2000 to 2015, and stabilizing from 2015 to 2020. NDVI was mainly distributed in the southwestern and northeastern areas, while NPP was primarily found in the central and northern parts, gradually evolving from a uniform distribution to a fragmented one. AAT mainly affected the central and southern areas, while PD was concentrated in the northern region, showing a diffusion trend. Additionally, NTL never became the most important driving factor in any spatial area.

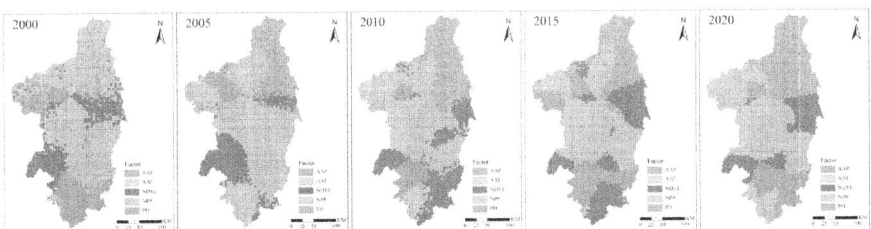

Fig. 3. Spatial distribution changes of the most important driving factor in the same space

From the numerical perspective, the area changes of the most important driving factors for LERI in the same space showed a clear differentiated trend across different years (Table 4). NPP consistently occupied the largest area, but it showed an overall decreasing trend, dropping from 34.68×10^3 km^2 in 2000 to the lowest value of 21.63×10^3 km^2 in 2015, then rising again to 23.75×10^3 km^2 in 2020. AAP and NDVI exhibited significant fluctuations. AAP was higher in 2000 (13.89×10^3 km^2), then sharply decreased to 3.97×10^3 km^2 in 2005, increased again to 12.51×10^3 km^2 in 2015, and decreased to 9.10×10^3 km^2 in 2020, showing considerable volatility. NDVI remained relatively stable, but dropped to 23.75×10^3 km^2 in 2020. AAT and PD rapidly increased after 2005, with PD growing from 3.40×10^3 km^2 in 2000 to 6.31×10^3 km^2 in 2020. In contrast, NTL remained at 0.00 throughout.

Table 4. Area changes of the most important driving factor in the same space.

Driving factor type	Year				
	2000	2005	2010	2015	2020
AAP	13.89	3.97	5.50	12.51	9.10
AAT	2.06	11.65	13.73	10.63	16.64
NPP	11.39	11.03	14.22	15.02	9.61
NDVI	34.68	26.25	23.15	21.63	23.75
PD	3.40	12.52	8.83	5.64	6.31
NTL	0.00	0.00	0.00	0.00	0.00

As shown in Fig. 4, from 2000 to 2020, the correlation among the six driving factors exhibited certain dynamic changes. However, the overall trend indicated a relatively stable strong positive correlation among AAP, NDVI, NPP, and AAT, particularly between 2000 and 2015. Over time, especially in 2015 and 2020, the correlation between some variables significantly weakened. Notably, the negative correlation between AAP and PD, as well as AAP and NTL, became more pronounced (e.g., in 2020, the correlation between AAP and PD was −0.20). Meanwhile, NTL, as an indicator associated with forest cover and urban greening, exhibited a distinct negative correlation with other variables in multiple years. For instance, the correlation between NTL and AAP was −0.30 in 2000, −0.29 in 2005, and −0.23 in 2010. However, this relationship shifted in 2015 and 2020, turning into positive correlations of 0.30 and 0.03, respectively.

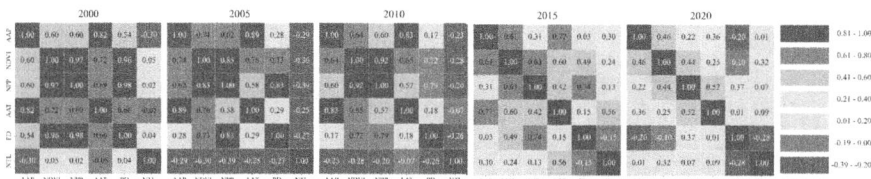

Fig. 4. Correlation changes among driving factors

4.3 Independent Spatial-Temporal Evolution Characteristics of LERI Driving Factors

As shown in Table 5, from 2000 to 2020, the spatial importance of various factors showed significant trends. AAP saw a sharp decline in very low-importance zones (56.39×10^3 km^2 to 16.71×10^3 km^2) and a dramatic increase in very high-importance zones (0.03 × 10³ km² to 15.81 × 10³ km²). AAT exhibited a major contraction in very low-importance zones (59.08 × 10³ km² to 16.29 × 10³ km²), while very high-importance zones peaked at 5.59 × 10³ km² in 2015 before slightly declining. NDVI showed a decline in very low-importance zones (36.48 × 10³ km² to 16.20 × 10³ km²) and a substantial increase in very high-importance zones (2.34 × 10³ km² to 26.18 × 10³ km²). NPP experienced a sharp drop in very low-importance zones (33.85 × 10³ km² to 6.47 × 10³ km²) and exponential growth in very high-importance zones (0.03 × 10³ km² to 22.16 × 10³ km²). PD saw very high-importance zones surge from 0.12 × 10³ km² to 18.21 × 10³ km², while very low-importance zones declined by half. NTL was dominated by very low-importance zones early on (65.42 × 10³ km² in 2000), which then contracted, while very high-importance zones peaked at 6.84 × 10³ km² in 2015 before declining. Overall, all factors showed a consistent trend of shrinking very low-importance zones and expanding very high-importance zones, particularly after 2010.

As shown in Fig. 5, from 2000 to 2020, the spatial distribution of importance zones across factors exhibited both commonalities and distinct regional trends. Overall, very low-importance zones initially dominated the landscape but gradually shrank, while very high-importance zones emerged and expanded outward, forming a concentric, band-like structure with decreasing importance from the core. AAP, AAT, and PD all showed an initial concentration of very high-importance zones in the northern and northwestern regions, which later expanded southward or outward. The spatial distribution of NDVI and NPP also followed a similar trend, with very high-importance zones emerging in the northwest and northern areas, then expanding southeastward. Notably, NDVI exhibited regional phases of merging and fragmentation, while NPP maintained a more continuous outward spread. NTL differed slightly, as the study area was dominated by very low-importance zones until 2010, after which very high-importance zones emerged centrally and expanded until 2015, before contracting in the northwest by 2020. Across all factors, very high-importance zones consistently grew after 2010, often clustering in key regions before radiating outward, while low- and middle-importance zones formed transitional bands between core high-importance areas and peripheral low-importance regions.

Table 5. Area changes of different factors at different importance levels (Unit: 10^3 km²)

Type	Level	Value range	Year				
			2000	2005	2010	2015	2020
AAP	Very low	0.000–0.200	56.39	48.78	33.68	24.11	16.71
	Low	0.201–0.300	5.90	7.74	12.29	13.26	12.62
	Middle	0.301–0.400	2.29	3.51	7.19	6.79	13.77
	High	0.401–0.500	0.81	1.32	5.02	3.51	6.52
	Very high	>0.501	0.03	4.07	7.24	17.75	15.81
AAT	Very low	0.000–0.200	59.08	51.46	22.27	16.17	16.29
	Low	0.201–0.300	5.66	9.80	25.86	26.94	26.62

(*continued*)

Table 5. (*continued*)

Type	Level	Value range	Year				
			2000	2005	2010	2015	2020
	Middle	0.301–0.400	0.67	2.38	11.76	13.36	13.61
	High	0.401–0.500	0.00	1.64	3.51	3.36	5.16
	Very high	>0.501	0.00	0.14	2.01	5.59	3.74
NDVI	Very low	0.000–0.200	36.48	26.80	13.34	10.12	16.20
	Low	0.201–0.300	14.77	12.89	9.73	6.27	8.71
	Middle	0.301–0.400	7.79	11.12	11.18	8.95	6.96
	High	0.401–0.500	4.05	8.13	8.73	7.98	7.37
	Very high	>0.501	2.34	6.47	22.44	32.11	26.18
NPP	Very low	0.000–0.200	33.85	24.96	13.47	12.92	6.47
	Low	0.201–0.400	22.18	24.08	20.31	13.82	15.20
	Middle	0.401–0.600	6.65	9.61	13.80	10.58	12.69
	High	0.601–0.800	2.71	4.60	8.90	8.02	8.90
	Very high	>0.801	0.03	2.17	8.94	20.08	22.16
PD	Very low	0.000–0.100	24.43	18.48	10.30	13.57	11.95
	Low	0.101–0.300	27.24	27.78	31.42	28.42	22.13
	Middle	0.301–0.500	10.35	12.04	5.81	2.34	9.50
	High	0.501–0.700	3.28	6.45	7.88	2.50	3.63
	Very high	>0.701	0.12	0.67	10.01	18.60	18.21
NTL	Very low	0.000–0.040	65.42	65.42	54.58	32.77	31.96
	Low	0.041–0.080	0.00	0.00	6.17	14.70	14.83
	Middle	0.081–0.120	0.00	0.00	2.50	7.86	10.86
	High	0.121–0.160	0.00	0.00	1.71	3.26	3.00
	Very high	>0.161	0.00	0.00	0.46	6.84	4.76

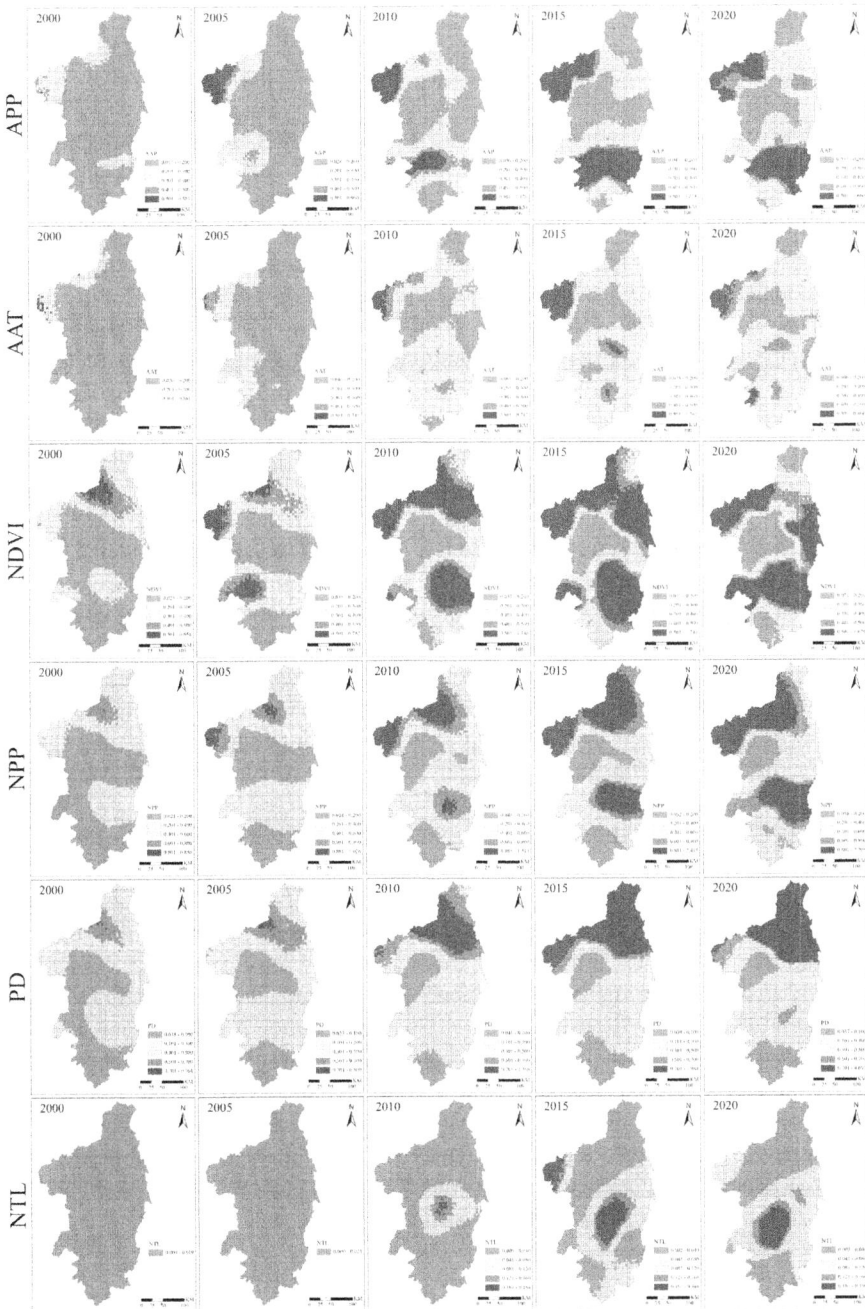

Fig. 5. Spatial distribution changes of different factors at different importance levels

5 Discussion

5.1 Analysis of Spatial-Temporal Evolution Characteristics of LERI

From 2000 to 2020, the spatial pattern of LERI in the study area remained generally stable, exhibiting a "high in the north, low in the south" distribution pattern. The very high-risk zones were primarily concentrated in the northern part of the study area, including Hongze Lake, Gaoyou Lake, the Yangtze River Basin, as well as the southern regions around Shijiu Lake and Nanyi Lake. Notably, the fragmented patches in the southern part gradually evolved into more cohesive clusters. High-risk zones were distributed around the very high-risk zones, while middle- and low-risk zones occupied a larger proportion, forming an interwoven distribution in planar or scattered patterns. The very low-risk zones were mainly located in the southern part of the study area. This distribution pattern is largely determined by topography and hydrological conditions. The southern region is dominated by mountainous and hilly terrain, with higher elevations and relatively stable ecosystems, resulting in lower LERI (Zeng, et al. 2024). In contrast, the northern region consists mainly of plains with lower elevations and a dense water network, including large lakes such as Hongze Lake and Gaoyou Lake, with the Yangtze River flowing through the area. Additionally, Shijiu Lake and Nanyi Lake are located in the central and southern parts. Due to frequent human activities and improper land use, ecosystems in these lake and riverine areas experience higher levels of disturbance, leading to high LERI (Wu and Chen 2020). Furthermore, the distribution of water systems has also influenced the formation of risk gradients. The very high-risk zones typically appeared as banded or clustered distributions along water bodies, transitioning outward into lower-risk zones. This finding is largely consistent with the results of (Wang, et al. 2025b).

From 2000 to 2020, the most significant decrease was observed in the area of the medium-risk zones, which declined by 1.25×10^3 km^2 (a reduction of 5.76%). Conversely, the most notable increase was in the high-risk zones, which expanded by 0.39×10^3 km^2 (a growth of 8.11%). The areas of the very low-, low-, and very high-risk zones remained relatively stable. This trend indicates that while the overall LERI pattern in the study area remained stable, certain local regions experienced changes in risk levels, demonstrating a tendency toward polarization. The reduction in the medium-risk zones may be attributed to the accelerated urbanization process in some areas, where increased land development intensity has led to ecosystem fragmentation, causing a shift toward high-risk zones (Song, et al. 2023). On the other hand, some medium-risk areas may have undergone ecological restoration, land rehabilitation, and environmental management initiatives, leading to ecosystem recovery and a transition to low-risk zones (Song, et al. 2023).

5.2 Analysis of Spatial-Temporal Evolution Characteristics of LERI Driving Factors

NPP, NDVI, and AAP were the primary driving factors influencing LERI changes. NPP was mainly concentrated in the central and northern regions, where its distribution has gradually evolved from a uniform pattern to a fragmented one. NDVI was primarily distributed in the southwestern and northeastern regions, while AAP had a more significant impact in the southern and northwestern parts of the study area. AAP exhibited an overall decreasing trend from 2000 to 2015 but remained relatively stable from 2015 to 2020. The spatial distribution changes of NPP and NDVI reflected variations in vegetation growth conditions and the response of ecosystems to climate change and land-use changes. The fragmented distribution of NPP in the central and northern regions indicated a decline in vegetation productivity and an increase in landscape fragmentation, which further affects ecosystem stability and regulatory capacity. In contrast, higher NDVI in the southwestern and northeastern regions suggested relatively good vegetation cover, which provided a buffering effect against ecological risks (Karimian, et al. 2022). Meanwhile, AAP played a crucial role in the early stages by supplying moisture to the ecosystem. Its reduction over time may have led to localized ecosystem degradation, contributing to an increase in landscape ecological risk (Yang, et al. 2024a).

From the perspective of the most important driving factor in the same spatial area, NPP consistently occupied the largest area but showed a declining trend, decreasing from 34.68×10^3 km^2 in 2000 to its lowest point of 21.63×10^3 km^2 in 2015, before rebounding to 23.75×10^3 km^2 in 2020. Meanwhile, PD exhibited a significant upward trend, increasing from 3.40×10^3 km^2 in 2000 to 6.31×10^3 km^2 in 2020. This indicates that in the early stages of the study period, NPP played a dominant role in controlling LERI, as higher NPP values correspond to more stable ecosystems and lower ecological risks. However, over time, the influence range of NPP gradually contracted. Additionally, the rapid increase in PD suggests that human activities have become increasingly influential in the evolution of ecological risks, likely linked to urban expansion, changes in agricultural land use, and infrastructure development (Lv, et al. 2024). This shift suggests that the driving mechanism of LERI may be transitioning from being predominantly controlled by natural factors to being increasingly driven by human interventions. Specifically, the regulation of ecological risk, which was previously centered around climate, hydrology, and vegetation as part of the natural ecosystem, is gradually shifting toward a human-driven mechanism dominated by land use changes and population growth.

6 Conclusion

This study constructed an LERI model and integrated it with the GWRF model to analyze the spatial-temporal evolution of LERI and its driving factors in the Nanjing Metropolitan Area from 2000 to 2020. The key findings are as follows: (1) The spatial pattern of LERI in the Nanjing Metropolitan Area remained relatively stable, exhibiting a general trend of "high in the north and low in the south." The area of medium-risk zones significantly decreased, while the area of high-risk zones substantially increased, indicating a growing threat to regional landscape ecological stability; (2) NPP, NDVI, and AAP were identified as the primary driving factors, with PD also exerting a considerable influence on LERI. NPP was mainly distributed in the central and northern regions, NDVI in the southwestern and northeastern regions, AAP had a stronger impact in the southern and northwestern areas, while PD was concentrated in the northern region. The driving mechanism of LERI was undergoing a transition from being dominated by natural factors to being increasingly influenced by human interventions; (3) AAP, AAT, NDVI, and

NPP exhibited a relatively stable strong positive correlation, suggesting a synergistic role in ecosystem regulation. This study aimed to provide a scientific basis for regional ecological risk management and sustainable landscape planning.

Acknowledgments. This research was supported by the National Natural Science Foundation of China (NSFC) Key Project "Research on the Reconstruction of Contemporary Construction System Based on the Integrative Mechanism of 'Architecture-Human-Environment' in the Chinese Context" (Grant No. 52038007).

Disclosure of Interests. The authors declare that they have no known competing financial interests or personal relationships that could have appeared to influence the work reported in this paper.

References

Bryan, B.A., et al.: China's response to a national land-system sustainability emergency. Nature **559**, 193–204 (2018)

Cao, Q., et al.: Multi-scenario simulation of landscape ecological risk probability to facilitate different decision-making preferences. J. Clean. Prod. **227**, 325–335 (2019)

Du, L., et al.: Spatial-temporal evolution of land cover changes and landscape ecological risk assessment in the Yellow River Basin, 2015–2020. J. Environ. Manage. **332**, 117149 (2023)

Guo, J., et al.: Past dynamics and future prediction of the impacts of land use cover change and climate change on landscape ecological risk across the Mongolian plateau. J. Environ. Manage. **355**, 120365 (2024)

Karimian, H., et al.: Landscape ecological risk assessment and driving factor analysis in Dongjiang river watershed. Chemosphere **307**, 135835 (2022)

Li, J., et al.: Study of identification and simulation of ecological zoning through integration of landscape ecological risk and ecosystem service value. Sustain. Cities Soc. **107**, 105442 (2024a)

Li, K., et al.: An ecological perspective for understanding regional integration based on ecosystem service budgets, bundles, and flows: a case study of the Jinan metropolitan area in China. J. Environ. Manage. **305**, 114371 (2022)

Li, M., et al.: Application of geographical detector and geographically weighted regression for assessing landscape ecological risk in the Irtysh River Basin, Central Asia. Ecol. Indicat. **158**, 111540 (2024b)

Li, S., et al.: Exploring new methods for assessing landscape ecological risk in key basin. J. Clean. Prod. **461**, 142633 (2024c)

Liu, H., Tang, D.: Ecological zoning and ecosystem management based on landscape ecological risk and ecosystem services: a case study in the Wuling Mountain Area. Ecol. Ind. **166**, 112421 (2024)

Liu, W., et al.: Spatial-temporal distribution and driving factors of regional green spaces during rapid urbanization in Nanjing metropolitan area, China. Ecol. Indicat. **148**, 110058 (2023)

Luo, F., et al.: Assessing urban landscape ecological risk through an adaptive cycle framework. Landsc. Urban Plan. **180**, 125–134 (2018)

Lv, L., et al.: Spatial drivers of ecosystem services supply-demand balances in the Nanjing metropolitan area, China. J. Clean. Prod. **434**, 139894 (2024)

Peng, Y., et al.: Analysis and prediction of the spatial-temporal characteristics of land-use ecological risk and carbon storage in Wuhan metropolitan area. Ecol. Ind. **158**, 111432 (2024)

Ran, P., et al.: Exploring changes in landscape ecological risk in the Yangtze River economic belt from a spatial-temporal perspective. Ecol. Ind. **137**, 108744 (2022)

Song, S., et al.: Functional regionalization of land resources considering eco-efficiency in Nanjing Metropolitan Area, China. Ecol. Indicat. **155**, 110964 (2023)

Wang, J., Wang, J., Zhang, J.: Optimization of landscape ecological risk assessment method and ecological management zoning considering resilience. J. Environ. Manage. **376**, 124586 (2025b)

Wang, W., et al.: Determining the main contributing factors to nutrient concentration in rivers in arid northwest China using partial least squares structural equation modeling. J. Environ. Manage. **343**, 118249 (2023)

Wang, X., Zhu, T., Jiang, C.: Landscape ecological risk based on optimal scale and its trade-off/synergy with human activities: a case study of the Nanjing metropolitan area, China. Ecol. Indicat. **170**, 113040 (2025b)

Wu, C., Chen, W.: Indicator system construction and health assessment of wetland ecosystem—taking Hongze Lake Wetland, China as an example. Ecol. Indicat. **112**, 106164 (2020)

Xu, D., et al.: Influences of urban spatial factors on surface urban heat island effect and its spatial heterogeneity: a case study of Xi'an. Build. Environ. **248**, 111072 (2024)

Yang, N., et al.: Landscape ecological risk assessment and driving factors analysis based on optimal spatial scales in Luan River Basin, China. Ecol. Indicat. **169**, 112821 (2024a)

Yang, Y., et al.: Constructing child-friendly cities: comprehensive evaluation of street-level child-friendliness using the method of empathy-based stories, street view images, and deep learning. Cities **154**, 105385 (2024b)

Zeng, J., Wu, J., Chen, W.: Coupling analysis of land use change with landscape ecological risk in China: a multi-scenario simulation perspective. J. Clean. Prod. **435**, 140518 (2024)

Zhang, Y., et al.: Optimizing urban green space configurations for enhanced heat island mitigation: a geographically weighted machine learning approach. Sustain. Cities Soc. **119**, 106087 (2025)

Author Index

C
Cai, Zhi 245, 267
Chen, Fenglei 295
Chen, Hongmei 191
Chen, Xiaohui 150, 167
Cheng, Yan 295

F
Fan, Hanming 267
Fan, Zipei 86, 118, 139
Feng, Ziruo 295

G
Gao, Haiyan 267
Geng, Xing 295
Guo, Limin 245
Guo, Xiangzhong 70

H
Han, Wei 139
Hu, Yike 295
Huang, Haolan 295
Huang, Tianlv 139

K
Kang, Zhihao 295

L
Li, Jiaqi 219
Li, Li 99
Li, Min 295
Li, Sheng 267
Li, Xiang 219
Li, Xiao 202
Li, Yong 35, 54
Li, Zongrong 1
Liang, Haojian 202
Liang, Yu 118

Liao, Hanwen 267
Lin Ye, 167
Liu, Chang 202
Liu, Haiyan 150
Liu, Weijia 245
Liu, Yu 139
Liu, Zhaoge 20
Lu, Junting 99
Lu, Yimin 70

M
Ma, Zhihui 191
Mei, Qiang 35, 54
Mei, Yiduo 99

P
Pang, Yuanyuan 35

R
Ren, Fang 219

S
Si, Junjun 99
Song, Weijie 20
Song, Xuan 86, 118
Su, Cheng 202
Su, Junyou 118
Su, Xing 245
Su, Yunlei 1

T
Tan, Bin 118

W
Wang, Deze 167
Wang, Hongrong 1
Wang, Lihua 86
Wang, Peng 35, 54

© The Editor(s) (if applicable) and The Author(s), under exclusive license to Springer Nature Singapore Pte Ltd. 2026
Y. Liu et al. (Eds.): SpatialDI 2025, LNCS 15838, pp. 313–314, 2026.
https://doi.org/10.1007/978-981-95-3102-8

Wang, Shaohua 202
Wu, Guolong 70

X

Xiao, Kehong 219
Xiao, Qing 191
Xu, Chenfeng 295
Xu, Dachuan 202
Xue, Tong 54

Y

Ye, Lin 150
Yuan, Yi 118

Z

Zhang, Bing 150, 167
Zhang, Ran 150, 167
Zhao, Wufan 1
Zhao, Yunpeng 167
Zheng, Jiayi 202
Zheng, Mingqi 150, 167
Zhong, Yang 202
Zhou, Junyuan 202
Zhou, Lihua 191
Zhou, Meiqi 139
Zhu, Zibo 295
Zou, Linzi 99
Zou, Zhengyang 295

Made in the USA
Monee, IL
03 May 2026

49438650R00181